J. Ambrose Raftis

A Small Town in Late Medieval England

Godmanchester, 1278-1400

Owing to historiographical traditions that treat almost exclusively of cities or villages, the town does not have a well-developed role in social and economic histories of medieval Europe. An attempt is made to correct this deficiency by this study of the town of Godmanchester, lying across the river from Huntingdon, and possessing an extraordinary series of records from the late thirteenth century. Three-weekly court records that survive in an almost unbroken series from the 1270s have made possible the nominal identification of more than thirteen hundred families for the period under consideration. Court records also provide ample opportunity to envisage the active application of custom to family and town life.

Supplementary records for the late thirteenth and early fourteenth centuries, such as the very detailed Hundred Roll for 1279, lay subsidy rolls and subletting lists, also make possible an interesting overview of the settlement pattern of the town as well as the relation of Godmanchester to a local agrarian region and a wider commercial region. The town was able to absorb much of the new clerical and commercial expertise of the day — often by admitting outsiders to the freedom of the town — without apparent loss of character. Families too were able to manipulate their customs to ensure survival despite the hazards of replacement and the tensions of entrepreneurial ambitions.

This study of Godmanchester concludes that town organization was sufficiently distinct from village and city to warrant investigation of other towns as models of valuable social and economic experience. At the same time, it is hoped that many of the records and much of the data provided in this volume will be found useful for a wider analysis by historians of the family, demographers, students of custom and those interested in settlement patterns as well as the geography of regions.

STUDIES AND TEXTS 53

A SMALL TOWN
IN LATE MEDIEVAL ENGLAND

Godmanchester 1278-1400

BY

J. A. RAFTIS

PONTIFICAL INSTITUTE OF MEDIAEVAL STUDIES

ACKNOWLEDGEMENT

This book has been published with the help of a grant
from the Social Science Federation of Canada,
using funds provided by the Social Sciences
and Humanities Research Council of canada.

CANADIAN CATALOGUING IN PUBLICATION DATA

Raftis, J. A. (James Ambrose), 1922-
  A small town in late medieval England

(Studies and texts, ISSN 0082-5328 ; 53)
Bibliography: p.
Includes index.
ISBN 0-88844-053-7

1. Godmanchester (Huntingdonshire) - History.   2. Godmanchester (Hunting-
donshire) - Social conditions.   I. Pontifical Institute of Mediaeval Studies.
II. Title.   III. Series: Studies and texts (Pontifical Institute of Mediaeval
Studies) ; 53.

DA690.G58R33   942.6´5403´7   C81-094380-8

PRINTED BY UNIVERSA, WETTEREN, BELGIUM

To the Memory
of
P. G. M. Dickinson
late archivist of Huntingdon

Contents

PART THREE   THE PEOPLE OF THE COURT ROLL

MAPS

TABLES

Preface

This is the story of a small English town called Godmanchester from the late thirteenth through the fourteenth century. Though it was at the time still technically a royal manor, we shall call it a town since Mary Bateson thought it worthy of inclusion in her study of borough customs[1] and the size and activities of the place were much the same in the fourteenth century as when Godmanchester did become officially a borough in 1604. It is more important, whatever their official status, that the Godmanchester people were keenly aware of their special identity from the thirteenth century and have left the historian a heritage of records that surpasses in continuity many great estate complexes and most boroughs of any size.

Despite this great heritage, the trials of World War II and the rapid changes thereafter that led to the incorporation of Godmanchester with Huntingdon by 1964, almost brought about the loss of this invaluable collection. It was that gifted "amateur," the late P. G. M. Dickinson,[2] brought to the town by the exigencies of his career, whose keen eye first suspected and finally detected the whereabouts of the Godmanchester records that had apparently been buried away below ground level for safekeeping during the war and then forgotten.[3] As borough archivist, Dickinson then saw to the preservation of these records in their present excellent condition.

His decisive action occurred none too soon for it is evident that valuable records had already been lost. Godmanchester was administered during the Middle Ages by two courts, the view of frankpledge and a manorial court. Customs recorded in the view of frankpledge, particularly for 1324 (17 Edw. II), form much of the basis for the useful account of town administration in the *Victoria County History* of Huntingdonshire written in 1932. However, neither P. G. M. Dickinson, his successors nor this

---

[1] *Borough Customs* (London, 1906); see further Appendix 1 to Chapter 1.

[2] For a brief appreciation of Dickinson, see David Renton, *Records of Huntingdonshire*, Huntingdonshire Local History Society, 1977, no. 1, part 8, pp. 2-3.

[3] This information was conveyed to me by P. G. M. Dickinson in personal conversation.

writer have been able to find any surviving frankpledge rolls prior to the fifteenth century. Whether any manorial court rolls have been lost over the past fifty years is difficult to determine. Again, the *VCH* account says that the court rolls are preserved from 1271, and there may have been others since there is no evidence that all surviving records were checked by the writer of this account. In any case, a search of the present collection shows that there are no extant court rolls between 1 and 5 Edward I.

The reason for the dedication of this volume to P. G. M. Dickinson is, then, obvious enough. Dickinson's successors at the Huntingdon County Record Office, Mr. P. J. Locke and Mr. A. D. Hill, have continued to be fully cooperative in my Godmanchester investigations. At the request of Mr. Dickinson, The Borough Council gave permission for the microfilming of the Godmanchester records — an absolute essential to the overseas scholar. I was assisted by Edward Britton and Ellen Wedemeyer Moore in the tedious task of transcribing names and entries from the court rolls. Something of what this volume owes to the devoted services of my research assistant, Miss Beryl Wells, may be indicated by putting on record that she transposed names and entries of all Godmanchester people from the transcriptions, constructed the chart of family relationships as well as other tables, drew the maps and typed the manuscript. The Social Sciences and Humanities Research Council (formerly the Canada Council) generously funded microfilming and research assistants' costs. The special debt owed to Anne and Edwin DeWindt for making available some of their research materials is acknowledged at the appropriate places in this volume. As always, it is a pleasure to be able to thank my colleagues, L. E. Boyle and M. M. Sheehan, who made their expert knowledge available at several technical points of textual interpretation.

Abbreviations

a	acre
Bateson, *Borough Customs*	Mary Bateson, *Borough Customs*, Selden Society, vol. 21 (London, 1906).
English Medieval Towns	Susan Reynolds, *An Introduction to the History of English Medieval Towns* (Oxford, 1977).
Family and Inheritance	Jack Goody, Joan Thirsk and E. P. Thompson, eds., *Family and Inheritance: Rural Society in Western Europe 1200-1800* (Cambridge, 1976).
1279 Hundred Roll	*Rotuli Hundredorum*, eds. W. Illingworth and J. Caley, Publications of the Records Commissioners (1812-1818), 1: 591-597.
Patent Rolls	*Calendar of Patent Rolls*, Henry iii ff., Public Record Office (1893-).
r	rod
Raftis, and Hogan, *Lay Subsidy Rolls*	J. Ambrose Raftis and Mary P. Hogan, *Early Huntingdonshire Lay Subsidy Rolls* (Toronto, 1976).
Sheehan, *The Will in Medieval England*	Michael M. Sheehan, *The Will in Medieval England* (Toronto, 1963).
VCH	*The Victoria History of the County of Huntingdon*, vol. 2, edited by William Page, Granville Proby and S. Inskip Ladds (London, 1932).

Note: Godmanchester Court Roll references are signified by date, box, and bundle numbers. Abbreviations for Table 26, "Family Data," are given below, p. 236.

Introduction

The small and middle sized country towns have not enjoyed much of a press among medieval historians. In great part this omission may be explained by a historiography that established such a clear dichotomy between the city of the Mediterranean world and the rural life of the Germanic north. In consequence, towns of any size tend to be equated with cities and the study of the towns and countryside of northwestern Europe followed parallel but non-converging lines. This traditional approach to northern towns is best depicted by the classical investigations into the origins of towns by Henri Pirenne — origins to be found in natural phenomena such as harbours or artificial constructions such as forts or the shrines, but not as normal components or outgrowth of the economy of the time. In parallel fashion, decades of research into the rural economy of great western European land mass could be summarized in the magisterial study of Georges Duby[1] without even posing the question of the rise of towns. Towns were not a part of the "original" rural economy (p. 7) while on the other hand the study of towns was a specialization beyond the ken of the rural historian (p. 128).

No one who glances through the histories of medieval town and country written over the past one hundred years can fail to recognize that this traditional historiography has been immensely productive. The different sources and differing social and economic complexities have made, and continue to make this longtime division of labour eminently practicable. Furthermore, as the recent study of Reynolds[2] illustrates, this traditional approach has still much to offer. At the same time, nothing would seem to be gained by hardening these two parallel town and country historiographical traditions into exclusive approaches that would

---

[1] *Rural Economy and Country Life in the Medieval West*, tr. by Cynthia Postan (Columbia, S.C., 1968). Page references in the following sentence are to this English translation.

[2] Susan Reynolds, *An Introduction to the History of English Medieval Towns* (Oxford, 1977).

negate the possibility of more intermediate analysis of town and country.[3] Research has gradually blurred the neat premises of these two historiographical models. For example, the "Pirenne-like" explanation of the rise of towns in England from their status as royal boroughs does not account for the many towns with borough characteristics, though without official borough status. As the recent article of R. H. Britnell clearly establishes, the bulk of trade both "rural" and "urban" was carried on outside all the sets of privileges, lay or ecclesiastic, even in the heyday of feudal organization.[4] In turn, archaeological research on the rather remote village of Wharram Percy indicates that the village economy was not isolated from more highly specialized trade centres.[5] Indeed if this reader understands rightly the more recent assessments of the doyen of English medieval economic history, that great surge of economic development prior to the fourteenth century was a mutual affair of town and country: "By, say, 1250 medieval England had come to be covered by a network of urban centres, most of them serving relatively small regions and occupied in commercial and industrial activities cast on a small and purely local scale."[6]

Such assessments show the need of additional models to understand small town development in medieval Europe. One town does not a model make. Such models may require new data which, if not deliberately ignored by traditional models, have not been deemed necessary to their understanding. This study of Godmanchester is presented, primarily, in order to illustrate the type of data that still require much investigation in the medieval town and, secondarily, in order to make the case for a new model, or at least a stronger historical image, of the smallish town in medieval society. For Godmanchester was not a royal borough, nor endowed with special charters of market or fair privilege, nor an ecclesiastical centre, nor even identifiable with any commercial specialization. Yet, Godmanchester gained special royal recognition and was attractive to merchant and ecclesiastic alike. In short, Godmanchester

---

[3] Robert S. Lopez, "The Trade of Medieval Europe: The South," in *The Cambridge Economic History of Europe*, 2 (1952), p. 327: "... few historians have regarded them [market of middle-sized industrial cities] worthy of attention."

[4] R. H. Britnell, "English Markets and Royal Administration before 1200," *The Economic History Review*, Second Series, 31, No. 2 (1978), 183-196.

[5] See the forthcoming article by J. G. Hurst in the volume on recent peasant studies to be published by the University of Toronto Press.

[6] M. M. Postan, *The Medieval Economy and Society: An Economic History of Britain 1100-1500* (London, 1972), p. 210. The more specific research questions to be probed in order to flesh out Postan's general statement are given in Reynolds, *English Medieval Towns*, pp. 59-60.

exercised a vital role in a wide sector of the economy of medieval England. How could this happen?

The answer to this question cannot be given in the traditional terms of borough status, town government and gild, merchant or ecclesiastical privilege. The answer must be reconstructed from the lives of the townsmen. But, first of all, something must be said of the geographical and historical setting of our investigation.

*
* *

Godmanchester lies today across the Ouse River from the town of Huntingdon. It was formerly in the county of Huntingdonshire and now in the new enlarged county of Cambridgeshire. Godmanchester is some twenty miles west of Cambridge by the old Roman road (Via Devana no. A604) and 65 miles northeast of London on the central Roman road called Ermine Street (now A14). The parish embraces nearly 5000 acres, largely of easily worked gravelly soil together with a band of rich, though in earlier times frequently flooded, meadow along the river.

Godmanchester ("Gumcestre" in the medieval manuscripts employed in this study and in a traditional local dialect) had a long history before the period under study in this volume. While there was undoubtedly prehistoric activity in the area, the modern name and town derive from the period of Roman settlement. The Ouse river remained for some time the frontier of the invading Roman armies and Godmanchester developed at a fording point of the river both as a fort and supply centre. More than twenty years of painstaking efforts by the archaeologist of the town, H. J. M. Green, have made it possible to identify the chief characteristics of the Roman fort of the first century, the Roman settlement with inn, baths and basilica over the second and third century, the Dark Age hamlet, the Danish burh and the Saxon town.[7] Throughout these periods Godman-chester remained a transportation focal point for the southeast and west roads from Cambridge and Sandy crossed by Ermine Street that ran north over the bridged Ouse. Major changes occurred in each identifiable period of the history of the town. The name "Godmundcestre" is to be found in Domesday Book, having replaced the Roman designation possibly "Duro-vigutum." It was in the Danish period, too, that for reasons of fortification the curious polygonal shape of the town roads took their origin.

Ironically, while it was a military purpose that seems to have dictated the line of Godmanchester streets, the greater military importance of Huntingdon as a vantage point controlling the area north of the Ouse

---

[7] H. J. M. Green, *Godmanchester* (Cambridge, 1977).

drew the status of borough to the latter town rather than to Godmanchester. In assessing the economic importance of Godmanchester, the
modern student must keep in mind that the whole fen country, stretching
to within a dozen miles of Godmanchester, was largely traversed by water
transport before modern drainage. Furthermore, for more than a
thousand years after the coming of the Romans (until the building of a
bridge at St. Ives in the twelfth century), the Ouse river was still a frontier
to overland transportation and the bridge at Godmanchester, perhaps fifty
miles by water from the sea, was the lowest on the Ouse river. While
Huntingdon borough gained notoriety as a royal mint and fortified burh
and castle over the late Anglo-Saxon and early Anglo-Norman centuries,
it will be important for an understanding of the Godmanchester economy
to keep in mind that the locational advantage of Godmanchester had not
altered. From its pivotal location, then, Godmanchester remained one of
those "primary towns" described by Alan Everitt, although it did not
develop the administrative and legal functions to be expected of this
category.[8]

On the surface, the rise of Huntingdon reduced Godmanchester to a
manorial backwater. For two hundred years after Domesday Book[9]
information about Godmanchester is the sort to be found for most rural
estates. This substantial manor of fourteen hides had paid £40 to the king
in the time of Edward the Confessor and William the Conqueror. By the
time of Richard I the manor was farmed for £50. In 1212, under King
John, the manor was granted "to the men of Godmanchester" to be held
in fee-farm for the rent of £120 a year. Of course, one cannot discover
who these "men of Godmanchester" were in 1212 and how they were
able to pay a rent almost two and one half times that demanded by
Richard I only twenty-two years before.[10] It is interesting to note that by
the thirteenth century the farm of Godmanchester was three times that
paid to William the Conqueror and, as will be seen below, the tenants of
the town given in the Hundred Roll of 1279 numbered more than three
times the 80 villagers (*villati*) and 15 bordars of 1086.

*
**

In the seventh decade of the thirteenth century the people of Godmanchester first appear individually to the historian. In the three weekly court

---

[8] A. Everitt, "The Banburys of England," *Urban History Yearbook* (1974).
[9] VCH, pp. 286-295.
[10] P. D. A. Harvey, "The English Inflation of 1180-1220," *Past and Present*, No. 61
(November 1973), pp. 1-30, suggests one explanation.

rolls that survive from the time and in occasional supplementary records, beginning with the Hundred Roll of 1279, thousands of Godmanchester people are noted. These people were so closely indentified with their town that even their names provide us with a general overview of the main physical characteristics of the place. There was a family located near the entrance to the church (*ad schalam ecclesie*), a family near the town cross (*ad crucem*), a family on the bank of the river (*ad ripam*) and another close to some water (*ad aquam*), a family at the town well or spring (*ad fontem* or "atte well"), a family at the green ("atte grene"), another at the entrance gate ("atte barre") and another at the edge of the town (*ad capud ville* or "atte towneshende"). Some of the ancient wall of the town must have survived for one family had the name "*super murum*" or "on ye wal." No family took its name from the main streets of the town, but one family was identified with a lane (*in venella* or "atte [*or* in] the lane") and another family with the end of the lane ("attelaneshende"). In the earliest map of Godmanchester, that of 1514, a cluster of buildings are identified in the meadow to the northeast of the town as The Rushes. A family took its name from this location in our earliest records (*ad cirpos* or *ad rissis*). Other families located outside the town were Hill (*super montem*, "super le hill," "on ye hill"), "of the moor" and "of the thorpe."

As a source for surnames, toponymics were very exceptional at God-manchester. In the land conveyances from this time it is quite clear, however, that there were three arable fields (Eastfield, Westfield and Depden), meadow held in severalty along the river and numerous closes about the town. The general contours of the town that greet us in the 1270s were, then, much the same as those to be found in maps from the sixteenth century and in the earlier maps reconstructed by H. J. M. Green.

If the names of Godmanchester provide us with a brief glimpse of the topography of the town, they are much more important as a starting point for the study of Godmanchester social and economic life. Such is indeed the case and the identification of 6,000 Godmanchester individuals and families provide the basic data for what follows. Since this material (Table 26 "Family Data") which charts relationship patterns within the town is the "basic text" of the volume, it is presented in Parts Two and Three as an independent study. To a great degree, the scope of this volume is determined by the possibilities and adequacies of the information charting family relationships. At the same time this is but a text, based upon the manuscript text of the court rolls, and not intended in its original purpose to be a complete social and economic record. The inadequacies of this source will be obvious enough. What is more remarkable, perhaps, is the fact that such records should reveal as much as they do about the

social and economic life of the time. It becomes as important, therefore, to understand why such records reveal a wide variety of data as what data are actually revealed.

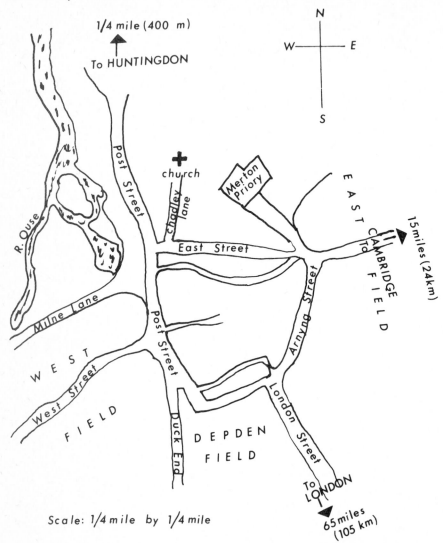

MAP 1. LATE THIRTEENTH-CENTURY GODMANCHESTER

To this end it must be heartily recommended that the student suspend any bias toward evolutionary categories in the study of historical social organization and approach the data more as a social possibility in its own right. That is to say, there is more to the story of Godmanchester than is

revealed by the notion of a borough or guild manqué. As we seek today varieties of local and regional socialization in order to mount a healthy decentralization of economy and government, it may be useful to recall that before the advent of modern government a vast amount of human energy was expended in a great variety of involved and inventive ways in the ordering of everyday lives. This point is not raised to suggest odious comparisons between the professional civil servant and the dedicated amateur and much less any romantic return to the past, but quite simply to indicate that recognition of greater variety of human experience in the past may excite our imagination about possibilities for the future.

What this general train of thought means for the case at hand, the history of Godmanchester, may be suggested by a series of questions. Were the people of Godmanchester content with their local government? Were they ill at ease vis-à-vis the borough across the river? Was Godmanchester well served by the town administration? In turn, this is to raise the questions: Who served in the administration? What varieties of social needs were served by it? Could a variety of local as well as "outsider" requirements be managed? Could the town adjust to those changing social and economic conditions that we now know strongly differentiated each generation of the fourteenth century?

Certainly in the historical period under consideration in this volume Godmanchester seemed well content with its manorial status and its charter of privileges. The royal charters were renewed under each king of the thirteenth century and, together with other records, carefully kept in a special repository from at least the late thirteenth century. This collection and set of privileges were to be long-lived. One finds written with a modern hand on a court of Thursday before the feast of St. Mark, 9 Edward I (25 April 1282):

> Examined by Edward Martin of Godmanchester who took this memorandum July 10th, 1838 aged 68, being then Mayor for the second time since the passing of the Municipal Bill on the 9th September, 1835. At this Time a cause being to be tried at the ensuing Assizes at Huntingdon on 26th July. The Corporation versus Phillips (a taylor) for stocking with 2 cows the West Common, he not being a Freman, but only occupying a Commonable House. The said Edward read all the old Rolls and Books to prove the exclusive rights of Freemen.

The King's little writ of right was used by plaintiffs as late as 1805 and the town system of tenure was basically still that of ancient demesne of the crown into the twentieth century.[11] How could such an apparently

---

[11] vch, p. 289.

anachronistic system function over so long a period of history with any vitality? To answer this question we must begin with the fundamental role of custom in the town of Godmanchester.

Parts One and Two of this volume give the analysis of data presented in detailed form in the subsequent sections. In the first part, Chapter 1 will demonstrate custom at work in the life cycles of people of Godmanchester. In Chapter 2 Godmanchester custom will be seen in local government and certain economic controls. Both of these chapters present the intriguing picture of custom flourishing in conjunction with an open land market and a regional economy. The sources for the study of Godmanchester at this time, dealing so largely with the landed people only, are not adequate to an analysis of the full social consequences of these policies demonstrated in Chapter 1 and 2. However, it is possible in Chapter 3 to present a considerable amount of information on the family settlement patterns and the occupational map, in Chapter 4 to attempt an introduction to the people of Godmanchester, and in Chapter 5 to sketch the changing role of wealth among the townsmen.

Part Three is the main backdrop to Parts One and Two. The extraction of demographic data from court rolls has been rightly called an exercise in "demographic archaeology." Since the formation of the table entitled "Family Data from Godmanchester Court Rolls" is such a distinct methodological process Part Two has been devoted to the description of this process and to some of the data while Part Three is the "Family Data" itself. There is the further stylistic reason for the separation of parts, of course, that some hundred pages of a table are ill-suited to the sequence of the earlier chapters. At the same time, the information in the "Family Data from Godmanchester Court Rolls" is worth printing in its own right since it is rather rare for this early period, the analysis of Part One depends on it, and it is of possible future use for demographers in a wider context.

Part One

Custom and Change

1

Living with Custom

Customary law was, like common law or Roman law, a certain legal system. The court rolls of Godmanchester show that a system of customary law made possible a wide variety of social and economic arrangements. When that legal system worked, as with any legal system, recourse through the courts was not necessary. The system of customary law seems to have worked well at Godmanchester since the court was invoked rarely to establish claims with respect to many main elements of family property disposition — entry to property at legal age, dower, dowry, disposition of heirlooms and even challenge to the last will and testament. Furthermore, as is discussed in detail at various points throughout this chapter, the court roll formulary often remained vague with respect to the familial disposition of property.

From the point of view of social content, if not of strict legal definition, much could be said for describing the customs of a town or village like Godmanchester as "regulations for self government." Paradoxically, the very immediacy and success of this system of self government obviated the necessity of written records and custom was thereby virtually excluded as a source for the modern social historian. As a result, despite the insights from decades of productive work by social anthropologists centred about more observable modern custom, social historians are still struggling to have custom recognized as a legitimate field for research.[1]

A productive methodology for the study of societies governed by customary law cannot expect to follow the traditional methods of legal-social historians. Recorded customs are too small a part of the whole customary legal system. Surviving snippets of recorded custom are often late in terms of the history of their social function and lend more to the

---

[1] For a recent example, see Cicely Howell, "Peasant Inheritance Customs in the Midlands, 1280-1700," in *Family and Inheritance*, pp. 112-115.

traditional derogatory opinion of customs as ossified life than to an understanding of more vital social realities. It is ironic, given the view that
regards custom as peripheral to the life of society, that its importance in
relation to other forms of law should become more evident the more the
day-to-day actions of the people can be reconstructed. This is first and
foremost the task of the social historian. It is precisely because social
historians have depended upon prior "theoretical" work by constitutional,
legal and economic historians that the study of custom has not received its
due.[2]

Following upon the above remarks, no attempt will be made in this
volume to recover the texts of customs of Godmanchester, as useful in
themselves, nor indeed to isolate customs from other legal forms peeping
through the records. Rather, custom will be left in its context as part of the
normal wider social and economic experience of the time.

A beginning can be made in our understanding of the place of custom
in this social history by recognizing that the use of custom in thirteenth-
century Godmanchester was not simply succumbing to the weight of
tradition but the result of a deliberate choice. Recent studies of the royal
manor of Havering, Essex, have established that the use of local customs
for the vill was deliberately promoted by both the king's lawyers and local
men in the very heyday of common law developments.[3] Undoubtedly, for
the people of Godmanchester, too, one of the reasons for jealously
preserving royal charters from the time of King John would have been the
fact that "privileges" included local customs. The royal grant was a grant
of self-government:

> Therefore We will and firmly command that Our aforesaid Men of God-
> manchester have and hold of Us and Our heirs the aforesaid Manor of God-
> manchester, truly and in peace, freely quietly and surely, with all privileges
> belonging to the said manor....[4]

---

[2] The acute observation of Ruth Benedict is applicable here: "Customs did not
challenge the attention of social theorists because it was the very stuff of their own
thinking; it was the lens without which they could not see at all. Precisely in proportion as
it was fundamental, it had its existence outside the fields of conscious attention" (*Patterns
of Culture*, Mentor Books [Boston, 1948], p. 8). Although this book was first printed in
1934, it is employed here to underline how long twentieth-century scholars have been
struggling with a methodology for custom. It is noteworthy that so long ago, too, Ruth
Benedict threw out a challenge to historians to resolve the issue; see especially ibid.,
pp. 214-215.

[3] M. K. McKintosh, "The Privileged Villeins of the English Ancient Demesne," *Viator*,
7 (19), 295-328.

[4] "Translation of the Charter of King John to the men of Godmanchester 20 May,
1212," by P. G. M. Dickinson in *Records of Huntingdonshire*, 1967, no. 1, p. 46.

Customs remained as a system of local government for so long because customs were capable of change. As with the byelaws of the open field villages that might have to be reissued with new seasons,[5] so the local community at Godmanchester had the view of frankpledge and its appointed inquisition as regular vehicles for the reassessment of customary requirements. Like microcosms of parliament, village communities and manorial town communities such as Godmanchester enacted new statutes with pompous self-importance.[6] Since custom derived its legitimacy from being recognized as an established practise, the changing of custom appears rather anomalous to modern eyes. However, for people of the time, there seemed to be no contradiction in juxtaposing change with permanency. Mary Bateson points out[7] how the customs of Godmanchester were changed several times over the late medieval period. And yet the whole community had commissioned the two bailiffs and twelve jurors of the view of frankpledge held 2 January 1324, "to treat and consult on the articles following, and what they should decide thereon was to be established for ever."[8]

Undoubtedly, however, customary law remained attractive and adequate for the people of a place like medieval Godmanchester most of all because the heart of the customs was the regulation of the family disposition of property. It does not explain very much to describe these family customs as private law, for "private" and "public" have had different social meanings over history.[9] Indeed, there would be a certain validity in describing the contents of this chapter as "the public face of a private sector." But it does help to answer the surprised questions of the modern inquirer about the knowledge and implementation of law evidenced by these pre-industrial peoples[10] to remark that customs touched the lives of each individual through marriage and the family. As anthropologists, expert in the study of family and inheritance, finally turned to pre-industrial Western Europe,[11] it is not surprising that the study of custom emerged as a necessary corollary to their investigations.

---

[5] W. O. Ault, *Open-Field Farming in Medieval England: A Study of Village By-Laws* (New York, 1972); J. A. Raftis, *Tenure and Mobility* (Toronto, 1964).

[6] See Appendix, "Godmanchester Customals, 1324 and 1465," below, pp. 431-442. Legal historians have been well aware of this flexibility of custom. See T. F. T. Plucknett, *A Concise History of the Common Law*, 4th ed. (London, 1948), pp. 290-291.

[7] *Borough Customs*, p. xxix.

[8] Ibid.

[9] The volume of Philippe Aries, *Centuries of Childhood* (New York, 1962), has served to highlight this fact, despite the controversial nature of his conclusions.

[10] John P. Dawson, *A History of Lay Judges* (Cambridge, Mass., 1960).

[11] The best review of this work still remains that by Lutz Berkner, "Recent Research

One may go further and suggest that the family inheritance customs of Godmanchester have such a distinct institutional thrust that they may be conveniently classified separately from other customs of the town. These other customs deal in large part with "public" administration. As such, they would be recorded to guarantee implementation by various officials and in the minds of the local citizenry they would be remembered by the penalties invoked for their violation. Such administrative customs were the election of bailiffs, the date of election of officers, payment of the king's farm, custody of the rolls, borough accounting, a view of frank-pledge, officers' accounting, the assizes of bread and beer, protection from compensation for certain kinds of disaster, royal carriage dues, use of correct names in pleading, duty of constable, delivery of seisin, game laws, labour laws, hearing of accounts, order in court and contravention of ordinances. Customs dealing with petty offences included fines for letting fald to foreigners, fines for digging near the highway, fines for impleading burgesses outside the liberty, for alienating land to foreigners and fines to exclude them from pasture as well as for the regulation of larceny.[12]

Owing to the disappearance of thirteenth and fourteenth-century frank-pledge rolls, very little formal organizational description about this "second administration category" of customs survives for the period studied by this volume. Some interesting social and economic consequences of this system of town government or administration do surface in surviving records and form the substance of Chapter 2. The present chapter will concern itself with the more specific data to be found in court rolls about the context of implementation of family custom. Whether this division of family and town administration is quite valid is a question to be raised in Chapter 5.

*
**

Fortunately, enough texts have survived because present in the edition of Mary Bateson to indicate how custom must have covered the main stages of the family cycle. Some of these texts are of a general nature such as the age of the son and daughter inheriting. However, most of these texts concerning customary regulations were clearly written up only because of some specific issue regarding inheritance and the disposition of the

---

on the History of the Family in Western Europe," *Journal of Marriage and the Family*, 35 (1973), 395-405.

   [12] For the complete list, see Mary Bateson's Introduction to *Borough Customs*, p. xxix; later versions of these texts may be found below in Appendix 1.

dower.[13] The fact remains that the most detailed written customary survivals would still be far from the complete social history of the families. As has already been noted, the exigencies possible to the biological, economic and social life of a family were manifold. Customs allowed for these exigencies but written records did not pretend to record them all.

Nevertheless, the splendid series of courts rolls for Godmanchester do contain enough cases involving custom to reconstruct its outlines for the family in the social and economic life of the town. Historians have recently begun to give a more orderly approach to the problem of surviving information about customs by employing the framework of the family cycle.[14] That is to say, customs, mainly dealing with help and support of the family, may be more fully appreciated in the "womb to tomb" sense over a term of one generation than as isolated facets of familial practise. This family cycle framework is employed in the following pages for presentation of the practises at Godmanchester from the time of the establishment of a family, through support of children by gifts, then of their parents by maintenance, until transmission of property to another family by will. In order to illustrate more precisely the cycle within the context of single family units, references to various stages of support for specific families are given at the close of this chapter.

THE DOWER

The customs of Godmanchester make clear that marriage is a matter for ecclesiastical jurisdiction.[15] As a result, the courts of Godmanchester make no effort to record the marriage arrangements of the people. Nonetheless, that most tangible evidence for the establishment of a family, the grant of a dower to the wife by her husband, was a clearly recognized title to property in Godmanchester courts. One of the most interesting features of this dower (*dos*) in the courts of Godmanchester was the way in which this form of property could be maintained in an active land market. The dower was simply protected by a phrase "save the dower." Examples of this were the purchase by John son of Robert Dosyn of meadow from William Dosyn, save the dower of Cristina Dosyn (1326); the receipt by William son of Nicholas Edward of land from executors of his father, save the dower of Pellagia (1312); the bequest to Alexander and William

---

[13] See the 1324 Customs below in Appendix 1.
[14] See *Family and Inheritance*, s.v. developmental cycle.
[15] See the transcript of the 1465 Customal below in Appendix 1.

sons of William Goni of land by Reginald Goni, save the dower of Reginald's widow Margaret (1312), the distribution of land to the heirs of Godfrey in the Lane by John and Reyner Gransden, save the dower of Isolda Gransden (1316); the sale of property by Henry Wilde and his wife Juliana, save the dower of the latter (1320).

Examples of the disposal of dowers are equally varied. In 1294 Mabel Bovetun sold one half acre of property, formerly her dower, to William Manipenny. In 1309 John son of Simon *de* Graveley purchased the dower of Sarra *de* Graveley. In 1281 Emma Puttok sold to Thomas Clerk land that she had held in dower. Most commonly, entries dealt with the sale from the mother's dower, as in 1291 when John Pellage sold one half acre from the dower of his mother Pellagia and in 1319 Lawrence Pays sold one half acre from the dower of his mother. Husbands could also dispose of the dower of their wives, as in 1288 when John Vecharem sold land from the dower of his late wife Felicia. A few texts may better illustrate this movement of dower holdings. As the third text below illustrates, not all claims to dower were legitimate.

> Thomas *de* Gowel is seized of one acre of land in a croft formerly belonging to William the son of Simon Clerk and bought from William the son of William the son of Simon Clerk as the dower of Elena the mother of the said William the son of William the son of Simon Clerk which dower the said Elena had in that acre of land, defending for the usual amount.[16]

> Again, the said Reyner [Garlop] is seized of one half acre abutting on Auhowebroc bought from Cristina super Montem and of one croft lying in West crofts next the place of William *le* Rede *de* Huntingdon containing 30 cris. This same croft the said Cristina had in gift of William super Montem her husband from his perquisites, defending for the usual amount. Then Walter on *le* Hil delivered over all his rights in any of the tenements that Cristina his mother sold in any fashion.[17]

> It is to be noted that in the same day Agnes, widow of Hugh *de* Mattishall *de* Huntingdon, came into the full court of Godmanchester and

---

[16] Box 4, bundle 3. 21 September 1329.
Thomas de Gowel sesitus est de una acra terre in crofto quondam Willelmi filii Simonis Clerici empta de Willelmo filio Willelmi filii Simonis Clerici una cum dote Elene matris predicti Willelmi filii Willelmi filii Simonis Clerici quod dictam dotem predicta Elena habuit in predicta acra terre ad defendendum pro fine debita.

[17] Box 4, bundle 1. 11 October 1331.
Reynerus Garlop cepit sesinam. Item dictus Reynerus sesitus est de dimidia acra abuttante super auhowebroc empta de Christina super Montem et de uno crofto iacente in Westcroftes iuxta placem Willelmi le Rede de Hunt' continente triginta cras quod dictum croftum dicta Christina habuit de dono Willelmi super Montem mariti sui de perquisitis suis ad defendendum pro fine debita. Unde Walterus on le Hil sursum dedit totum ius suum omnium tenementorum que Christina mater eius vendidit aliquo modo.

claimed one rod of meadow in Damgars as her dower. This same rod of meadow was found to be fully in the possession of Lord Phillip *de* Hemington. Therefore, the above Lord Phillip pleaded peaceful possession of that rod of meadow and this is granted to him through the hands of the bailiffs after consideration by the whole court.[18]

Given this clear recognition of *dos* as a title to property in Godmanchester courts, it is remarkable that the courts never employed the term *dos* in describing the establishment of family property arrangements. In this respect, Godmanchester courts would seem to have been technically perfect in avoiding interference with the jurisdiction of ecclesiastical courts. At the same time, by *not* employing the term *dos* Godmanchester courts may have left themselves free to enroll a great variety of *de facto* endowments of the wife by her husband. In any case, such seems to be the thrust of texts such as the following:

> Reginald in the Lane grants and concedes to Mariota his wife that principal messuage to be held for the term of Reginald's life.[19]

> Roger the son of Reginald Spruntyng and Reginald his father give into the hands of the bailiffs all their rights in one messuage and two acres of land along with one and one half rods of meadow for the use of Albrida daughter of Nicholas and wife of Roger. This tenement formerly belonged to Godfrey Juel and defends for the customary farm amount. Whence this land is to be taken in seisin after the death of the said Reginald father of the said Roger. And if it should happen that the said Roger and his children should die without heir to the above then the said tenement should revert to Reginald and after his death be sold and [the money] distributed for their souls.[20]

---

[18] Box 4, bundle 3. 13 July 1329.

Memorandum quod eodem die venit Agnes quondam uxor Hugonis de Matesale de Huntyngden in plena curia de Gumecestre et calumpniavit unam rodam prati in damgars nomine dotis sue de qua roda prati Dominus Philippus de Hemington inventus fuit plenarie presesitus. Ideo predictus Dominus Philippus postulavit pacem in predicta roda prati habenda et concessa est pax in eadem per considerationem totius curie de manu ballivi.

[19] Box 7, bundle 1. 28 February 1320.

Reginaldus in venalla dedit et concessit Mariote uxori sue istum principale mesuagium ad terminum vite sue dicti Reginaldi.

[20] Box 7, bundle 1. 18 August 1317. (The bracketed sums after texts are entry fines from the margin of the manuscript and not the farm payment.)

Rogerus filius Reginaldi Spruntyng et Reginaldus pater suus redd < ider > unt sursum in manus ballivorum ius suum unius mesuagii et duarum acrarum terre et unius rode et dimidie prati ad usum Albride filie Nicholai uxoris dicti Rogeri de tenemento quondam Galfridi Iuel ad deffendendum pro firma debita. Unde sesitus est Rogerus post obitum dicti Reginaldi patris dicti Rogeri, et si contingat quod dictus Rogerus et pueri sui obierint sine herede de se procreato dictum tenementum dicto Reginaldo rediet et post obitum suum vendetur et distribuatur pro animabus suis. (iid.)

It is to be noted that William the son of William Manipenny delivered into the hands of the bailiffs to the use of Roger Manipenny a messuage and six acres of land which tenement Reginald Goni gave to Margaret his wife in free marriage whence the said Roger is seised under the condition namely that if the said Margaret the wife of this Roger should outlive him that then she should have full tenure of that tenement, namely the messuage and six acres of land, for the term of her life. And this Roger fully concedes so that nevertheless it should descend to the heirs of the said Roger and Margaret should these be legitimately procreated and survive them. And should the said Roger survive Margaret he will hold and possess all the above tenement to do as he will with it. And the said Roger will have celebrated for this grant one annual [mass] for the soul of the above Reginald Goni and of all christians. Also that if the said Roger should die before the said Margaret without living heirs legitimately procreated by them that then the said tenement after the death of this Margaret should be sold and by her executors distributed among the poor of Godmanchester for the souls of the above[21] Roger, Margaret and Reginald.[22]

It is to be noted that Hugh son of Henry *de* Gidding came into the full court and delivered into the hands of the bailiffs the whole of the tenement land and meadow that he had or is able to claim in the vill of Godmanchester, whether in fields or meadows of the same, to the use of Elizabeth his wife and heirs procreated by them. And the said Elizabeth takes full seisin of the same to be defended by the usual [farm].[23]

---

[21] For marriages of Margaret, see below pp. 215, 303.

[22] Box 7, bundle 1. 19 February 1316.

Memorandum quod Willelmus filius Willelmi Manipeny reddidit sursum in manibus ballivorum ad usum Rogeri Manipeny < ius suum unius > mesuagii et sex acrarum terre quod dictum tenementum Reginaldus Gony dedit Margarete uxori sue in libero maritagio, unde dictus Rogerus sesitus est sub tali condicione quod si dicta margareta uxor dicti Rogeri dictum Rogerum supervixerit predictum tenementum scilicet mesuagium et sex acras terre plenarie tenebit ad terminum vite sue et dictus Rogerus bene concessit. Ita tamen quod descendat heredibus predictorum Rogeri et Margarete si aliquis inter illos legitime pervenerit et dictos Rogerum et Margaretam supervixerit; et si dictus Rogerus dictam Margaretam supervixerit totum predictum tenementum tenebit et possidebit ad suam voluntatem faciendam. Et dictus Rogerus celebrare faciet pro predicta concessione unum annuale pro anima predicti Reginaldi Gony et omnium christianorum. Ita tamen quod si dictus Rogerus obierit antequam dicta Margareta nec aliquis inter illos heres vivens sit procreatus, tunc predictum tenementum post obitum dicte Margaret vendetur et per executores suos distribuetur inter pauperes Gomecestre pro animabus predictorum Rogeri Margarete et Reginaldi antedicti.

[23] Box 6, bundle 1. 2 May 1297.

Memorandum quod Hugo filius Henrici de Gidding venit in plenam curiam et reddidit in manibus ballivorum totum tenementum terram et pratum quod habuit vel habere potuit in villa de Gomecestre in campis et in pratis eiusdem ad usum Elizabet uxoris sue et heredum ex ipsis procreatorum et dicta Elizabet plenam ibidem cepit sesinam pro defensione debita.

Richard Rome junior takes seisin of one messuage on Longelane bought from William Papworth and his wife Cristina, defending for $\frac{1}{2}$d. at the proper term, under this condition, that Joan the wife of this Richard should receive full possession of this messuage after his death if she should outlive him and after the death of both this is to be sold and distributed for the good of their souls.[24]

The dower was directed so much to the assistance of the wife and possible children, should the husband die, that for all practical purposes the dower and grant by will must have performed much the same function. For example, in the following text one may have a dower arrangement confirmed by will:

Matilda Mustarder takes seisin of nine and one half acres and one half rod of land from the gift of John Mattishale formerly her husband, as is contained in the will of John.[25]

Occasionally, the more formal marriage arrangements peep through our records, as in the following grant[26] in "free" and "legitimate" marriage:

It is to be noted that Cristina Godchild, widow of Henry *le* Warenter of Godmanchester, came into the full court of Godmanchester and delivered into the hands of the bailiffs four acres warnot with appurtenances in Godmanchester along with one croft that lies at Hinewellewelle to the use of Roger her son by which it is conceded to the same Roger in legitimate marriage. And at once the same Roger pays an entry fine for the said property and is conceded seisin of these four acres warnot with appurtenances and the croft by the bailiffs. It is also to be noted that the said Cristina Godchild after this seisin and payment of entry fine came to that Roger her son seeking the said croft lying at Hinewellewelle and one acre and one half of that land and meadow that she had previously granted to that same Roger, that this be returned to her. At first he did not grant this, but at length, at the request of friends and to obtain a mother's blessing the said croft and three and one half acres of land and meadow were willingly given to Cristina his mother and into the hands of the bailiffs delivered to

---

[24] Box 6, bundle 1. 7 October 1316.

Ricardus Rome junior cepit sesinam de uno mesuagio in longelane empto de Willelmo Papp[worth] et Christina uxore eius ad defendendum pro obolo ad terminum sub hac conditione quod Johanna uxor dicti Ricardi plenarie dictum mesuagium recipiat post obitum suum si diutius vixerit et post decessum amborum vendetur et distribuatur pro animabus eorum.

[25] Box 7, bundle 1. 20 March 1320.

Matilda Mustarder cepit seisinam de ix acris terre dimidia acra et dimidia roda de dono Johannis Matesale olim mariti sui prout in testamento Johannis continetur. (iis.)

[26] For other grants under this title, see below pp. 21-23.

her use, on condition that if the said Cristina or any of her assignees at any time should wish to sell the property, the same Roger would have prior right of purchase. And the above Cristina conceded the same and for the above croft and three and one half acres of land and meadow quitclaimed to Roger her son all that land first granted to him in marriage and transferred in the court namely one half acre of land at Potterismade next Richard Acry, also one half acre of land at Fourehowys next John Manipenny, also one acre and one rod at Rygweis next Richard Tinctor, also one half acre on Holebroc next Godfrey Dosyn, also one acre and one foreland called Randolfishabyr, also two rods in Madecroft next the forland of Felicia Seman, also one rod in Wigmere next Reginald Alred, also one half acre on Schiterishul next Thomas Balle, also one half acre in Berinscroft next Henry Rode, also one half acre on Helderstubfurlong next Godfrey son of Robert, also one half acre on longlundhavedin next Lytlewille, also one rod facing Depedenbroc next the Prior of Merton, also one and one half rod at Greyorn next the heirs of Martin super *le* Wal, also one rod of meadow below Aldorp next Godfrey the son of Matilda, also one rod in Rowismade next the heirs of Cristina Penytour by one year in the other year one rod in Le Redmade and one rod on Hulmade, also one swat at Bramtomibus, also one rod on Hodepol next John ad Cirpos.[27]

[27] Box 7, bundle 1. 23 May 1297.

Memorandum quod Cristina Godchild relicta Henrici Le Warenter de Gomecestre venit in plenam curiam de Gomecestre et reddidit sursum in manus ballivorum quatuor acras warnot cum pertinenciis in Gomecestre et unum croftum quod fuit apud Hinewelle-welle ad usum Rogeri filii sui sicut alias eidem Rogero in legitimo matrimonio concesserat, et statim idem Rogerus predictam terram cum pertinenciis ibidem gersummavit, et ballivi predicto Rogero de predictis quatuor acris warnot cum pertinenciis et de predicto crofto sesinam plenam contulerunt, memorandum eciam quod predicta Cristina Godchild post predictam sesinam et gersummam datam venit predicto Rogero filio suo petens predictum croftum iacens apud Hinewalwelle et unam acram et dimidiam terre et prati de terra que prius eidem Rogero dedisset redonare sibi, qui eciam primo non concessit sed tandem prece amicorum et pro benedictione materna possidenda predictum croftum et predictas tres dimidias acras terre et prati predicte Cristine matri sue voluntarie dimisit et in manibus ballivorum ad usum illius sursum reddidit, tali quoque condicione quod si predicta Cristina vel aliquid suorum assignatorum aliquo tempore valent predictum croftum vendere, idem Rogerus pre omnibus aliis possit illud emere et predicta Cristina concessit et eadem Cristina pro predicto crofto et predictis tribus dimidiis acris terre et prati in quietum clamavit Rogero filio suo totam illam terram quam prius ei in matrimonio et in curia dedisset, videlicet dimidiam acram terre apud Potterismade iuxta Ricardum Acry. Item dimidiam acram terre apud Fourehowys iuxta Johannem Manip. Item unam acram et unam rodam terre apud Rygweis iuxta Ricardum Tingtorem. Item dimidiam acram supra Holebroc iuxta Galfridum Dosyn. Item unam acram cum una forera que vocatur Randolfishabyr. Item duas rodas in Madecroft iuxta foreram Felicie Seman. Item unam rodam in Wigmere iuxta Reginaldum Alred. Item dimidiam acram super schiterishul iuxta Thomam Balle. Item dimidiam acram in Berinscroft iuxta Henricum Rode. Item dimidiam acram super Helderstubforlong iuxta Galfridum filium Roberti. Item dimidiam acram supra Longlandhanedin iuxta Lytlewille. Item unam rodam versus Depedenbroc iuxta priorem Merton. Item unam rodam et

Dowry

Godmanchester court policy with respect to the property that the bride brought to the marriage — her dowry (*maritagium*) would seem to have been much the same as that concerning the *dos*. At the same time, unlike the title *dos*, the term *maritagium* is not carefully preserved as a title to property. In part, this may be explained by the fact that the courts referred to the settlement of land on sons (and, one may assume, the wife although she is not named) as free marriage arrangements. The few cases of these have been included in the previous section since for all practical purposes such arrangements were the same as "endowing" the couple. In large part, however, the courts were simply concerned to register gifts, such as the first example in the following text, that were tantamount to dowries, but without being technically described as such. Some of the relatively few explicit references to such "dowry" arrangements are given below:

> Isolda wife of Robert Alryth took seisin of one acre of land and one rod of meadow and 12 beddis of curtilage in West crofts by the gift of Dyonisia her mother. This defends as five rods at the proper term.[28]

> Nicholas the son of Roger *le* Barbour *de* Huntingdon is seised of a half acre of land in gift from Joan his mother, which land John *de* Hamerton her [father] gave to that Joan in marriage.[29]

> Cristina, wife of Richard *le* Taylor, formerly daughter of Roger Maddermonger, took seisin of a half acre of land on Dekwelebroc facing the forland formerly of Roger *de* Strateshylle, chaplain and of one rod of land lying on Shitersile as gift of her mother in free marriage. Furthermore, the same Cristina is seised of one cottage lying between the place of Edward Kyne on one side and the place of John Glewe on the other, which cottage Isolda Pikering gave to the same Cristina and her heirs in free marriage. On the same day, Richard Cissor, husband of the above Cristina was seised of that same cottage to have and to hold in gift of the above Isolda Pikering in

---

dimidiam apud Greyorn iuxta heredes martini super Le Wal. Item unam rodam prati sub Aldorp iuxta Galfridum filium Matilde. Item unam rodam in Rowismade iuxta heredes Cristine Pentur per unum annum et in alio anno unam rodam in Le Redmade et unam rodam super Hulmade. Item unam swat apud Bramtomibus. Item unam rodam super Hodepol iuxta Johannem ad cirpos.

[28] Box 6, bundle 1. 2 June 1306.

Isolda uxor Roberti Alryth cepit sesinam de una acra terre et una roda prati et duodecim beddis curtilagii in Westcroftes de dono Dyonisie matris eius ad defendendum pro v. rodis ad terminum. (vid.)

[29] Box 7, bundle 1. (?) 1313-1314.

Nicholas filius Rogeri le Barbour de Hunt. sesitus est de una dimidia acra terre de dono Johanne matris sue quam Johannes de Hamerton < pater > eius dedonavit dicte Johanne in matrimonii. (iid.)

free marriage until the end of the life of that same Richard, except for 12d. to be paid to that Isolda as long as she lives. The above three rods of land owe as the custom of the vill as determined by the new ordinance enacted by the whole community.[30]

Isabella, daughter of Margaret daughter of William *de* Warmington, clerk, is seised of an entire messuage that lies in Longelane next the [curtilage of] the Prior of Merton, coming to the above Isabella after the death of Margaret her mother by right of inheritance. This same messuage, William Clerk formerly gave to Margaret his daughter and mother of this Isabella in free marriage along with one rod of land lying at le Madecroft and one rod of land abutting on Shepenbroc of the above donation. In addition, she is seised of one rod of land lying at le Heyhavenden bought from Godfrey the son of Amicia, to defend for the due obligation.[31]

Agnes, wife of Reginald Godwar, took seisin of 18 cris of curtilage lying in Wynewal, which same 18 cris this Agnes had from the gift of William Clerk her father in free marriage, to defend for the due obligations.[32]

William the son of Thomas Mileward and Emma his wife took seisin of a place ... and five rods of land ... which said tenement this William and Emma had by gift of Simon Persoun in free marriage. And if this same Emma should die without heir of her body then this tenement indicated in the above seisin, should revert to the heirs of Simon Persoun, saving the

---

[30] Box 7, bundle 1. 21 March 1325.

Christina uxor Ricardi le Taylor quondam filia Rogeri Madirmonger cepit sesinam de dimidia acra terre supra dokwelebroc versus foreram quondam Rogeri de Stratesille capellani et de una roda terre iacente super shitersile de dono matris sue in libero matrimonio. Iterum eadem Christina sesita est de uno cotagio iacente inter placeam Edwardi Kine ex una parte et placeam Johannis Glewe ex altera quod dictum cotagium Isolda Pikering eidem Christine dedit et heredibus suis in libero matrimonio. Eodem die Ricardus Cissor maritus predicte Christine sesitus est de predicto cotagio habendo et tenendo de dono predicte Isolde Pikering in libero matrimonio ad terminum vite predicti Ricardi, salvis duodecim denariis solvendis predicte Isolde dum vixerit. Predicte tres rode terre debent defendi prout consuetudo ville exigit de nova ordinatione facta per totam communitatem. (ivd.)

[31] Box 4, bundle 3. 21 November 1331.

Isabella filia Margareta filie Willelmi de Warmington clerici sesita est de uno mesuagio integro sicut iacet in Longelane iuxta le [curtilagium] Prioris de Merton accidente predicte Isabelle post obitum Margarete matris eius iure hereditario, quod dictum mesuagium Willelmus Clericus quondam dedit Margarete filie eius et matri dicte Isabelle in libero matrimonio et de una roda terre iacente apud le madecroft et de una roda terre abuttante super Shepenbroc de donatione predicta. Item sesita est de una roda terre iacente apud le Heyhavenden empta de Galfrido filio Amicie ad defendendum pro fine debita. (iiid.)

[32] Box 4, bundle 3. 12 December 1331.

Agnes uxor Reginaldi Godwar cepit sesinam de xviii cris curtilagii iacentibus in Wynewal quas dictas xviii cras dicta Agnes habuit de dono Willelmi clerici patris eius in libero matrimonio ad defendendum pro fine debita. (id.)

dowry of the above William Mileward. This property defends for the due service.[33]

Isolda, widow of John Quenyng, took seisin of land three cris in width which lies between the messuage of Reginald the son of Robert on one side and the messuage of John Quenyng on the other and heads on the King's Road at one end and at the other on the common bank leading towards the mill of Godmanchester. She also took seisin of a place of land lying between the messuage of John Manipenny and the *divisa* of John Quenyng and abutting at one end on the same and at the other on the messuage of John Quenyng next his gore where there is now a certain small building. And these two parts ought to defend for one rod. She was also seised of one rod and one half of meadow at Wilewinestub and of a half acre of land at Fowerehowes, to defend for one rod. In addition she was seised of one messuage which formerly belonged to her father and lies in West Street between the messuage of Godfrey Clerk on one side and William in the Lane on the other and abuts at one end on the King's Road and on the other on the field called Madecroft, along with 12 acres of land in the fields of Godmanchester from which the same Isolda holds four acres of land by title of free marriage and eight acres as heir and for these she pays the due services.[34]

GIFT

In places such as Godmanchester where specific laws governed the disposition of family property at death of the parent (or parents), the gift of

---

[33] Box 4, bundle 3. 9 March 1340.

Willelmus filius Thome Mileward et Emma uxor eius ceperunt sesinam de una placea ... et v rodis terre ... que dicta tenementa dicti Willelmus et Emma habuerunt de dono Simonis Persoun in libero matrimonio. Et si dicta Emma obierit absque herede sui corporis ex tunc dicta tenementa in presenti sesina prenotata redient heredibus Simonis Persoun salva dote predicti Willelmi Mileward ad defendendum pro fina debita. (ivd.)

[34] Box 6, bundle 1. 3 March 1295.

Isolda relicta Johannis Quenyne cepit seysinam de tribus cris terre in latitudine que iacent inter mesuagium Reginaldi filii Roberti ex parte una et mesuagium Johannis Quenyne ex altera et abutant ad unum capud super viam regiam et ad aliud capud super communem ripam que fluit versus molendinum de Gomecestre. Item de una placea terre que iacet inter mesuagium Johannis Manipeny et divisam Johannis Quenyne et abbuttat ad unum capud super predictam et ad aliud capud super mesuagium Johannis Quenyne iuxta garennum suum cum quadam parva domo in eadem sita, et hec due partes debeant defendi pro una roda. Item de una roda et dimidia prati apud Wilewinestub et de una dimidia acra terre apud Fowerehowes ad defendendum pro una roda. Item de uno mesuagio quod quidem mesuagium quondam fuit patris sui et iacet in Westrata inter mesuagium Galfridi Clerici ex una parte et Willelmi in venella ex altera et abutat ad unum capud super viam regiam et ad aliud capud super campum qui dicitur Madecroft et de xii acris terre in campis de Gomecestre de quibus dicta Isolda tenet iiii acras terre nomine liberi maritagii, et viii nomine hereditatis et debent defendi pro servicio debito.

property during the life of the donor was the main means of providing for non-inheriting — or even inheriting but momentarily needy — members of the family. As we have seen in the texts in the previous section, the dowry arrangement was one form of gift for Godmanchester girls. An element of gift as a basic feature of the family society[35] would underly intra-familial sales and various features of bequests. Some of the practical results of settlement of property on family members during the lifetime of the donor will be seen in the final section of Chapter 5 below.

The term gift (*ex dono, de dono,* etc.) actually is employed with regularity only after 1300. For the generation prior to 1300 there is but the one reference to gift in 1296. In the courts before 1300 and to some degree afterwards gifts were apparently included under the general formula of surrender of land in the hands of the bailiffs (*sursum reddidit,* etc.). That is to say, a vast number of properties were conveyed to other members of families without employing the technical term "gift." In short, parallel to avoidance of the terms dower and dowry, the courts of Godmanchester may have found the simple conveyance entry an adequate protection for the gift.[36] However, taking for the moment only those court roll entries that employ the technical term "gift," some interesting uses of the gift may be identified.

There are 153 entries emplying the term "gift" for the courts between 1300 and 1326. This figure does not allow for the fact that *inter vivos* and *post obit* gifts were frequently noted in the same court roll entry. Among the 118 conveyances by gift where the family relationship has been specified, 43 of the recipients of the gifts were male and all of these were sons, except for the five gifts received from brothers and one from a wife. Of the remaining approximately two thirds of the recipients who were female, 62 were single daughters and four were married. The remaining gifts were given to two daughters in seven other families, to three daughters in three families, to two sons and two daughters in another family and to one son and four daughters in yet another family.

One can perhaps see the important role of endowed women in late medieval Godmanchester as much from the donors as recipients of gifts. Only five gifts were given by both parents. About one third of the gifts

---

[35] Beginnings of the contemporary rediscovery of the role of the gift in pre-industrial society may be traced in Marcel Mauss, *The Gift: forms and functions of exchange in archaic societies,* trans. Ian Cunnison, introduction by E. E. Evans (London: Pritchard, 1966).

[36] That the gift could be employed as a legal fiction to protect women of the family is illustrated below, p. 227.

were given by fathers. But well over one half of the gifts were granted by mothers. Most of these gifts by mothers were to daughters although 16 were donations to sons. The majority (9) of the remaining donors were brothers. In short, the use of gift by mothers, and especially in relation to unmarried daughters, parallels similar practise in last wills in England at this time.[37]

Here are some examples of the actual forms that these gifts took at Godmanchester:

> Cristina, daughter of Nicholas Drewe, took seisin of two acres and one half rod of land in gift from that same Nicholas Drewe, to defend for one acre Warnoht and one penny at the proper time. This same Cristina will also have the messuage of the above Nicholas after his death, except for the house in which Agnes Baker lives and four crops from the half acre of land lying in Stonilond after the death of the same Nicholas.[38]

> It is to be noted that Emma, daughter of Edward Goni, took seisin of the gift of the said Edward her father, namely of one house, and of the following land, that is, of one croft which is called Mottiscroft, also of one rod of land on Nutteforlong and one rod of land on Littlewong in Le Mers and of one acre at Grenehowebroc and of one half acre at Litelhul and of one acre of land at Holebroc and of one half acre of land at Heyham along with one rod of meadow on Hodepol with two Delys abutting on Madehavid — to defend for two acres and a $\frac{1}{2}$d. at the term in East Street. The same [Emma] also took seisin of one half of one half acre of land on Collefurlong next the road. All these lands the above Edward gave to Emma his daughter except for the half of all reserved to himself.[39]

> Cristina, the daughter of Albrit Morgrove, took seisin of one and one half rods lying in Flexmer and of one swat of meadow lying on Le Morlond

---

[37] See Sheehan, *The Will in Medieval England*, pp. 263-264.

[38] Box 6, bundle 1. 3 August 1301.
Cristina filia Nicolai Drewe cepit sesinam de duabus acris terre et dimidia roda terre ex dono predicti Nicolai Drewe ad defendendum pro una acra warnoht et uno denario ad terminum. Item dicta Cristina habebit mesuagium predicti Nicolai post decessum eiusdem preter unam domum in qua Agnes Baker manet et quattuor vesturas unius dimidie acre terre iacentis super Stonilond post decessum eiusdem Nicolai. (iiiid.)

[39] Box 6, bundle 1. 7 May 1299.
Memorandum quod Emma filia Edwardi Goni sesinam cepit de dono predicti Edwardi patris sui videlicet de una domo et de terra subscripta videlicet de uno crofto quod vocatur Mottiscroft. Item de una roda terre super Nutteforlong et de una roda terre super Littlewong in Le Mers et de una acra apud Grenehowebroc et de una dimidia acra apud Littlehul et de una acra terre apud Holebroc et de una dimidia acra terre apud Heyhom cum una roda prati super Hodepol cum duobus Delys super Madehavedin abuttantibus ad defendendum pro duabus acris et obolo ad terminum in Estrata. Item eadem cepit sesinam de medietate unius dimidie acre terre super Collefurlong prope viam. Hanc quidem terram predictus Edwardus dedit Emme filie sue salva sibi medietate tocius.

next John Pentel and of one rod of land lying in Le Mers and of one rod of land lying next the forland of Cristina Marewele next Le Mers and of one half acre in Bermerscroft next the land of Roger Kyng and the half acre abutting on Le Mar' next the Canouneswong and the half acre on the upper end of Shepdenbroc and the half acre lying on Waterslond in Depden and the half acre lying on Le Westlayes next Henry Rode and the half acre of meadow lying at Le Eldebyrystede in Westmade and the one half swat of meadow next to the head del bene and the three "curti" swat abutting on Hodepolhavden and the half acre of land lying on Le Pesefurlong in Bernescroft and the one rod of land lying at Overewell. All these above holdings the said Cristina had in gift from Isolda her mother to be received legally into her power after the death of the said Isolda and her husband Albrit and by the understanding that she will and truly defend for the due obligations just as her father and mother before her. In addition, the same Cristina on the same day in open court took seisin from the original gift of Isolda her mother of one rod of land lying on Corunland in Depden along with one quarter of land on Duhowebroc and one rod of meadow lying in Le Bene in Westmade, to defend for the usual obligations.[40]

MAINTENANCE AGREEMENTS

While most of the 153 gifts discussed in the previous section were to take immediate effect, twelve of the gifts by mothers and eight by fathers were to take effect after the death of the respective parents. Furthermore, as is exemplified by the texts above under the section on Gifts, the *post obit* arrangement could take many forms. All, or only a portion of the property could be conveyed at any time as one method of providing for

---

[40] Box 5, bundle 9. 25 September 1337.
    Christina filia Albrici Morgrove cepit sesinam de una roda et dimidia terre iacente in Flexmere, et de uno swat prati iacente super le morlond iuxta Johannem Pentel, et de una roda terre iacente in le mers, et de una roda terre iacente iuxta foreram Christine Marwel iuxta le mers, et dimidia acra in bermerscroft iuxta terram Rogeri Kynge et dimidia acra abuttante supra le mar' iuxta le Canouneswong, et dimidia acra supra superiorem partem de Shepdenbroc et dimidia acra terre iacente supra Waterslond in depden, et dimidia acra iacente super le Westlayes iuxta Henricum Rode, et dimidia acra prati iacente apud le Eldebyrystede in Westmade, et dimidio swat prati ad proximum capud del bene, tribus curtis swat abuttantibus super hodepolhaveden et dimidia acra terre iacente super le pesefurlong in bernescroft, et una roda terre iacente apud Overewell. Que supradicta tenementa dicta Christina habuit de dono Isolde matris eiusdem in sua legitima potestate recipienda post obitum dicte Isolde et Albrici mariti sui et sub forma quod se bene et honeste habeat penes patrem et matrem ut prius ad defendendum pro forma debita et consueta. Item eadem Christina eodem die in plena curia recepit sesinam de dono pristino Isolde matris sue de una roda terre iacente super Corunlond in depden, una quadrote terre supra Duhowebroc, et una roda prati iacente in le bene in Westmade ad defendendum pro forma debita. (xd.)

members of the family. Another method was the immediate transfer of property by the parents (or parent) while the recipient guaranteed maintenance of his or her parents (or parent). The details for only some half dozen such maintenance agreements are to be found under conveyance by gift. However, this type of agreement was common in traditional societies and very likely was frequent at Godmanchester too although it was not found necessary to record many of these agreements. Nevertheless, about a score of such agreements were recorded for the late thirteenth and early fourteenth centuries and show us the varied form of these important intra-family contracts.

In some instances a very casual arrangement of non-specified support would seem to have been adequate. Among these examples, it may be noted that a family relationship is indicated in one, a gift in another and simply a rental agreement for the others:

> Margaret, widow of Alexander Grigory, came into the full court and surrendered into the bailiffs hands all that land that she had in the fields of Godmanchester as well as meadow and croft to the use of Simon le Rede and his heirs in return for the food for her maintenance for the rest of her days. And that Simon took seisin of that land, meadow and croft.[41]

> Reginald Warde took seisin of two rods of land in gift from Matilda Grinde, defending for one rod, in return for the sustenance of that same Matilda. Of this land one rod lies in Benecroft and one rod at Deutwel-broc.[42]

> Felicia, daughter of John Ede, is seised of one half acre of land at Todalysbroc, one rod of land at Pottersmade, one rod of land at the upper end of Corpdenebroc, one swat of meadow under le Hilmade in gift from John her father, to defend for the due farm. And if that John should become needy in any time during his life she may be expected to assist him.[43]

---

[41] Box 6, bundle 1. 20 March 1292.

Margareta relicta Alexandri Grigorii venit in plenam curiam et reddidit in manibus ballivorum totam terram quam habuit in campis de Gomecestre cum prato in eadem et crofta ad opus Symonis le Rede et heredum suorum pro sustentatione sui victus in usque in extremis diebus suis et quod Symon cepit seysinam de predicta terra et prato et crofta.

[42] Box 7, bundle 1. 29 January 1316.

Reginaldus Warde cepit sesinam de duabus rodis terre de dono Matilda Grynd' ad deffendendum pro una roda pro sustentatione eiusdem Matilde unde una roda iacet in Benecroft una roda apud Dutwelbroc. (id.)

[43] Box 4, bundle 3. 17 February 1340.

Felicia filia Johannis Ede est seysita de una dimidia acra terre apud Todalysbroc, una roda terre apud Pottersmad', una roda terre ad superiorem finem de Corpdenebroc, una swat prati sub le Hilmad' de dono Johannis patris sui ad deffendendum pro firma debita et si dictus Johannes indigerit per tempus vite sue licite possit ipsum auxiliare. (iid.)

Joan Ede took seisin of three rods of land on Hamhyl bought from Cristina Boneville, and to defend for one half acre, under this condition that the said Cristina may receive one bushel of grain each year according to the grain that has been sown that year until the end of the life of that Cristina.[44]

An agreement was made between Vincent *de* Dunton on one hand and Mariota the daughter of Simon Atenock on the other, as follows: That the said Mariota should let all her land for a term of nine years to that Vincent and that same Vincent should support that Mariota during that same time. And the above Vincent may dispose and order the use of the above land and meadows as he wills and he will give to that same woman each year six bushels of barley.[45]

In most texts support is more specified and tends to suggest that a regular form was in common use:

It is to be noted that William the son of John Clere surrendered into the hands of the bailiffs all his rights in his whole messuage, two acres and one rod of land and one half acre of meadow to the use of John Millicent and his heirs. Whence the said John took seisin for himself and his heirs, defending for the due farm. Said John and his heirs will provide for that same William all that he may need in food, drink and clothing in return for this grant and the said William will continue to work in the service of this John and his heirs so long as he is able to do so. And he gives as entry fine 1d.[46]

John, son of Eusebius Pope, surrendered into the hands of the bailiffs all his rights in all his tenements for the use of Agnes his mother, to defend for

---

[44] Box 7, bundle 1. 3 September 1310.
Johanna Ede cepit seysinam de iii rodis terre super hamhyl emptis de Christina Bonevyle ad deffendendam pro dimidia acra sub hac forma quod dicta Christina recipiet unum buccellum bladi quolibet anno quando seminetur de tale blado quale seminetur videlicet ad terminum dicte Christine. (iid.)

[45] Box 7, bundle 1. 28 October 1317.
Convenit inter Vincencium de Duntone ex una perte et Mariotam filiam Symonis atenock ex altera, videlicet quod predicta Mariota dimisit totam terram suam usque ad terminum ix annorum predicto Vincencio et predictus Vincencius exibebit predictam Mariotam durante termino predicto et predictus Vincencius disponet et ordinabit de omnibus predictis terris et pratis pro libito sue voluntatis et dabit predicto mulieri per annum vi buccellos ordei.

[46] Box 7, bundle 1. Date uncertain, 1315-1316.
Memorandum quod Willelmus filius Johannis Clere reddidit sursum in manus ballivi totum ius suum totius mesuagii sui et duarum acrarum et unius rode terre et dimidie acre prati ad usum Johannis Milisent et heredum suorum, unde dictus Johannes cepit sesinam pro se et heredibus suis ad deffendendum pro firma debita dictus Johannes et sui heredes invenient dicto Willelmo que sibi neccessaria sunt in cibis potibus vestimentis pro dicta concessione et dictus Willelmus in servicio dicti Johannis et suorum heredum laborabit dum poterit et dedit gersumam unum denarium. (id.)

the due farm. And for that gift the same Agnes will make available to that above John her son all that he should need, namely lodging, food and drink, clothing both linen and woollen, to the end of his life. And it is not permitted to that above named Agnes, nor to anyone in her name, to diminish or sell any part of those said tenements during the life of that same John.[47]

John son of John son of William son of Simon Clerk, gave to that above John [his father] all his rights in a messuage and one acre of land, to defend for the due farm. This grant was given on condition that the said son of William should live with that same John his son at his expense save lodging for Roger his brother. Whence he is given seisin. Should the said John become needy and sell the above messuage or in that same messuage at some time should wish to live then the said Roger may be removed from that lodging.[48]

William Juel surrendered into the hands of the bailiffs all the tenements that he had and was able to have to the use of Hugh Gile, to defend for the due farm. Whence the said Hugh is seised of these lands on condition that Hugh will provide for that William for the rest of his life all that he should need in food, drink, lodging and clothes as well as a bushel of peas each year and at his death 100 shillings and one sheep to the vicar immediately as mortuary.[49]

John Bonis took seisin of a messuage lying in Post Street next Gilbert Clerk in gift from William his father. This was on condition that the said

[47] Box 7, bundle 1. 18 November 1316.
Johannes filius Eusebii Pope reddidit sursum in manibus ballivorum totum ius suum omnium tenementorum suorum ad usum Angnetis matris sue ad deffendendum pro firma debita, et pro dicta donaccione predicta Agnes inveniet et tribuit Johanni filio suo antedicto omnia sibi neccessaria videlicet hospicium, cibum et potum, vestimenta linena et lanena ad terminum vite sue, nec licebit Angneti antedicte nec alicui nomine eius aliquam partem de dictis tenementis minuere vel vendere dum dictus Johannes advixerit. (xviiid.)
[48] Box 7, bundle 1. 16 February 1324.
Johannes filius Johannis filii Willelmi filii Simonis Clerici dedit Johanni suo [patri] predicto totum ius suum unius mesuagii sui unius acre terre ad deffendendum pro firma debita. Ita quod dictus filius Willelmi demoratur cum dicto Johanne filio suo antedicto ad sumptus suos. Unde est seysitus salvo hospicio Rogero fratri suo, quousque dictus Johannes indigeret dictum mesuagium vendere aut in ipso mesuagio antedicto quando-cumque voluerit moram suam facere, tunc deinceps dictus Rogerus de dicto hospicio carebit. (ivd.)
[49] Box 7, bundle 1. 31 May 1324.
Willelmus Juel reddidit sursum in manus ballivi omnia tenementa sua que habuit et habere potuit ad opus Hugonis Gile ad deffendendum pro firma debita. Unde dictus Hugo est seysitus sub tali condicione: dictus Hugo inveniat dicto Willelmo ad terminum vite predicti Willelmi omnia sibi necessaria in cibis, potibus, hospicio, vestura et quolibet anno unum buccellum pisarum et in obitu suo C.s. et unum bidentem vicario cito pro principale. (xiid.)

John should sustain the above William his father in a suitable manner for the rest of the life of that William. And if the above John should be lacking in any way in providing sustenance in a suitable manner for that William, then it will be allowed for that William to sell or alienate the above messuage to whomever and whenever he wishes. Furthermore, if Richard the son of that William should return home after the death of that William, or prior to his death, one half of that messuage may be his to hold and enjoy in the form by which the said John Bonis is enjoined and as this obligation would pertain to the half of that messuage.[50]

John Puttock and his wife Alditha took seisin of a messuage lying in Post Street next Gilbert Clerk in gift from William Bonis. This was on condition that the above John and Alditha his wife should sustain William Bonis for the rest of his life in a proper manner in food and in clothing. And if the said John and Alditha his wife should default in this sustenance of the above William in any manner at any time that then the said William Bonis may have and enjoy possession of that messuage to sell or let to whomsoever and whenever he might wish without obligation to anyone.[51]

The requirements of the corrody[52] and customary "state of life" were specified in some texts:

Agnes the daughter of John Pellage was seised of three acres of land along with appurtenances from the land of Richard the son of Simon

---

[50] Box 7, bundle 1. 26 December 1325.

Johannes Bonys cepit sesinam de uno mesuagio iacente in poststrate iuxta Gilbertum clericum de dono Willelmi patris sui. Ita quod dictus Johannes sustineat predictum Willelmum patrem suum congruo modo prout decet ad terminum vite predicti Willelmi. Et si predictus Johannes in sustentatione predicti Willelmi defecerit quin honeste sustineat deinde bene liceat dicto Willelmo predicto mesuagium vendere vel alio modo alienare cuicumque et quandocumque voluerit. Item si Ricardus filius dicti Willelmi in patriam redierit post decessum dicti Willelmi vel ante, medietatem predicti mesuagii habeat et gaudeat in forma per quam dictus Johannes bonys ligatus est et pro forma qua honorata est medietas dicti mesuagii. (iiid.)

[51] Box 7, bundle 1. 5 June 1326.

Johannes Puttok et Alditha uxor eius ceperunt sesinam de uno mesuagio iacente in potestrate iuxta Gilbertum Clericum de dono Willelmi bonys. Ita quod predicti Johannes et Aldytha uxor eius predictum Willelmum bonys honeste sustineant ad terminum vite predicti Willelmi victu et vestitu, et si dictus Johannes et Aldytha uxor eius in sustentatione predicti Willelmi defecerint aliquo tempore deinde dictus Willelmus Bonys bene teneat et gaudiat predictum mesuagium et vendat vel dimitat cuique et quandocumque voluerit sine conditione alicuius. (viid.)

For some reason that we do not know, the previous arrangement with John Bonis seems to have been waived for this agreement with John Puttock and his wife Alditha.

[52] The corrody as an insurance arrangement for more wealthy members of society has been frequently studied. For a useful picture from a town not too far from Godmanchester, see "Corrodies at the Carmelite Friary of Lynn," by the late A. G. Little, ed. by Eric Stone, *Journal of Ecclesiastical History*, 9 (1958), 8-29.

Notting, to be defended at the proper term. This was done by agreement that the above Richard should have food and clothing from the Abbot of Ramsey and if there is default John Pellage as heir will recover the above agreement. These were the witnesses: Reginald son of Robert, Thomas Balle, then bailiffs, and others.[53]

Cristina daughter of John Pellage was seised of three acres of land and one rod of meadow that John, called Pistor, surrendered to her through the hands of the bailiffs on condition that the corrody of one brother at Ramsey in the money of the Abbot should be paid. And if it should happen that this corrody should be wanting in any manner then his land should revert to him.[54]

Gilbert the son of Eusebius in the Lane took seisin of all the tenements coming to him as heir upon the death of Matilda his mother, to be defended for the due farm. Also, of one acre of land on Blakelond bought from the executors of Richard the son of Augustine Turk, to be defended for one half rod. Furthermore, Eusebius, father of that said Gilbert, surrendered into the hands of the bailiff to the use of that Gilbert all his rights in all his lands, except for the one acre and one rod of land reserved at the will of that said Eusebius, to defend for the due farm. And the said Eusebius is to receive from that Gilbert every year for his life for that gift lodging, food and clothing according to his dignity and state of life along with the crop of one half acre sown with barley and the half of all the grain on the above tenement. On the death of the said Eusebius the will is to be administered according to his wishes. And if the said Gilbert should be deficient in any matter of the agreement to detriment of the above mentioned Eusebius all the above tenements are to be returned unconditionally to his possession and enjoyment.[55]

[53] Box 6, bundle 1. 23 April 1282.

Agnes filia Johannis Pelage seysita fuit de tribus acris terre cum pertinentiis de terra Ricardi filii Symonis Noting ad defendendum propter terminum in his pactis quod predictus Ricardus habebit victum et vestitum suum de Abbate de rammiseye et si deficit ibi Johannes Pel[age here]des suos parcabunt predictum pactum hiis testibus: Reginaldo filio Roberti, Thoma Balle tunc ballivi et aliis.

[54] Box 6, bundle 1. 14 May 1282.

Christiana filia Johannis Pelage seysita fuit de tribus acris terre et una roda prati quas Johannes dictus Pistor ad opus eius reddidit in manibus ballivorum ad opus eius, hiis condicionibus quod corrodum unius fratris apud rammeseye de denario Abbatis percipiet, et si contingat ipsum [a] dicto corrodio distrandari mitis suis in exigentibus quod terram suam habebit retrorsum.

[55] Box 7, bundle 1. 28 July 1317.

Gilbertus filius Eusebii in the Lane cepit sesinam de omnibus tenementis sibi accidentibus hereditàrie post decessum Matilde matris sue ad deffendendum pro firma debita. Item de una roda terre super Blakelond empta de executoribus Ricardi filii Augustini Turk ad deffendendum pro dimidia roda. Item Eusebius pater dicti Gilberti reddidit sursum in manus ballivorum ad usum dicti Gilberti totum ius suum omnium tenementorum suorum preter unius acre terre et unius rode reservandarum ad

Other arrangements would seem to reflect less trust and sense of security between the parties involved:

> It is to be noted that Reginald Spruntyng and Roger his son took seisin of a messuage lying in Arnyng Street along with two acres of arable and a rod and a half of meadow that Godfrey Grinde had totally surrendered to the use of the above Reginald and Roger through the hands of the bailiffs, to defend for the due farm, under this condition: That the above Reginald and Roger and their heirs or assignees should provide to the above Godfrey Grinde as long as he lives whatever should be necessary, namely in food, drink, clothing and shoes, lodging and each year the sustenance of one sheep over the winter and the ploughing of one rod of land at the convenience of that said Godfrey. In addition, the above Reginald, Roger and their heirs or assignees should provide lodging to Mabel [wife] of that Godfrey so long as she survives him and provide her each year with a chemise. If, God forbid, the above Reginald, Roger or their heirs or assignees should default in any degree against the above Godfrey then through the view of friends and neighbours of the above Godfrey satisfaction is to be made in the proper measure. The above Reginald and Roger find pledges for themselves and their heirs and assignees, namely [?] ad Crucem and Henry Spruntyng.[56]

On the same day Henry Rode took seisin of the tenements listed below in gift of John Elys, to defend for two acres at the term, computed as a $\frac{1}{2}$ d. at

---

voluntatem dicti Eusebii ad deffendendum pro firma debita, et dictus Eusebius recipiet de dicto Gilberto ad terminum vite sue quolibet anno pro dicta donatione hospitium victum suum et vestimentum secundum honorem et statum suum et vesturam unius dimidie acre seminate cum ordeo et medietate omnium bladorum super dictum tenementum, in obitu dicti Eusebii testamentum ad voluntatem suam ministratur et si dictus Gilbertus contra Eusebium antedictum in dicta conventione deficitur omnia tenementa predicta recipiet sine conditione alicuius et gaudebit. (xiid.)

[56] Box 7, bundle 1. 16 September 1311.

Memorandum quod Reginaldus Sprunting et Rogerus filius eius ceperunt seysinam de uno mesuagio iacente in le Arningstrate et de duabus acris terre arabilis et de una roda prati et dimidia unde Galfridus Grynd' totum ius suum ad opus predictorum Reginaldi et Rogeri in manibus ballivorum sursum reddidit ad defendendum pro firma debita sub hac forma: quod predicti Reginaldus et Rogerus ac heredes sui sive assignati predicto Galfrido Grynd' que sunt necessaria donec vixerit attribuent, videlicet in cibis potibus vesturis ac calceamentis hospicio et quolibet anno sustentationem unius bidentis per tempus hyemale et arraturam unius rode terre ad comodum dicti Galfridi. Predicti vero Reginaldus Rogerus et eorum heredes sive assignati Mabili [uxori] dicti Galfridi dum idem Galfridus superstites sit hospicium invenire et quolibet anno unam camisiam sibi dabunt. Et si predicti Reginaldus, Rogerus aut eorum heredes sive assignati in perte sua aliquid contra predictum Galfridum forisfacerint quod absit tunc per visum amicorum et vicinorum predicto Galfrido satisfacere debent. Ad hanc rem ratam habendam predicti Reginaldus Rogerus pro se et heredibus suis seu assignatis plegios invenerunt videlicet [illeg.] ad Crucem et Henricum Sprunting. (vid.)

term as well as receiving from Cristina Gildene a $\frac{1}{2}$d. at term. And the said Henry Rode and his heirs will provide to that John reasonable sustenance for the rest of his life in return for that gift both in meat and other requirements as well as clothing, linen and woollens along with lodgings. And if the said John should outlive Henry and his heirs should default in the above mentioned distribution to that John, though may this not happen, then the said John will repossess all the said tenements for the rest of his life in such a manner that after his death they should fully revert to the heirs and assignees of the said Henry. Of these tenements one rod of land abuts on the ditch of Henry in the west field, one rod on the Le Refulong, one half acre at Balleswelles, one rod on Colbefurlong, one rod on Annowe, one rod at the head of Annonebroc, one rod at the same place next the three rods formerly of William Manipenny, one half rod on Grethorn, three rods at Le Mare, one half rod on Waterleneland and a fourth part in Ontysgoren in the west meadow and a half swat one year and one rod abutting on the head of the said Goren in another year and a half of one rod and a half on Le Benefurlong to be received with Godfrey Aylred and one piece of curtilage in Westcroftes.[57]

William Goni surrendered into the hands of the bailiffs to the use of his son William all his lands and tenements completely except for three one half acres of land and one half acre of meadow. Whence the said William son of the same William is seised under this form: That the said William will provide to William his father above mentioned for the rest of his life all that may be necessary for his honourable livelihood, namely, food, drink and clothing. And if it should happen that the above William junior should fail in the above, all those lands should revert to the said William senior for his life, nor is it permitted to the said William to sell or alienate in any part from the above tenements to anyone during his life. Accordingly the above

[57] Box 7, bundle 1. 18 November 1316.

Eodem die Henricus Rode cepit sesinam de subscriptis tenementis de dono Johannis Elys ad deffendendum pro duabus acris ad terminum computus super obolum ad terminum et recipiet de Christina Gildene obolum ad terminum. Et dictus Henricus Rode et heredes sui pro dicta donatione victum rationabilem dicto Johanni tribuent et invenient ad terminum vite sue tam bovum quam alicui servorum suorum ac vestimenta linena et lanena hospicium. Et si dictus Johannes dictum Henricum supervixerit et heredes sui in distributionem antedictam defecerint versus dictum Johannem quod absit tunc dictus Johannes omnia dicta tenementa ad terminum vite sue possidebit eo quod post decessum eius plenarie heredibus et assignatis dicti Henrici redeant; de quibus tenementis una roda terre abuttat super duitum Henrici in campo occidente, una roda super le Refurlong, una dimidia acra apud Balleswelles, una roda super Colbefurlong, una roda super Annowe, una roda ad superiorem de Annonebroc, una roda ibidem iuxta tres rodas quondam Willelmi Manipeny, dimidia roda super Grethorn, tres rodas apud le Mare, dimidia roda super Waterlanelond et quartam partem in Ontysgoren in prato occidente et dimidia swat uno anno, et una roda abuttat ad capud dictorum Goren alio anno et medietas unius rode et dimidie super Le Benefurlong percipienda cum Galfrido Alred, et una pecia curtilagii in Westkroftes.

William son of the same William will receive those entire lands after the latter's death. And under this form he is seised, to defend for the due farm nor is it permitted to the said William to sell anything from those above holdings during the lifetime of his father William.[58]

It is to be noted that on the day of the Ascension of Our Lord in the Eleventh year of King Edward III John son of John Colowot of West Street of Godmanchester junior surrendered into the hands of Thomas Hopay then bailiff of Godmanchester to the use of Cristina daughter of Robert Garlop and to the use of the children procreated by Robert Denne and the same Cristina all his rights in one capital messuage lying between the messuage of Reginald Denne on the east side of West Street and the messuage of William Parson on the west side in West Street along with all his arable lands pasture curtilages and other tenements and of any other goods mobile or immobile which the said John has or by any title should come to him at any time. Accordingly, that same Cristina must support that said John for the rest of the days of John well and decently as the said John and Cristina and the children of this Cristina and Robert Denne should be able to live for better or for worse. And if anyone either of the said John and Cristina should outlive the other all the tenements and goods of the said John are to be retained for the life of the surviving party entire without sale or alienation in any part. And after the death of both, namely John and Cristina, all the tenements and all the other moveable goods of the said John Colowot entirely and without any diminution shall come to the children begotten between Robert Denne and the said Cristina Garlop in equal portions[59] to each of the several children. And should it happen that the said Cristina should contract marriage with any man and be well supported in food and clothing the said John will have support from the above agreement as so indicated while the same John is released from the obligation of the custody of the said Cristina Garlop. According to which after the separation of the said John from the custody of the above Cristina

[58] Box 7, bundle 1. 4 July 1308.
Willelmus Gony reddidit sursum in manibus ballivorum ad usum Willelmi filii sui totam terram suam et tenementa sua plenarie exceptis iii dimidiis acris terre et una dimidia acra prati, unde dictus Willelmus filius eiusdem Willelmi seysitus est sub hac forma: quod dictus Willelmus Willelmo patri suo predicto ad terminum vite sue omnia que sibi neccesaria sunt honorifice inveniet videlicet in cibis et potibus et vestimentis. Et si contingat quod predictus Willelmus junior de predictis cessaverit, omnia predicta tenementa predicto Willelmo seniori redibunt ad terminum vite sue tenenda, nec liceat dicto Willelmo de predictis tenementis alicui vendere et alienare nec ad terminum vite sue. Ita quod predictus Willelmus filius eiusdem Willelmi dictum tenementum integrum post eius decessum recipiet et sub hac forma seysitus est ad deffendendum pro firma debita nec licebit dicto Willelmo aliquid de predictis tenementis ad terminum [vite] Willelmi patris sui vendere. (iis.)
[59] For some discussion of the implications of this stress upon equality among children, despite the custom of ultimogeniture, see below, Chapter 5, Section III.

the said Robert Denne may have in custody the said John and all his goods in the name of the children of that Robert and Cristina until the said children should come of age. Once coming of age has been determined the above custody of that John and all his tenements and moveable goods may be fully assumed and maintained under the form of the agreement for the maintenance of John as above. And the said John is not to be released from the custody of the said Robert and Cristina for some accidental reason brought about by those who spread malicious gossip, unless it can be proved as reasonably and as openly as possible by the neighbourhood that the aforesaid Cristina and Robert or their children had behaved badly towards John, breaking the above agreement.[60]

[60] Box 5, bundle 9. 29 May 1337. (In this unique entry the date given here is taken, of course, from this entry rather than from the date of the court session.)

Memorandum quod die Ascensionis Domini anno regni Regis Edwardi tercii a conquestu undecimo Johannes filius Johannis Colwot de Westrate de Gumecestre junior reddidit sursum in manus Thome Hopay tunc Ballivi de Gumecestre ad opus Cristine filie quondam Roberti Garlop et ad opus puerorum inter Robertum Denne et dictam Cristinam procreatorum totum ius suum unius mesuagii sui capitalis iacentis inter mesuagium Reginaldi Denne ex una parte orientali in Westrate et mesuagium Willelmi Persoun ex altera parte occidentali in le Westrate et omnium terrarum suarum arabilium pratorum curtilagiorum et omnium aliorum tenementorum suorum seu omnium aliorum bonorum suorum mobilium et inmobilium, que dictus Johannes habet vel aliquo iure sibi accidente habere poterit usque in sempiternum. Ita quod dicta Cristina dictum Johannem sustineat ad terminum vite dicti Johannis competenter et decenter prout bona dictorum Johannis et Cristine et puerorum dicte Cristine et Roberti Denne predictorum exigerint prout casus melioris seu peioris sustentationis contigerit. Et si quis vel que dictorum Johannis et Cristine alium vel aliam supravixerit omnia tenementa et bona mobilia dicti Johannis ad terminum vite illius superstitis penes se integre sine vendicione seu aliqua alienacione retinebit et habebit. Et post obitum utriusque videlicet Johannis et Cristine omnia tenementa et omnia alia bona mobilia dicti Johannis Colwot integre et sine aliqua diminucione et destrucione dant pueris inter Robertum Denne et dictam Cristinam Garlop procreatis equali porcione inter eosdem pueros divisura. Et si contingat quod dicta Cristina cum aliquo viro matrimonium contraxerit et bene se in victu et vestitu penes dictum Johannem habuerit sustentacionem ex utraque parte observatam: stet in suo robore convencio supradicta, sin autem bene liceat dictus Johannes [sic] a custodia Cristine Garlop predicte separare. Ita quod post separacionem dicti Johannis a custodia Cristine predicta, dictus Robertus Denne dictum Johannem custodiat et omnia bona eiusdem habeat nomine puerorum dictorum Roberti et Cristine quousque predicti pueri omnes pervenerint ad plenam etatem, qua etate probata supradicti pueri predictam custodiam predicti Johannis et omnia tenementa et omnia bona mobilia illius plenarie poterit reassumere et custodire sub forma convencionis supradicte eidem Johanni tenende. Et non liceat dicto Johanni a custodia dictorum Roberti et Cristine seu puerorum pro aliqua causa accidenter [separare] per procuracionem aliquorum maliciosam sugestionem proponencium nisi racionalius et apercius fuerit probatum per vicinos citra sedentes sic probantes quod dicta Cristina vel dictus Robertus seu pueri predicti penes dictum Johannem contra convencionem supradictam se male habuerint. Insuper quod neutra pars supradictorum vendicionem dictorum tenementorum seu alicuius partis inde faciat in vita dicti Johannis. Et dictus Johannes omnimoda opera operabitur secundum quantitatem potestatis sue et dicta Cristina domos in placea dicti Johannis edificatas cooperiet et supportabit ad totum tempus suum et reparabit. (vid.)

Buying and Selling within the Family[61]

From the late thirteenth century there is an increasing use among immediate members of families of the usual court roll formula for sales (*cepit sesinam*, etc.) with entry fines. In addition, the word purchase (some form of *emptio*) was also gradually adopted over the last decade of the century to become frequent from the early fourteenth century. There are only about one half dozen entries of this sort in the 1280s, these still number a mere 20 in the 1290s, but over the next two and one half decades some 175 such entries are to be found. Only infrequently do the entries inform us about the actual cash considerations in these intra-family conveyances. These entries do at least prevent us from falling into the easy assumption that intra-family sales were mere euphemisms for gifts. One such rare entry is that for the Paxton family in 1326, when Agnes daughter of Nicholas Paxton paid 20 marks for six acres acquired from her father and Cristina daughter of Nicholas Paxton also paid 20 marks for a six acre purchase from her father.

The very different pattern of family involvement in buying and selling does serve to suggest that this form of conveyance performed a distinct function from that of the gift. A sister only figured clearly in one gift, but among intra-family sales 17 sisters (or groups of sisters) bought property and 28 sisters sold property. As sellers sisters numbered almost as many as mothers (28) who had predominated in the handling of gifts. On the other hand, only 25 of the purchasers were daughters while the vast majority were sons. Again, a distinct difference from the relative numbers involved in receiving gifts. A different pattern is also found with males selling property, since fathers were sellers in only 52 instances but sons in more (55). Altogether, then, the economic dynamics of the intra-family land market is seen most clearly when one notes that 121 sons (or groups of sons) purchased property from brothers, sisters, mothers or fathers.

The common use of reversion clauses in the various texts already given in this chapter shows the desire of families to keep property in the family. Although only in the unusual case of Cristina Godchild[62] is a right of pre-emption clause to be found in these texts, the number of intra-familial sales suggest that such pre-emptive rights were in practice to be expected. The above statistics indicate that intra-familial sales complemented gifts. Whereas gifts flowed more often from parent to child, sales facilitated the

---

[61] For the right of the boy or girl to sell or demise property upon coming of age, see the Godmanchester customs of 1324, no. 3(b), p. 431.

[62] See above, pp. 19-20.

movement of properties horizontally among siblings. In turn, it was only to be expected that brothers should purchase property frequently from sisters as the latter married, became needy or simply were physically unable to work the land. Unfortunately, such reasons for sales do not appear in the cryptic court roll entries. Since the sale of property among members of a family does not follow a form in court roll entries differing from other sales, texts of these sales are not illustrated here.

INHERITANCE

In sharp contrast with the limitations imposed by the common law in England, there is nothing in the customs of Godmanchester forbidding the disposition of land by will.[63] Next to sales, more entries in Godmanchester court rolls deal with conveyance of property by inheritance than with any other form. This does not mean that the court was employed as a record for wills. Indeed, as has been noted above, in the surviving customs testaments are specifically relegated to the jurisdiction of ecclesiastical courts. Only after the Black Death were some wills recorded in what would appear to be their more full formal language. References to inheritance had occurred in the courts as part of that increasing information about family property management from the late thirteenth century. The language, therefore, was varied and casual rather than formal, as the texts below will illustrate.

There were only 40 references to inheritance in courts of the 1280s and 1290s and, over these same two decades, only one reference to executors apart from wills. However, between 1300 and 1326 there may be found 183 entries dealing with inheritance and a further 62 entries recording the acts of executors in the court rolls of Godmanchester. Furthermore, in contrast with information about dowers, dowry and maintenance, references to inheritance continued to be a regular feature of court rolls throughout the fourteenth century. As a result, much can be learned about the role of inheritance, the will and the executor in the management of family properties.

As the following breakdown of figures for the pre-1326 period indicates, a wide range of family beneficiaries are indicated in court roll references to bequests. In about 20 per cent of the wills (41 of 219)[64] the

---

[63] For a general review of the literature on the devise of land by will in boroughs and manors of ancient demesne, see Sheehan, *The Will in Medieval England*, pp. 274-281.

[64] In twelve cases a will is noted as directed to a different beneficiary in two different years; in one case a will noted different beneficiaries in three years. Since all these multiple notices involved children of families they have been included in the following list as one will (hence 233 − 14 = 219).

relationship of the beneficiary to the testator is not specified. One bequest was to the church and seven bequests are to parties not clearly specified. While most of the bequests are to children, as might be expected, a goodly number are to other relatives. One third (53 of 160) of the testators bequeathing to indicated relations were women. In only six of these 53 cases were wives identified with husbands as testators. The wife bequeathed alone in the remaining cases (19 as mother, though identified by name as wife also; eight as mother only; six as wife only; nine as daughter; four as sister; one as sister-in-law).

TABLE 1. TESTATORS AND BENEFICIARIES, PRE-1326

Number of Testators	Beneficiaries
47	1 son
17	2 sons
2	3 sons
2	4 sons
30	1 daughter
6	2 daughters
1	3 daughters
1	4 daughters
2	1 son and 1 daughter
2	2 sons and 2 daughters
4	1 son and 2 daughters
2	3 sons and 6 daughters
1	2 sons and 1 daughter
6	wives
3	husbands
17	brother
3	2 brothers
8	sister
1	sister-in-law
1	2 sisters
1	2 uncles
1	aunt
1	mother
1	grandmother
1	2 daughters and an uncle

Totals: Individuals as Testators: 160; Number of Beneficiaries: 240

Although the extant court rolls series are not as complete for the second quarter of the fourteenth century, the same considerable spread of testators and beneficiaries is to be found in the use of the will. Of the 59 clearly identifiable testators, 21 were fathers, nine wife and mother, four

sons, four mothers, four brothers, one husband and wife, two husbands, one uncle, one grandfather, one sister, as well as eight males and two females whose kinship has not been specified. As the following list presents, these 59 testators bequeathed property to 82 individuals, exactly 50 per cent to males and 50 per cent to females.

TABLE 2: TESTATORS AND BENEFICIARIES, 1375-1400

Number of Testators	Beneficiaries	
19		1 son
2		2 sons
1		4 sons
1		1 grandson
8		1 daughter
1		2 daughters
1		3 daughters
2		4 daughters
1		1 son and 1 daughter
1		2 daughters and 1 son
1		2 sisters
1		1 sister
3		1 brother
2		wife
3		mother
1		niece
8	Male	heirs of no specified relationship
8	Female	

Totals: Individuals as Testators: 59; Number of Beneficiaries: 82

While there are only a half dozen references to reception of property by will in the last quarter of the fourteenth century, over the 1350s and '60s more than 60 conveyances are reported under the title of wills. Over one half of the identifiable beneficiaries are women. However, owing to the fact that one third of the beneficiaries cannot be clearly identified in the present condition of these rolls, and for another third the relationship to the testator is not given, generalization from these data would be misleading.

Some early texts may be cited to illustrate the pragmatic, ad hoc nature of references to inheritance in these court rolls. In one of the earliest references to testaments, to be found in a fragmentary court dated as Vigil of the Feast of the Apostles Peter and Paul, 1 Edward ɪ (28 June 1273), Cecilia Gylekoc was seised in full court of property (not fully identifiable) from her sister Ivetta as bequeathed by the will of the said Ivetta (*ex*

testamento dicte Ivette legato). A few years later, that is on the Thursday after the Feast of St. Matthew the Apostle, 14 Edward I (26 September 1286), one finds an entry to the effect that William the son of Roger Rede was seised of one quarter land and messuage from Robert *le* Rede his brother and that the same William petitioned for his total inheritance from his brother (*et predictus Willelmus petebat totam hereditatem fratris sui Roberti sicut rectus heres et junior*). Testaments are also referred to in the following entries:

> Be it noted that Reginald Gony of Godmanchester surrendered into the hands of the bailiffs to the use of Margaret, daughter of Richard in the Lane, a messuage along with six acres in the fields, which came to her as heiress. [These] are to be defended as three acres and 3d. at the term. Whosoever of the above Reginald and Margaret should live the longest will hold that messuage and land for life and after the death of both that tenement is to be sold and the money thereby acquired distributed for their souls. And if any boy or girl should be born of them and outlive them he will have that tenement in the above manner.[65]

> Hugh, son and heir of Simon Fole, William his brother, John brother of the same and Roger, sons of that same Simon, recovered seisin of land and tenements in which their father, the above Simon, died vested and seised. They gave 4d. as entry fine but this was condoned by decision of the court.[66]

> Cristina, widow of Robert le Carter, took seisin of a rod of meadow lying in Westmade between Le Brokys. She fell heir to this from Isolda Bindewynter to whom she was the nearest heir. This is to be defended by the customary farm.[67]

---

[65] Box 6, bundle 1. 2 May 1303.
    Memorandum quod Reginaldus Gony de Gomecestre reddidit sursum in manus ballivorum ad usum Margarete filie Ricardi in the Lane unum messuagium cum sex acris terre infra campis que accidit ei heredi ad deffendendum pro iii acris et iiid. ad terminum et quis predictorum Reginaldi et Margarete longius vixerit dictum messuagium cum dicta terra ad terminum vite sue tenebit et post amborum decessum vendatur dictum tenementum et pecunia inde recepta distribuabitur pro animabus illorum, et si aliquis vel alique inter illos sit procreatus et vitam post obitum illorum habuerit dictum tenementum possidebit in formam predictam. (xiid.)

[66] Box 6, bundle 1. 12 May 1300.
    Hugo filius et heres Simonis Fole Willelmus frater eius Johannes frater eiusdem et Rogerus filii dicti Simonis recuperauerunt sesinam de terra et tenementis in quibus predictus Symon pater eorum obiit vestitus et sesitus et dederunt in gersumam iiiid. sed condonatur per considerationem curie.

[67] Box 6, bundle 1. 12 May 1300.
    Christina que fuit uxor Roberti le Carter' cepit sesinam de una roda prati iacente in Westmade inter Le Brokys que terra ei accidit ex hereditate Isolde Bindewynter quia propinquior erat sibi eres ad defendendum pro firma consueta.

Cristina, daughter of William Onty, took seisin of an acre and three rods of land and meadow lying within the liberties of Godmanchester coming to that same Cristina by hereditary right after the death of William Onty father of the same Cristina. This is to defend for the farm owed.[68]

Cristina, wife of John Sly of Hemingford Abbots, took seisin of a messuage in Arnyng Street along with three acres and one rod of land and meadow in the fields and meadows of Godmanchester, coming to her by hereditary right after the death of William the son of Reginald Alred.[69]

In addition to these regular references to inheritance as the title by which seisin was acquired, there are enough lawsuits on the same subject to indicate the range of operation of customary regulations. In the text below, for Godfrey the son of Reginald in the Lane, one sees the application of the principle of Borough English. A mother's dowry was at stake in the case of recovery with respect to Robert the son of John the son of John and his brother William. The specificity possible to customary regulations is manifested by the capacity of the aunt (Amicia Hopay) to recover from her nephew. This latter case also gives us a welcome glimpse of a split decision in the court.

Be it noted that Godfrey, son of Reginald in the Lane, came into full court and requested seisin of the whole messuage along with all the lands and tenements of which his brother John died vested and seised. Reginald, as brother of the same, requested a half of that messuage, land and tenement. Then both parties placed themselves on the judgement of the court. The court indeed rendered in judgement that the above Godfrey should have the messuage whole and entire without the participation of anyone else and one half of the tenement and land in the fields since he was the younger brother and proper heir. Reginald, as older brother, may have nothing of the capital messuage but is to have one half of the remaining tenement and [ ] land in the fields, as is the custom of the vill.[70]

[68] Box 4, bundle 3. 7 December 1346.

Christina filia Willelmi Onty cepit sesinam de una acra et tribus rodis terre et prati iacentibus infra libertatem de Gumecestre accidentibus eidem Christine iure hereditario post obitum Willelmi Onty patris dicte Christine ad defendendum pro firma debita. (ivd.)

[69] Box 4, bundle 3. 22 September 1362.

Christina uxor Johannis Sly de Hemyngford Abbatis cepit sesinam de uno mesuagio iacenti in le Arningstrate et de tribus acris et una roda terre et prati iacentibus in campis et pratis de Gumecestre accidentibus sibi iure hereditario post mortem Willelmis filii Reginaldi Alred. (iiis. ivd.)

[70] Box 6, bundle 1. 17 January 1297.

Memorandum quod Galfridus filius Reginaldi in venella venit in plenam curiam et postulavit sesinam de toto mesuagio et de tota terra et tenementis in quibus Johannes frater suus obiit vestitus et sesitus. Reginaldus ut frater eiusdem postulavit medietatem

Be it noted that Robert, son of John the son of John, and William his brother, came to this court and sought, as they had done at the preceding court, peaceful possession of their land. Whence they paid the entry fine and took seisin upon the death of their father John, namely of one half of 21 acres of arable and one half of two and one half acres and one rod of meadow. This land and meadow Amicia, widow of John the son of William parent of the above Robert and William who are his sole heirs, held in dower as assigned to her by the above John (her husband's) father and his brother Reginald. Then, they say, that John their father and a certain Reginald his brother, after the death of John son of William the latters' father, took seisin of the above tenements and after the death of the above Amicia. And so they complained that Reginald the son of John, their uncle wrongly impeded their entry. And since they were not at all able to work that land and have their part in it seisin was given to them in full court according to the custom of the manor. And the above Reginald was present in the court, as at the preceding court, and willingly conceded that he and their father had seisin and that these had the same. And he willingly conceded that they should have entry to that land if they know or are able to find out just where that land and meadow lie. And the court asked the above Reginald voluntarily to make a peaceful settlement with them by a legal view of men. And since he was unwilling to do this it was ordered that the above Reginald should be distrained and one horse was taken as distress to have him make peace with the above Robert and William about the above dower and in order that he should come to this court. But now he has not come to this court. So he was distrained by a horse yet was unwilling to do anything nor would he justify himself by distraint. So, it was granted by the whole court that through a view of good men who were named to the jury that property from the above dower should be divided between them before the next court.[71]

---

dicti mesuagii terre et tenementi. sed utraque pers posuit se tandem in iudicium curie. Curia vero dedit in judicium quod predictus Galfridus haberet mesuagium totum et integrum sine perticipatione alicuius et medietatem tenementi et terre in campis. quia erat iunior frater et rectus heres. Reginaldus ut senior frater nichil haberet de mesuagio capitali sed medietatem haberet ceteri tenementi. et [*blank*] terre in campis propter consuetudinem ville.

[71] Box 6, bundle 1. 21 March 1297.

Memorandum quod ad curiam istam venerunt Robertus filius Johannis filii Johannis et Willelmus frater eius et petierunt pacem sicut alias ad curiam precedentem super terram suam unde fecerunt gersumam suam et ceperunt sesinam suam post mortem Johannis patris sui scilicet de medietate xxi acrarum terre arabilis et medietate ii. acrarum prati et dimidie et i rode quam terram et pratum Amicia que fuit uxor Johannis filii Willelmi avi predictorum Roberti et Willelmi cuius unus heredum ipsi sunt tenuit in dotem de asignatione predicti Johannis patris sui et Reginaldi fratris sui et unde dicunt quod Johannes pater eorum et quidam Reginaldus frater eius post mortem Johannis filii Willelmi patris eorum ceperunt sesinam de predictis tenementis et post mortem Amicie predicte inter eos et heredes eorum forent participanda. Et unde queruntur quia

Richard le Rede and Amicia Hopay requested in the full court of Godmanchester that they be given seisin of a messuage, seven acres of arable
and two acres of meadow with appurtenances in Godmanchester, which
tenement ought to descend to them on the occasion of the death of a certain
Thomas Hopay nephew of that Amicia. John, son of Eustace Hopay, and
William his brother came and defended seisin saying that they had a greater
right in that tenement than the above Richard and Amicia because a certain
Henry Hopay, uncle of that John and William, died vested and seised
thereof so that the right descends as in domain fee and right and ought to
descend to Thomas Hopay as his son and heir. And the same Thomas died
without heir of his body. Therefore the above John and William asked that
seisin to that tenement be granted to them since in pure hereditary fashion it
ought to descend to them as by the death of the son of a brother to the sons
of the brother. The above Richard and Amicia came and defended seisin
against the above John and William and say that said tenement [first] ought
to descend to them rather than to the above John and William in as much
as the said Henry Hopay, through whose death that John and William
claim that tenement, was brother of said Amicia. And since the said Amicia
was nearer in blood to the said Henry than the above John and William,
therefore the said Richard and Amicia being closer they say the said Amicia
is the heir. And on this they seek seisin. Accordingly, certain members of
the court of Godmanchester acknowledge that Amicia to have the nearest
claim as heir because of the obvious explanation and they request that
seisin be granted to her. But certain other members of that court did not
grant that she was heir and therefore sought to have seisin postponed until
the next court. But to this certain members were unwilling to agree so that
on that very day they obliged the bailiffs to deliver seisin to the above
Richard and Amicia and they were seised.[72]

Reginaldus filius Johannis avunculus eorum iniuste eos impedit et quia minus possunt in
terram illam manuoperare et terram pertem suam habere sicut sesita fuit illis et liberata in
plena curia secundum consuetudinem manerii. Et predictus Reginaldus alias ad curiam
proximam precedentem fuit presens in curia et bene concessit quod ipse et pater eorum
ceperunt inde sesinam et ipsi similiter fecerunt. Et bene concedit quod eant < super >
terram et habeant si sciverint sive scire possunt ubi predicta terra et pratum jacet. Et
dictum est per totam curiam predicto Reginaldo quod faciat pacem inter eos per visum
legem virorum gratis. Et quia noluit, preceptum fuit quod predictus Reginaldus
distringeretur et fuit districtus per 1. equum ad faciendum predictis Roberto et Willelmo
pacem suam de predicta dote et quod sit ad istam curiam et modo ad istam curiam non
venit. Et fuit districtus per 1. equum nec aliquid inde facere voluit nec per districtionem se
iusticiare voluit. Et concessum est per totam curiam quod per visum bonorum virorum
quorum nomina fuit in panella fiat pertitio inter eos de predicta dote infra proximam
curiam.

[72] Box 6, bundle 1. 8 October 1293.

Ricardus le Rede et Amicia Hopay optulerunt se in plena curia de Gomecestre et
petierunt seysinam < de > uno mesuagio* de septem acris terre arabilis et duabus acris

Lawsuits could be avoided by *inter vivos* arrangements. Such arrangements might guarantee the release of rights in property, as with the following entry for William the son of Roger *le* Rede of Godmanchester. Without such a precaution, the heirs could recover property of which their parents died seised, as in the instance of Isabella Petyt which follows.

> William, son of Roger le Rede of Godmanchester, took seisin of a messuage and a croft bought from Robert Julian, defending in each instance as one rod. Godfrey, son of the above Robert Julian indeed surrendered into the hands of the bailiffs the whole right and claim that he had or was able to have in the above messuage and croft, formerly belonging to his ancestor Eustace le Masun, to the use of the above William le Rede. Millicent, sister of the above Godfrey, indeed likewise surrendered her whole right in claim to the said messuage and croft into the hands of the bailiffs to the use of the above William le Rede. The same William le Rede acquired seisin of the above messuage and croft in full court. He also [acquired seisin] of a croft in Arnyng Street, lying between the messuage formerly belonging to Henry Sibily on one side and the messuage of Roger le Rede on the other, bought from Alexander, son of Godfrey Ese, defending as one rod.[73]

---

prati cum pertinentiis in Gomecestre quod quidem tenementum eis decendere debuit ex decessu cuiusdam Thome Hopay nepotis dicte Amicie. Johannes filius Eustacii Hopay et Willelmus frater eius venerunt et defenderunt illam seysinam et dixerunt se maius habere ius in illo tenemento quam predictos Ricardum et Amiciam [*sic*] eo quod quidam Henricus Hopay avunculus dictorum Johannis et Willelmi inde obiit vestitus et seysitus die quo obiit tamquam in dominico feodo et iure suo decendit illud ius et decendere debuit Thome Hopay tamquam filio et heredi. Et idem Thomas obiit sine herede de corpore suo. Ideo predicti Johannes et Willelmus petunt seysinam eis tribui de dicto tenemento tamquam de pura hereditate sua que eis decendere debuit per decessum de filio fratri ad filios fratris. Predicti Ricardus et Amicia venerunt et defenderunt seysinam dictorum Johannis et Willelmi quam petebant et dicunt quod predictum tenementum prius† eius debuit decendere quam predictis Johanni et Willelmo eo quod dictus Henricus Hopay per cuius decessum dicti Johannes et Willelmus clamant tenementum habere fuit frater dicte Amicie. Et quia dicta Amicia propinquior sanginis fuit dicto Henrico quam predicti Johannes et Willelmus ideo dicti Ricardi et Amicia propinquiorem dicunt dictam Amiceam esse heredem. Et super hoc petunt seysinam. Unde quidam de curia de Gomecestre propter rationem extremam concesserunt dictam Amiciam propinquiorem esse heredem et petebant seysinam sibi largire sed quidam alii de dicta curia non concesserunt ipsam esse heredem quare petebant illam seysinam prolongari usque ad proximam curiam sed ad hoc noluerunt quidam consentire sed eodem die coegerunt ballivum predictis Ricardo et Amicie tribuere seysinam et seysiti fuerunt.

* *uno mesuagio*: interlineary additions.

† MS *frius* (?).

[73] Box 6, bundle 1. 16 April 1299.

Willelmus filius Rogeri le Rede de Gomecestre cepit sesinam de uno mesuagio et de uno crofto emptis de Roberto Julian ad defendendum pariter pro una roda. Galfridus vero filius predicti Roberti Julian reddidit sursum in manus ballivorum totum ius et clamium

Godfrey Breton and William his brother pleaded again with a royal writ
of right against Benedict, son of Michael, and his sister Isabella seeking 11
acres and a half of land that the said Benedict and Isabella his sister wrongly
withold from them. For they say that this was done unjustly since a certain
Isabella Petyt, their mother, died seised and in seisin as of her domain fee of
this land and tenement. Therefore the said Godfrey and William seek that
land and tenement as rightful heirs and nearest by blood after the death of
their mother Isabella. And this they state to be a true judgement. In reply,
the above Benedict and Isabella said that in fact a certain Isabella, called
Petyt, at a certain time and year enfeoffed and granted the above land and
tenement to that Benedict and his wife Joan and as warranty for this they
appeal to the common rolls. [*and skipping to the conclusion of the case*] And
therefore, an inquisition was held. And afterwards it was discovered by the
same inquisition that the above Godfrey had a greater right in that land just
as they sought through their writ. Also, that the above Benedict and
Isabella, in so far as that Isabella Petyt died vested and seised as of her
domain etc., never were let that property. Therefore it is judged that the
above G. and W. should recover seisin of that 11½ acres [*illeg.*] in Godmanchester. And they are given complete seisin in full court through the hands
of the bailiffs and there they pay an [*illeg.*] entry fine according as [*illeg.*] of
the manor requires.[74]

---

quod habuit vel habere potuit in predicto mesuagio et in predicto crofto qui quondam
erant Eustachii Le Masun antecessoris sui ad usum predicti Willelmi Le Rede. Milisent'
vero soror predicti Galfridi totum ius et suum clamium similiter sursum reddidit in manus
ballivorum de predictis mesuagio et crofto ad usum predicti Willelmi Le Rede, et idem
Willelmus Le Rede de predictis mesuagio et crofto in plena curia sumpsit sesinam. Item de
uno crofto in Arningstrate quod iacet inter mesuagium quondam Henrici Sibily ex una
perte et mesuagium Rogeri Le Rede ex altera empto de Alexandri filio Galfridi Ese ad
defendendum pro una roda.

[74] Box 6, bundle 1. 28 August 1298.

Galfridus Bretun et Willelmus frater eius optulerunt se sicut prius cum breve domini
Regis de Recto versus Benedictum filium Michaelis et Isabellam filiam eius petentes
undecim acras terre et dimidiam quas dicti Benedictus et Isabella filia eius deforciant
iniuste ut dicunt et hoc iniuste quia quedam Isabella Petyt mater eorum de dicta terra et
dicto tenemento obiit sesita et sesitam habuit in dominico suo feodo unde dicti Galfridus et
Willelmus petunt dictam terram et tenementum sicut recti eredes et propinquiores
sanguine post discessum [*sic*] Isabelle matris sue et hoc per iudicium fidelium. Predicti
vero Benedictus et Isabella respondendo dixerunt quod quedam Isabella dicta Petyt certo
tempore et anno predictam terram et tenementum predicto Benedicto et Johanne uxore
sue infeofavit et donavit et hoc petunt ad warentizationem communem rotulorum.
predicti vero Galfridus et Willelmus petunt iudicium curie in defenso. Quia sicut ipsi prius
narraverunt quia Isabella Petyt mater eorum de dicta terra et dicto tenemento obiit vestita
et sesita et sicut in dominico feodo. Dicti Benedictus et Isabella respondendo defenderunt
ius Galfridi et Willelmi et non defenderunt ius neque sesinam predicte Isabelle Petyt
matris eorum sicut recta brevis exigit unde petunt iudicium de ipsis tamquam in
defensione et predictus Benedictus et Isabella filia eius dixerunt quod satis et sufficenter
responderunt. Et super hoc ponunt se in iudicium curie. Galfridus et Willelmus similiter

The most powerful instrument for the disposition of property rights was of course the written testament.[75] Nevertheless, the written instrument could be forged and proven to be false as was the case with Mariota, widow of Roger Tinctor, given below. The written testament had various practical purposes, such as the opportunity for specification of the disposal of purchased property (see Henry the son of John the son of Reginald, below) and the designation of liturgical allowances. Most commonly on the other hand, the court found it adequate to make a very general reference to the last will and testament by such general expressions as the following examples taken from a court around 1290:

... by bequest in the will of the said Robert Faber....

... Godfrey, son of Eusebius Anice, took seisin of one half acre of land beyond Longlondhaved, according to the will of Agnes his mother....

John, son of Eusebius Anice, took seisin of one half acre of land in Le Mor bought from the executors of his mother Agnes....[76]

Nicholas, son of Roger Tinctor of Huntingdon, appeared in full court and sought seisin of the land and tenement in which the above Roger his father

---

fecerunt. Unde tota curia de communi assensu dicit pro iudicio quod predicti Benedictus et Isabelle filia eius non defenderunt ius neque sesinam predicte Isabella Petyt sicut recta brevis exigit etc. propter quod predicti Galfridus et Willelmus petunt sesinam de predictis terris et tenementis prout habuerunt iudicium curie indefenso.

After several other entries, the court repeats the main statements of claimants and defendants and concludes as given here:

Et Benedictus et Isabella filia eius venerunt et defenderunt vim et [blank] et jus predictorum G. et W. et dicunt quod non deforciant predictos Galfridum et Willelmum de predicta terra eo quod predicta Isabella Petyt temporibus retroactis feoffavit predictum Benedictum et quondam Johannam uxorem suam et quod predicta Isabella Petyt non obiit vestita et sesita in dominico suo ut de feodo. Et quia iidem G. et W. sunt propinquiores heredes predicte Isabelle Petyt et maior ius habent in sua petitione per predictam brevem de predicta terra. Quia predicti Benedictus et Isabella habent in sua tenencia ponunt se super iudicium inquisitionis. Et ideo capiatur inquisitio. Et postea inventus fuit per eandem inquisitionem quod predicti Galfridus et Willelmus maior ius habent in predicta terra sicut petierunt per brevem suum. Quam predicti Benedictus et Isabella eo quod predicta Isabella Petyt obiit vestita et sesita in dominico suo etc. numquam se demisit. Ideo consideratum est quod predicti G. et W. recuperant sesinam predictam undecim acrarum terre et dimidie [illeg.] in Gomecestre. et data est illis plena sesina in plena curia per manus ballivorum et ibidem dederunt [illeg.] gersummam prout [illeg.] manerii exigit.

[75] See Sheehan, *The Will in Medieval England*.

[76] Box 6, bundle 1.

... ex legatione in testimonio dicti Roberti Fabri....

... Galfridus filius Eusebii Anicie cepit sesinam de i dimidia acre terre extra Longlondhaved secundum testimonium Angnetis matris sue....

Johannes filius Eusebii Anicie cepit sesinam de dimidia acre terre in Le More empte de executoribus Angnetis matris eius ad....

died seised and vested in the manor of Godmanchester. However, Mariota, widow of that Roger le Tinctor of Huntingdon, appeared with a certain will containing the following: I, Roger Tinctor of Huntingdon, bequeath to Mariota my wife and the children begotten of our body all the lands that I have in the fields of Godmanchester and in the meadow of the same place. Nevertheless, since several people said that the above will was false, being neither faithful nor true, therefore, by judgement of the court the bailiffs conferred upon the above Nicholas the son of Roger seisin of the above lands and tenements. And he gave as entry fine 12d.[77]

On the same day, Henry the son of John, the son of Reginald of Godmanchester, Thomas and Gilbert brothers of that Henry and Cristina their junior sister received seisin of a messuage that Reginald the son of Robert bought from William, John and Robert, sons of Simon Clerk, to defend for the amount owed. Thence, the above Reginald bequeathed that messuage by his will to the above H.T.G. and the junior Cristina for the farm owed, saving the right that anyone may have in that property....[78]

Be it noted that William Millicent junior, executor of the will of John Millicent, surrendered into the hands of the bailiffs one and one half rods of meadow to provide services [at the church called] the Blessed Virgin Mary of Godmanchester. Whence, Roger de Strateshille, chaplain, took seisin to provide that service. He is to have and to hold for life that meadow which

---

[77] Box 6, bundle 1. 22 October 1299.

Nicholaus filius Rogeri Tinctor de Huntingdon' optulit se in plenam curiam et petiit sesinam de terra et tenemento in quibus Rogerus pater suus predictus obiit sesitus et vestitus in manerio de Gomecestre. Mariota etiam relicta dicti Rogeri Le Tenturer optulit se cum quoddam testamento in quo continebatur sequens Ego Rogerus Tingtori de huntingdon' Lego Mariote uxori mee et pueris de corpore nostro procreatis omnes terras quas habeo in manerio de Gomecestre et in pratis eiusdem. Sed quia plurimi dicebant predictum testamentum esse falsum et non fidele nec verum, ideo per considerationem curie ballivi contulerunt predicto Nicholao filio Rogeri sesinam de predictis terris et tenementis et dedit in gersummam xiid.

[78] Box 6, bundle 1. 5 January 1301.

Eodem die Henricus filius Johannis filii Reginaldi de Gomecestre. Thomas et Gilbertus fratres ipsius Henrici et Cristina junior soror eorundem receperunt sesinam de uno mesuagio quod Reginaldus filius Roberti emit de Willelmo Johanne et Roberto filiis Simonis Clerici pro defensione debita unde predictus Reginaldus predictum mesuagium in testamento suo predictis H. T. G. et Cristine iuniori legavit pro firma debita salvo iure cuiuslibet. Item predictus Henricus filius Johannis cepit sesinam de una acra terre versus depdenbroc super Longe de terra Reginaldi filii Roberti predictus Thomas filius Johannis predicti cepit sesinam de maiori dimidia acra terre apud Depdenebroc empta de Johanne Pelage et dimidia acra terre in berniscroft empta de Roberto Cokayn, Cristina iunior filia predicti Johannis cepit sesinam de una dimidia acra terre apud Ontyscroft et dimidia acra terre in Berniscroft iuxta Rogerum Le Rede. Item Gilbertus filius predicti Johannis cepit sesinam de una acra terre que iacet super le biriforlong inter Le Litlehow et [blank] Cristina filia predicti Johannis cepit sesinam de dimidia acra [blank] empta de Eusibio Albryt et dimidia acra [blank] empta de Galfrido Onty. Walterus filius Johannis predicti cepit sesinam de una acra terre iacente similiter super Biriforlong in Westfeld.

lies in Westmade. And if it should happen that the said Roger, chaplain, should make good men of Godmanchester his patrons, the same meadow will belong to whoever performs those services in that place after the death of Roger, defending for one rod at the term and not being redistributed among the people of Godmanchester. In addition, the same Roger took seisin of rents to be received from the land of Richard de Hartford, namely, from Simon ad Crucem 2s. at Michaelmas and 2s. at Easter for a rod of meadow on smalhowis, from Henry of Thodenham 1s. at Michaelmas and 1s. at Easter for a rod of land on Brynwong, from Helen le Goldsmyt 1d. at Michaelmas and 1d. at Easter for a rod and a half of land at Wynewelbrok, from John de Luton 2d. at Michaelmas and 2d. at Easter for a half acre on Lose, from Reginald the son of John $\frac{1}{4}$d. at Michaelmas and $\frac{1}{4}$d. at Easter, from Pellagia Balle 1s. at Michaelmas and 1s. at Easter, from Richard Acry $\frac{1}{4}$d. at Michaelmas and $\frac{1}{4}$d. at Easter, from Robert Danlys 1d. at Michaelmas and 1d. at Easter, from William Swytman 1d. at Michaelmas and 1d. at Easter.[79]

The frequent appearance of the excutor at Godmanchester is an indication of the wide use of the will.[80] Executors supplemented the ordinary machinery of family inheritance and, as might be expected thereby exercised a more impersonal role in Godmanchester court records. This does not mean that executors were not friends or relatives of the family. Of the few instances where executors were named in the first quarter of the fourteenth century, most were related to the testator.

[79] Box 6, bundle 1. 10 March 1306.
Memorandum quod Willelmus Milisent junior executor testamenti Johannis Milisent reddidit sursum in manibus ballivorum i rodam prati et dimidiam ad usum servitii [ecclesie] beate virginis marie de Gomecestre unde Rogerus de Strateshille capellanus cepit sesysinam ad dictum servitium celebrandum quod dictum pratum iacet in Westmade habendum et tenendum ad terminum vite sue et si contingat quod dictus Rogerus capellanus bonos homines de Gomecestre de suis omnibus tenementis ueros faciat patronos dictum pratum quibuscumque dictum servicium post mortem dicti Rogeri celebrantibus in loco predicto in pace manebit ad deffendendum pro i roda ad terminum sed non redistribuantur communiter de Gomecestre. Item dictus Rogerus cepit sesinam de redditu assissu recipiendo de terra Ricardi de Herforde videlicet de Simone ad Crucem iis. ad festum Michaelis et ad Pascham iis. pro una roda prati super smalhowis. Item de Henrico de Thodenham is. ad festum Michaelis et ad Pascham is. una roda terre super Brynwong de Helena Le Goldsmyt id. ad festum Michaelis et ad pascham id. pro una roda terre et dimidia apud Wynewelbrok. Item de Johanna de Luyetone iid. ad festum Michaelis et ad Pascham iid. pro dimidia acra super lose. Item de Reginaldo filio Johannis iq. ad festum Michaelis et ad Pascham iq. Item de Pelagia Balle is. ad festum Michaelis et ad Pascham is. Item de Ricardo Acry iq. ad festum Michaelis et ad Pascham iq. Item de Roberto Danlys id. ad festum Michaelis et ad pascham id. Item de Willelmo Swytman id. ad festum Michaeli et ad Pascham id.
[80] For the general development of the role of the executor in thirteenth-century England, see Sheehan, The Will in Medieval England, pp. 148-161.

TABLE 3: TESTATORS AND EXECUTORS

Testator	Executor
Aylward, Bartholomew	1306: Godfrey Cokayn
	1307: Godfrey Ingelond, Richard Freville and John Ironmonger
Colowot, John	1322: Sarra, his daughter
Gidding, Hugh *de*	1303: Alice Buxston
Haveley, Agnes wife of William *de*	1298: William, her husband
Huntingdon, Richard *de*	1304: John, his son
Millicent, John	1303: Godfrey Kutere and William Millicent junior
Millicent, William	1308: William Millicent and John *de* Graveley
Millicent, Simon	1308: William, son of Simon Person
	1322: Thomas Witman and wife
Rede, Martin *le*, *de* Hunts	1311: William senior, his brother
Smalle, Robert *le*	1325: Sybil, his daughter

If one may judge by the Godmanchester court rolls, executors were not frequently called upon to administer estates. When executors were found conveying property in the courts it is most often to sons or daughters who have by now apparently reached their majority. Furthermore, the bailiffs carefully listed "heirs" rather than executors in inventories of those owing obligations to the royal farm.[81] By far the most active role of executors in the Godmanchester court rolls had to do with the sale of property:[82]

TABLE 4: NUMBER OF LAND CONVEYANCES BY EXECUTORS
IN GODMANCHESTER COURT ROLLS, 1280 TO 1399

Year	No.	Year	No.	Year	No.	Year	No.
1280	1	1302	2	1313	6	1324	4
1281	2	1303	3	1314	5	1325	4
1282	2	1304	5	1315	2	1326	4
1283	1	1306	2	1316	6	1327	7
1284	2	1307	6	1317	5	1329	4
1286	1	1308	7	1318	3	1330	2
1296	1	1309	6	1319	1	1331	1
1297	1	1310	3	1320	2	1332	4
1298	2	1311	5	1321	2	1335	4
1301	2	1312	6	1322	9	1338	2

[81] See below, Chapter 3, especially p. 000.

[82] This function of course differed from that of executors under common law where disposal of chattels, especially for debt, was pivotal. See Sheehan, *The Will in Medieval England*, pp. 154 ff. However, the implementation of this custom never seems to have been the charge of the town courts.

Year	No.	Year	No.	Year	No.	Year	No.
1339	1	1350	9	1366	2	1387	2
1340	7	1351	4	1368	2	1388	7
1341	5	1353	3	1369	2	1389	2
1342	3	1354	3	1371	1	1390	4
1343	1	1357	1	1373	3	1391	5
1344	10	1359	1	1377	3	1393	1
1345	16	1361	8	1378	4	1394	2
1347	1	1362	5	1379	1	1395	1
1348	5	1363	2	1380	1	1397	1
1349	17	1364	1	1386	1	1399	2
						Total:	287

These property sales recorded in the Godmanchester court rolls are but the most minimal record of the activities of executors. It may be useful, therefore, to quote from a contemporary eyre roll[83] in order to obtain a better appreciation of the possible power of executors with respect to the distribution of property:

> An assize comes to declare whether William Pack, of Huntingdon, William Teynturer, Reginald, son of Robert of Godmanchester, Reyner, vicar of the church of Godmanchester, Simon, vicar of the church of Blessed Mary of Huntingdon, John of the Trinity, the prioress of Huntingdon, Adam Grinde, Ralph son of Martin Rede, John Manning, Mary Pollard, Roger, parson of the church of All Saints of Huntingdon, Adam of the Trinity, of St. Neots, John of Hardwick of Huntingdon, and John le Orfevere unjustly disseised Nicholas of Sparkford of his free tenement in Huntingdon and Godmanchester, and whereupon he complains that they disseised him of one messuage, four acres of land with appurtenances in Huntingdon, and 41 acres of land and two acres of meadow with appurtenances in Godmanchester.
>
> William Pack and the others come, and Ralph, son of Martin Rede comes, and he responds for himself as the tenant of that messuage in Huntingdon and of a half acre of land in Godmanchester, and regarding the messuage and land he says that he committed no injury or disseisin, for he says that he entered into those tenements by the grant and enfeoffment of William Teynturer and Reginald, son of Robert; and whatever befalls concerning this assize, he vouches them to warrant. They are present and freely warrant him.

[83] This translation from the eyre of 1286 has been kindly made available by the editors of that roll. See A. R. DeWindt and E. B. DeWindt, *Royal Justice and the Medieval English Countryside* (Toronto, in press).

The prioress of Huntingdon, through her bailiff, regarding the two acres of land which she holds in Huntingdon, Simon, the vicar of the church of Blessed Mary in Huntingdon, regarding the one acre of land he holds in Huntingdon, and Roger, the parson of the church of All Saints in Huntingdon, regarding the one acre he holds in Huntingdon, answer for themselves as tenants of those tenements, and they say that they committed no injury or disseisin, because they entered into these tenements through William Teynturer and Reginald, son of Robert, and not through disseisin.

William and Reginald answer for themselves and the others, and they say that the aforesaid messuage and four acres of land were the right and acquisition of a certain Thomas Gos, whose executors they are, who devised those tenements on his deathbed, as it was permitted him according to the customs of that borough of Huntingdon, that those tenements were to be sold by those executors, and that they were to dispose of them as they deemed it more profitable. And they say that by that legacy, they took seisin of those tenements and sold them, as was permitted them, and that they committed no injury or disseisin. And concerning this, they put themselves on the assize.

And regarding the tenements, whereupon this assize has been summoned, they [William and Reginald] say that the assize should not be held, for they say that [all] the tenements in Godmanchester are ancient demesne of the crown of the lord King, where no writ runs except the little writ [of right] close, according to the customs of the manor of Godmanchester, and concerning this they put themselves on the assize, and Nicholas does the same. Therefore, let the assize be taken.

The jurors say on their oath, regarding the tenements in Godmanchester, that those tenements and all the tenements in Godmanchester are ancient demesne of the crown of the lord King, where no writ runs except the little writ according to the custom of the manor. And regarding the four acres of land in Huntingdon, they say that those tenements were a certain Thomas Gos's who, dying, willed them to be disposed of by William and Robert, his executors, for his soul. And they say that, immediately after the dead body of Thomas was carried to the tomb, a certain William Pack, nephew and heir of Thomas, put himself in those four acres of land until those executors, returning from the tomb, expelled him, and did not permit him to have any further seisin. And they say that these executors, by that bequest, held themselves in seisin, until, wishing to make a profit of them, they sold them to the prioress, Simon and Roger, as it was permitted them according to the custom of that vill of Huntingdon, because all purchased tenements can be devised. And because those tenements in Huntingdon were the right and acquisition of that Thomas, who, according to the custom of that vill, devised them, as was permitted him, and because tenements in Godmanchester are ancient demesne of the crown of the lord King, it is adjudged that the prioress, and all others except Ralph go without

a day, and that Nicholas take nothing by this assize, but is in mercy for a false claim. And let Nicholas take action by another writ, if he wishes.

Later, Nicholas came and, regarding the one messuage in Huntingdon and the half acre of land in Godmanchester which he put in his view, and of which he claimed to have been disseised by Ralph, son of Martin Rede of Huntingdon, he withdrew. Therefore, Ralph goes without a day, and Nicholas and his pledges for prosecuting are in mercy. Let the names of the pledges be sought.

Later, the fine is excused at the request of John of Lovetot, and afterwards there was an agreement between them, namely: that Nicholas released and completely quitclaimed, for himself and his heirs, to Ralph and his heirs all his right and claim that he had or in any other way could have in that messuage in Huntingdon and in the half acre of land in Godmanchester with appurtenances, perpetually. And in return for this, Ralph will give Nicholas 40s., which he will pay him next Christmas. And unless he does this, he grants that the sheriff may levy it from his lands and chattels.

SOME GENERAL OBSERVATIONS

By now it will have become abundantly clear that the court rolls of Godmanchester were in no way a record of the implementation of the customs of the town. In simple statistical terms alone, the several hundred legal acts referred to in the previous pages of this chapter represent but a small percentage of the customary legal conveyances that might be expected. That is to say, even for the period of more complete "family" conveyances in the early fourteenth century, entries average out to fewer than one for each known family. In the normal family life cycle one might expect at least five or six acts of property conveyance (dower, dowry, gift, maintenance, will, executor).

Why then was the Godmanchester court employed at all for recording the conveyance of properties covered by a customary title? One answer to this question might be the need that certain townsmen felt for greater legal security. That is to say, the Godmanchester court of conveyance was employed to supplement customary acts. There is an *a priori* evidence to support this explanation since families that employed the courts most for intra-familial property conveyances were families with obvious concerns for security. The Begenore, Grantesden, Spicer and Essex families will be given in illustration of this point.

The Begenore's were a family from across the river in Huntingdon who had established a foothold in Godmanchester. Under the apparent pressure of poverty, the court records of Godmanchester show the family having to remove from the latter town. As the following text indicates,

William Begenore bequeathed property to his sons Peter and Paul in 1314. However, within the year William's wife Mariota had to sell off rights in five acres of property to settle debts accumulated by her husband. In turn, Peter bequeathed property to his brother Paul in 1322 but the latter seemed to have found it necessary to sell this land within the year.

At the very time that the Begenores were falling on evil days a family with the surname *de* Grantesden (*Grantsden*) was establishing itself in Godmanchester. The court rolls indicate purchases of property by John *de* Grantesden from 1298. The family seems to have become firmly established when John's father William obtained liberty of the vill in 1306. William would seem to have desired this liberty in order to invest more fully in Godmanchester land for in that same year he purchased five different pieces of meadow. A good amount of property moved back and forth among the members of the family over the next decade by purchase and sale as well as the grant of a dower. The degree to which this family was simply involved in the land market may be seen by the operations centering around John *de* Grantesden for two or three years. In 1315 John sold a half acre of land plus a swath of meadow and with his wife Pellagia a further one half acre of land and a rod of land. This pattern continued in 1316 when John sold a half acre by himself and with Pellagia two half acre units along with a swath of meadow and a further rod of meadow. In 1316 with his brother Reyner, John sold various units of meadow (one swath plus a half swath plus a half swath plus two swaths plus four beddis) as well as arable (one half rod plus a half rod plus one rod plus one rod plus a half acre plus 1d. of rent). Later that same year John and Pellagia sold a croft along with one rod and one and one half rod unit of land. John had received land from his father and mother Isolda in 1315 as well as property from his brother Reginald. Around this same time John and Pellagia began to make arrangements for the term of their life when they sold seisin in a orchard which they kept for life. Nevertheless, in 1317 John took seisin of three units of land (one quarter acre plus one quarter acre plus one half rod) to be received after the death of his mother Isolda. Some of this land (one half acre plus a quarter acre) he already arranged to release.

In contrast to the Begenores and Grantesdens, there was the Spicer family, or Apotekarius as they were known in the late thirteenth century, establishing itself at Godmanchester by the profits of trade. A Henry Spicer is first noted in 1282 when he sold one half acre of land to Ralph Mercator, following a common pattern of merchants dealing in land. In the next year of 1283 a John *le* Spicer is noted as subletting one rod, and by 1286 with his wife who is not named they sold a built messuage. By

1291 he again sublets three rods of land and one and one half acre of land. His trade must have been flourishing as by 1295 he sublets one half acre of land plus another half acre and a house plus a swat and further pieces of land. He bought a house in 1297 plus one acre of land; 1299 sees John buying land again. John and his wife "procreated" two boys and two girls. His daughter Agnes in 1293 followed in her father's footsteps and bought or sublet two rods of land. John's other daughter Mabel in 1301 buys a house, presumably from her father, and in 1302 he gives her a gift of three rods of land.

John's two sons also had a hand in the land market of that era. Reginald bought one half acre of land that formerly belonged to John *le* Ironmonger in 1301 and this may be noted as typical of how merchants dealt frequently with one another in land. In this same year he bought two acres of land and another one acre from the executors of Edward Goni. In the next year, 1302, John, Reginald's father surrenders one messuage and 12 acres of land to Reginald and Reginald's wife Agnes, who is the daughter of Alan Lutgate. Edward the other son of John *le* Spicer also had one half acre of land that his father surrendered to him, and this was not to be sold while his father lived (in the year of 1302), and by 1304 Edward buys one acre plus one rod of meadow from John (his father) who holds for life.

Texts from a generation of the family with the surname *de* Essex provide us with good information about the place of wives and widows in family property management. One may begin in 1297 when John *de* Essex surrendered to the use of his wife Matilda and her heirs six acres of land inherited from his father Nicholas. Over the next half dozen years John and his wife Matilda were involved in at least three dower exchanges with John's mother Agnes. John's sister Cristina had also obtained property from her father in 1297. Agnes, the widow of Nicholas also purchased land from John in 1299. By 1303 John was dead[84] and his widow Matilda was letting some land to her sister Cristina. John and Matilda had a daughter who was also named Cristina and in 1319 the latter purchased property from her mother. The two daughters of John and Matilda, Agnes and Cristina, received land in gift from their mother in 1313. Property took a further circulation in the Essex family in 1315

---

[84] According to the Goal Delivery Roll entry of 15 May 1302, John *de* Essex was convicted of burglary of a house in Canonstret, Huntingdon, and his chattels were described as 3s. plus land worth 3s. 8d. a year. I owe this reference to Barbara Hanawalt. As far as one can gather from the court rolls, the Essex family property continued in the family after the hanging of John.

when Matilda purchased property from her son John. The Essex family had land dealings, of course, with other than immediate members of their family: in 1297 John exchanged a rod of property with Simon Ingelond; in 1298 there were further property exchanges or purchases with the Kutere family, perhaps implying some marriage relationship with the latter.

*
**

While these four families provide us with interesting illustrations of family use of the courts, such data do not go far to explain the overall court practice. Why were there not more references to family marriage arrangements and maintenance agreements? Security reasons surely could have been invoked by dozens more families! Alternatively, why were there fuller references to bequests over a longer period and the more complete use of the courts by executors?

The answer to these questions seems to be simply a deliberate choice by the people of Godmanchester. Whether for reasons of experimentation at a time of legal development or some sense of pride as a burgeoning "borough," the courts of Godmanchester became more detailed in their records and were used by many more families from the late thirteenth century. From the second quarter of the fourteenth century, however, whether the costs of family settlements became too prohibitive in the town courts,[85] or simply the fact that the mature procedure of ecclesiastical courts was now considered adequate to all intra-familial conveyances, the townspeople of Godmanchester increasingly withdrew their family affairs from the town court from the second quarter of the fourteenth century.

It would be a mistake to interpret this early fourteenth-century experiment at Godmanchester as a frustrated development. Increasingly, as has been noted at the beginning of this chapter, historians now see the claims to ancient demesne by various manors as the desire for the customs of royal manors, not as a revulsion against customary law as such. There is nothing in this fourteenth-century experiment to suggest that the people of Godmanchester were unhappy to live with custom. They would do so for centuries to come. The courts of Godmanchester remain a tacit tribute to the successful functioning of a system of custom in those areas of

---

[85] On clerical costs, see Chapter 2 below, p. 70. Fines were infrequently indicated in the court rolls at the beginning of the surviving series of records. However, there is evidence that fines increased in both their range and amounts over the early fourteenth century.

human relations that in the fourteenth — as well as the twentieth century — were complex and costly.

Furthermore, despite those statistical limitations of court roll data that have been noted again and again in this chapter, we know that the system of property disposition available to the people of Godmanchester was flexible and varied. Taken in isolation, those various property conveyances illustrated in the texts of this chapter are familiar enough to the historian. Less noted is the fact that *in toto* these texts reveal an extraordinary capacity for property redistribution in the very heyday of custom. Requirements of various stages in the life cycle were more proximate forces in the land market than they might be in a different economic structure. But the land market was none the less deserving of the name.[86] Change in demand conditions was a phenomenon dictated by the changing life cycles of hundreds of individuals. Change in supply of land in response to demand was dictated by the rules of custom. In consequence, at Godmanchester custom was very much a stimulant of the land market system.

Nevertheless, the question must be asked: did custom remain supreme at Godmanchester at the price of progress? Progress in the thirteenth and fourteenth centuries has often been described in terms of the rise of the new intellectual and economic estates. How did the "customary town" of Godmanchester fare with respect to these new clerks and merchants? To these questions we turn in the following two chapters. In a later chapter (5), we shall return to a more detailed assessment of resource distribution in Godmanchester by custom as well as other market forces.

---

[86] Karl Polanyi et al., *Trade and Market in the Early Empires: Economics in History and Theory* (Glencoe, Ill., 1957), is a pioneer study of market forms alternative to the capitalist system. Unfortunately, the volume has as yet made little impact on medieval historians.

2

Government by Custom

The fact that custom should remain central to the administration of the different stages of the family cycle may not be too surprising. After all, in this tradition a family is a society in its own right with considerable powers of self-government. The very fact that family life normally functioned without redress to the courts is itself proof of this self-sufficiency. But what of the wider administrative and economic needs of the town? How, for example, did Godmanchester compete in the larger economy of its day without compromising its independence to merchant privilege and how did it satisfy its need for clerical ministration without subordinating its customs to the clerical privileges of the day?

In fourteenth-century England, as at other times in history, economic competition could lead to violent conflict. At St. Albans, within a day's journey to the south of Godmanchester, tension between the townsmen and the abbey simmered for generations before a violent eruption at the time of the Peasants' Revolt. At Cambridge, nearer to Godmanchester than St. Albans, townsmen's attack on the university has been made famous by their oft-quoted cry of "away with the learning of the clerks." The resolution of economic issues in a little country town such as Godmanchester was less likely to be recorded in the annals of the age. But the numerous surviving records of the town make possible a considerable reconstruction of the various elements that were at play in the social and economic life of Godmanchester. Who really governed Godmanchester? Was this control centred in an identifiable economic group? If so, did this group buttress its strength by such various means as intermarriage and the exclusion of competitors, especially outsiders to the town? Questions of this nature will be proposed in the following chapter.

Logically, a beginning of the history of government in Godmanchester ought to be made with analysis of some of those embryonic acts of

borough administration, namely the royal farm [1] and the collection of toll. We do know the actual amounts of the payment of the farm at Godmanchester from bits and pieces of surviving accounts,[2] as well as central government documents.[3] But little is known of the machinery for collecting this farm before the fifteenth century.[4] In similiar fashion, we do know the names of the toll collectors at one time in the late thirteenth century,[5] but nothing more before the fifteenth century. Logic apart, therefore, the historian must begin with surviving documents.

A. LOCAL GOVERNMENT PERSONNEL

The Bailiffs

One has only to glance at the earliest customs of Godmanchester, and the application of such customs in court rolls, to realize that the practical government of the town lay in the hands of the annually appointed bailiffs. The function of the bailiffs was indeed a more "on the scene" power than that of their manorial counterparts, the lord's stewards. For, in the neighbouring manors of Ramsey Abbey, at least, the Ramsey steward presided over village courts regularly but twice a year. Bailiffs administered the entry of outsiders to the liberty, the conveyance of property, the court fee for such conveyance and the farm to be paid from the conveyed properties. Could such power rest lightly upon the shoulders of annually elected bailiffs? Or, alternatively, what could annual "election" really mean in such a context? A beginning of the answer to such questions must be sought in identifying the actual historical personnel of Godmanchester bailiffs.

While properties were conveyed through the hands of bailiffs from the earliest extant court rolls, only from 14 March 1280 do the court records

---

[1] See Reynolds, *English Medieval Towns*, chap. 6, for a summary of these standard elements in the growth of towns over the twelfth and thirteenth centuries.

[2] A half dozen receipts for payment of the royal farms over the late thirteenth and fourteenth centuries survive among Godmanchester records.

[3] The vCH volume for Huntingdonshire which covers Godmanchester makes good use of these sources.

[4] See below, however, Chapter 3, on various surviving assessment inventories.

[5] On the back of the court roll for 1272 (box 5, bundle 1) is written in a contemporary hand: "The following received ale tolls — West Street, Edward Colonot, pledge Godfrey Clerk; Earning Street, Thomas Balle, pledge William Clerk; Post Street, William son of Simon Clerk, pledge Henry Maddermonger; East Street, William de Hartford, pledge Nicholas Parson."

give the names of bailiffs. Only in 1280, too, do we discover that Godmanchester did not have a court house. The court would very likely meet
in the more spacious premises of the town. The first recorded meeting
place of the court was in the hall of the prior of Merton on 14 March
1280. The next court session was in the garden (*in horto*) of Henry *le*
Maddermonger on 4 April. Of the nine further sessions recorded for the
hall of Merton, eight were over the period from 1280 to 1282. In the
meantime, the court began to meet more often at a place called Leyrstowe
(*in uno loco vocato*) (1280 – 1; 1281 – 6; 1282 – 10; 1283 – 7 + ;
1284 – 11 + ; 1285 – 12; 1286 – 18 July to 14 November inclusive). For
several courts the place of meeting is not indicated but this was very likely
at Leyrstowe, the scene of previous sessions (the plus (+) sign above
indicates their inclusion in the total). Of course, not all court sessions have
survived (noticeably those of the first six months of 1286) so that the
above numbers are not complete. After December 1286, the place of the
court meeting is never again mentioned. The logical assumption to be
taken from this is that a regular court house had been built by this time.
Owing to the increasing preference for "the place called Leyrstowe" it
might also be suggested that the court was built on that "place." Nevertheless, as will be seen below, it can also be suggested that the court met in
the house of a prominent clerk from this time.

    Prior to 1287, the court met more intermittently at other places. On 27
November 1281, 18 December 1281 and 19 February 1282 the court met
in the garden "formerly of Henry *le* Maddermonger" (or *le* Warenter).
The court met once in the garden of Simon Seman (31 October 1280). The
court showed a preference also for the gardens of John Manipenny (24
July 1281, 3 June 1283), Godfrey Gildene (9 August 1285) and Reginald,
son of Robert (16 November 1284). The court was said to have met in the
hall (*aula*) of Godfrey Gildene (25 September 1281) and of Reginald, son
of Robert (4 April 1282; 10 December 1282; 18 October 1285). On 31
December 1282, the court met in the house (*in domo*) of Adam Grinde
and on 5 December 1286 in the house of Henry *le* Warenter (*le*
Maddermonger). The most frequented house for court sessions was that of
Eusebius *le* Masun (27 June 1280; 14 May 1282; 21 January, 11
February, 4 March 1283; 27 January, 24 February 1284), although on 26
June 1281, the court was said to have been held in the hall of Eusebius *le*
Masun.

    The 1279 Hundred Roll for Godmanchester confirms that the court
was meeting on the premises of the more wealthy men of the town. In one
case at least, that of Adam Grinde, the site of the meeting probably
represented a prime commercial site for he was not yet among the more

wealthy landowners but this site was to bring the proprietor to a position of great wealth by the time of the first surviving local lay subsidy roll. Unexpectedly, for wealth will prove to be a general criterion, only one of the owners of the court meeting places, Reginald son of Robert, was also a bailiff over this time. Reginald son of Robert was one of the more wealthy men of the town in the Hundred Roll of 1279. A few months after Reginald's name disappeared from among the bailiffs, John son of Reginald is listed as one of the bailiffs. A John son of Reginald also appeared in 1279 as a wealthy landholder. In one entry, that of 22 February 1291, John son of Reginald is designated as clerk.

Names of the bailiffs of Godmanchester read like a short-list of God-manchester wealth. Again, excepting Clerks for the moment, Godman-chester bailiffs illustrate families that thrived over the greater length of the period of this study as well as families whose prominence was confined to the special entrepreneurial skills and fortunes of one or two of its members. Of the former, most prominent were the Aylreds and Manipennys. A Manipenny functioned as a bailiff in 1280-1281, 1315-1316, 1321-1322, 1329-1332, 1341-1342, 1346-1348, 1350-1351, 1356-1358, 1362-1363, 1366-1369 and 1370. An Aylred was a bailiff in 1309-1311, 1323-1326, 1329-1330, 1335, 1337, 1338, 1343-1344, 1347, 1353-1354, 1360-1366, 1390-1391, and 1394 to 1397. After two flourishing generations as bailiff (1291-1299, 1300-1311, 1316-1318, 1321-1322 and 1331-1332) the Rode family never recovered its economic leadership and never once placed a bailiff following the Black Death. A good many families, that flourished in numbers over the whole of our period, had bailiffs restricted to very few exceptional individuals. Examples of such families were Balle, Gildene, Glewe, Goni, Lane, Millicent, Pensel, Pernel, Rede, Quenyng and Willem. On the other hand, an equally large number of families failed to maintain representatives among bailiffs owing to the fact they faltered for demographic reasons. Examples of this category are the Acry, Garlop, Grinde, Hopay, Kuter, Maddermonger (Warenter), Mason and Witman families.[6]

Despite the persistence of certain family names, therefore, and the obvious significance of wealth, the following list of Godmanchester bailiffs represents a fairly wide range of town families.

---

[6] For further comments on this demographic feature of Godmanchester, see below, Chapter 5, C. "Mobilizing Wealth Through the Family," p. 201.

TABLE 5: THE BAILIFFS OF GODMANCHESTER, 1278 TO 1399

Name	Bailiff from	to	
William Clerk	14 March	12 December	1280
Reginald son of Robert	14 March	4 April	1280
William Manipenny	27 June	12 December	1280
Thomas Atterissis	2 January	27 November	1281
William Manipenny	2 January	27 November	1281
Reginald son of Robert	—	18 December	1281
Thomas Balle	—	18 December	1281
Reginald son of Robert	8 January	31 December	1282
Thomas Balle	8 January	31 December	1282
Reginald son of Robert	21 January	2 December	1283
Thomas Balle	—	2 December	1283
Reginald son of Robert	13 January	6 December	1284
Thomas Balle	13 January	6 December	1284
Reginald son of Robert	1 March	? November	1285
Thomas Balle	1 March	? November	1285
William son of Simon	18 July	5 December	1286
Roger Goni	18 July	5 December	1286
William Clerk	20 February	3 April	1287
Reginald son of Robert*	9 October	18 November	1287
John son of Reginald, clerk	1 July	28 October, 9 December	1288
Robert le Warenter	1 July	28 October, 9 December	1288
Robert le Warenter	20 January	16 June, 23 December	1289
John son of Reginald, clerk	20 January	16 June, 23 December	1289
Robert le Warenter	20 July	9 November	1290
Nicholas de Essex	20 July	9 November	1290
John son of Reginald, clerk	22 February	13 December	1291
Henry Rode	22 February	13 December	1291
John son of John	15 March	—	1291
John son of Reginald	10 January	31 July	1292
Henry Rode	10 January	31 July	1292
Nicholas Rede	2 April	18 November	1293
William Millicent	2 April	5 November	1293
William son of Simon Clerk	8 December	31 December	1293
Henry Rode	8 December	31 December	1293
William son of Simon Clerk	25 March	23 December	1294
Henry Rode	25 March	23 December	1294

* Reginald son of Robert was the only acting bailiff for the months of October and November 1287.

Name	Bailiff from	to	
Henry Rode	20 January	24 November	1295
William son of Simon Clerk	20 January	22 September	1295
Godfrey le Clerk	13 October	24 November	1295
Henry Rode	2 August	27 December	1296
Godfrey le Clerk	2 August	27 December	1296
Godfrey le Clerk	3 January	19 December	1297
Henry Rode	3 January	19 December	1297
Richard Pernel	9 January	30 October	1298
Robert le Maddermonger (le Warenter)	9 January	30 October	1298
Henry Rode	20 November	31 December	1298
Richard Acry	20 November	31 December	1298
Henry Rode	22 January	3 December	1299
Richard Acry	22 January	3 December	1299
Hende	26 March	—	1299
Richard Pernel	30 October	—	1299
Robert le Warenter	30 October	—	1299
Henry Rode	7 April	15 December	1300
Richard Acry	7 April	24 November	1300
Adam Grinde	—	15 December	1300
Adam Grinde	9 January	7 December	1301
Henry Rode	9 January	7 December	1301
Henry Rode	4 January	20 December	1302
Adam Grinde	4 January	20 December	1302
Henry Rode	10 January	8 August	1303
Adam Grinde	10 January	8 August	1303
William son of Simon	19 September	19 December	1303
Godfrey le Kutere	19 September	19 December	1303
Godfrey le Kutere	2 January	29 December	1304
William son of Simon	2 January	29 December	1304
Henry Rode	—	16 December	1305
William le Mason	—	16 December	1305
William son of Simon	12 August	2 December	1305
Godfrey le Kutere	12 August	2 December	1305
William le Mason (of Post Street)	6 January	17 November	1306
Henry Rode	6 January	29 December	1306
Henry Rode	April	21 December	1307
Richard Pernel	16 May	21 December	1307
Richard Pernel	11 January	31 October	1308
Henry Rode	11 January	31 October	1308
Reginald son of John	10 July	12 December	1308
Stephen Clerk	10 July	12 December	1308
Stephen Clerk	2 January	19 June	1309
Reginald son of John	2 January	19 June	1309
Henry Rode	31 July	11 September	1309

Name	Bailiff from	to	
Henry Rode	4 December	18 December	1309
Godfrey Aylred	4 December	18 December	1309
Henry Rode	21 May	17 December	1310
Godfrey Aylred	21 May	17 December	1310
Henry Rode	7 January	9 December	1311
Godfrey Aylred	7 January	9 December	1311
Adam Grinde	—	30 December	1311
John Millicent	—	30 December	1311
Adam Grinde	? January	7 September	1312
John Millicent	? January	7 September	1312
Reyner Garlop	9 November	21 December	1312
William son of Simon	9 November	21 December	1312
William son of Simon	? February	? October	1313
Reyner Garlop	? February	13 December	1313
Adam Grinde	8 November	13 December	1313
Reyner Garlop	3 January	—	1314
Adam Grinde	3 January	—	1314
Stephen Clerk	—	26 December	1314
John Millicent	—	26 December	1314
Stephen Clerk	16 January	21 August	1315
John Millicent	16 January	21 August	1315
Thomas Witman	27 November	18 December	1315
Roger Manipenny	27 November	18 December	1315
Thomas Witman	1 April	14 October	1316
Roger Manipenny	1 April	14 October	1316
Reyner Garlop	28 October	30 December	1316
Henry Rode	28 October	30 December	1316
Henry Rode	20 January	15 September	1317
Reyner Garlop	20 January	15 September	1317
Henry Rode	9 February	16 August	1318
Reyner Garlop	9 February	16 August	1318
Eusebius Clerk	19 October	14 December	1318
William son of Simon	19 October	14 December	1318
Eusebius Clerk	14 January	19 April	1319
William son of Simon	14 January	19 April	1319
Stephen Clerk	25 October	27 December	1319
John son of Thomas Quenyng	25 October	27 December	1319
Stephen Clerk	10 January	4 September	1320
John son of Thomas Quenyng	10 January	4 September	1320
Reyner Garlop	19 February	17 September	1321
Thomas Witman	19 February	17 September	1321
Godfrey Manipenny	8 October	31 December	1321
Henry Rode	8 October	31 December	1321
Henry Rode	21 January	9 September	1322
Godfrey Manipenny	21 January	9 September	1322
John Pensel	30 September	11 November	1322

Name	Bailiff from	to	
John Pensel	7 April	29 September	1323
William Aylred	13 October	15 December	1323
William Colion	13 October	15 December	1323
William Aylred	5 January	? December	1324
William Colion	5 January	? December	1324
Godfrey Oundle	18 January	26 September	1325
Godfrey Glewe	18 January	26 September	1325
William son of William Aylred	24 October	26 December	1325
Gilbert in Venella (Lane)	24 October	26 December	1325
William son of William Aylred	9 January	18 September	1326
Gilbert in Venella	9 January	18 September	1326
Henry Willem	9 October	11 December	1326
Reyner Garlop	9 October	11 December	1326
Reyner Garlop	8 January	20 September	1327
Henry Willem	8 January	20 September	1327
Henry Manipenny	16 February	21 September	1329
Thomas Witman	16 February	21 September	1329
Godfrey Manipenny	5 October	21 December	1329
William Aylred	5 October	21 December	1329
Godfrey Manipenny	18 January	27 September	1330
William Aylred	18 January	27 September	1330
Henry Manipenny	18 October	29 November	1330
Andrew Bonis	18 October	29 November	1330
Henry Manipenny	10 January	19 September	1331
Andrew Bonis	10 January	19 September	1331
Henry Rode	11 October	13 December	1331
Godfrey Manipenny	11 October	13 December	1331
Henry Rode	3 January	10 September	1332
Godfrey Manipenny	3 January	10 September	1332
John son of Godfrey	1 October	24 December	1332
Thomas Hopay	1 October	24 December	1332
Thomas Witman	14 January	4 February	1333
John son of Godfrey	14 January	23 September	1333
Thomas Hopay	25 February	23 September	1333
John Glewe	6 October	29 December	1334
Richard son of William le Rede	6 October	29 December	1334
Henry Colowot	6 October	—	1334
Richard Aylred	19 January	—	1335
John Glewe	19 January	28 September	1335
Richard le Rede	9 February	28 September	1335
William Aylred	2 October	18 December	1337
Henry Mileward	2 October	18 December	1337
William Aylred	13 January	24 September	1338
Henry Mileward	13 January	24 September	1338
Henry Colowot	14 October	21 December	1339
Henry Colowot	6 January	14 September	1340

Name	Bailiff from	to	
John Gildene	6 January	14 September	1340
John son of Godfrey	5 October	28 December	1340
Godfrey Atterissis	5 October	28 December	1340
John son of Godfrey	18 January	27 September	1341
Godfrey Atterissis	18 January	27 September	1341
William le Rede	18 October	20 December	1341
Godfrey Manipenny	18 October	20 December	1341
Godfrey Manipenny	10 January	19 September	1342
William le Rede	10 January	19 September	1342
William Aylred	2 October	25 December	1343
William Gile	2 October	25 December	1343
William Gile	15 January	23 September	1344
William Aylred	15 January	23 September	1344
Henry Willem	4 November	16 December	1344
Henry Willem	6 January	15 September	1345
John Glewe	6 January	15 September	1345
Henry Colowot	29 September	8 December	1345
William le Rede	29 September	8 December	1345
Henry Colowot	13 January	28 September	1346
William le Rede	13 January	28 September	1346
Godfrey Manipenny	19 October	21 December	1346
Alan Aylred	19 October	21 December	1346
Alan Aylred	11 January	20 September	1347
Godfrey Manipenny	11 January	20 September	1347
Henry Manipenny	11 October	13 December	1347
Richard le Rede	11 October	13 December	1347
Henry Manipenny	3 January	12 June	1348
Richard le Rede	3 January	18 September	1348
John son of Alexander Goni	26 June	18 September	1348
Henry Colowot	9 October	11 December	1348
Henry Willem	9 October	11 December	1348
Henry Willem	8 January	20 August	1349
Henry Colowot (died June 1349)	8 January	28 May	1349
John Skinner	18 June	20 August	1349
Godfrey Millicent	13 January	? July	1350
William Clervaux	13 January	? July	1350
Godfrey Manipenny	23 September	16 December	1350
Henry Willem	23 September	16 December	1350
Godfrey Millicent	13 January	21 December	1351
William Clervaux	13 January	21 December	1351
Henry Willem	13 January	4 August	1351
Godfrey Manipenny	13 January	4 August	1351
Godfrey Millicent	5 January	27 September	1352
William Clervaux	5 January	27 September	1352
Godfrey Millicent	? March	26 December	1353
William Clervaux	? March	? November	1353

Name	Bailiff from	to	
Alan Aylred	3 May	October	1353
Thomas Pernel	3 May	—	1353
Henry Aylred	31 October	26 December	1353
Godfrey Millicent	6 February	25 December	1354
Henry Aylred	6 February	25 December	1354
Roger atte Barre	1 March	—	1354
John son of Alexander Goni	29 January	17 December	1355
Thomas Clerk	29 January	17 December	1355
John son of Alexander Goni	12 January	15 September	1356
Thomas Clerk	12 January	15 September	1356
John Quenyng	6 October	29 December	1356
William Hors	6 October	29 December	1356
John Quenyng	19 January	? August	1357
William Hors	19 January	? August	1357
Thomas Gildene	12 October	28 December	1357
John Manipenny	12 October	28 December	1357
Thomas Gildene	29 March	13 September	1358
John Manipenny	29 March	13 September	1358
John Skinner	7 February	26 September	1359
William son of Thomas Goni	7 February	26 September	1359
John Goni	? February	—	1360
Alan Aylred	8 October	10 December	1360
John Munderford	8 October	10 December	1360
Alan Aylred	1 January	23 December	1361
John Munderford	1 February	23 December	1361
Alan Aylred	13 January	20 October	1362
Richard Oxenford	1? October	18 December	1362
John Manipenny	1? October	18 December	1362
Richard Oxenford	5 January	14 September	1363
John Manipenny	5 January	14 September	1363
Alan Aylred	29 September	28 December	1363
Thomas Pernel	29 September	28 December	1363
Alan Aylred	17 January	19 December	1364
Thomas Pernel	17 January	? October	1364
Thomas Gildene	17 October	19? December	1364
Thomas Gildene	10 January	18 September	1365
Alan Aylred	10 January	11 December	1365
John Mundeford	9 October	11 December	1365
Alan Aylred	1 January	30 July	1366
John Mundeford	1 January	30 July	1366
Thomas Clerk	1 October	24 December	1366
John Manipenny	1 October	24 December	1366
Thomas Clerk	14 January	23 September	1367
John Manipenny	14 January	23 July	1367
Thomas Gildene	12 October	14 December	1368
John Manipenny	12 October	14 December	1368

Name	Bailiff from	to	
Thomas Gildene	4 January	13 September	1369
John Manipenny	4 January	13 September	1369
John Manipenny	17 October	19 December	1370
Thomas Balle	17 October	19 December	1370
Thomas Balle	9 January	18 September	1371
John Manipenny	9 January	18 September	1371
William le Longe	7 August	11 December	1371
William in ye Lane	7 August	11 December	1371
William le Longe, clerk	1 January	23 December	1372
William in ye Lane	1 January	9 September	1372
John Manipenny	? February	—	1372
Thomas Clerk	? October	23 December	1372
Thomas Clerk	13 January	22 September	1373
William le Longe	13 January	22 September	1373
John Chadeslee	13 October	15 December	1373
William Hartford	13 October	15 December	1373
John Chadeslee	6 January	14 September	1374
William Hartford	6 January	14 September	1374
William le Longe, clerk	16 November	28 December	1374
Thomas Balle	16 November	28 December	1374
William le Longe, clerk	18 January	27 September	1375
Thomas Balle	18 January	27 September	1375
John Donewych	—	20 December	1375
William Peek	—	20 December	1375
John Donewych	10 January	11 December	1376
William Peek	10 January	28 August	1376
John Curl	? September	11 December	1376
John Curl	1 January	10 September	1377
John Donewych	1 January	10 September	1377
William Peek	26 February	23 April	1377
John Aleyn	1 September	24 December	1377
Thomas Balle	1 September	24 December	1377
Thomas Balle	14 January	23 September	1378
John Aleyn	14 January	23 September	1378
John Curl	14 October	16 December	1378
William Peek	14 October	16 December	1378
John Curl	6 January	15 September	1379
William Peek	6 January	15 September	1379
John Plomer	8 December	29 December	1379
William Hartford	8 December	29 December	1379
John Plomer	? January	11 October	1380
William Hartford	? January	11 October	1380
John Curl	? September	20 December	1380
William Chapman	? September	20 December	1380
John Curl	10 January	19 September	1381
William Chapman	10 January	19 September	1381

Name	Bailiff from	to	
John Donewych	10 October	12 December	1381
John Plomer	10 October	12 December	1381
John Donewych	2 January	11 September	1382
John Plomer	2 January	11 September	1382
William le Longe	5 February	17 September	1383
John Donewych	5 February	17 September	1383
John Curl	20 October	22 December	1384
John Willem	20 October	22 December	1384
Thomas Balle	12 October	14 December	1385
William Hartford	12 October	14 December	1385
John Curl	10 August	21 September	1385
Reyner Outy	? November	—	1385
Thomas Balle	4 January	19 April	1386
William Hartford	4 January	19 April	1386
John Curl	? September	6 December	1386
John Willem	? September	6 December	1386
John Willem	13 January	25 July	1387
John Curl	13 January	25 July	1387
John Plomer	7 November	28 November	1387
Thomas Pernel	7 November	28 November	1387
John Plomer	9 January	25 June	1388
Thomas Pernel	9 January	25 June	1388
John Curl	12 November	17 December	1388
John Frere	12 November	17 December	1388
John Curl	7 January	16 September	1389
William Hartford	20 January	29 September	1389
John Frere	7 January	16 September	1389
Simon Dicere	28 October	23 December	1389
Simon Dicere	20 January	29 September	1390
Thomas Gildene	22 October	24 December	1390
Thomas Aylred	22 October	24 December	1390
Thomas Aylred	12 January	31 August	1391
Thomas Gildene	12 January	14 December	1391
John Donewych	12 October	14 December	1391
Thomas Gildene	3 January	12 September	1392
John Donewych	3 January	12 September	1392
William Peek	3 October	26 December	1392
John Curl	3 October	26 December	1392
William Peek	16 January	25 September	1393
John Curl	16 January	25 September	1393
John Manipenny	16 October	18 December	1393
Thomas Robyn	16 October	18 December	1393
Thomas Robyn	8 January	17 September	1394
John Manipenny	8 January	17 September	1394
Thomas Gildene	29 October	31 December	1394
Thomas Aylred	29 October	31 December	1394

Name	Bailiff from	to	
Thomas Gildene	21 January	19 August	1395
Thomas Aylred	21 January	19 August	1395
John Curl	12 October	14 December	1396
Thomas Aylred	12 October	14 December	1396
John Curl	4 January	13 September	1397
Thomas Aylred	4 January	13 September	1397
John Donewych	17 October	19 December	1398
John Copegray	17 October	19 December	1398
John Donewych	9 January	18 September	1399
John Copegray	9 January	18 September	1399

THE CLERKS

In addition to prominent landholders of the town, it is immediately apparent that clerks appear consistently as bailiffs. Whether that Reginald son of Robert who was bailiff in the 1280s to be succeeded by his son John came from the main clerk family cannot be determined since the probable father of Reginald, Simon Clerk, is a rather shadowy historical person in the more sparse court rolls of the 1270s. It is clear, however, that a clerk family acquired a hereditary monopoly over the clerk role in Godmanchester from the 1280s, if not earlier. A patriarchal figure, William Clerk appears as a bailiff in 1280, reappears frequently as a bailiff from 1286 for the rest of the century, and intermittently in the early fourteenth century until 1319. William was one of those important personages easily identifiable to his contemporaries and variously referred to as William Clerk, William the son of Simon and William the son of Simon Clerk. Over the late 1290s, Godfrey *le* Clerk appeared often as a bailiff. Godfrey *le* Clerk is identified as brother of Simon. Over 1318-1319, Eusebius, the son of Godfrey Clerk, appeared often as a bailiff. From 1308, Stephen Clerk, the son of William, began to appear as bailiff and continued until 1320. The Thomas Clerk who functioned as a bailiff from 1355 to 1366 was very likely the grandson of William although the line of descent of his father Reginald cannot be clearly established.

The Clerk family's dominance over the profession of clerk can be established from their role as bailiffs. From this same role, one series of court dates tell us how remunerative the office of clerk could be. For the court of the Thursday after the feast of St. Barnabas the Apostle, 13 Edward II (12 June 1320), the bailiffs were announced as Stephen *le* Clerk and John son of Thomas Quenyeve. To the heading of the court is added,

"And Stephen Clerk receives the entry fines from this court: 2s. 10d." (*Et Stephanus Clerk recepit gersumas de ista curia*), surely an extraordinarily generous reward for recording eleven entries (4 ongoing pleas, 2 entries to property for which no fine was paid and 5 entries with fines). In the next three courts it is also noted that Stephen Clerk receives the entry fines, although these are not totalled as was the case for 12 June. However, totals do come to 3s. 3d., 5s. and 2s. for these courts — altogether, a payment of over eleven shillings for these four brief courts.

At the same time, it should be remarked that the work of the clerk was quite distinct from that of the bailiff. In other words, clerks would have to perform their tasks for the court and for the town, whether or not they were bailiffs for that session. This makes all the more remarkable the fact that one family could maintain a monopoly over this lucrative office. Yet, to judge by the Clerk surname, such a monopoly may not have been uncommon. A geographical mapping of the name Clerk in Huntingdonshire lay subsidy rolls shows a remarkably even, and controlled, incidence of the name Clerk.[7] Furthermore, in view of the feverish involvement of ecclesiastics in the Godmanchester land market, Clerks other than the family cited above appeared very rarely among land conveyances. To all appearances the family of William the son of Simon Clerk kept out other clerks.

Over the whole of our period, only a score of clerk "outsiders" are noted in Godmanchester courts. Most of the references to Clerks — William of Broughton, 1279; John of Brampton, 1279; Thomas of Huntingdon, 1280; William Clerk of Stukeley, dead by 1282; John of St. Ives, 1285; Robert *le* Clerk of Brampton, 1295; Henry, of Olney, living in West Street, 1356; Margaret wife of William Clerk of Huntingdon, 1364 — deal with small parcels of land that betray no signs of such Clerks performing their occupational roles in Godmanchester.

Many of these Clerks would seem to have gained an entry to Godmanchester through relatives. Such was clearly the case for Clerks holding land in Godmanchester from neighbouring Hemingford. John Clerk of Hemingford, who sold some thirty small pieces of property at Godmanchester over 1329-1330 was specified as "brother of Alice wife of Simon Miller." Over 1329, William son of John Clerk, of Houghton, sold eleven small pieces of property that very likely came to him by inheritance. A John Clerk from Over had interests in Godmanchester through his wife,

---

[7] This study was done in an unpublished paper by Malcolm Burson from lay subsidy rolls and other available lists of names.

Agnes Mattishale. He acquired a few smallish pieces of property in the town over the late 1320s and was said to be living (*manens*) in Godmanchester. One may suggest that this John Clerk retired to the town since he appears only briefly in the above-noted context. Emma wife of Thomas Clerk of Offord Cluny acquiring property in 1280 and selling it in 1281, was the sister of Elena West. Some entries show no particular interests in the town, as in 1329 when John Clerk of Huntingdon appeared only in the role of attorney.

THE CLERGY

The spiritual government of Godmanchester — *cura animarum* in technical canonical terms — was a powerful force in material matters of the town as well. In the gift of Merton Priory, Surrey, the one parish church had brought the local or sub-priory at Godmanchester considerable holdings by the late thirteenth century. According to the Hundred Roll of 1279 the church was endowed with 48 acres of arable, held 15 acres of meadow in severalty for the tithes of all the meadow (*totius feni*) and also received 26s. 8d. as tithing from the mills.

Despite these considerable economic resources, there is no evidence after the Statute of Mortmain (1279) that the courts of Godmanchester allowed property to be conveyed into the hand of the priory. Perhaps the last conveyance of this sort was recorded in the Godmanchester court of 13 May 1277, when Thomas, bailiff of the prior of Merton took seisin in the name of the prior of one rod of land from Eusebius Albrit. Thereafter, the statute seems to have been strictly enforced. For example, on 17 July 1326 the Church of All Saints of Huntingdon was refused entry to one swath of meadow because this was of lay fee. Occasionally, the courts would remind purchasers of property that these were not to be alienated to religious houses. One instance of this occurred in 1310 when William son of Thomas atte Lewe was receiving three acres at the hands of the bailiffs. As we shall see below, the bailiffs were much more careful to remind those seeking liberty of the town that the statute was enforced. Of course, the customs of Godmanchester gave a separate title to this statute forbidding properties coming into the hands of religious houses.[8]

No such restraint held back the secular clergy of Godmanchester around the end of the thirteenth century. Their market performance provides evidence to vindicate the worst fears of the fourteenth-century friar or the modern anticlerical. The land market record of Reyner Vicory

---

[8] See Appendix 1, "Godmanchester Customals," p. 433.

in the late thirteenth century and Roger *de* Stratishill over the next generation vies with that of leading townsmen such as Adam Grinde and William Millicent. As the following list of conveyances from the court rolls indicate, these clergy must have kept a ready eye on the land market.

TABLE 6: LAND ACQUISITIONS OF REYNER VICORY

Date	*Property*
1280	1r + 1r meadow + ½a + 1r + 1a + 1a + 3r
1281	3r + ½a + 1r meadow + 1 messuage + 1r meadow + 1½a + 3r + 1 place + 8a + 1 messuage + 1 cris + 1a + 1r meadow + ½a
1282	2 butts + 1r meadow + ½a + ½a + ½a + ½a + 6 heres of land + 1r + ½a + ½a + 1½r + 3r + 1 swath meadow
1283	1a + 1 swath of meadow + ½a + ½a meadow + ½a + ½a + 3 pieces of land + ½a meadow + 2r
1284	½a + ½a + ½a
1286	1a + ½a + 3½a + 1a meadow.

TABLE 7: LAND ACQUISITIONS OF ROGER *DE* STRATESHILL

Year	*Property*
1291	1r + ½a + 3r + 1a + 1a + 1½r + 1r + 3r + 1r + ½a + 1r + 3 ob. rent + 1 messuage + 1 messuage + 1 area + 1 house
1292	1 forera + 1r + 1r meadow + 2d. rent + ½a + 1 messuage + 3r + 1½r
1293	5 year lease from Walter son of Elias Ede
1295	½a + 2r + 1 messuage + 1½a + 1½a + 1½a + 1r + ½r + 1r
1296	1 messuage + ½a
1297	3r meadow + ½a meadow + 1r + 1 forera + ½a
1298	½a + 1½r + 1½r + 1 ob. rent
1300	½a
1301	9 beddis
1302	9 cris + 6 cris + ½a + 1d. q. rent
1306	1½r meadow + rent of ½d. + ½d.
1308	9 beddis
1309	½a + ½a

Roger *de* Strateshill died in or around the year of 1322.

Whether or not from pressure of the Statute of Mortmain cannot be immediately discerned, but this concentration of property in the hands of a few clergy began to taper off in the early fourteenth century.[9] In their

[9] Property presumably of spiritual rather than lay fee continued to be conveyed among clergy. During 1288, for example, Thomas Clerk acquired a half acre of meadow and an acre of arable from Simon, vicar of the church of Godmanchester.

place appeared a great variety of chaplains. This growth of the clerical estate appears in our records through the entry of many small gifts to these men under the title of chaplain. The number of chaplains associated with Godmanchester alone is considerable in the court rolls, as shown by Table 8.

TABLE 8: CHAPLAINS OF GODMANCHESTER

Martin, the chaplain	1279
Balle, Robert	1282
Furnam, William ad	1291
Scot, Lord John	1299
Balle, William	1304
Atequene, William	1308
Atequene, William	1313
Denne, Robert	1326
Manipenny, Reginald son of John	1332
Abraham, Robert *de* Cononwestrate	1342
Balle, Robert	1343
Goni, Lord Robert	1345
Kyne, John	1349
Batweye, William	1343
Banastre, John, clerk	1350
Dicere, Thomas	1350
Garlop, Hugh	1350
Rudham, Alan	1351
Marny, Thomas	1351
Aleyn, William	1354
Botman, John	1356
Outy, William	1359
Balle, Robert	1366
Taburer, Simon	1372
Wythgrane, Henry	1372
Wayte, John	1378
Awnfleys, Nicholas	1380
Hyndale, William	1380
Moore, Simon of the	1391
Hilgar, Thomas	1394

Usually under the title of "chaplain" the list of clergy from outside Godmanchester with a finger in the local land scene shows a geographical spread almost comparable to that of merchants. However, the amounts of land involved were usually quite small.

TABLE 9: CHAPLAINS APPEARING IN GODMANCHESTER COURT ROLLS
FROM OUTSIDE THE TOWN

Name	Place	Date
Walter	Buckworth	1279
Hotot, Roger *le*	Eleen	1289
Lord Martin	Bromham	1292
Sen, Lord Simon	Hunts	1296
William	Elsworth	1297
Garlop, Reyner son of Richard	Warboys	1308
Lord Elias	Luton	1310
Garlop, Reyner son of Richard	Warboys	1311
Lord Walter	Stukeley	1312
Lord Roger	Iselham	1315
Warmington, Walter, canon of	Lincs	1316
Welle, Walter atte	Great Stukeley	1324
William	Burtonsteye	1327
Lord Peter	Eton	1329
Walter	Elsworth	1329
Lord Walter	Stukeley	1331
Utting, John	Hunts	1340
Gonnfayon, William	Buckworth	1340
John	Mildenhall	1342
Beaugrant, Lord Roger	Mildenhall	1346
Bewschampe, Lord William canon of	Hunts	1349
John	Caxton	1349
John	Kent	1350
John	Fen Stanton	1351
Fulborne, Robert	Papworth	1355
Whyte, John	Hunts	1361
Tanne, William	Brampton	1364
John	St. Neots	1365
Lincoln, the chaplain of church of	Great Paxton	1378
Burke, John of Cam	Lincoln	1378
Barker, John, of church of St. John	Great Paxton	1378
Berne, Walter, of church of St. John	Great Paxton	1378
Russel, John, of church of	Knapwell	1387
Drayton, William, of church of All Saints	Cambridge	1389
Michel, Adam son of John	Hartford	1394

That these commercial activities of the clergy, especially outsiders, caused friction with lay competitors may be expected. The nature of surviving records is such, however, that friction does not come to our attention. Only an exceptional case, a *cause célèbre* that reached the royal courts, gives us a glimpse of what could happen. On 10 June 1332, William Colion and Andrew Bonis of Godmanchester were charged before William *le* Moigne, sheriff of Huntingdon at his tourn in Toseland, with murdering John *de* Raveley, parson of All Saints church in

Huntingdon. Along with Colion and Bonis eighteen other men were charged with aiding and abetting: Simon Parson, Richard his son, John Hardy, taylor, John Notting, smith, Gilbert son of John Notting, Robert Denne, clerk, Godfrey Manipenny, Thomas Hopay, John Godman, John Hilde, Henry son of Reginald son of John Hilde, William son of Alan *le* Mileward, John Baronn, Roger Manipenny, John Glewe, butcher, Andrew Mundeford, John *le* Longe, smith and Lamberois LenyWyere.[10] While all these men were acquitted, it is difficult to imagine that so many important personages from Godmanchester were involved in an incident deriving from a momentary homicidal impulse.

More than likely such friction was in great part muted by the commitment of townsmen to religious activities and, to some degree, by the commitment of clergy to the town, even by marriage. In short, through the increasing role of chaplaincies monitored by guilds, the people of Godmanchester remained closely identified with many clergy, and the disposition of funds for spiritual purposes, over the fourteenth century. Names of custodians of guilds only appear after the mid-century, but these were clearly the more affluent members of the town.[11] Members of the Confraternity of St. John the Baptist were John Skinner, William Nottyng, Lord Reginald Manipenny, Richard Taylor, John *de* Hyl, John Hoggh', Robert Howman, William Mileward, John Stirtloe, Roger atte Barre and John Drewry (May 1351); Custodians of The Blessed Mary were John Ede (1361), William Graveley and John Ridel (June 1366); Custodians for the Guild of All Saints included Simon Dicere holding this office in January 1354, July 1373 and August 1391 and John Othewold in August 1391. The Custodian for the Guild of the Sacred Body of Christ was William Walton around 1340 and the Custodian for the Guild of St. Mary in Perpetuate was John Aleyn in 1377. It is noteworthy that the guilds were able to buy and sell property in the courts. For example, in June 1366 Cristina daughter of John Colion sold a certain amount of land to a guild and a guild sold a shop to William Longe in 1367. In both instances it was the Guild of Blessed Mary that was involved.

There is a good deal of incidental information in Godmanchester court rolls about property bequeathed for spiritual purposes. For example, in

---

[10] I am indebted to Barbara Hanawalt for this information from gaol delivery rolls. Hanawalt argues to economic causes as the main source of friction behind other crimes in Huntingdonshire. See her "Community Conflict and Social Control: Crime and Justice in the Ramsey Abbey Villages," *Mediaeval Studies*, 39 (1977), 402-423.

[11] The text of the establishing of a chaplaincy service in 1306, given above in Chapter 1, pp. 47-48, also features two wealthy families of the town, the Millicents and Hartfords.

1312 William Aylred made arrangements through an attorney to follow the will of his sister-in-law (late wife of Richard Acry) who had left two rods of land to supply a light in the parish church. Over the previous year Henry Rode had given three rods of meadow and Reginald, son of John, one rod of arable for services by the parish church. In 1302 Godfrey Clerk had surrendered property to the bailiffs (one acre of arable and one and one half rods of arable, one dole of meadow, a croft, a parcel and a halfpenny rent) in honour of St. James to maintain one poor man each year. On the whole, however, such references are infrequent. Much more significant was that fact that wills left to the discretion of executors the disposal of their property for spiritual purposes. We have frequent reference in the *inter vivos* disposition of property to this executorial discretion "should there be no children." Significantly, the executors are always to sell the property and to employ the sale price for spiritualities. The large numbers of property sales by executors has been noted above.[12] One cannot escape the conclusion that the executor performed the key role in preventing the spread of clerical control over property at Godmanchester.

B. OUTSIDERS AT GODMANCHESTER

When one begins to calculate the outsiders involved in one way or another with Godmanchester and its people the numbers involved become very large. In following chapters we will attempt a more detailed assessment of the role of outsiders in the economy of the town. It is the concern of this chapter to indicate the numbers of these non-Godmanchester people and how the town reacted in order to avoid being overwhelmed.

In the 1279 Hundred Roll, after the listing of property holders with messuages who appear to be residents,[13] there appears a number of property holders without messuages:

Joan Froyl, 1½a
William Squier, 2½a ½r
Walter *de* Kent, 1a 3r
Elelina Ayleve, ½r
Henry Spicer, 1a
Herbert Manipenny, 13a 1r

[12] See p. 49.
[13] See further below, Chapter 3.

William Palmer 1½a
Henry Palmer, 2a
Richard King, 1r
Peter *le* Masun, 1r meadow
Richard Tinctor, 3a + 1r meadow
Ralph *de* Garsinhale, 2½a
William *de* Hemington, 2½a ½r
John *de* Croxton, 1a 1r
Stephen *de* Aula, 5a ½r + ½r meadow
Benedict Buxton, 16a 1r + 1a ½r meadow
Chichely Gilekoc, 3a 1r
Richard *de* Paxton, 7a 3½r + 3r meadow
Ralph *de* Spalding, 2a 3½r
Simon Marshall, 5½a + ½a meadow
Gunnilda Diver, 23a + ½a meadow
Robert *de* Hiche, 10½a
William *de* Stukeley, clerk, 5½a ½r + ½a meadow
Godfrey Marshall, 2a meadow
Robert Buldir, 4a 1r
John Anfred, 3a
Andrew Buxston, 20a + 3r meadow
Cristina Corveiser, ½a
William Boneville, ½a
Sarra Aubin, 3r
Berenger Tinctor, 1a
Nicholas Caperon, 11a ½r + 1r meadow
John Regus, 11a 1r + 2½a meadow
Stephen Piscator, 3r
Parvus Willelmus, 5a ½r + ½a meadow
William Pistor, 1a
Walter Page, 1a
Roger Kors, 8a 1r
Godfrey *de* Ripton, ½a
Robert Prepositus, ½a
Nicholas Pollard, ½a
Henry Marshall, 5a 3r
John Crane, 1a 1r
Lawrence ad Pontem, 20a 3r + ½a ½r meadow
Helen daughter of William Buldir, 3½a
Helen Buldir, 2a 1½r + 1r meadow
Henry Page, 3a ½r + 1r meadow
Roger Hardwyne, 3a ½r + 3r meadow
Robert Wombe, 3r
Andrew Carnifex, 3a 1r + 1r meadow

William, chaplain of Trinity, $1\frac{1}{2}$a
John Aurifaber, $1\frac{1}{2}$a + 2a meadow
William son of Goscelin, 1a + 1r meadow
William, vicar of St. Ives, 1a
Roger Tinctor, $3\frac{1}{2}$r
William Page, 1r
Robert *de* Croxton, 3a
Godfrey Bretun, $2\frac{1}{2}$a $\frac{1}{2}$r
Andrew Kroylard, $3\frac{1}{2}$r
Henry Corveiser, 11a 1r + 1a 1r meadow
Martin Sutor, $2\frac{1}{2}$a
Ranulph Fet, 2a $3\frac{1}{2}$r
Godfrey *de* Hamerton, $1\frac{1}{2}$a + 1r meadow
Robert Warinot, $1\frac{1}{2}$a $\frac{1}{2}$r
Nicholas *de* Hardwich, 2a 1r
Ranulph Palmer, $\frac{1}{2}$a $\frac{1}{2}$r
Edelina *de* Offord, 3r
William Gardener, 1a 1r
Reginald, son of John Ede, $1\frac{1}{2}$a
Walter Rote, $1\frac{1}{2}$a
Reginald Gale, 3r
John Gentil, 3r
Sarle Tinctor, 1a 1r + $1\frac{1}{2}$r meadow
Simon *de* Hemingford, 1a 1r

Many of the larger property holders in this list may be identified as Huntingdon people. Some of these individuals may have been labourers or practised special trades at Godmanchester while living with someone of the town. Another dozen names of outsiders not in the Hundred Roll and without messuages could be added to the list. In any case, these 74 names of individuals holding 263 acres and one half rod of arable and 17 acres of meadow could easily be all outsiders to judge from the land market activities of other Godmanchester recogds.

From the surrounding band of villages and the town of Huntingdon scores of people appeared on the Godmanchester scene, for the most part interested in land. As a second category, thirty-three individuals from Huntingdon alone engaged in agricultural activities at Godmanchester according to the sowing and sheep list of ca. 1341. More incidental information from the court rolls allows a summary of these to be made.[14] There is a third category of outsiders who appeared in Godmanchester

[14] See below, Chapter 3, p. 134.

often to finally settle there, but for what initial purpose contact was made the surviving records hold no information. Nonetheless, it is clear that the interaction was a continuing process, as Table 27 "Outsiders Appearing in Godmanchester Court Rolls, 1278-1399"[15] demonstrates with 92 appearances noted between 1278 and 1300, 63 between 1301 and 1325, 66 between 1326 and 1348 and 132 between 1349 and 1399. Owing to the uneven survival of records for the last half of the century, and the decline in detail for those that do survive, the longer period has been taken to be a more useful average.[16] Along with the continuing process, the geographical spread among towns and villages was quite wide, as the accompanying Map 2 "The Provenance of Outsiders at Godmanchester, 1278-1348" illustrates. It may not be surprising, therefore, that where individuals can be traced in town or village (as is the case for Ramsey Abbey manors), nothing exceptional may be found for those who appear at Godmanchester. In short, all the evidence points to a regional society in which town and country were complementary.

At first glance, the ease with which many of these outsiders could "play" the land market of Godmanchester without living in the town seems rather contradictory in view of the proud heritage of customs to which the townsmen were so endeared. A closer look at the court rolls reveals, however, that the townsmen were not blind to the danger of losing control over their birthright to outsiders. Despite the relative silence of late thirteenth and early fourteenth-century courts about customs, over the full length of our period town policies become reasonably clear. Outsiders who were not resident in Godmanchester took a special oath to pay to the royal farm and other town obligations.[17] Those who wished to live in Godmanchester and enjoy the full privileges of the town were expected to take up the liberty of the town. Each one of these policies will be discussed in turn.[18]

---

[15] See below, Chapter 8, "Outsiders in Godmanchester."

[16] As the information stands, there are 82 entries for the period 1349-1374 and 50 for the period 1375-1399.

[17] The list of pledges for Huntingdon people in Table 13 "Sowing and Sheep Inventory No. 2, ca. 1341," pp. 115-116, would suggest that such outsiders also required pledges. Court roll entries do not specify such pledges.

[18] Despite the great amount of scholarly work on freemen of various cities, and perhaps because of the concentration upon constitutional and economic aspects of these liberties, very little attention has been given to the "social" aspect of early town liberties that seems to lie behind so many Godmanchester arrangements under the first policy. For an excellent example of the current state of study of city freemen, see the Introduction by Margery M. Rowe and Andrew M. Jackson, *Exeter Freemen 1266-1967* (Exeter, 1973).

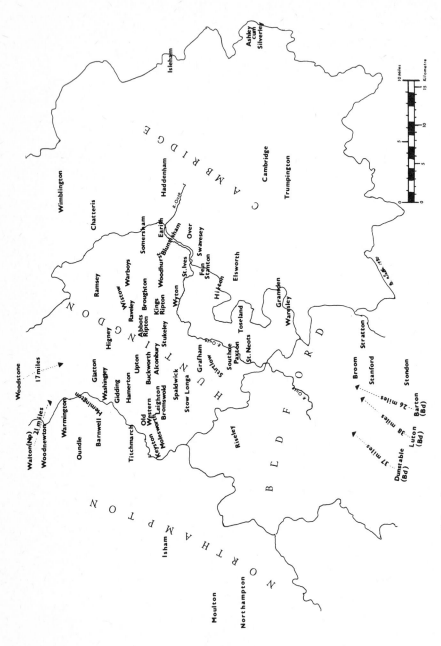

MAP 2A. THE PROVENANCE OF OUTSIDERS AT GODMANCHESTER, 1278-1348

MAP 2B. THE PROVENANCE OF OUTSIDERS AT GODMANCHESTER, 1278-1348

Only in the fourteenth century did the court rolls bother to give more detail about the first policy. In 1334 this entry occurs: "William Osemund *de* Hemingford Abbot takes the oath according to usage, etc. And on the same day this William took seisin of two and one half acres of land and of one swath of meadow which he had in gift from his wife Margaret Ingyl, which property he is to defend for the farm that it customarily pays (2s. 10d.)."[19] John Wryte (6s. 8d.), Thomas Benewyck (8s.) and John Faukener *de* Over (6s. 8d.) are described as taking property under the same form in 1334. The sum in parentheses is the amount each individual had to pay as fine.

By 1397 the court expresses this policy in a slightly different form: "Simon Tayler *de* St. Ives is admitted in the manner usual to outsiders who are tenants and he took the oath along with his wife. The same Simon took seisin. (3s. 4d.)"[20] John Sayer *de* Huntingdon (2s.) and Nicholas Overton *de* Brampton (2s.) were admitted as tenants under the same form in 1397 and Nicholas Overton immediately paid further an entry fine (*gersuma*) for seisin of six acres and three and one half rods. The court records remained rather casual about this form, however, since an entry of 1395 simply states that John Penyr *de* Offord took the oath and paid 40 pence and in the previous year William Martyn *de* Hemingford Abbots took the oath (2s.) and paid an additional 3 pence for entry fine to a property.

It is this casual entry form that was traditional and considered sufficient. In 1349 Thomas Swafham *de* Sundone was given a gift of one messuage and paid 3s. fine. John Balle took the oath and swore to keep the customs of the vill in 1359, fine of 6d. Henry Wille *de* Yelling was given a gift of one messuage plus 11 acres from John *de* Essex and took the oath and swore to follow the customs of the town (3/4d.) in 1364 and in this same year Alice Bryd also took seisin of one messuage which was given to her by Mabel wife of John Stirtlehowe and she paid 2s. and entered the property right away. In the following year (1365) John son of Nicholas Moregrove received land by bequest of his sister Sybil (two and one half acres plus one and one half rod) (5d.). Nine years later (1374)

---

[19] Box 5, bundle 1. 19 May 1334.

     Willelmus Osemund de Hemyngford Abbatis iuratus est ut mos, etc. Et eodem die idem Willelmus cepit seysinam de duabus acris et dimidia terre et uno swath' prati quas habuit de dono Margaret Ingyl uxoris eius ad defendendum pro firma debita et consueta. (2s. 10d.)

[20] Box 8, bundle 1. 14 September 1397.

     Simon Tyler *de* Sancto Ivone admissus est sicut toti tenentes forinsici et iuratus est ut uxor etc. Idem Simon cepit sesinam. (3s. 4d.)

Thomas son of Nicholas Trappe *de* Hemingford Abbots received land (one half of three acres) which was formerly held by his father Nicholas and Thomas took the oath and paid 12d. Thomas' brother John also took the oath and paid 12d. for the other half of the property which belonged to his father. In the year of 1380 William and his son John *de* Stamford come into the court and took the oath (3/4d.).

Information about the "policy" of pressing outsiders to take up the liberties of the town, is considerably more detailed. For the period under study in this volume there are 208 formal references to receipt of the liberty of Godmanchester. These names are listed chronologically below (Table 10) together with the fines assessed for obtaining the liberty. It will be immediately apparent that the size of the average fine gradually increased over the fourteenth century. Furthermore, there could be considerable variations among the fines of various individuals at any one period. A quick glance at the land market readily explains the reason for this fine differential among contemporaries. Those with more substantial wealth were more heavily taxed to be able to use the privileges of the town.

In keeping with the brevity to be found in other entries, the court form for entry to the liberty of Godmanchester in the early fourteenth century tended to be terse "one line" statements. The entrants took the liberty, swore the oath and paid the fine. The monotony of these entries is pleasantly broken in 1338 when Robert Howman applied for liberty. Howman was very wealthy and his application seems to have thrown the court into something of a dither. In any case, the entry may have justified a fine more than ten times the size of other fines of the period: "Robert Howman came before those present in full court and requested the liberty of Godmanchester offering the said court for this liberty as above (20s.) By order of the bailiffs he then withdrew from the court; then they considered [the matter] and at length granted that liberty to the same Robert. The latter at once swore the oath and so entered the liberty."[21]

The Black Death brought an interesting development as a flood of people requested liberty of Godmanchester. Among these were twelve individuals in 1349 who earlier must have relinquished their Godmanchester birthrights since their entries describe them as recovering (*recupe-*

---

[21] Box 5, bundle 9. 13 June 1338.

Robertus Howman venit in plena curia presenti et postulavit de Gumecestre et optulit dicte curie pro dicta libertate habenda ut supra. De precepto ballivi subtraxit de curia unde omnes sedentes in curia predicta inde consuluerunt et tandem eidem Roberto dictam libertatem concesserunt. Qui continuo juravit fidelitatem et sic intravit libertatem. (20s.)

ravit) the liberty. Variations in fines were such that it is impossible to discover whether these twelve were penalized or discounted for the recovery. As the heavy influx to Godmanchester continued over the 1350s, the townsmen found it necessary to "bond" six individuals to the amount of 20 shillings each.[22] At least this is what the rather enigmatic entry (*pro forfaitura*) would seem to imply since it was not noted on the margin as a collected fine and the actual fines collected from these six were not exceptionable.

> Adam ye Poyser de Conter, haberdasher, came into the full court of God-manchester, and having recovered said liberty by a special grace of the community of Godmanchester and for a bond of twenty shillings, he received seisin of that liberty.[23]
>
> Bartholemew ye Taylour came into the full court of Godmanchester, and having recovered said liberty by a special grace of the community of God-manchester and for a bond of twenty shillings, he took the oath to the bailiffs [*illeg.*] to stay in residence [*illeg.*].[24]
>
> Robert Tedbold ... as above ... (12d.)

References to "recovery" and to the 20 shillings do not occur after 1360 although the fines increase substantially. For some time the entries remained fairly brief with slight variations from time to time. In 1376 Adam Feltewelle "took seisin of the liberty of Godmanchester, was sworn according to the customs of the court and gave as above. (6s. 8d.)"[25]

Three entries for 1334 followed the style of Lawrence Donewale "by a special grace of the whole community he was admitted to the liberty of Godmanchester, was sworn according to the customs of the court and gave as above. (6s. 8d.)"[26] "Williamus Mychel de Hallysbery ... as above. (6s. 8d.)"[27] "Roger Gardener and John his son ... as above. (6s. 8d.)"[28]

---

[22] Unfortunately the manuscript is in poor condition for the courts of these years.

[23] Box 5, bundle 9. 26 July 1352.

Adam ye Poyser de Conter habidirdayser venit in plena curia Gumecestre et ressiit libertatem predictam ex speciali gratia comunitatis Gumecestre et pro forfaitura xxs. ad predictum argentum cepit sesinam de predicta libertate. (18d.)

[24] Box 5, bundle 9. 6 September 1352.

Bertholemeus ye Taylour venit in plena curia Gumecestre et ressiit libertatem predictam ex speciali gratia comunitatis Gumecestre et pro forfaitura xxs. et juravit ballivis co [*illeg.*] ad facienda residencia plena in [*illeg.*]. (12d.)

[25] Box 5, bundle 1. 23 April 1376.

Adam Feltewelle cepit seisinam de libertate de Gumecestre et iuratus est secundum consuetudinem curie et dedit ut supra. (6s. 8d.)

[26] Box 5, bundle 1. 13 May 1334.

Laurentius Donewale ex speciali gratia totius comitatis admissus est ad libertatem de Gumecestre et iuratus est secundum consuetudinem curie et dedit ut supra. (6s. 8d.)

[27] Box 5, bundle 1. 13 May 1334.

[28] Box 5, bundle 1. 1 December 1334.

Roger Gardener et Johannes filius eius... . (6s. 8d.)

In contrast with the wide variety of social and economic interests that lay behind the generality of immigration to Godmanchester, the purchase of liberty was strictly an economic venture in order to gain access to the land of the royal manor. For only a half dozen purchases are the family of the purchaser (wife and/or children) mentioned. Purchasers were invariably men. The purchaser of the liberty immediately invested in Godmanchester property, often in the same court session.

Unlike those listed in Table 10, applicants for liberty in a number of instances were not assessed specified fines. While there is no further reference in the court rolls to a number of these applicants, the entries do not indicate that they had been refused liberty. Those individuals in this category are listed in Table 11.

As might be expected where a number of specialized crafts were involved,[29] some of those acquiring liberty of Godmanchester may have had *pieds-à-terre* in various places. Where there is evidence, however, it is clear that Godmanchester had no difficulty in absorbing their newly-accepted townsmen, rich or poor. The family of the wealthy Robert Howman, who received liberty in 1338, continued on at Godmanchester for the rest of the century. Of that large influx of people after the Black Death, who, if one may judge from the demand for bonds, the town officials were rather uncertain about, at least 50 per cent can be traced in even skimpy records carrying on in the town. Some of these were of more modest means, as were William *de* Bumstead, *le* shepherd and Richard *de* Hemingford Grey, *ye* gardener, both received in 1351. But the same pattern is to be found for the more prominent, Henry Clerk *de* Olney (1356) who came to live in West Street and the John Legat, miller (1358).

*
**

The fact that late thirteenth-century Godmanchester had a charter of privileges, its own seal and a "sense of history" that required conservation of its records was not idle pretension. This town was able to absorb the new clerical and economic expertise of the time, apparently without loss to its own identity. How was this possible? One explanation must be found in the powerful resiliency of customary family organization. An historical understanding of this social phenomenon has hardly begun.[30] In the first chapter of this study we presented some evidence of the family "using" the market system. More of the results of this practise will be seen in Chapter 5.

[29] See below, Chapter 3, B. "The Occupational Roll at Godmanchester."
[30] See Goody, ed., *Family and Inheritance.*

A second explanation must be sought in the complex local government practices of thirteenth-century towns and villages. The bright, rosy-cheeked clerk approaching on the road from Cambridge and the astute old merchant crossing the bridge from Huntingdon were not coming upon a resort of awe-stricken country bumpkins. Godmanchester people were well schooled in the administration of their own affairs and sensitized by everyday experience to the economics of rights in common and severalty. One must, of course, be careful in assuming that the administration of Godmanchester was the same in 1300 as after 1400. But the administrative structure of the town after 1400 does not appear to have changed greatly over the previous one hundred years. Over this period, however, the town had absorbed a virtual reformation in attitude and influence of the clerical estate as well as scores of new families. The customary government of the town, no less than family customs, provided a powerful tool for the redistribution of social control.

TABLE 10: RECEIPT OF LIBERTY INTO GODMANCHESTER
EITHER BY FINE AND OATH OR BY PROPERTY

Date	Name	Fine
1301	Ripton, William *de*	12d.
	Stonle, Alexander *de*, living in Hunts	40d.
1308	Kingston, Robert *de*, cook	1d.
1309	Maryot, Thomas *de* St. Ives	3s. 4d.
1312	Merton Thomas *de*	2s.q.
1313	Fanner, Robert son of Roger	12d.
1323	Stirtlehow, John son of John	4d.
1324	Houghton, John, pelliparius	2s.
1329	Kingston, Roger *de*, wodeward	2s.
1330	Weston, John son of Alan *de*	12d.
	Reder, John	1d.; 4s. gersuma
1331	Borel, William son of Simon	5s. gersuma
1332	Berkingg', William *de*	12d.
	Murum, John son of John super	12d.
	Larke, William	12d.
	Marchaunt, John	4s.
	Grafham, John *de*	12d.
	Sutor, John and Henry sons of Ralph	2s.
1338	Howman, Robert	20s.
1340	Gounfayoun, William *de* Buckworth, chaplain	23s. 4d.
1341	Crepkyne, Robert	7 (d.)
1343	Beaustrat, Roger, chaplain	12d.
1344	Lodelowe, John	[ ]
	Stukeley, Nicholas *de*	[ ]
1346	Swethon, Hugh *de*	20s.
1347	Clervaux, William	20s.

Date	Name	Fine
1349	Benewyk, John	6d. recovery
	Berton, William son of Simon	(fine)
	Commandrour, Walter *le*	3s.
	Cook, John *de* Deopham	6d. recovery
	(Cook), Richard	12d. recovery
	Ely, Thomas *de*	12d.
	Gotte, John *de* Hartford	22d.
	Hamerton, Richard *de*	18d. recovery
	Haue (Hunter?), William	12d. recovery
	King, John son of John *de* Lt. Stukeley	12d. recovery
	Maryot, Thomas	12d.
	Mileward, Hugh	12d.
	Morbo[ur], Robert	18d.
	[Northborg], William *de*	?
	Pakerel, Thomas son of John	12d. recovery
	Plomer, John *de* Westakre	12d.
	Ramsey, Robert	40d.
	Roo, William *le*	9d.
	Russell, Simon	3s.
	Salmon, William	16d. recovery
	Swafham, Thomas *de* Sundon	3s. (messuage in gift, no liberty)
	Taylor, Simon	12d.
	Thresshere, [Simon] *de* Cornwall	22d. recovery
	Wollemonger, Nicholas	9d.
	[P], John son of John *de* St. Ives	2s. recovery
	[G], Walter	40d.
	[ ]uli, John	20d.
1350	Benyt, Hugh	2s.
	Bonde, Richard	12d. (capital messuage pays 1d.)
	Coyper, John *de* Gidding	12d.
	King, John	3s.
	Malmisbery, John *de* Hunts	3s. 1d. recovery
	Somerdere, John *de* Broughton	12d. recovery
	Turnere, Walter and his children	12d.
1351	Borsworth, William	40d.
	Sumter, William *de* Therny'g	12d.
1352	Poyser, Adam ye,	
	de Conter Habirdayste	18d.
	Taylor, Bartholomew	[ ] 12d.
1353	Grimsby, William *de*	40d.
1355	Isham, John	12d.
	Plowrighte, Thomas	20s. bond + 12d. to enter liberty
	Rudham, Thomas *de*	40d.
	[Sigor], Richard	18d.
1356	Cheyld, Henry	18d.
	[Dean], Simon	5s.
	Hilton, William	20s. bond + 12d. to enter liberty
	T'nngct, John	12d.
1357	Bee'[ryth], William son of John	20s. bond + 40d. to enter liberty
	Dally, Robert	20s. bond + 20d. to enter liberty
	Freman, William	20s. bond

Date	Name	Fine
	Mason, John *de* Hartford	6s. 8d.
	Staci, Hugh *de* Bekingham	2s. 8d.
1358	Legat, John	3s.
	(Cur)teys, Richard	20s. bond + 5s. to enter liberty
1359	Balle, John	6d. sworn, no liberty
	Essex, Henry	2s.
	Stretham, Robert *de*	20d.
	Taylor, Thomas son of Bartholomew	20d.
	Wigar, John *de* St. Ives	2s.
1360	Broun, William and children, John Godfrey and Cristina	3s.
1361	Custaunce, Robert	3s. 4d.
	Houghton, John *de*	3s.
	Robert, John son of, *de* Paxton and daughter (Margaret)	3s.
1362	Cook, John junior	2s.
	Danewych, John	fine obligation
	Faukes, William	3s.
	Stoke, John *de*	5s.
1363	Ffythe, William	[5s.]
	Freysol, John *de* Long Stanton	5s.
1364	Lungespy, John	3s. 4d.
	Wille, Henry *de* Yelling	3s. 4d. oath, received gift of 1 messuage + 11 acres, no liberty
1365	Balton, John *de* Quy	3s. 4d.
	Borel, John	2s.
	Bryd, Alice	2s. no liberty; a messuage was bequeathed to her and she entered the property straight away
	Moregrove, John son of Nicholas	5d. no liberty; $2\frac{1}{2}$a + $1\frac{1}{2}$r bequeathed to him from his sister Sybil
	Peek, William	10s. + 1 messuage bought 3d.
	Wright, Nicholas	3s. 4d.
1366	Clerk, William, butcher	[3s.] 8d.
	Hekedoun, Sayerus and son John	6s. 8d. (3s. 4d. at two terms)
	Hert, John and son William	3s. 4d.
	Newman, John *de* Southoe	13s. 4d.
1367	Cage, Robert	2s.
	Douce, William, butcher, and son John	3s. 4d.
	Lockyngton, Agnes, Alice and Richard	3s. 4d.
1369	Bate, Robert	10s.
	Boroughbrygge, John	2s.
	Brydlyngton, Richard	3s. 4d.
	Sandone, Richard and son William	2s.
	Wetyng, William	6s. 8d.
1371	Howelond, John and wife Elena *de* Yelling	10s.
1372	Baroun, John	40d.
	Cook, Thomas	8s.

Date	Name	Fine
	Dalby, Lord John	40d.
	Glover, Thomas	2s.
	Palmer, Richard	3s. 4d.
	Robyn, Thomas son of John	10s.
	Ruddek, William	5s.
1373	Chapman, Bartholomew	3s. 8d.
	Freman, Thomas	10s. (+)
	Well, John atte, smith	2s.
1374	Ameneye, John *de*	3s. 4d.
	Dedale, John	3s. 4d.
	Haukyn, Edmund	3s. 4d.
	Ruscheton, John *de* Stanton	12s. 8d.
	Trappe, Thomas son of Nicholas *de* Hemingford Abbots	12d. sworn for $^1/_2$ of 3a. from father, no liberty
	Trappe, John son of Nicholas *de* Hemingford Abbots	12d. sworn; receives the other half of property from father, no liberty
1375	Burman, Roger	6s. 8d.
	Campion, John senior	3s. 4d.
1376	Feltewelle, Adam	6s. 8d.
1377	Knytte, John and wife Margaret and son John	no amount
	Manyhas, John and wife Emma and children, William and Thomas	6s. 8d.
1378	Doraunt, Ralph and all his sons	6s. 8d.
	Grene, John atte and wife Matilda	6s. 8d.
	Herle, John and wife Joan	6s. 8d.
	Simon, Richard [son of]	8s.
	Wrythe, Alan *de* St. Ives	6s. 8d.
1379	Annaipa[us], Nicholas, priest	13s.
	Londonwalle, Thomas	6s. 8d.
	Lytlebody, William	6s. 8d.
	Panter, John	6s. 8d.
	Raldet, John	6s. 8d.
1380	Carpenter, John and son John	6s. 8d.
	Frene, Thomas and sister Margaret	6s. 8d.
	Hewerard, John *de* Hemingford Abbots	no amount
	Leffeyne, Godfrey (and John)	6s. 8d.
	Jemys, Richard and son Philipp	6s. 8d.
	Porthos, Nicholas and all his sons	3s. 4d.
	Rynghold, John	6s. 8d.
	Stamford, William and son John	3s. 4d. no liberty
	Tame, Matilda and daughter Margaret *de*	10s.
	Thorley, John and all his sons	3s. 4d.
1382	Lockyngton, Walter	6s. 8d.
	Poterel, William	6s. 8d.
	Reynold, Thomas *de* Dickleburgh	10s.
1384	Donewale, Lawrence	6s. 8d.
	Gardener, Roger and son John	6s. 8d.
	Michel, William *de* Hallysbery	6s. 8d.

Date	Name	Fine
1385	Benewyk, Thomas	8s. no liberty
	Faukener, John *de* Over	6s. 8d. no liberty
	Osmund, William *de* Hemingford Abbots	2s. 10d. no liberty
	Wryte, John	6s. 8d. no liberty
1386	Delethorpe, John *de* Hemingford Abbots	10s.
	Lister, Simon *de* St. Ives, spicer	6s. 8d.
	Olethorpe, Edmund	3s. 4d.
1387	Judd, John	6s. 8d.
	Wyke, Richard	6s. 8d.
1388	Fisher, Andrew *de* Offord	6s. 8d.
	Merle, Robert, butcher	5s.
1389	Fisher, John	6s. 8d.
	Wrawby, John	6s. 8d.
1390	Herde, Thomas *le*	13s. 4d.
	Robyn, John	6s. 8d.
	Walsh, Walter	10s.
1391	Beverle, William, wright	6s. 8d.
	Prentys, Richard	13s. 4d.
1392	Atthemeer, Richard	6s. 8d.
	Bochere, Robert junior	6s. 8d.
	Clophale, William	10s.
	Derlyng, John	6s. 8d.
	Gynys, John	6s. 8d. (40d. at two terms)
	Lawnder, Simon	8s.
	Pertenhall, Thomas	10s.
	Warde, John	6s. 8d.
1393	Kele, Thomas, taylor and son John	7s.
	Sewestere, Thomas	6s. 8d.
1394	Althryton, William, hosier	6s. 8d.
	Brown, John and sons John and Thomas	6s. 8d. (40d. at two terms)
	Martyn, William *de* Hemingford Abbots	2s. sworn, no liberty + 3d. for property
	Porter, John, fisher	6s. 8d.
	Ruscheton, John	6s. 8d.
	Ruscheton, William	6s. 8d.
	Spaldwick, Robert, and sons William, Simon and Henry	10s.
	Stalygton, William, wright	6s. 8d.
1395	Crofton, John	6s. 8d.
	Penyr, John *de* Offord	40d. sworn, no liberty
	Pye, Edmund, wright	6s. 8d.
1397	Anable, Joan *de* Staunford	6s. 8d.
	Overton, Nicholas *de* Brampton	2s. sworn, no liberty
	Palmer, John	3s. 4d.
	Sayer, John	2s. sworn, no liberty
	Tyler, Simon and wife *de* St. Ives	6s. 8d. sworn, no liberty

Date	Name	Fine
1398	Pere, John	6s. 8d.
1399	Baret, John	6s. 8d.
	Brigge, William atte	8s.
	Meyre, John *de* Ramsey	6s. 8d.
	Taylor, William	6s. 8d.

TABLE 11: APPLICANTS FOR LIBERTY NOT PAYING FINES,
APPEARING IN GODMANCHESTER, 1349-1399

Date	Name
1349	Barbour, John
	Bercarius, Reyner
	Mohaut, John
1350	Dicer, Thomas, chaplain
	Horsley, John *de*
	Kent, John *de*, chaplain
	Mayden, John
	Nocemo, Roger
	Swetecok, John, taylor
1351	Bumstead, William *de*, *le* shepherd
	Richard *de* Hemingford Grey, *ye* gardener
	Man, Richard *de* Hartford
	Radwell, Robert son of Simon *de*
	Rudham, Alan *de*
1352	Stanton, Thomas, brother of John, chaplain, *de*
	Tedbold, Robert
1353	Carnifex, John *de* Weston
	Pokesbrok, John *de*
	Roger, Cristina *de* Abbots Ripton
1356	Botman, John, vicar of Godmanchester
	Clerk, Henry *de* Olney
	Mor, John on ye
	Thorpe, John *de*, chaplain
1360	Balle, Thomas *de* Offord Cluny
	Bretoun, William
1361	White, John, chaplain
	Wulle?, John, clerk
1362	Cook, John, junior
	Spalding, William
	Ulf, John
1363	Engle, William son of John, *de* Hemingford Abbots
	Forthe, William atte
	Houlot, John, *de* Hartford
	Luton, Thomas *de* Hartford
1366	Ayshere, Roger *de* Hemingford Abbots, shepherd
	Goselyn, Richard
	Peek, Thomas

Date	Name
1367	Castel, Nicholas
1369	Herny, Richard
	Leticia, William, couper
1372	Thykthorn, William
	Wright, Roger
1373	Gyssing, Adam *de*
1374	Pikerell, Thomas
	Wedale, John atte
1375	Walcote, Richard *de* Hunts
1377	Baroun, John *de* Hemingford
	Boscep, John
	Pysford, William and wife Matilda
	William, John
1380	Plumpton, John *de*
1386	Leicester, Simon *de* St. Ives
1390	Robyn, Thomas, butcher
1394	Marshall, John son of John *de* Hartford
	Marshall, Thomas son of John *de* Hartford
	Michel, Adam son of John, *de* Hartford, chaplain
	Simon, William and his son William
1395	Est, John *de* Hemingford Abbots

3

Settlement Patterns
and Occupational Divisions

To this point we have been investigating the manner by which custom governed the lives of specific families, the role of individuals and families in town government and the policy exercised towards certain types of outsiders. In this chapter we shall attempt to look at the results of these customs and policies in terms of the whole town. First of all, what did Godmanchester people look like "on the ground" or, in the current parlance of archaeologists and geographers, what was the settlement pattern of the town? Secondly, what was Godmanchester like in terms of economic sophistication? Lacking obvious industrial development, such as the cloth industry at neighbouring Huntingdon, without a prominent fair and market, such as at nearby St. Ives, was Godmanchester simply a larger village? And finally, do Godmanchester families fall into residential classifications familiar to towns or, do they remain very much the same as the family groupings to be found in villages of Huntingdonshire?

A. THE PROPERTY GRID AT GODMANCHESTER

The substantial farm of £120 that Godmanchester paid yearly to the crown (or some assignee of the crown) imposed a considerable administrative burden upon the town. The bulk of the court roll entries dealing as they do with property conveyances indicate the need for continual adjustment of farm obligation records. How could payments to this farm be assessed upon the multiple familial revenues from property and those bits and pieces of land revolving more or less rapidly among non-residents as well as the people of Godmanchester itself? Bailiffs were kept busy changing the lists, and by the very fact of these many changes, lists quickly became obsolete and not worth keeping in the town records.

Some references will be given below [1] to evidence for stroking out some entries and adding others in farm assessment lists.

It was in relation to obligations owed to the world beyond that Godmanchester records were more conservatively preserved for this relationship was a more static affair. Hence, the central government preserved the comprehensive Hundred Rolls of 1279. In turn, Godmanchester was at pains to maintain records of farm payments as well as charters of liberties and various preliminary surveys employed in preparing assessments for the lay subsidies. In relation to such more static sources the surviving local administrative lists employed for the calculation of the annual farm to the king are but bits and pieces. Nevertheless, these bits and pieces do serve to illustrate the administrative task facing the bailiffs. More importantly, however, all the above records were in their earliest stages prepared by local people who would tend to employ familiar techniques despite the new or infrequent purpose of the assessment. For this reason, most of the surviving records of Godmanchester can be fitted together in an attempt to reconstruct the settlement plan of the town.

The most completely preserved records for Godmanchester are, then, the 1279 Hundred Roll and several lay subsidy lists. Incomplete local assessment lists complement the lay subsidy rolls still preserved at the Public Record Office in London and these published local lists may now be further supplemented by a fragmentary inventory of crops sown and fleeces obtained for one year. Fragments also survive of two kinds of lists obviously employed by the bailiffs for calculation of the royal farm. These are here termed "subletting lists" and a "messuage and meadow list." More description of all lists will be given below as these are analyzed.

The Godmanchester Hundred Roll of 1279 may be taken as a point of departure for the study of the economic life of the town since this roll is the most detailed medieval inventory for Godmanchester. According to the 1279 inquisition, there were 2,511½ acres, ½ rod of arable (*terra*), 395 acres, ½ rod of meadow (*pratum*), 85 acres of pasture (*pastura*), along with 378 messuages and 199 crofts. The Hundred Roll lists 53 odd bits and pieces of property obviously considered of lesser value by nature of their relative payments to the royal farm: 19 *divisie*, 8 headlands, 8 *havedin*, 6 *reggevees*, 5 river meadows (*holme*), 3 gores of meadow, 1 *berewordislond*, 1 place, 1 smithy (*fabricum*) and one place for manufacturing (*domus fabricationis*).

---

[1] See below, pp. 120-121.

The Hundred Roll begins with the largest landholder of the town, the prior of Merton who held the church in gift and therefore the 48 acres of arable by which the parish was endowed as well as the 15 acres of meadow pertaining to the same church for tithes of the "fen." In addition, the prior of Merton held $66\frac{1}{2}$ acres of arable, $8\frac{1}{2}$ acres of meadow and two messuages pertaining to the priory itself. The Hundred Roll concluded in turn with the above-mentioned two score and more of small bits and pieces of property, in the majority of cases the sole property of smallholders. This does not mean that the Hundred Roll entries were graduated according to wealth in feudal fashion by surveys such as Domesday Book. On the contrary, the remaining 400 and more entries present a persistent pattern of scatter of the differing degrees of wealth. For example, next to Eusebius Albrit with a messuage, a croft, 15 acres of arable and $2\frac{1}{2}$ acres of meadow (for which he paid 11s. 8d. to the royal farm) one finds Richard *de* Mundeford with a messuage and three rods of arable (paying only 6d. to the farm). Or, next to John Millicent with a messuage, a croft, 10 acres, 3 rods of arable and 2 acres, 1 rod of meadow, was Godfrey Nunne with only one messuage. One could present more than 50 examples of these extreme instances of the top and bottom of the propertied scale listed cheek-by-jowl.

It gradually becomes apparent from observations such as the above that the Hundred Roll presents this peculiar pattern of wealth because it reflects the itinerary through the town of the Hundred Roll inquisitors at work. After listings of the holdings of the church (and so, Merton Priory) are to be found 11 messuages obviously built upon church property. The Hundred Roll investigators then moved along Post Street for, after a reference to the property of the priory, are to be found a series of names familiar to Post Street in later lists (Simon *le* Longe, Ede, Goni, Balle...).[2] In a forthcoming work, an attempt will be made, with the assistance of the archaeologist of Godmanchester, H. J. M. Green, to reconstruct Godmanchester at this period. For the immediate purposes of this volume, it may only be noted that the itinerary ends[3] with a series of property holders, in some instances quite large, several of whom would seem to be outsiders or tradesmen from their surnames who were non-residents to judge by their lack of messuages. The itinerary was concluded[4] by a number (among those tenants of odd bits and pieces noted above) who held

---

[2] See the lists discussed below in this chapter.

[3] That is, the two columns on p. 596 of the summary of the Hundred Roll.

[4] That is, from the bottom of the second column on p. 596 to the end of the columns on p. 597 in the summary of the Hundred Roll.

messuages only. These messuages were for the most part of little value, to judge from their obligations, so one may deduce that this concluding list of messuage holders was composed in part at least of poorer "squatters" who had spread beyond the town with population pressure of the late thirteenth century. In short, messuages on the lanes and roads beyond the four streets of the town were merely cottages and contrasted with those estate complexes which will be discussed in the conclusion to this chapter.

From the perspective of this itinerary, several elements of the Hundred Roll take on more meaning. In most instances, the listing of a surname in more than one part of the town indicates that some families have two or more well-established branches. In this fashion 41 families can be identified with more than one well-established branch. As may be seen in Table 26 "Family Data from Godmanchester Court Rolls" given below, the majority of these multi-branch families continued throughout the decades after 1279.[5] The few families that did not continue in more than one branch are smallish ones (Chichely, ad Crucem, Drewe and Juel) or ones that cannot be shown to have continued because of ambiguity arising from patronymics (Gilbert, Henry, Robert) or place-names (Croxton and Paxton). The following is a list of families with more than one well-established branch to be found in the Hundred Roll of Godmanchester: Aylred, atte Barre, Balde, Balle, Bole, Bonis, Buxton, Ede, Edward, Essex *de*, Glewe, Goni (Gony), Graveley *de*, Hartford *de*, Inhewyn, John, Julian, Lane, Legge, Manipenny, Marshall, Mason (Masoun), Millicent, Nottyng (Notting), Page (Pays), Quenyng, Rede, Rode, Scot, Seman and Wal, super le (super le Murum).

This does not mean that the concentration of wealth was levelled out by family requirements. Two separate individuals each held three of the classical medieval living units, the messuages. Forty-three individuals held two messuages apiece. Many of the larger property holders were competing with lesser men of the town for those odd bits and pieces of property listed at the end of the Hundred Roll. This very likely explains why members of more wealthy families held messuages of greater value than those held by other tenants at the end of the list. For example, members of the Lane family held messuages of the value of 18d. and 3s. respectively whereas the messuage of a Robert *le* Swon paid 2d., that of Richard Bonis 2d., that of Cristina Bonis 2d., Godfrey Hot 2d. and so forth.

---

[5] At the same time the actual number of married family units over the late thirteenth and early fourteenth centuries greatly exceeded this number of multiple homestead settlements. For further comment on this point, see Chapter 4, p. 161.

At the same time, the family spread of property goes far towards explaining the juxtaposition of large and small tenants in the Godmanchester Hundred Roll. In some thirty instances individuals with the same family surname follow one another. As the following list shows, in a great many of these instances such listing suggests a splitting of family property. That is to say, a member of a family either because he is old or young may be settled on a residence (messuage) with a small supporting estate or, conversely, hold a small property with no messuages since he or she presumably still has residence on the family messuage. This list follows the sequence of entries as these are to be found in the Hundred Roll edition. The farm value of the properties is given in brackets after the entries that follow the usual short form (m = messuage, cr = croft, mea = meadow, a = acre, ar = arable, r = rod).

John *le* Longe, senior: 1 m (2d.)
John *le* Longe, junior: 1 m, 2a ar, $^1/_2$r mea (17d.)

Richard Gildene: 2 m, 1 cr, 12$^1/_2$a ar, 1a mea (16s. 6d.)
Gosceline Gildene: 1 m, 1 cr, 3a ar, $^1/_2$a mea (2s. 4d.)

Adam Gyle: 1 m, 1 cr, 8a ar, 1a ar, 1r mea (6s. 2d.)
John Gyle: 1 m, 4a ar, $^1/_2$a mea (3s.)

Godfrey Ingelond senior: 1 m, 3r ar (6d.)
Godfrey Ingelond junior: 1 r ar (2d.)
Simon Ingelond: 1r ar (2d.)

Cristina Balde: 1 m, 1a ar (12d.)
John Balde major: 1 m, 1a ar (8d.)
John Balde minor: 1a ar (8d.)

Eusebius in Venella (Lane): 1 cr, 7a ar, 2$^1/_2$a mea (6s. 4d.)
Godfrey in Venella (Lane): 3a ar (2s.)

Roger Scot: 1 m, 1 cr, 9a ar, 2a 1r mea (8s. 10d.)
Richard Scot: 1 cr, 7a ar, 3a mea (6s. 8d.)

Richard in Angulo: 6a ar, $^1/_2$a mea (4s. 4d.)
Reginald in Angulo: 1m, 1 cr, 12a ar, 2a mea (9s. 4d.)

Godfrey Togod: 1 m, 4a ar, 1r mea (24d.)[a]
Isolda Togod: $^1/_2$a ar (4d.)

William Ede: 1 m, $^1/_2$a ar (4d.)
Thomas Ede: 1 cr, 3a ar, $^1/_2$a mea (2s. 4d.)
Isolda Ede: 1 m, 2 cr, 9a ar, 1a 3r mea (7s. 2d.)

---

[a] The considerable property of Roger son of John (2 m, 24a. ar etc.) comes between the Togod's in this list and the latter would appear to have acquired their holdings from Roger.

Sarra Frere: 1 m, 6½a ar (4s. 4d.)
Richard Frere: 1 m, 4a ar, 3r mea (3s. 2d.)

John Aylward: 2 m, 7a ar, 1a 1r mea (5s. 6d.)
Simon Aylward: 1 m, 1 cr, 3a 1r ar, 3r mea (32d.)

Godfrey Alrich: 1 m, 1 cr, 10a 1½r ar, 2a mea (8s. 3d.)
Robert Alrich: 1 m, 7a 1r ar, 1a mea (5s. 6d.)

Godfrey Juel: 1a ar (8d.)
Richard Juel: ½a ar (4d.)

Thomas Hildemar: 1 m, 4a ar, 2a 1r mea (4s. 2d.)
Nicholas Hildemar: 1 m, 1 cr, 6a ar, 2a ½r mea (5s. 5d.)

Bartholomew Goni: 1 m, 6a ar, 1a 1r mea (4s. 10d.)[b]
Roger Goni: 1 m, 1 cr, 3a 3r ar, 1a 1r mea (3s. 4d.)
John Goni: 2 m, 1 cr, 6a 1½r ar, 3r mea (4s. 9d.)
Nicholas Goni: 1 m, 1 cr, 1½a ar, ½a mea (16d.)

Agnes Ese: 3½r ar, ½r mea (8d.)
Eustace Ese: 1 m, 8a ar, 1a mea (5s. 4d.)

William Parson: 1 m, 1 cr, 8a 1r ar, 1a mea (6s. 2d.)
Simon Parson: 1 m, 1 cr, 6a ar, 1a mea (4s. 8d.)

Reginald son of Simon: 1 m, 3a ar, ½a mea (2s. 4d.)
Agnes daughter of Simon: 1a 3r ar, ½a mea (18d.)
William son of Simon: 8½a ar (5s. 8d.)

Sybil Inhewyn: 1 m, 5½a ar (3s. 8d.)
Beatrix Inhewyn: 1 m (1d.)

Robert Rode: 1 m, 4½a ar, 3r mea (3s. 6d.)
Phillipa Rode: 1 m, 8a ar, 2a mea (6s. 8d.)
Henry Rode: 2 m, 2 cr, 20a ar, 2a mea (14s. 8d.)

John Seman: 1 m, 2 cr, 18a ar, 4a mea (14s. 8d.)
William Seman: 2 m, 1 cr, 14a 3r ar, 1a mea (10s. 6d.)

William Mason: 2a ar, 1r mea (18d.)
Eusebius Mason: 1 m, 1a 3r ar, 1r mea (16d.)

Thomas Balle: 1 m, 2 cr, 26a 1r ar, 5a mea (21s. 10d.)
Reginald Balle: ½a ar, 1r mea (6d.)
William Balle: 1a ar (18d.)
Alexander Balle: 1 m, 4a ar, ½a mea (3s.)[c]

---

[b] Agnes Pick, holding only 1 messuage with 1½ acres of arable comes between Roger and John Goni on the list.

[c] Godfrey Legge with the small holding of one croft and one acre comes before Alexander Balle in the list.

William Spruntyng: 1 m, 4a ar, 1r mea (34d.)
Reginald Spruntyng: 1 m, 1r ar (2d.)

Henry son of John: 1 m, 1 cr, 2a ar, 1r mea (18d.)
John son of John: 2a ar, 1r mea (18d.)
William son of John: 2a ar, 1r mea (18d.)

Roger *le* Rede: 2 m, 2 cr, 18$\frac{1}{2}$a ar, 4a mea (15s.)
Simon *le* Rede: $\frac{1}{2}$a, 1r mea (6d.)

Matilda daughter of Henry: 1 cr, 3a ar, 1r mea (2s. 2d.)
Amicia daughter of Henry: 1 cr, 3a ar, 1r mea (2s. 2d.)

William Palmer: 1$\frac{1}{2}$a ar (12d.)
Henry Palmer: 2a ar (16d.)

Helen daughter of William Buldir: 3$\frac{1}{2}$a ar (28d.)
Helen Buldir: 2a 1$\frac{1}{2}$r ar, 1r mea (21d.)

Godfrey in the Lane: 1 m (18d.)
Eusebius in the Lane: 1 m, 1$\frac{1}{2}$a ar (2s. 6d.)
Richard in Venella (Lane): 1 m (3s.)[d]

Aside from members of the above family groupings, very few tenants in the main body of the Hundred Roll were without messuages. On the other hand, an interesting sprinkle of the non-family or single individuals held very little property. After the first ten names of substantial tenants come Godfrey Hot (1 messuage, 1$\frac{1}{2}$ acres) and Godfrey Tileman (1 messuage, 1$\frac{1}{2}$ acres, $\frac{1}{2}$ acre of meadow); after 11 more substantial townsmen comes the name of Adam Grinde (1 messuage, 1 croft, 4 acres); seven names later comes William Cokayne (1 messuage) followed after one name by Robert *de* Stukeley (1 messuage, 3 rods). Then after the modest Ingelond family, come three names: Roger Pywyv (1 messuage, 3 rods), John Ailmer (1 messuage) and John Hanaper (1 messuage, 2$\frac{1}{2}$ acres). Among the next ten tenants we find Eustace Grinde ($\frac{1}{2}$ rod), Robert *le* Carter (1 rod) next to Richard Lacy (1 messuage) and Simon *de* Stanford (1 messuage, 1 rod) next to Alan *de* Wodestone ($\frac{1}{2}$ acre). This pattern of small propertied individuals living singly, in pairs and in clusters is found repeated throughout the rest of the main body of the Hundred Roll.

Some of these people who were poorer in landed wealth in 1279, and tended to be isolated among substantial landowners, were merchants with a bright future in Godmanchester. As we shall see in more detail below,

---

[d] Henry Cunator with one messuage is listed before Richard in the Lane. It should be noted that Eusebius and Godfrey occur previously in this list.

William Cokayn, who held a modest messuage in 1297, was the progenitor of an important trade family. Adam Grinde and Richard Garlop were only beginning to accumulate land in Godmanchester in 1279. A great many of the grouped people with little property had occupational surnames or surnames indicating that they had come from beyond Godmanchester. Many of these apparently failed to improve their lot. For example, the court rolls show no sign of improvement for Godfrey Tileman, Richard Mercator, Emma Piscator, Robert *le* Mileward, Thomas Faber, Walter Fanner, Walter Russel and Godfrey *le* Bedel. Among outsiders who had not continued were Richard *de* Mundeford, Simon Waleys and Robert *de la* Batayle.

The interesting scatter of large and small tenants along Godmanchester streets is confirmed by a series of local assessment lists[6] (see above, p. 94) of the more finished or static kind compiled as surveys to assist in drawing up lay subsidy lists. These surveys show the land use of rural properties as well as throwing an unusual amount of light on the nature of an assessment procedure about which we know so little. It is clear that the Godmanchester assessors began their work with an inventory of sown acres. This does not mean that Godmanchester officials would necessarily differ from other assessors by not making surplus the basis of tax capacity.[7] Rather, this assessment procedure does suggest that sown acres may have been taken as a more rough and ready basis of surplus than the complicated criteria for surplus now generally accepted by scholars. However, in contrast with this method of assessing corn, the produce of meadow may have been measured simply in terms of fleeces and lambs available for sale. Incidentally, the listing of such fleeces confirms the recent opinion about the importance of sheep and their wool from smaller properties as well as the large estates.[8] Finally, since these lists complement the printed lay subsidy lists, they are reproduced here in full except that the numbers of sown acres and of fleeces and lambs are given in tabular form.[9]

[6] Godmanchester records, Box 1, bundle 1, no. 1 and no. 71.

[7] For the most recent analysis of this topic, see R. E. Glasscock, *The Lay Subsidy of 1334* (London, 1975).

[8] A. R. Bridbury, "Before the Black Death," *Economic History Review*, 2nd series, 30 (1977), pp. 398-399.

[9] These lists were not included in the edition of Godmanchester lay subsidy materials (*Early Huntingdonshire Lay Subsidy Rolls*) owing to the fact that an adequate understanding of Godmanchester names depended upon the construction of Table 26 "Family Data from Godmanchester Court Rolls," below, pp. 241-408.

The first "sowing" list (Table 12 – ca. 1334) is fragmentary, but 199 names can be distinguished. From this list, the first more affluent individual, Henry Willem, is the first name to be found in the Godmanchester lay subsidy list for 1332. The second more affluent individual, Richard Rede, would seem to represent the Rede property paying tax in 1332 under the name of Agnes *le* Rede (the second name in the lay subsidy list for 1332). The third more affluent individual in the following list John Peysel (Pentel), occurs as the third name in the 1332 lay subsidy list. The fourth more affluent individual in the sowing list, Godfrey Rississ, atte (Ateriffis, *ad Cirpos*), occurs as the twenty-second name in the lay subsidy list of 1332. However, before Godfrey occur at least nine names that can be found in regular sequence as more wealthy people listed in the sowing and sheep register. Altogether, at least 44 names from the sowing and sheep lists can be identified in the 1332 lay subsidy list. These 44 of the 199 names on this surviving fragment do not all have sufficient sown acres and sheep to warrant taxation. As will be seen below, their tax would be assessed upon commercial chattels.

It is clear that the sowing list is later than that of the 1332 lay subsidy. In the sowing list the widow of Robert *le* Rede holds his property and the widow of John Glewe holds his land. Both Robert and John were living at the time of the 1332 assessment. Very likely, this sowing list was drawn up prior to the 1334 lay subsidy assessment. To indicate the relationship of these two records, in the following sowing list names to be found in the 1332 lay subsidy list are identified by an asterisk. It will be immediately apparent that the Hundred Roll pattern is here found reproduced. Henry Willem comes after three relatively poor townsmen. Richard Rede comes after six poorer townsmen, and so on. Robert and John Red, John Peysel, and his son Thomas, Thomas Chapman and daughter Sybil, four Bartelots and so on, are found listed next to one another.

The second list of sown acres and sheep (Table 13 – ca. 1341) comes somewhat later in the second quarter of the fourteenth century so that it bears much less relation to the 1332 lay subsidy list. Only 28 of the 124 individuals on this second list had appeared in the 1332 tax record. Since only nine of these 124 individuals had also appeared in that first sowing list discussed above, the two sowing lists are to some degree complementary. The list of ca. 1341 has the further complementary value of listing 24 individuals from Huntingdon with land in Godmanchester, 16 of these individuals being identifiable on the 1332 lay subsidy lists for Huntingdon. Two of the 10 individuals from Papworth Agnes, one of the four from Hemingford and three of the three from Offord Cluny are also to be found in the 1332 lay subsidy lists for these villages.

TABLE 12: SOWING AND SHEEP INVENTORY NO. 1, CA. 1334 [a]

Name	Wheat	Barley	Peas	Oats	Rye	Dredge [b]	Fleeces	Lambs
Henry Pope	1r	1a 1r	1a	—	—	—	6	4
Matilda Tymmis	—	1a ½r	3r	—	—	—	6	4
Thomas Mason	—	½a	½a	—	—	—	5	4
*Henry Willem [c]	4a 3½r	6½a	11a 1½r	3a 1r	1a	—	27	10
John Inhewyn	—	—	½a	½a	—	—	—	—
Robert Red	1a 1½r	4a 3r	7a	3r	—	—	12	7
John Red	½a 1½r	3a ½r	5a 1r	—	—	—	5	3
Thomas Underwode	1r	1a	1a 3½r	—	—	—	5	4
John Alconbury	—	2r	2r	—	—	—	(1)	(1)
*Richard Rede	4a	17a	14a	7a	3a	—	54	16
Simon Pernel	—	1a	3r	1r	—	—	—	?
Reginald Warde	—	—	2r	—	—	—	4	—
*John Peysel (Pentel)	3½a	8a	7½a	1½a	1a	—	160	10
Thomas, son of John Peysel	2r	1a	2a 1r	1r	—	—	—	—
*Godfrey Rissis atte	3½a 1r	7½a ½r	9a 1½r	2a 1r	½a	—	39	18
Cristina daughter of John Aylred	1r	½a	—	—	—	—	—	—
Thomas Chapman	—	1a	1a	1a	—	—	2	1
Sybil, daughter of Thomas Chapman	—	—	—	1a	—	—	—	—
Nicholas Bartelot (Bartheloth)	1a	3a	2a 3r	½a	3r	—	7	—
Godfrey his son	1r	1r	1a	—	—	—	2	—
William Bartelot (Barteloth)	—	1a ½r	—	—	—	—	—	—
Millicent his sister	—	—	—	1r	—	—	—	—

[a] Box 1, bundle 1. Owing to the fragmentary condition of these manuscripts, some entries are uncertain (as indicated by numbers in brackets) while other entries are totally illegible (as indicated by question marks).
[b] Dredge (*dragetum*): a coarse grain.
[c] Names to be found in the lay subsidy rolls are indicated by an asterisk.

Name	*Wheat*	*Barley*	*Peas*	*Oats*	*Rye*	*Dredge*	*Fleeces*	*Lambs*
Richard Aylred	3r	3½a ½r	5a 1½r	5r	3r	—	27 with the tithes of the rector	12 with tithes
Alan, the son of 'G' Aylred	2a	3a 3r	3a 3r	?	1a 1r	—	15	—
John Goni	1a 3r	3a 3r	4a 1r	3 × ½a	½a½r	—	11	7
Roger Goni	—	2a 1r	3 × ½a	1a	—	—	12	3
*William, son of Nicholas	1a 3r	3a	3½a	3r	½a	—	16	—
Nicholas Goni	—	3r	3r	½a	—	—	7	2
*Robert, son of John	3a	4½a	6a ½r	3 × ½a	½a	—	—	—
Robert Goni	—	1r	—	1r	1r	—	3	2
*John Gilligg (Yelling?)	1½r	3a	2a 3r	2r	1a	—	10	2
Thomas Hopay	3a 1r	12½a	15a 3r	3 × ½a	2a 1r	—	20	3
Emma Thresher	2½a	½a	3r	½a	—	—	1	1
William Valey	—	½a	1a	—	—	—	—	—
*Reyner Aylred	1a	2a 1½r	2a 3r	3r ½a	3½r	—	33	14 with the tithe of the church
Richard Rode	1r	1a 1½r	3a 3r	3r	—	—	—	—
*the widow of Robert Rede	2r	1a 1r	3 × ½a	½a	—	—	—	1
*John, son of Eustace	3r	4a ½r	4½a	3½r	½a	—	9 with tithes of the church	5
*Bartholomew Hildemar	(2a) 3r	5a 3r	6½a	3a 3r	5r	—	32	9
Henry Pa[ ]r	3r	1½a ½r	2½a	1a 3r	½a ½r	—	12	—
Henry [Comene]	—	?	2a 3½r	—	—	—	—	—
Agnes W[ymer]	—	½a	—	—	?	—	—	—
John Pays [Page]	? ½a	3a	3a	—	1r	—	?	?
Robert [Rene]	? ½a	2a	2 ?	?	2r	—	?	?
Emma Ese	—	—	(1r)	—	—	—	—	—
*Emma Undele (Oundle)	3 × ½a ½r	5a?	?	5r	5r	—	23	9

Name	Wheat	Barley	Peas	Oats	Rye	Dredge	Fleeces	Lambs
*John Balle	1½r	3½a ½r	3a 1r	?	1r	—	?	?
*John Mason	1a 3r	3a 1r	4a	1a	2r	—	15	1
*John son of Nicholas	3×½a	1a 3r	3a ½r	—	1r	—	1	1
John Caterina	3r	2a 3r	4a 1r	1a 1r	1r	—	—	—
Richard Rome	½a	2a 3r	3½a	1a	—	—	3	—
Elena Balle	1a	2a 3r	2a	1a	3×½a	—	20	1
Millicent Bonere	—	2r	—	—	—	—	—	—
Godfrey her son	—	2r	—	—	—	—	—	—
Dionysius Bulion	—	½a	½a	—	—	—	—	—
Albrida Pernel	3½r	2a	2a	5r	3r	—	13	4
William Caterina	3×½a 1r	2a 3½r	4a 3½r	3×½a	2½r	—	with tithes 14	4
Nicholas Strut	1r	1a	3×½a	½a	1½r	—	with tithes 9	3
Reginald Aylred	1a	3a ½r	3a	½a	1r	—	25	11
*Godfrey Outy	½a	2a 1r	2a 1r	½a ½r	1a	—	with tithes 13	2
*William son of John	1a 1½r	4a 1½r	4½a	1½a 1r	—	—	9	4
John Dosyn	—	1r	1a	—	—	—	—	—
Nicholas Stircup	—	2½a ½r	—	½a	—	—	9	3
John son of Lawrence Pelliparius	—	—	½a	—	—	—	—	—
Richard Taylor	—	½a	—	—	—	—	—	—
*Gilbert Loxsmyth	2½a	5½a ½r	8½a	3×½a	3r	—	13	?
William Page	½a ½r	2a 1½r	3½a	—	—	—	4	2
William Baccon	1r	—	½a	—	—	—	—	—
Roger Kingston	3r	3×½a	2½a	½a	—	—	15	4
Pellagia Rome	—	1a 3r	1a	—	—	—	—	—
*Reyner Doketon	1a	3a	3a 3½r	1a 3r	½a	—	?	?
Robert Denne	3a ½r	6a	8a 1½r	—	1½a	1a 3r	33	5
William Hors	7a	16½a	8a	3r	?	—	?	?

Name	Wheat	Barley	Peas	Oats	Rye	Dredge	Fleeces	Lambs
Lord Richard, vicar	2½a	6a 1r	2½a	—	—	3r	?	?
Richard Loxsmith	3r	2r	3r	1r	—	—	5	2
John son of Ralph	1a	?	?	?	?	?	?	?
William Colyon (Colyn)	1a	?	—	1r	—	—	?	?
Phillip Cooperator	?	?	?	?	?	?	?	?
John Croxton	½a	?	?	?	?	?	?	?
Godfrey Bate	3½r	½a	2a?	?	—	?	?	1
Cristina Cecely	—	½a	½a	—	—	—	5	
William Roo	½a	½a	3r	1r	—	—	—	
Nicolas de Wistow	—	—	5r	1r	1r	—		?
William Horold	3r	3 × ½a	2a	3 × ½?	1r	—		
the wife of Eustace Parson (Person)			½a	—	—	—		—
Reginald Underwode	—	3r	3r	—	—	—	3	1
*John Elys	3r	2a	2½a	?	?	?	?	?
William Austyn	1r	2r	2r	?	—	—	3	?
Simon Isham	—	5r	3r	½a	—	—	?	?
William Ese	—	1a 3r	1a 3r	?	?	?	?	?
Felicity widow of John Glewe	—	2r	1r	—	—	—	?	?
Agnes Manipenny	1a	1a	3½r	—	½a	—	?	?
Simon Aylred	—	3 × ½a	?	? 1r	½r	—	?	
Mabel daughter of Simon Aylred	—	—		—	½a	—	—	
Roger? brother of same	—	3r	3r	—	—	—		
the widow of William Swan (Cristina)	—	—		—	—	—		
Godfrey (her son)	?	?	1r	?	?	?	?	?
Cristina Gylemyn	2½a	8a?	?	2a 1r	2a	?	?	?
William Aylred	1r	3 × ½a	?	?	½r	—	?	1
Walter Pernel	3 × ½a	—	—	—	3r	—	53	?
William Pernel			—					

Name	Wheat	Barley	Peas	Oats	Rye	Dredge	Fleeces	Lambs
Simon Legge	—	½a	—	—	—	—	2	?
Edward Rode	—	½a	1r	—	—	—	3	1
Robert Pernel	—	3r	1½a	—	½a	—	?	?
Isolda Julian	1r	½a	2a 3r	—	1r	—	?	?
Elena Cook	—	—	3a 3r	2r	?	—	?	?
John Desere	—	—	1r	½r	—	—	?	?
John Pikerel	—	½a	½a	?	—	—	?	?
William Hopay	1r	3r	1a	?	?	—	?	?
Matilda Balle	—	½a	2½r	?	?	—	?	?
*John Marchaunt	2r	½a	1a	?	?	?	?	?
John Grafham	—	—	1a	½a	—	—	?	?
Robert Balle	—	5r	1a ½r	?	?	—	?	?
*John Gildene	2a 1r	4a 1r	?	—	1½a	—	?	?
Cristina Balle	1a 1r	3a	—	4a	1½a	—	?	?
Henry son of Ralph	—	1a ½r	1½a	—	1r	—	4	?
William de Stevech	—	½a	1r	—	1r	—	1	?
William Notting	1r	2a	2a	?	1r	—	?	?
Godfrey Quenyng	½a	3a	?	?	1r	—	?	?
William Legge	½a	3r	1r	—	3r	—	?	?
Richard Langeley	3½r	4a	?	(7)	3r	—	?	?
Nicholas Reynold	—	—	1r	—	—	—	?	?
Reginald Cook	—	—	3r	—	—	—	3	1
Amicia Ray	—	3r	5 ?	—	2r	—	?	1
Thomas Coronour	—	1r	—	1r	—	—	?	
Roger Godchild	2r	1a 1r	4a 3r	?	3r	—	?	?
Cristina dau of [Roger or Reginald] Seman	1½r	?	2½a	—	1r	—	5	3
Cristina Cook	?	—	—	?	—	—	?	3
Robert Penyman	?	—	—	½a	—	—		?
Roger? Croxton	3r ?	—	—	½a	?	—	8	4

Name	*Wheat*	*Barley*	*Peas*	*Oats*	*Rye*	*Dredge*	*Fleeces*	*Lambs*
[ ]ston	1r	—	1r	—	—	—	2	1
[?]	—	1r	1r	—	—	—	—	—
[?]	—	—	—	—	1r	—	3	1
[?]	?	3 × ½a	3a ½r	1a	—	—	?	?
Sybil Statehele (Strateshylle)	?	?	3r	?	?	—	2	1
*Reginald Seman	3½r	3a (7r)	3½a ½r	1a	?	—	9	5
*William Rede	2a 1½r	5a + ?	6a	2r	—	—	14	8
Godfrey Seman	3½r	3a + ?	2a 1r	½a	3r	—	5	3
*Cristina Rede	3 × ½a ½r	3a 3½r	4a 1r	1a 3r	1r	—	15	2
Godfrey Caterina	3 × ½a ½r	2½a	5a 3½r	1a	½a	—	20	6
Roger atte Gate	1r	3 × ½a ½r	2a ½r	—	—	—	6	2
Henry Aylred	2a ½r	2a 3r	4a 1r	—	—	—	19	11
Cristina Outy	—	1r	—	—	—	—	—	—
Pellage Cook	—	1r	½a	—	—	—	3	1
*William Manipenny	3a	6a ½r	7a 1r	2a	1a 3r	—	10	2
Cristina Hilde	—	—	—	—	—	—	5	4
*Thomas Gildene	1a 3½r	5a	4½a	3 × ½a	½a	—	35	8
Roger Rede	3 × ½a	3a 1r	3½a 1r	2a	—	—	17	9
Cristina Legge	3r	1a	1a 3r	½a	—	—	10	3
*John atte Brok	—	1r	½a	—	—	—	—	—
Isolda Valey	1r	½r	2r	—	—	—	4	2
*Henry Rode	10a 1½r	16a	16a	—	5a 1½r	11a 3r	86	27
Simon Aula (atte Hall)	—	2r	3r	—	—	—	—	—
John Ridel	—	1a 1½r	5r	—	½a	—	2	1
Thomas Maddermonger	1½r	2a	1a 1r	½a	1r	—	4	2
*John Mariny (Marnier)	1a 3r	2a	2a 1r	1a	1r	—	—	—
John Barthelot	2a ½r	3a + ?	3a + ?	2½a + ?	1½a + ?	—	—	1
John son of Alan	1a 1r	2a ½r	2½r	1r	2½r	—	9	?
Robert Thrumbold	—	½a	—	—	—	—	—	—
Reyner Willem	1a	4a 1r	6a	—	1a	—	6	—

Name	Wheat	Barley	Peas	Oats	Rye	Dredge	Fleeces	Lambs
John Goni	—	1a 3r	5r	3 × ½a	1a	—	?	?
*Alan Miller	2½a	?	?	?	1a ½r	—	?	?
*William Collon	?		?	?				?
John son of W[?]no	3r	?	?	?	?		?	?
Henry Reynol[d]	? ½a	3½r	?	?	1r		?	?
*Reginald in ye Lane	½a + ?	1a	1a	?	?		?	?
Reginald Lavendar	1r	1r	2r		?		?	
Nicholas Cook		2r			?		—	—
Robert Howman	1r	3a 1r	2a	1a	?		7	2
John Goni		3 × ½a	3½r		½a		6	2
*John Scot	½a	3 × ½a	2½a	1a	1a ½r			
John Quenyng	3r	1a	3r					
Thomas Mariot		1a						
John Prikke		½a	—	½a				
John Brond	2r	3r	1a					
Roger Cowper		1r	3½r					
Cecilia Stirtlehowe (Stirtloe de)		½a	½a				2	2
*Simon Parson		1a 1r			1r		11	4
William Syros		½a						
Richard Per[fery?]	1a 2r	—		3 × ½a	1r		4	2
*Richard Howman	1r	4½a	4a 1r	1r	1r			
Agnes Thrambold		3a	2r					
Cristina Thrumbold	1½a	½a	3½r	3r	1r		5	3
*John Baroun	3a 3r	2½a	3a 3r	2½a ½r	2a 1r		3	1
*Gilbert in ye Lane (in Venella)	1a 3r	5a 3r	8a				17	?
Henry Mileward		5a 1r	5½a		3r	3a	6	?
Richard in ye Lane (in Venella)	3r	2r	2½a		3r		7	[4]
Margaret Marshall		—	3r				—	—

Name	Wheat	Barley	Peas	Oats	Rye	Dredge	Fleeces	Lambs
Agnes Colion	3r	3 × 1/2a + ?	1a 1 1/2r	1r	3r	—	5	4
John Skinner	2a	6a 2 1/2r	5a 1r	3 × 1/2a	3r	—	12	5
Godfrey Skinner	1/2a	1a 1r	3 × 1/2a	1/2a	—	—	4	—
Andrew Bonis	3 × 1/2a	2a 3r	3a 3r	—	—	—	11	2
Robert atte Gate	1/2a	—	1/2a	—	—	—	—	—
Thomas Boteler	—	—	3r	—	—	—	2	—
Isabella Balte	—	—	1r	—	—	—	—	—
*John son of Alexander Goni	1 1/2a 1/2r	4a?, 1 1/2r + 1/2r	7a 1r	—	—	6a 1 1/2r	?	?
*William Swaneslee	2r	1a 3r	1/2a	—	—	—	11	2
Reginald Alk' (Alconbury)	—	1r	1a 3r	—	—	—	5	1
Thomas Notting	1a 3r	—	1/2a	—	—	—	3	1
Richard Chapman	1a	2a + ?	2a 3r	—	—	—	7	4
*William Mason	1r	2a	3a 1r	5r	1a	—	—	—
[Thomas] Wrighte	—	1r	—	—	—	—	—	—
Adam Gildersowe	2r	—	1r	1r	—	—	—	—
Cristina [Fyshe]	2a 2 1/2r	1r	2a	?	?	—	6	2
John Godman	3r	(2a) 1r	7a 1 1/2r	1a	1/2a	—	20	5
*Hugh Gile	1a	5 1/2a	3a	2a	1a 1 1/2r	—	(2)	(2)
Stephen Gile	—	3 × 1/2a 1/2r	?	?	1r	—	?	?
John Grinde	—	? + 1 1/2r	[1/2r]	?	?	—	?	?
John Taylor	—	1/2a	?	?	?	—	—	—
[John] Notting	—	?	7a 1/2r	?	?	—	—	—
Walter Glewe	1a + ?	3a 1r	3a 3r	1/2r	?	—	?	?
*Walter Ede	1a + ?	2a 1 1/2r	6a 1r	1/2r	?	—	—	—
John Pikering	—	5a 1 1/2r	11a	2 1/2a	—	—	30	?
Walt?[ ]	?	—	?	?	?	?	?	?
Will.[ ]	?	?	?	?	?	?	?	?
Will.[ ]	?	?	?	?	?	?	?	?
John [ ]	?	?	?	?	?	?	?	?

TABLE 13: SOWING AND SHEEP INVENTORY NO. 2, CA. 1341[a]

Name	*Wheat*	*Barley*	*Peas*	*Oats*	*Rye*	*Dredge*	*Fleeces*	*Lambs*
Simon ad Leirstowe	3r	1a	3a	—	1r	—	?	?
*Robert Bluntisham	—	1½a	2a 1r	—	—	—	—	—
John, son of John atte Well	1r	1½a	1a	3r	—	—	?	(6)
Matilda Gildene	—	1½a	3a 3r	2r	1½r	—	—	—
*Cristina Godchild	½a ½r	1a 3r	2½a ½r	—	1a	—	3	2
Amicia widow of John Goni	—	½a	—	—	—	—	2	—
John Graveley	1a 3r	2a 3r	?	—	2r	2a 1r	9	—
Cristina Paxton	1a	1½a	2a	½a	½a	—	2	—
*John on ye Wal	3 × ½a	3a ½r	—	—	2r	—	23	6
*John Graveley senior (dead)	—	—	3r	—	—	—	?	?
John Walton	—	1a 3r	1a 3½r	—	—	—	3	1
*John Quenyng, carnifex	1a	1a	2a	1a	½a	—	5	?
Thomas Seman	½a	½a	½a	½a	—	—	2	?
*William Rede	3a	4a 3r	7a 3½r	3½a	3a ½r	—	20	3
*Albric Moregrove	5r	3a	3a	2a	2r	—	5	6
Thomas Ese	3r	3 × ½a (1½r)	3 × ½a 1r	1r	½a	—	(6)	(6)
Godfrey Ede	5½r	3a ½r	4a 1r	1r	—	—	—	—
Reginald Quenyng	1a 1½r	4a 1½r	5a	2a	1½a	—	15	(5)
John son of Gosceline	1a	1a 1½r	3a	1½a	1a	—	5	1
*Godfrey in ye Lane	4a 1½r	5a 3r	7a ½r	2a 3r	2a ½r	—	20	5
Felicity widow of Godfrey Gildene	1a 3r	4a ½r	5a 3½r	1a	½a	—	—	—
*Roger Longe	2a 1½r	3a ½r	5a 1r	1½a	1a	—	9	2
Roger Longe junior	½a	½a	½a ½r	—	—	—	—	—
John Chipenham	2a 3½r	5a ½r	10a 3r	2a 1r	2a ½r	—	—	—
Emma *de* Abbots Ripton	1½a	3a 3r	4a	—	3r	1½a	—	—

[a] Box 1, bunle 1.

Name	Wheat	Barley	Peas	Oats	Rye	Dredge	Fleeces	Lambs
Elias Barker	—	—	$3\frac{1}{2}$r	—	—	—	1	—
*John Hildemar (dead)	1a 1r	2a 3r	5a 1r	1a 1r	$1\frac{1}{2}$r	—	(15)	3
Sybil Manipenny	—	5r	1a	—	—	—	—	—
*John Manipenny	1a $\frac{1}{2}$r	(2a) 3r	(2a)	1a	$1\frac{1}{2}$r	—	15	?
*Robert Fanner	$1\frac{1}{2}$a	(1a) $\frac{1}{2}$r	$3\frac{1}{2}$a	5r	1a	—	11	2
Godfrey Kyne	—	3r	1r	$\frac{1}{2}$a	—	—	(2)	1
Simon Grinde	$\frac{1}{2}$a	$\frac{1}{2}$a $\frac{1}{2}$r	2a	$\frac{1}{2}$a	$\frac{1}{2}$a	—	—	—
John son of William Page	—	$\frac{1}{2}$a	—	—	—	—	3	1
Godfrey Desore	1r	$3\frac{1}{2}$r	$2\frac{1}{2}$r	—	—	—	(13)	2
*William Parson	2a	2a	3r	$2\frac{1}{2}$a $\frac{1}{2}$r	3r	—	5	2
*William Frere	1a	2a $\frac{1}{2}$r	4a $\frac{1}{2}$r	1a 1r	1r	—	9	5
William Page	—	1a 1r	$2\frac{1}{2}$r	—	—	—	3	(2)
Godfrey Page senior	—	1r	2r	—	—	—	4	3
Robert son of Godfrey	—	—	2r	—	—	—	—	—
Reyner Alrich	—	$\frac{1}{2}$a	1a	$\frac{1}{2}$a	—	—	—	—
*Henry Aylred	3r	3a $\frac{1}{2}$r	1a	1r	—	—	?	4
widow of John Sorner (Serner?)	1r	$\frac{1}{2}$a	$1\frac{1}{2}$a	3r	$\frac{1}{2}$a	—	—	—
William Goni	—	2a	3r	—	$\frac{1}{2}$a	—	—	—
Agnes Pentour (Peyntour)	1a	$3\frac{1}{2}$r	$1\frac{1}{2}$a $\frac{1}{2}$r	—	—	—	—	—
John Kok (Cook)	5r	2a $3\frac{1}{2}$r	6a $\frac{1}{2}$r	$3 \times \frac{1}{2}$a	$3\frac{1}{2}$r	—	3	1
John son of Godfrey	1a $1\frac{1}{2}$r	5a 3r	$5\frac{1}{2}$a	2a 3r	1a 1r	—	—	—
*John Gildene	—	3r	3r	—	1r	—	—	—
Godfrey Lincoln	$2\frac{1}{2}$a	$4\frac{1}{2}$a $1\frac{1}{2}$r	7a 2r	2a	2a	—	16	8
Reginald Denne	6a	1a	$3 \times \frac{1}{2}$a	$1\frac{1}{2}$r	1a 1r	—	4	2
William Larke	—	3r	1a	—	—	—	4	1
William Inhewyn	3r	1a 3r	2a $\frac{1}{2}$r	1a	2r	—	2	1
John Lambehird	—	1a $\frac{1}{2}$r	1a	—	—	—	1	1
Thomas Acry	1r	3r	1r	—	—	—	1	1
John Juel	$1\frac{1}{2}$r	$\frac{1}{2}$a	3r	1r	—	—	—	—
Richard Acry	—	3r	$\frac{1}{2}$a	—	—	—	—	—

Name	*Wheat*	*Barley*	*Peas*	*Oats*	*Rye*	*Dredge*	*Fleeces*	*Lambs*
Margaret Acry	—	—	½a	—	—	—	—	—
Robert Abraham	4a	9½a	10½a	4a + ?	1½a	—	(17)	2
John Quenemen	3r	1½a	2a 1r	3r	½a	—	—	—
widow of John Frere	1a 1r	2a 3r	2½a	1a 1r	½a	—	(13)	3
Onti	—	½a	—	--	—	—	5	2
daughters of John Frere	½a	5r	1a 3r	½r	½a	—	3	1
Henry in ye Lane	—	3½r	1a	1r	½a ½r	—	—	—
Godfrey in ye Wal	1a	1a 3½r	3a	1a	2r	—	8	3
Parvus John (John Small)	1a 3r	2½a	3a	3½r	1a 1½r	—	9	2
*William Elys	1½a ½r	2a	4a ½r	5r	3r	—	5	2
*Henry Manipenny	3a 1r	7a	10a 3½r	1a	1½a	—	36	8
Alexander Savage	—	1½a	1a	—	—	—	5	2
Roger Hathewolf	—	1r	—	1r	—	—	—	—
Thomas Hardy	—	3r	½r	—	—	—	5	1
Robert Ramsey	—	½a	—	—	—	—	—	—
the daughters of John Elys	—	1r	3r	1½r	1r	—	—	—
Godfrey in ye Lane	3r	1a 3r	2a ½r	2r	½a	—	10	1
John Brows (Brous)	3½r	1½a	2½a	½a	1r	—	3	1
Hugh Bonde	—	—	1r	—	—	—	4	2
Robert son of Hugh	½a	½a 1½r	? + ½r	—	—	—	—	—
Cristina wife of Eusebius Clerk	2a 3r	3a	4a 1r	1a 3r	2r	—	8	2
Godfrey Clerk	1a	3a	3a	—	—	—	1	—
William Parmenter	—	2r	½a	—	—	—	5	1
Godfrey son of William Pennyman	2½r	1½a	2½r	3r	—	—	4	?
Godfrey son of Godfrey Pennyman	—	½a	—	1r	—	—	3	—
Gasse Pennyman	—	—	—	1r	—	—	2	—
Simon Pennyman	—	1a ½r	1½r	½a	—	—	(11)	—
Emma Cokayne	—	1a 1r	—	1a	—	—	—	—
Roger Dosyn	1r	1a	1½a ½r	1r	—	—	5	?
*John Scot	2½r	1a	4r	½a	1r	—	9	4

Name	*Wheat*	*Barley*	*Peas*	*Oats*	*Rye*	*Dredge*	*Fleeces*	*Lambs*
John Glewe	2½a	12a 1r	11a	7a	3a 1r	—	20	5
John Quenyng	1a 1½r	3a 1r	4a	2½r	1r	—	5	2
Roger son of William Aylred	—	1r	1r	—	—	—	—	—
*John Parson	—	½a	½a	1r	—	—	—	—
John son of Hugh	3r	2½a	5r	2½r	½r	—	6	2
William his brother	—	½a	1r	—	—	—	—	—
Reyner Ede	2r	3r	5½r	—	—	—	5	2
John son of Godfrey Bole	—	—	1r	—	—	—	—	—
John son of Matilda Balle	—	½a	1a	½a	½a	—	5	2
Elena Bole	½a	½a	2a	1½a ½r	—	—	7	2
[b] Godfrey her son	—	—	1r	—	—	—	—	—
William Dosyn	½a	1a	1a	1a	1r	—	—	—
*John Millicent	6a	12a ½r	15a 1½r	8½a	4a 3½r	—	42	5
*William his son	—	5r	1½a	½a	—	—	30	4
John son of Roger Manipenny	—	—	1a	—	—	—	—	—
Lambert Moulton	½r	3r	2r	2r	—	—	5	1
William Waryn	1r	2r	½a	1r	—	—	5	1
*John Startle	1r	3r	3r	—	—	—	—	—
Cristina Warde	—	1r	—	—	—	—	—	—
Thomas Hortoy (Hopay?)	6a	1a	1a	½a	—	—	2	1
*Matilda Glewe	1r	1r	½a	—	3r	—	—	—
*John son of Martin	1a 3r	2a	3½a	2r	1a	—	—	—
*John Glewe	3r	5r	3½r	3r	1r	—	5	2
John Drury	1r	½a ½r	1½r	1r	—	—	1	1
Caterina Hadenham	1a	1a	2a	3r	1r	—	14	5
the widow of Godfrey Pellage	3r	1a ½r	2r	6½r	—	—	13	2

[b] This entry has been crossed out in the manuscript.

Name	Wheat	Barley	Peas	Oats	Rye	Dredge	Fleeces	Lambs
Sybil Dosyn	1a	½a	1a	1r	1r	—	—	—
John son of William Cowter	1½a 1r	1a 3r	5r	½a	—	—	—	—
*Henry Lister	1½a	2a	2a 3r	1a	1½a	—	3	2
John Graveley	2a	(3a)	2a 3r	3a	1r	—	40	4
William Cowter junior	2a	4½a	7a 3r	2½a	3r	—	22	2
John Fole	—	1½r	½a	½a	1½r	—	2	1
*Robert Dosyn	1a	2½a	2a 3r	5r	1r	—	7	1
Simon Norreys	—	1r	2r	1r	—	—	3	—
Cristina Trely	2r	1r	3r	1r	—	—	—	1
Thomas Bole	2½a	4a	6½a 1r	2a	½a	—	14	?
Simon Scot	½a	—	½a	—	—	—	—	—
Henry Colowot	3a 3r	13a	9½a	—	2½a	3a	19	3
John [Boni]	1a 1½r	4a + ?	5a	2a	1a 1r	—	3	1
Simon Dosyn	1r	3r	(½a)	—	—	—	—	—
PAPWORTH								
John Hokerylle			vacant					
Reginald Squire			4a 3r	1a				
*Thomas Waryn			2a	1½a				
William Freman			3r	1½a				
William Barton			2a 3r	3a 1r				
Simon Barton, chaplain			2a	4a				
Walter Barton			3a	3a				
Thomas Hogoun			1a	—				
*John Aylwyne (Aleyn)			1a	—				
William de Papworth			½a	—				
Simon Longe			vacant					

Name	Wheat	Barley	Peas	Oats	Rye	Dredge	Pledges
HEMINGFORD							
Thomas Marshall			vacant				
Simon Everard		1r?					
Nicholas Robyn			vacant				
John Robyn			vacant				
YELLING (GILLING)							
Godfrey Mileward		1r					
Thomas Duraunt		1a					
Lord Rector de Graveley		3 × 1/2a				?	
OFFORD							
*John Chapman			2				
*the wife of Richard Chapman			vacant				
John Baroun			1a				

Summary on the side of the manuscript is incomplete.

Name	Wheat	Barley	Peas	Oats	Rye	Dredge	Pledges
HUNTINGDON							
*John Lorimer	—	8a	4a 1r	—	—	2a	
William Hemingford	—	8a 1r	2a 1r	—	—	2a	
*Paul Begenore	—	4a 1r	1a	—	—	2a	
*Robert Hocchene (Hitchin)	—	4a	(1a) 1r	—	1a 1 1/2r	2a + ?	
Emma de Hocchene (Hitchin)	1 1/2a	—	1/2a	—	?a		
(de Hocchene)	1a	—	1/2a	—	1/2a		
*John Serle	1a 3r	8a	(2 1/2a 1r)	—	1a		John Serle
*John Richardyn	5a 1r	6 1/2a 1/2r	2a	—	1a	1 1/2a	

Name	Wheat	Barley	Peas	Oats	Rye	Dredge	Pledges
William Scot	1a	5a 1r	4a 3r	—	—	½a	John Wymer
*John Wymer	½a	3a 3r	3a	—	—	—	William Scot
*John Beverle	1a	2a 3r	3a	—	—	1a 1r	Godfrey Quenyng
*Walter Bronne	2½a	4½a	4½a	—	3r	(1a?)	John Hemington
John Hemington	3r	—	½a	—	1r	—	Walter Bronne
*Robert Alyous	1a	2a 3r	(2a) 3r	—	—	—	Martin Rede
John Thomeston	3r	—	(1½a)	—	½a	—	Lord John Chippenham
Margeret de Hocchene (Hitchin)	2r	—	—	—	1r +	1r	Gilbert Goni
*Thomas Godoun	—	—	1a	—	—	—	Henry (?)
*John Bolder	1a	—	—	—	—	1a	John Richardyn
*Ralph Rede	3½a	1½r	1a 1r	—	—	(1)a	
*Martin Rede	3r	½a	2a	—	½a	—	
William Sadeler	—	—	1r	—	—	—	
*William Waleys	—	vacant	vacant	—	—	—	
*John de Hamyrton (Hamerton)	2a	4a	3a	½a	—	2a	
*John Waldecote (Walcot)	3 × ½a	—	½a 1r	½a	½a	—	
Roger Scot	1a 1r	—		—	—	—	
William Waltebec			vacant				
Matilda Wenewec			vacant				
Simon Haubaken			vacant				
John Hayilmar			vacant				
Emma de Luton			vacant				
John Marshall			vacant				
Robert Marshal			vacant				
Sabina Hundpetil	—	—	1½r	—	—	—	

Acres of wheat 24; acres of rye 7 acres + 2 rods; barley 62 acres + 2 rods; dredge 19 acres + 3 rods; peas 11 acres + 1 rod

Our understanding of the spread of people and property at Godmanchester can be further enlightened from surviving fragments of farm assessments of the town. Three of these deal in large part with temporary leasing and are considered below under the title of subletting lists. The remaining fragment is singular and small as well as being in poor condition. Nearly all the names can be further identified in the court rolls so it is possible to date this document as ca. 1340. According to this record, the bailiffs compiled lists of those holding "street" properties (mainly messuages) as well as meadow (either in acres and rods along the river or small units called "cris" or "cras" in croft enclosures) distinct from arable holdings (Table 14).

Although only some fifty names and their entries can be deciphered, this is enough to demonstrate familiar patterns. At one extreme are those individuals apparently not having their own home property or messuage: William and John, sons of John Frere, Cristina Page, Robert Ramsey, John Bole, Lawrence Bole, John Startle. At the other extremes were those with not only messuages but large amounts of meadow: William Elys ($17\frac{1}{2}$ acres), John son of Godfrey Quenyng ($11\frac{1}{2}$ acres), John Millicent ($64\frac{1}{2}$ acres) and William Millicent (14 acres, 1 rod).

TABLE 14: MESSUAGE AND MEADOW LIST[a]

The bracketed sum after the land entry is the amount to be paid to the farm from this property, the bracketed sum is not added where the damaged record makes the total uncertain.

Godfrey [Wran]dale	1 messuage (2d.)
[Thomas] Acry	1 messuage (6d.) 5 acres + 1 rod + 1 swath of meadow
Richard Acry	$\frac{1}{2}$ d. etc.?
[illeg.]	1 messuage (3d.)
William son of Simon	messuage in West Street ($1\frac{1}{2}$ d.)
Reginald? Alrych	messuage next to William Alred ($1\frac{1}{2}$ d.)
William and John sons of John Frere	3 acres 1 rod of meadow
Henry Manipenny	messuage next to messuage formerly of Gilbert in the Lane ($2\frac{1}{2}$ d.)
[illeg.], Lambert	messuage (3d.) + curtilage etc.?
John [illeg.]dinam	messuage next to Alexander Savage (2d.)
Alexander Warde	1 messuage ($1\frac{1}{4}$ d.) + $2\frac{1}{2}$ acres of meadow
Cristina Page	$2\frac{1}{2}$ acres + $1\frac{1}{2}$ rod of meadow
Robert Ramsey	3 rod + ?
William Elys	messuage + $17\frac{1}{2}$ acres of meadow
Henry Willem	messuage next to William Elys ($4\frac{1}{2}$ d.)
John son of Godfrey Quenyne	curtilage ($\frac{1}{4}$ d.) + $11\frac{1}{2}$ acres of meadow
John Brouse	messuage ($1\frac{1}{2}$ d.)

[a] Box 1, bundle 4.

Henry Bonde	messuage ($^3/_4$ d.) etc.
Henry Pademor	messuage in West Street (3d.)
heirs of John Ingelond	messuage (3d.) + 1 acre
Cristina Clerk	messuage next to William (Parmenter) (3d.)
William Parmenter	messuage (2d.) + 3 rods
Godfrey Pennyman, junior	messuage (2d.) + 1 curtilage in West Street + 6$^1/_2$ acres + $^1/_2$ swath of meadow
Roger Dosyn	1 messuage (1$^1/_2$ d.) + curtilage (1$^1/_2$ d.) + 7$^1/_2$ acres of meadow
John Scot	messuage (2d.) + 4 acres of meadow
John Parsons	messuage ($^3/_4$ d.) + curtilage in West Croft (1d.) + 1 acre 1 rod of meadow
Godfrey Bole	messuage ($^1/_2$ d.)
John Bole	1$^1/_2$ acres
Pellage Leman	messuage ($^1/_2$ d.) + curtilage in West Croft (1d.)
John Glewe	place formerly of William Millicent (3d.)
Pellage Frere	place formerly of William Millicent (3d.)
John Quenyng	place formerly of William Millicent (3d.) + 14 acres 1 rod of meadow etc.?
Godfrey Quenyng	le Garscroft next *le* West Bridge (6d.)
William Waryn	messuage next to *le* West Bridge ($^3/_4$ d.)
John Balle	messuage (1d.) + curtilage in West Croft ($^1/_4$ d.) + 3$^1/_2$ acres $^1/_2$ rod of meadow
Elena Bole	messuage (3d.) + curtilage (1$^1/_4$ d.) + meadow 7 acres 1 rod + Garscroft (1d.)
Lawrence Bole	$^1/_2$ acre
Thomas Plowrighte	curtilage in West Croft
William Dosyn	messuage (3d.) + 7 acres $^1/_2$ rod of meadow
John Millicent	capital messuage + curtilage (7$^1/_2$ d.) + 64$^1/_2$ acres meadow (17s. 6$^1/_2$ d.)
Cristina Warde	messuage (1d.) + curtilage ($^1/_2$ d.) + 1$^1/_2$ acres etc.?
John Startle	curtilage + 1 acre 1 rod of meadow
Godfrey Startle	1 messuage (3d.)
Thomas [Hortey]	6 acres etc. of meadow
heirs of Godfrey Glewe	messuage (2d.) etc.?
William [Tominson]	messuage (4$^1/_2$ d.) + curtilage
John Dosyn	curtilage ($^1/_2$ d.) + 3 acres of meadow
William Millicent	messuage (4$^1/_2$ d.) + curtilage (1d.) + 14 acres 1 rod of meadow (3s. $^1/_2$ d.)
John Glewe patissa˙	messuage (1$^1/_2$ d.) + curtilage (1$^1/_4$ d.) + 2 acres 1$^1/_2$ rods of meadow
heirs of William Pellage	messuage (2d.) + curtilage (2d.) + 4 acres 1 rod of meadow (17d.)
William Nunne	1 messuage ($^1/_4$ d.)
John Corner	messuage (2$^1/_2$ d.) + curtilage ($^1/_2$ d.) + 9 acres 1 rod of meadow
[heirs] of Henry Lister	messuage + curtilage (12d.) + (3 acres of meadow etc.)
[*illeg.*] Leicester	
[*illeg.*]	
[*illeg.*]	
[*illeg.*]	

SUBLETTING

The short-term lease of crops, houses and land was a convenient device for a community in the thirteenth century, as today. References to such leases in Godmanchester court rolls are not many, and these tend to be for more than the occasional seasonal opportunity. On 17 March 1272, Nicholas Tinctor conveyed one and one half acres of land to Reginald son of Robert and Henry *le* Maddermonger until "the term of St. John the Baptist" (29 August).[10] The ambitious Reyner Vicory rented a place to John Chese at five shillings per annum and exchanged property with Roger, son of William of Abbots Ripton, in an eight-year agreement.[11]

In a court of around 1280 with the heading lost[12] occurs the statement that Robert *de* Leche is given peaceful entry to one half acre of land let to him for six crops by William *le* Kuter. Around the same time, 20 November 1280, John *de* Hamerton was given seisin of one rod of land with the proviso that he pay five shillings to the bailiffs should he purchase that rod. In 1282 Vincent *de* Dunton obtained some land for nine years and in 1293 he leased a messuage and five acres for five years. Roger Glewe obtained land under a 12-year lease in 1292. Another five-year lease was given in 1293, a six-year lease in 1297, a $10^1/_2$-year lease in 1304 and a six-year agreement in 1312. William Savage entered a plea for

[10] Box 5, bundle 1.

Nicholaus Tinctor tradidit in manibus ballivorum ad opus Reginaldi filii Roberti et ad opus Henrici le Maddermonger tres dimidias acras terre in bernscroft usque ad terminum Nativitatis Sancti Johannis Baptiste ut pacaverit pactu quod erat inter ipsos et si vendita erat nemo debet emere praeter eos.

[11] Box 5, bundle 8. 27 March 1281.

Johannes Chese seysitus fuit de una placea inter terra Martini super Wal ex una perte et predicti Johannis Chese ex altera. quam Reyner Vicary ad opus suum reddidit in manibus ballivorum reddendo predicto vicario et suis assignatis v.s. per annum. videlicet ad festum Sancti Michaelis. ii.s. et vi.d. et ad festum Pasche. ii.s. et vi.d. et si in solutionem predictam deficiat predictus Johannes nichil iuris in predicta terra optinebit et de hoc invenit predicto vicario. ii. fideiussores scilicet Johannem Wecharin et Rogerum Glewe.

Hec est invencio facta inter dictum reynerum vicarius de Gomecestre' et inter Rogerum filium Willelmi de riptone abbatis. videlicet quod predictus R. vicarius dimisit et concessit predicto rogero illam terram quam habuit de Jacobo filio Stephani in cimiterio de Huntingdon' nomine custodi a termino .viii. annorum plene completorum. et pro hac concessione et dimissione predictus rogerus concessit predicto. R. Vicario tres acras de meliori terra quam eligere voluerit de tota predicta terra predicti Jacobi. et hoc ad totam vitam predicti R. vicarii ad defendendum pro .i. acra et dimidia. Et si contingat predictus. R. Vicarius infra terminum .viii. annorum in facto discedere licebit predicto vicario seu attornatis suis de predictis tribus acris disponere et ordinare usque terminum octo annorum continue completorum. Et post predictum terminum octo annorum predicte .iii. acre terre revertere predicto rogero seu eis assignatis.

[12] Box 5, bundle 1.

one crop in 1302 and the daughters (Emma and Cristina) of Nicholas Hildemar let land inherited from their father to Godfrey Oundle in 1309 for two crops. Obviously the court rolls were not designed to provide a record of subletting at Godmanchester so we are fortunate indeed to have supplementary records.

SUBLETTING LISTS

Whereas the sowing records could be placed in the context of lay subsidy lists, the subletting lists for Godmanchester are difficult to relate to other records. All are fragmentary with the heading missing. None are comparable with one another in terms of property entries. However, the nature and purpose of these records appears to be the same, for all are composed of lists of property held by various parties from the land of (de terra) some other townsmen followed by the size of the property in "farm" units, that is, the acreage or assessment amount of each unit of land.[13] It would appear, therefore, that the bailiffs of Godmanchester found it necessary to draw up annual lists of sublet of property at the time of the farm assessment. Since none of these entries occur in the court rolls, or in the other subletting lists, there is the further presumption that these lists indicate a practise of short-term, perhaps yearly (one-harvest) leasing, that need not be recorded in the court rolls. Such leasing pratices were to be found in other parts of England, even for villein tenements.[14] No records of this sort survive for after the Black Death, and indeed this series, in so far as its incompleteness allows, suggests a falling off of such subletting in the second quarter of the century. The short-term leasing nature of these records is further confirmed by the first surviving list in so far as numerous entries are stroked out and other added. In short, it is a picture of a rapidly changing market scene. In the manuscript for Table 15 "Subletting List No. 1," below, one entry has been stroked out under Robert Gile, John the son of William Manipenny, Roger Faber, Roger le Maddermonger, Albric Morgrove, [   ] Bole, John Startle junior, Stephen Clerk, William Millicent senior, John Warde, Godfrey son of Hugh, William Newman, Walter Quenyng, John son of William in ye Lane, Reyner Garlop, Martin super Murum and Richard Acry. Two entries

---

[13] In a few exceptional instances, however, holdings are listed as belonging (de proprie) to the tenant. Perhaps such properties have been recovered from lessees and are listed here for the convenience of the moment.

[14] For short-term subletting on neighbouring manors of Ramsey Abbey see J. A. Raftis, *Tenure and Mobility* (Toronto, 1964), pp. 74-81.

have been stroked out under William Manipenny, three entries under
Godfrey Bole and five entries under William *le* Rede. On the other hand,
properties have been added in another hand for a number of lessees: one
under William the son of William Manipenny and Stephen Clerk, two
under William Wenington, John Startle senior, Amicia widow of
Alexander super Murum, John *le* Frere and Reyner Garlop, three under
William Millicent and four under Adam Grinde. These additions are
included under the total number of properties for the Table but stroked
out properties are not included. A number of stroked out properties that
have already been cancelled because they ought to occur elsewhere, are
not included here. For example, the three one half acres held by John and
Godfrey, sons of Hugh, and their sister Isolda had originally been placed
under John's name but this entry was cancelled for a separate entry. As is
noted in Table 15, three names of lessees and their holdings have been
entirely cancelled and it can be corroborated from the court rolls that this
occurs owing to the demise of the lessor.

   In the following tables the figures in brackets are not conjectural but
incomplete. That is to say, every bracketed figure is "hard" or identifiable
and the bracket simply indicates that there are additions to these figures
that cannot be deciphered. In all cases, such additions are only one or two,
and from the context, small units of one or two rods. The acreage totals of
these tables are considerable. The first list (Table 15) may be presumed to
cover only about one quarter of the town despite the more than 220 acres
involved. The second list (Table 16) does not include East Street or
outsiders and still comes to nearly 400 acres. The third list (Table 17)
includes one (Arnyng) only of the four streets, along with outsiders, and
the total acreage is more than 150. Money rents in the lists are revenues
from more land and further enhance the acreage totals involved in these
records. However, since these rents were often held in complicated
fashion with others and sometimes involved bits and pieces of croft, these
are not added here.

   One can quickly identify the engrossing entrepreneurs of the day —
Grinde, Manipennys, Millicents, Spicer — in Table 15. At the same time,
subletting obviously provided a useful supplement to the family support
system outlined in Chapter 1 above. The "family" property demand is
quickly seen by maintenance of the titles of heirs and widows as well as
the first foothold in Godmanchester real estate being acquired by young
sons and married daughters. In the first subletting list, for example,
William, the son of John Gile and Hugh, the son of Robert Gile, are listed
as leasing respectively a pennyworth and 1 rod of land. Both of these sons
must have been quite young at this time since they do not appear in the

court rolls for at least another ten years. The three "sons of John," Gilbert, Thomas and Henry, appear to be in the same age category in the second subletting list (Table 16). Henry and John, sons of John Clerk, are in the same category in Subletting List No. 3 (Table 17). It has already been noted that in the surviving fragment of the second list 16 lessees were holding land from their father. The subletting lists also show properties being leased from wives and brothers.

What survives from the second "subletting list" (Table 16) is for the most part in good condition. As a result, we do appear to have the complete list for Arnyng and West Streets and a good portion of the Post Street list. Of the 170 entries in this list, 21 are for "heirs" of various God-manchester individuals and these serve to give an approximate dating for the record. Properties could remain in the hand of executors for years. However, this seems to have occurred less frequently for more wealthy townsmen such as the Manipennys and Millicents. Very likely then, this list may be dated as ca. 1315-1320 from entries to the "heirs of" John Manipenny (d. 1312), William Manipenny (d. 1312), Richard Acry (d. 1316), William Startle (d. 1315), Eusebius Pope (d. 1316) and Richard *de* Lincoln (d. 1310). Perhaps these lists, or part of them, were employed over several years when few changes were necessary. Dating is further complicated by the fact that the entries for West Street, although now gathered with other streets under the same number, appear to be in a slightly different and perhaps later hand. The terminal date of the manuscript as ca. 1320 is suggested by the fact we know that an important personage, Gilbert *de* Strateshylle, was dead by 1321 but not entered under heirs in this list.

The fact that this second subletting list is complete makes possible a better understanding of the record. Not only were properties held by heirs (*heredes*) to be found listed but, presumably because succession or leasing had been recently established, the entries for 16 individuals begin with property from his (or her) father. In eight instances a property is noted at the head of the individual's list as his or her "own" (*propria*). This latter category was also to be found for properties in the first subletting list. Perhaps the tenure of such properties was still *sub judice*, or but recently established. In any case, subletting (*de terra*) still embraces 99 percent of the entries on these lists. Furthermore, as the list indicates, properties continued to be leased from a very wide range of individuals.

A third subletting list (Table 17) would appear to be after No. 2 owing to the fact that reference is now made to heirs of Martin Aylred and Eusebius Clerk, both of whom were given as living at the time of Subletting List No. 2. The dating ca. 1320-1325 seems plausible for this

record. This shorter surviving manuscript (92 names in all) is for Arnyng Street and the tenants from neighbouring vills only. Again, however, it is a quite distinct record from the second subletting list since all the entries for Henry Rode, to take but one example, are different for each list. As can be seen quickly, in Table 17, there are also fewer properties leased in this fashion at this time. At the same time, the bailiff's task in maintaining an up-to-date list of those owing to the royal farm must have been an unenviable one. Owing no doubt to the sale of properties, a half-dozen properties were further identified in the following list as formerly (*quondam*) of someone else. More complicated is the fact that some of these sublet properties appear to have been sublet further. In five different instances it is noted that properties are actually to be assessed to others (*sed computabit*). In this fashion an acre held by Lawrence Julian is assessed to three others; among the properties held by the heirs of John Drew two and one half acres are assessed to four people; one half acre of the lands of the heirs of Eusebius Cook is assessed to Serle Tinctor; one rod of Simon Legge's land is assessed to two others and one half rod of the property of the widow of Roger *de* Upton was assessed in five units to four individuals.

TABLE 15: SUBLETTING LIST No. 1, CA. 1300[a]

Name of Lessee	No. of Properties	Land	Rent	No. of Lessors
William *le* Mason	2	2r	—	2
John *le* Couper	2	(1a)	—	2
Simon Mercator	1	—	$\frac{1}{2}$d.	1
Godfrey Glewe	6	(1a)	($\frac{1}{2}$d.)	6
John Frere	2	2a 2r	—	2
Simon Ingelond	3	(1a)	—	3
John Gile	6	(1a $\frac{1}{2}$r)	—	6
William son of John Gile	1	—	1d.	1
Godfrey Juel	6	(1a 1$\frac{1}{2}$r)	—	6
Walter Ede	3	(1$\frac{1}{2}$r)	—	3
Godfrey on *ye* Wal	2	3r	—	2
Robert Gile	5	—	(4$\frac{1}{4}$d.)	4
Hugh son of Robert Gile	1	1r	—	1
William Manipenny	18	(10a 1r)	(3d.)	18
William Wennington	4	(3$\frac{1}{2}$r)	—	4
William son of William Manipenny	4	(2$\frac{1}{2}$r)	—	4
John his brother	1	1r	—	1
Roger his brother	2	(2a $\frac{1}{2}$r)	—	2

[a] Box 2, no. 72.

Name of Lessee	No. of Properties	Land	Rent	No. of Lessors
Roger Faber	10	2a 2½r	2½d.	10
Walter Quenyng	3	2r	—	(3)
John Quenyng	3	1a ½r	¾d.	3
Adam Grinde	25	8a 3½r	6¼d.	23
Nicholas *de* Paxton	11	3a 2½r	¼d.	11
John *de* Graveley	5	1a 1½r	—	5
Roger *le* Maddermonger	1	1a 1r	—	1
Godfrey Gildene	3	5a	—	3
Albric' Morgrove	5	3a 2½r	1½d.	5

WEST STREET

Name of Lessee	No. of Properties	Land	Rent	No. of Lessors
William *le* Rede	18	(8a 3r)	(4¼d.)	16
William *le* Rede junior[b]	5	1a 2r	2d.	4
John on ye Wal	7	1a	2d.	7
John Bole	3	1a 1r	—	3
Robert Leman	1		2½d. messuage	—
heirs of Edward Glewe	3	2a 3½r	—	3
John Startle junior	11	4a 1r	2¾d.	11
Edward Glewe[c]	3	(4a)	(½d.)	2
Godfrey *le* Kutere junior	1	3a 2r	—	1
Godfrey *le* Kutere senior	8	5a 1r	(½d.)	7
Stephen Clerk	4	3r	—	4
Roger Glewe[d]	11	7a 1½r	1d.	11
John Startle senior	9	4a 2r	1¾d.	8
William *le* Wilde	1	—	2d. messuage	—
William Millicent senior	56	(22a 1½r)	(10¼d.)	50
Matilda Millicent	5	5a 1r	—	5
John Warde	1	3a	—	1
Godfrey Dosyn	7	9a	—	7
Richard Quenyng	3	2a	¾d.	3
Waryn *le* Webester	4	1a 3½r	½d.	4
William Millicent junior	7	(1a + ¼ land)	—	6
Reginald Ede	1	1r	—	1
[Godfrey] Pennyman	2	6a	—	1
[William Juel]	2	1a	—	1
John Glewe	4	(1a 1r)	—	4
Godfrey Bole	6	( )	—	5
William Newman	4	7a 1r	¼d.	3
Godfrey Clerk	15	(13a 1r)	(3½d.)	14
William son of Godfrey [Parminter)]	2	2a 1½r	—	1
John *le* Roo	3	—	1½d.	3

[b] This name and the entries following it have all been stroked out.
[c] This entry is entirely stroked out.
[d] This entry is entirely stroked out.

Name of Lessee	No. of Properties	Land	Rent	No. of Lessors
Peter *de* Dereham	4	(1a 3r)	—	3
John Bonis (Brus?)	6	2a	$^1/_2$d.	6
Walter Quenyng	7	(3a 3r)	—	7
Simon Miller	1	1a	—	1
[William] in ye Lane	13	3a 1r	—	13
[?] son of William in ye Lane	7	3a 3$^1/_2$r	—	7
John son of William in ye Lane	8	(3a 1$^1/_2$r)	( )	8
John Blaunche	8	3a 1$^1/_2$r + messuage	$^3/_4$d.	7
Thomas Miller	4	1a 1r	$^1/_4$d.	4
John son of John *de* Essex	1	2r	—	—
Richard *le* Rede	4	1a + messuage	$^1/_2$d.	3
William *de* Mattishale	4	2$^1/_2$r	$^3/_4$d.	4
John Hardy	1	1r	—	1
Amicia widow of Alexander *le* Wal	3	1a $^1/_2$r	1d.	3
John Faber	2	1$^1/_2$r	—	2
William *de* Wistow	3	1a 1r	1d.	3
heirs of Sarra *le* Frere	3	2a 3$^1/_2$r	—	2
John *le* Frere	3	1$^1/_2$r	—	3
Reyner Garlop	13	(messuage + 2a 2r)	(10d.)	12
Godfrey *le* Frere	6	5a	$^1/_2$d.	5
Martin super le Wal	5	2r + messuage (6d.) 2r	1$^1/_4$d.	4
Godfrey son of Martin le Wal	2	(1a 1$^1/_2$r)	—	2
Alan Scot	5	(2r)	—	5
Richard Acry	12	6a 2r + $^1/_4$ of land	2$^3/_4$d.	10
Robert Leffen	8	1a 2$^1/_2$r + messuage (3d.)	$^1/_4$d.	7

Total: 220 acres + 1$^1/_2$ rods + $^1/_2$ of land + 5 messuages
Rent: 6s. 4d.

TABLE 16: SUBLETTING LIST No. 2, CA. 1315-1320[a]

Name of Lessee	No. of Properties	Land	Rent	No. of Lessors
ARNYNG STREET				
Thomas Gildene	3	3a	(2d.)	3
John Gildene	6	(2a 1r)	2d.	6
Richard Gildene	9	6a 1r	$^1/_4$d.	7
Cristina Gildene	2	2a 1$^1/_2$r	—	2

[a] Box 2, bundle 6.

Name of Lessee	No. of Properties	Land	Rent	No. of Lessors
John Underwode	1	2r	—	1
Godfrey Pellage	3	1a $^{1}/_{2}$r	$^{3}/_{4}$d.	3
William son of John, son of Simon	2	1$^{1}/_{2}$r	—	2
Robert Legge	3	3a $^{1}/_{2}$r	$^{1}/_{2}$d.	3
Simon *le* Rede	8	13a	1d.	8
Roger son of Simon *le* Rede	1	1r	—	1
Henry Rode	26	(12a 3r + $^{1}/_{2}$ virg.)	(3$^{1}/_{2}$d.)	24
John apud *le* Brok	3	1a 1$^{1}/_{2}$r	—	2
William Manipenny	28	8a 3r	2d.	28
Godfrey Pademor	7	3a 1r	1$^{3}/_{4}$d.	7
Roger Edward	4	2a 3r	( )	4
Godfrey son of Edward	20	5a	8$^{1}/_{2}$d.	18
William *le* Rede	23	10a + $^{1}/_{2}$ 'virgate'	7$^{1}/_{2}$d.	21
Godfrey Seman	15	7a 3r	4$^{1}/_{4}$d.	13
John son of William Seman	9	7a 3$^{1}/_{2}$r	2d.	9
Henry son of John Clerk	3	3a 1r	1$^{3}/_{4}$d.	3
Isabella Julian	2	2a 3r	$^{1}/_{4}$d.	1
John son of John Clerk	2	3a	1$^{1}/_{4}$d.	2
Matilda daughter of John Clerk	—	1a	—	1
Roger de Croxton	1	$^{1}/_{2}$r	—	1
Simon ad Crucem	3	3a 2r	$^{1}/_{4}$d.	3
Reginald Seman	18	6a 2$^{1}/_{2}$r	7d.	15
[John] Bole	11	(1a 3$^{1}/_{2}$r)	(1$^{1}/_{2}$d.)	11
Stephen Clerk	13	(3a 1$^{1}/_{2}$r)	(2d.)	—
Reginald Mason	1	1a	—	1
John Waleys	1	1r	—	1
Eusebius *le* Cook	3	—	3$^{1}/_{4}$d.	3
John Longe junior	1	3r	—	1
Ralph Sutor	1	2r	—	1
Martin Aylred	3	5a	$^{1}/_{2}$d.	3
Millicent daughter of Martin Aylred	2	1r	2d.	2
Matilda Fressing	—	—	$^{3}/_{4}$d.	—
Reyner Clerk	1	$^{1}/_{2}$ 'virgate'	—	1
William son of Thomas Balle	3	$^{1}/_{2}$ 'virgate' + 6a 1r	$^{1}/_{4}$d.	3
Cristina daughter of Thomas [Balle?]	3	3a	$^{3}/_{4}$d.	3
Gunnilda Mendy	2	4a 3r	—	2
Alexander Balle	2	3a	—	2
Elena wife of Reginald *de* Papworth	2	3r	—	2
heirs	2	1r	$^{1}/_{4}$d.	2
Elena Cook	1	$^{1}/_{2}$r	—	1
William Aylred	10	(4a 2$^{3}/_{4}$r)	—	9
Reginald Spruntyng	3	1$^{1}/_{2}$r	$^{1}/_{2}$d.	3
heirs of John Cook	2	3r	—	2

Name of Lessee	No. of Properties	Land	Rent	No. of Lessors
Godfrey son of Eusebius Aniz	8	2a 3½r	½d.	8
Reginald son of Eusebius Aniz?	9	2a ½r	1½d.	8
Dionysia Aylred	6	8a	—	6
Henry son of William Aylred	6	3a ½r + croft (½d.)	¾d.	6
Nicholas Person	3	2r + croft (½d.)	—	3
Edward *le* Ray	3	3a ½r	¼d.	3
Lawrence Pays	2	1a	—	2
Simon brother of Lawrence Pays	1	3r	—	—
Elena Hilde	2	1½r	—	2
Millicent Hilde	1	1½r	—	—
William Pernel	4	3a 3r	1½d.	4
Walter his son	1	2r	—	1
Alan apud *le* Leirstowe	5	4a 3½r	—	5
Dionysia Drewe	1	2a	—	1
William son of Reginald Aylred	12	9a	1d.	12
heirs of Godfrey Legge	4	3a 3r	—	4
heirs of Lawrence Julian	7	4a 3½r	3½d.	6
William son of William Pernel	3	2r	4d.	3
WEST STREET				
heirs of John Manipenny	14	4a 2r	3d.	14
Lawrence ad Pontem	8	3a 1r	2d.	8
John Hildemar	5	1a 1r	1d.	5
Robert Carpenter	(2)	( )	( )	(2)
Alan *de* Bradenham	2	2r	—	2
Reyner son of William Peyntour	2	4a 2r	—	2
Henry Pentour	1	5a	—	1
John son of Godfrey	15	9a ½r	2d.	13
William Elys	1	1½r	—	1
heirs of John Gildene	4	2a	1d.	4
Robert Leffen	1	½r	—	1
Alexander Savage	1	2r	—	1
heirs of Richard Acry	1	1½r	—	1
John super *le* Wal	3	1a 2r	—	3
heirs of Alexander super *le* Wal	1	2r	—	1
Godfrey super *le* Wal	3	3r	¾d.	3
Reyner Garlop	12	5a	1¾d.	12
William *de* Mattishale	6	1a 1r	½d.	6
heirs of Thomas Miller	1	1a	—	1
Eusebius *le* Clerk	14	5a 3½r	1¾d.	14
William Pennyman	1	1r	—	1
Walter in Venella	1	1½r	—	1
Godfrey son of Walter Quenyng	3	(2½r)	—	3
John Brous	3	(1r)	(½d.)	3
Hugh *le* Bonde	1	1½r	—	1

Name of Lessee	No. of Properties	Land	Rent	No. of Lessors
William Millicent junior	3	(1a 1r)	—	3
heirs of Richard Quenyng	3	$3\frac{1}{2}$r	—	3
Simon Scot	4	1a $\frac{1}{2}$r	—	4
Godfrey Dosyn	1	$1\frac{1}{2}$r	—	1
John in Venella	3	3r	$\frac{1}{2}$d.	3
John *le* Frere	1	$1\frac{1}{2}$r	—	1
Robert *le* Fanner	4	$1\frac{1}{2}$r	1d.	4
John Millicent	16	4a 3r	$\frac{1}{2}$d.	14
heirs of William Startle	2	—	2d.	2
William Ede	1	1r	—	1
John Startle junior	3	$1\frac{1}{2}$r	$\frac{1}{4}$d.	3
Godfrey Bole	1	$\frac{1}{2}$r	—	1
John son of Roger Glewe	1	1r	—	1
Elena Glewe	1	1r	—	1
William Conter	1	2r	—	1
William Eusebius	2	1a	—	2
heirs of John Bole	1	2r	—	1
Robert Dosyn	1	1r	—	1
Thomas Bole	5	2a 1r	$1\frac{1}{4}$d.	5
Robert Cook	1	1r	—	1
John son of Robert son of Walter	1	1a 1r	—	1
William *le* Rede junior	7	2a 1r	—	7

POST STREET

John son of William *de* Wennington	3	3r	—	3
Cristina daughter of John son of Simon *le* Clerk	2	1r	1d.	2
[ ] Clerk	1	1r	—	1
[ ] Chaplain	17	(3a 2r)	($2\frac{1}{4}$d.)	(14)
Eustace Seman	1	2a	—	1
Roger Longe	7	$2\frac{1}{2}$r + $\frac{1}{3}$ of an acre	—	7
heirs of Richard Elys	1	2r	—	1
William Elys	—	( )	—	—
Godfrey in Venella	6	$2\frac{1}{2}$r	1d.	6
John son of Thomas Quenyng	8	1a $3\frac{1}{2}$r	$\frac{1}{2}$d.	8
John son of Ede	1	1r	—	1
Reginald Goni	4	3a 1r	1d.	4
Alexander Goni	1	2r	—	1
Albric Morgrove	5	1a $2\frac{1}{2}$r	$\frac{1}{2}$d.	5
Godfrey Gildene	3	1a 1r	$\frac{1}{4}$d.	3
Roger Maddermonger	5	2a 3r	—	5
John son of William *de* Graveley	10	4a $2\frac{1}{2}$r	$1\frac{1}{2}$d.	9
Nicholas Paxton	19	4a $1\frac{1}{2}$r	$1\frac{1}{2}$d.	18
Nicholas *de* Paxton	7	2a 1r	—	6
John super le Wal	3	1r	1d.	3
Henry Quenyne	2	2r + house ($\frac{1}{4}$d.)	—	1

Name of Lessee	No. of Properties	Land	Rent	No. of Lessors
John Quenyng, carnifex	8	3a 3r	—	8
Walter Quenyng	1	3r	—	1
heirs of Roger Faber	1	1r	—	1
heirs of Reginald son of Thomas Balle	6	8a 2r	1d.	6
John son of William *de* Leirstowe	1	—	$\frac{1}{2}$d.	1
heirs of William Manipenny	18	14a 1$\frac{1}{2}$r	$\frac{3}{4}$d.	15
Hugh Gile	2	2r	—	2
Robert Garlop	4	1a 2r	—	4
Walter Ede	3	2a $\frac{1}{2}$r	$\frac{1}{2}$d.	3
Godfrey super Murum	2	2r	—	2
William Juel	3	2a 3$\frac{1}{2}$r	—	3
William Gile	6	1a 3$\frac{1}{2}$r	—	(6)
heirs of Simon Ingelond	9	1a	1d.	(8)
John Pikering	9	4a $\frac{1}{3}$ of an acre + 2r	(2$\frac{1}{4}$d.)	(7)
John Pope	4	1a $\frac{1}{2}$r	—	4
heirs of Eusebius Pope	4	(1a $\frac{1}{2}$r)	—	4
Roger son of William Manipenny	8	(3r)	(1$\frac{1}{4}$d.)	8
John son of William Manipenny	3	$\frac{1}{2}$r	1$\frac{1}{2}$d.	3
Robert *de* Bluntisham	1	1r	—	1
John Mariner	3	1a 1r	—	3
William *le* Mason	3	$\frac{1}{2}$ 'virgate' + 3r	$\frac{1}{4}$d.	3
John Couper	1	—	1d.	1
Godfrey Cokayn	2	2r	1$\frac{1}{2}$d.	2
Godfrey apud *le* Barre	4	3r	—	4
John Balde	1	1a	—	1
William Bonis	3	3$\frac{1}{2}$r	—	3
Reginald Balle, sutor	1	1r	—	1
Emma Scot	3	3a $\frac{1}{2}$r	—	3
Gilbert son of Eusebius in Venella	7	6a 2r	$\frac{1}{4}$d.	7
heirs of Richard *de* Lincoln	5	1a $\frac{1}{2}$r	$\frac{1}{4}$d.	5
Richard Mercator	1	1r	—	1
John Miller	(9)	(2a 1r)	($\frac{1}{4}$d.)	(9)
William [Goni]	1	$\frac{1}{4}$a	—	1
heirs of [?] Augustine	1	3r	—	1
heirs of [?] Sutor	3	(1r)	(1d.)	3
Reginald Spicer	22	(5a 3$\frac{1}{2}$r)	(2d.)	(22)
John Scot	5	1a 3$\frac{1}{2}$r	—	5
Cristina Marewele	2	1a	—	1
Simon *le* Longe	1	2r	—	1
Godfrey son of Reginald in Venella	1	1a 2r	—	1
John Brond	2	1$\frac{1}{2}$r	—	2
Matilda in Venella	2	3a	—	1
John son of Reginald son of John	2	1a 2r	—	2
Alan Miller	11	4a 3$\frac{1}{2}$r	3d.	9

Name of Lessee	No. of Properties	Land	Rent	No. of Lessors
Gilbert son of John	(1)	3a 3½r	—	(1)
Thomas son of John	1	1½a	—	1
Henry son of John	1	(3r)	—	1
[?] Reginald son of John	5	2a	½d.	5
William Colion	2	1r	¼d.	1
Reginald son of Edward Goni	1	1r	—	1
Gilbert *de* Strateshylle	1	1r	—	1
John son of William Godisbrond	2	1½r	—	2
John son of Robert Maddermonger	4	1½r	¼d.	4
Elena Fayreheved	(1)	—	1d.	(1)

Total: 394 acres + ¼ rod + 2½ 'virgates' + 2 crofts + ⅔acre + 1 house
Rent: 10s. 1¼d.

TABLE 17: SUBLETTING LIST NO. 3, CA. 1320-1325[a]

Name of Lessee	No. of Properties	Land	Rent	No. of Lessors
ARNYNG STREET				
Henry Rode	20	10a 3r + messuage	2d.	16
Godfrey Pademor	2	2r	—	2
William son of William Manipenny	10	7a 3½r	—	9
Roger Edward	1	½a	—	1
John son of William Seman	1	—	½d.	1
Godfrey son of Eusebius	2	1a 3r	—	2
heirs of Richard Das	3	3r	½d.	3
Stephen son of John Seman	1	1½r	—	1
heirs of Reginald Frere	2	2r	—	2
John son of Thomas Gildene	9	2a 3r	2d.	9
Lawrence Julian	2	2a	—	1
John atte Broke	4	1a	—	4
heirs of John Drewe	1	3a ½r	—	1
Simon Legge	9	6a 1½r	2d.	6
heirs of Martin Aylred	3	2½r	½d.	3
William son of Reginald Aylred	5	1a 2½r	—	5
heirs of Eusebius Cook	3	1a 1½r	½d.	3
William *de* Gransden[b]	2	½a	½d.	2
Dionysia Aylred	3	1a 1r	—	3
William son of William Aylred	4	1a ½r	1d.	4
Robert Legge	3	1½a	—	3
Henry son of John Clerk	1	1r	—	1
John son of John Clerk	1	1r	—	1
Richard Gildene	4	1a 2r	1d.	4

[a] Box 1, bundle 1.
[b] This is entirely stroked out.

Name of Lessee	No. of Properties	Land	Rent	No. of Lessors
Henry Spruntyng	1	$^1/_2$r	—	1
William *le* Rede	4	1a	1$^1/_4$d.	4
William son of William *le* Rede	1	1r	—	1
Reginald Seman	4	3$^1/_2$r	—	4
Amicia Fole	1	2r	—	1
Godfrey Caterina	5	1a 2$^1/_2$r	1d.	5
John Seman	3	1a	—	3
Simon Julian	2	1a	—	2
heirs of William Clerk	5	1a 2r	—	5
Stephen Clerk	4	1a	$^1/_4$d.	4
heirs of Simon Godwar	1	—	1d.	1
John Longe junior	2	1$^1/_2$r	—	2
Nicholas son of Simon Parson	1	1r	—	—
William Outy	1	1r	—	1
Elena Cook	2	3r	—	2
Cristina Cook junior	1	1$^1/_2$r	—	1
Pellagia Cook	1	1r	—	1
Roger *de* Croxton	1	$^1/_2$r	—	1

OFFORD

Godfrey Chapman	1	1r	—	1
heirs of Ralph Palmer	1	2r	—	—

PAPWORTH

John Waryn	3	3r	—	3
Roger Hokerylle	1	1r	—	1
William Miller	1	1$^1/_2$r	—	1
heirs of Walter Barton	6	1a 3$^1/_2$r	—	6
John Roberd	2	3r	—	2
William *de* Kent	1	2r	—	1

HEMINGFORD

Thomas Marshall	4	1a	$^1/_2$d.	4
William Everard	3	2r	—	3
Ralph ad capud Ville	1	1r	$^1/_4$d.	1
John Ingel	2	1r	$^1/_4$d.	2
Robert *le* Newman	2	1$^1/_2$r	—	2
John Plomber, mercator	1	1r	—	1

HUNTINGDON [c]

Richard Bully	1	2r	—	1
heirs of William *de* Stukeley	5	4a $^1/_2$r	$^1/_4$d.	5

[c] Many of the names of these tenants at Godmanchester also appear as holding Huntingdon town properties from Hinchingbrooke Priory (Public Record Office: sc 11/ 10) and as witnesses to charters ("Chartulary of St. Mary's Priory, Huntingdon," British Library, Cotton Faust 1). I owe these references to Drs. Anne and Edwin DeWindt.

Name of Lessee	No. of Properties	Land	Rent	No. of Lessors
John *de* Hemington	4	1a 1r	$^1/_2$d.	4
heirs of John *de* Stirtloe	1	3r	—	1
St. Mary of the Church of All Saints	3	1a 1r	—	3
John Clerk *de* Houghton	12	4a 2$^1/_2$r	1$^1/_4$d.	11
John Aurifaber	4	1a 1r	$^1/_4$d.	4
Martin *le* Rede	19	6a 3r	4$^1/_2$d.	18
Mabel *le* Rede	2	1a	1$^1/_4$d.	2
Henry Underspitel, tinctor	1	—	—	1
John Anfred	1	1a	—	1
John Thomeston	6	1a	$^1/_4$d.	6
Stephen *de* Norfolk	2	2$^1/_2$r	—	2
Thomas *de* Luton	19	6a 2$^1/_2$r	3$^1/_4$d.	18
Nicholas *de* Hardley	11	3a 1$^1/_2$r	2$^1/_2$d.	11
William de Hemingford, clerk	2	2r	$^3/_4$d.	2
Paul Begenore	1	3r	—	1
Hugh *de* Gidding	9	4a 3r	1d.	8
Robert *de* Hitchin	3	4a 1r	$^1/_2$d.	3
John Marshall	13	3a 2$^1/_2$r	2$^3/_4$d.	13
Michael *de* Colne	1	1$^1/_2$r	—	—
widow of Little William	1	1r	—	1
John *de* Bilneye	8	2a 3$^1/_2$r	$^3/_4$d.	8
Little Roger	1	$^1/_2$a	—	1
Thomas Aldous	4	1a 2r	—	4
heirs of Reginald Godoun	5	1a 3r	—	5
widow of John Crane	1	$^1/_2$r	—	—
widow of Roger *de* Upton	2	1a 3$^1/_2$r	—	2
Hugh *de* Mattishale	7	1a $^1/_2$r	4$^1/_4$d.	5
Richard *de* Todenham	3	$^1/_2$r	1$^1/_2$d.	3
John Russell	7	2a 2$^1/_2$r	3$^1/_4$d.	7
Alice Silverle	1	—	$^1/_2$d.	1
heirs of Robert Buldir	1	—	$^3/_4$d.	1
widow of Serle Tinctor	8	1a 2$^1/_2$r	2$^1/_4$d.	8
Elias Tannator	3	1a $^1/_2$r	—	3
Lawrence Tinctor	23	13a $^1/_2$r	3d.	23
John son of Richard Tinctor	13	3a 1$^1/_2$r	1d.	12
John Clerk *de* Hemingford	22	4a 2r	4$^1/_4$d.	18

Total: 152 acres + 1$^1/_2$ rods + 1 messuage
Rent: 4s. 9$^1/_2$d.

Each of the above lists adds a new dimension to the simple horizontal perspective of Godmanchester property given in the Hundred Roll. Acres of arable become acres sown with this or that crop of grain, meadow becomes the producer of so many fleeces and lambs; the ownership of many units of lands revolves at a rather phenomenal rate. In short, each

dimension brings us one step closer to the complete picture of the disposition of wealth at Godmanchester around 1300.

The sowing and sheep lists suggest that there were considerably more individuals directly involved in the exploitation of property than the 453 indicated by the 1279 Hundred Roll. The 199 landholders of the sowing and sheep list of 1334 can probably be tripled to give a total of six hundred land-holders since the forty-four wealthier persons who appear on it are a third of the 131 individuals of the 1334 lay subsidy list. Despite the lack of precision of this sort of calculation, there are other indications that support evidence for a wider spread of landholding. Messuages apart, there are slightly fewer than 100 individuals with one acre or less in 1279 while in the 1334 fragment of sowing and sheep list there are about 50 individuals with sown lands of an acre or less.

The subletting lists show the considerable velocity in the turnover of land holding at Godmanchester rather than adding to our knowledge of the greater spread. In short, for the early fourteenth century at least, a *de facto* concentration of control over the productive use of large amounts of land could coexist with the wide spread of the legal tenure of the same properties.

GREATER AGRARIAN ZONE

Consideration of the property spread at Godmanchester cannot be limited to the people of the town and the perimeter of the parish. As has been discussed in the previous chapter, Godmanchester had a positive policy of encouragement for outsiders wishing to invest in the town.[15] Over the long run, the consistent pattern of outsiders in the town is as much a part of the local economic scene as the nature of family property spread throughout the town. A list of such people (Table 18) acquiring land as indicated in the court roll demonstrates a continuing interest in Godmanchester land from places within a four to five mile radius. It should be noted that a list from the court rolls differs from the large numbers of neighbouring people identified as subletting land (above, Table 17) and owning sown property and sheep at Godmanchester.[16] Whereas the latter were not resident, many of those acquiring land through the court roll became residents of Godmanchester.

---

[15] Undoubtedly Godmanchester people also looked beyond the town for economic opportunities, but our sources for such activity are too uneven to allow comparison. For example, in the Huntingdonshire *Calendar of the Feet of Fines* (ed. G. J. Turner [London, 1913]) only John in the Lane (1 messuage) and William Aylred (1 messuage) of Godmanchester held property in Huntingdon.

[16] See pp. 101-118.

A summary of those acquiring property at Godmanchester in this fashion is given in Table 18. The actual list of names (Table 28) better indicates the consistency and variety of individuals involved in acquiring Godmanchester lands.

TABLE 18: NEIGHBOURING VILLAGES ACQUIRING GODMANCHESTER LAND

	1278-1300	1301-1325	1326-1348	1349-1399
Brampton (3 miles west)	4	1	—	7
Graveley (5 miles south)	4	2	1	15
Hartford (2 miles north)	9	6	2	15
Hemingford (3 miles northeast)	5	3	23	43
Houghton (2½ miles northeast)	6	7	1	1
Huntingdon (¼ mile north)	4	28	79	100
Offord (3 miles southwest)	2	11	6	14
Papworth (4 miles west)	5	7	17	8
Yelling (5¼ miles south)	—	9	3	12

Radius: 4-5 miles

MAP 3. THE GODMANCHESTER LAND MARKET ZONE

B. THE OCCUPATIONAL ROLL AT GODMANCHESTER

The development of an adequate methodology for measurement of the economic value of natural and acquired skills in pre-industrial society is a task still awaiting the historian. In the era before the labour-saving devices of modern technology, the capital required by traditional skills is not easily assessed. When many skills were employed on a part-time basis, comparative wage scales are of little value. On the positive side, increasing help is forthcoming for the economic historian in judging the value of labour from detailed work on the history of technology, nor can the assistance of the historian of art be neglected in assessing the incidence of various skills.[17]

In the meantime there is abundant evidence to the effect that there was a highly developed division of labour in the small towns and villages of fourteenth-century England. Occupational surnames are a vital clue to this sophistication, albeit just the most superficial of indicators. For the town of Godmanchester itself occupational surnames before the Black Death indicate a wide range of specialization:[18] barber, barker (tanner), carter, carpenter, *cooperator* (couper), *carnifex* (butcher), combere, cook, coleman, faber (smith), fisher (*piscator*), flaxmonger, gardener, hering-monger, hosier, ironmonger, leter, locksmith, merchant (chapman, *mercator*, mercer), maddermonger (warenter), mason, miller, oylemaker, *pelliparius* (skinner), pellage (skinner), peyntour, *pistor* (baker), plowrighte (wheel-maker), ridilister, *seuster*, shepherd, speller, spenser, spicer, *sutor* (cobbler), *taberium*, taylor, *textor* (weaver), tileman, *tinctor*, waterleder, webester, wodeward.

For the period from 1349 to 1399 scribes appended the following occupations to surnames: *braciator*, brazier, butcher, carpenter, cook, *cooperator* (couper), draper, faber (smith), foster, garlickmonger, hay-ward, hosier, lockyer, maddermonger, malter, merchant (chapman, *mercator*, mercer), miller, mason, *pattisarius* (pastry maker), *piscator* (fisher), plowrighte (wheel-maker), shepherd, spayder, *sutor* (cobbler), taylor, thatcher, wollemonger and webester.

One of the most important aspects of the "expert" in pre-industrial society was his frequent association with considerable geographical mobility. In short, it was because specialized persons could service a large

---

[17] For some further analysis of economic implications of some occupations see Chapter 5 below, pp. 189-201.

[18] Parentheses indicate alternative forms employed from the late thirteenth century.

area that smallish towns and villages could afford to pay for such expertise and, in turn, a great variety of experts could make a living. The wide geographical range from which occupational specialists could be drawn upon at Godmanchester is indicated by the following lists. In the Huntingdonshire area[19] as for London itself,[20] the two generations and more before the Black Death were transitional in the use of occupational names as surnames. For this reason, in Table 19 the pre-1348 list of those with occupational surnames (Section A) has been distinguished below from those with occupational designations appended to the surname (Section B). From the mid-fourteenth century it may be taken for granted that occupational surnames, having long since dropped the telltale *le* designation, are no longer a guide to the actual practitioners of various specializations. As a result, Section C below is limited to individuals after 1348 whose occupation has been specified separately from their name.

TABLE 19: TRADES AND MERCHANTS, 1278-1399

Section A: 1278-1348

Trade Surname	1278-1325	1326-1348	Provenance[a]
Aurifaber, Nicholas	1279		Huntingdon
Aurifaber, William	1315		Huntingdon
Aurifaber, John	1315		Huntingdon
Barker, Robert		1342	Great Paxton
Barker, Richard		1346	Graveley (Cambs.)
Barker, Thomas		1330	Huntingdon
Barker, John *le*		1326	Huntingdon
Boweyer, Robert *le*	1295		Huntingdon
Candelmaker, Richard		1329	St. Ives
Carpenter, Richard	1301		Sawtry
Carpenter, Adam	1313		Henlow (Beds.)
Carpenter, Roger *le*	1302		Huntingdon
Carter, John	1316		Barnwell (Northants.)
Chapman, Ralph	1303		Offord
Chapman, Reginald	1298		Norfolk (Norf.)
Chapman, John	1281		Huntingdon
Chapman, John		1341	Offord
Chapman, Reginald		1331	Woodnewton (Northants.)
Chapman, Richard		1333	Little Stukeley
Cooperator, William	1311		Papworth (Cambs.)
Cooperator, William brother of William	1311		Papworth (Cambs.)

[a] All places are in Huntingdonshire unless otherwise noted. Places with an asterisk are unidentified.

[19] See Raftis, ed, *Beyond Town and Vill* (unpublished manuscript).

[20] Eilert Ekwall, *Studies on the Population of Medieval London* (Stockholm, 1956).

Trade Surname	1278-1325	1326-1348	Provenance
Cooperator, Phillip	1311		Papworth (Cambs.)
Combere, Robert	1280		Huntingdon
Corneseyer, Henry *le*	1301		Huntingdon
Couper, Robert	1321		Catworth
Couper, Hammond son of John	1321		Kinslingbury (Cambs.)
Couper, Roger		1340	Little Stukeley
Couper, Thomas *le*		1331	Sibthorpe (Notts.)
Couper, Thomas		1346	Huntingdon
Couper, Thomas		1327	Great Stukeley
Cook, Robert	1308		Kingston (Cambs.)
Faber, Ivo	1290		Papworth (Cambs.)
Faber, John	1279		Leighton
Faber, Richard	1278		Huntingdon
Faber, John		1340	Polesbrook (Northants.)
Fisher, Henry	1322		Huntingdon
Fisher, John	1321		Offord Cluny
Fisher, John	1322		Brampton
Fisher, Ralph		1330	Offord Cluny
Fisher, Richard son of Dany		1327	Paxton
Flaxmonger, Hugh		1332	Erle*
Goldsmith, John		1344	Huntingdon
Horseman, Walter *le*	1318		Huntingdon
Horseman, John son of Walter *le*	1318		Huntingdon
Lister, Lawrence *le*, son of William	1320		Huntingdon
Lister, Henry son of Lawrence		1327	Huntingdon
Lister, John son of Lawrence		1326	Huntingdon
Lorimer, Thomas	1279		Huntingdon
Lorimer, John	1319		Huntingdon
Lorimer, John and William sons of John		1330	Huntingdon
Mercator, Thomas		1329	Huntingdon
Miller, John	1308		Sawtry
Miller, Nicholas	1323		Papworth (Cambs.)
Miller, Godfrey	1323		Hemingford
Miller, Hugh	1310		Houghton
Miller, Godfrey son of Hugh	1310		Houghton
Miller, John	1310		Hemingford Grey
Miller, William son of Henry		1332	St. Neots
Milner, John *le*	1322		Eynesbury
Oylemaker, Roger		1346	Huntingdon
Parker, Godfrey *le*	1324		Buckden
Ploughwrighte, Thomas		1340	Stukeley
Shepherd, Nicholas		1332	Papworth (Cambs.)
Skinner, John		1335	Houghton
Spicer, Reginald	1303		Papworth (Cambs.)
Sutor, Gilbert *le*	1306		Hilton
Sutor, John	1311		Offord Cluny
Sutor, Reginald son of William	1280		Alconbury
Sutor, Ralph		1338	Offord Cluny

Trade Surname	1278-1325	1326-1348	Provenance
Taylor, William	1311		Shoreham/Scorham (Kent)
Taylor, Jurdan le	1298		Hemingford
Taylor, Walter le		1344	Dorchester (Dorset)
Tannator, John	1317		Buckden
Tannator, John son of John	1311		Croxton (Cambs.)
Tinctor, Richard	1321		St. Neots
Tinctor, Peter	1281		Hemingford
Tinctor, William le	1279		Huntingdon
Tinctor, Roger	1283		Huntingdon
Tinctor, Lawrence[b]	1299		Huntingdon
Tinctor, Richard	1279		Huntingdon
Triturator, Thomas	1316		Holland Wood
Vinur, Nicholas le	1296		Hemingford
Webester, Bartholomew		1345	Vicus Canonicorum
Yacher, William le	1302		Papworth (Cambs.)
Yacher, Richard	1302		St. Neots

Section B: 1278-1348

Surname	1278-1325	1326-1348	Trade	Provenance
Barbour, Gilbert le	1325		merchant	Sudbury (Suffolk)
Baroun, John son of Thomas de Merton	1325		merchant	Cambridge (Cambs.)
Benyt, Henry		1334	merchant	Oundle (Northants.)
Boy, William		1327	piscator	Huntingdon
Broughton, Robert	1316		piscator	St. Ives
Bully, Richard	1307		pistor	Huntingdon
Catworth, John	1299		carter	Catworth
Chaplain, Elias		1332	tannator	Huntingdon
Chatteris, John	1325		merchant	St. Ives
Cumberton, Warin	1302		textor	Comberton (Cambs.)
Gidding, Robert		1348	glover	Gidding
Godsweyn, Ralph	1320		triturator	Dunstable (Beds.)
Houghton, John	1324		pelliparius	Houghton
Kingston, Roger le		1329	wodeward	Kingston (Cambs.)
Leighton, John		1338	faber	Leighton
Leuman, John		1348	buyer	London
Lincoln, John	1312		sutor	Lincoln (Lincs.)
Quenyng, Henry	1325		tinctor	Biggleswade (Beds.)
Raveley, John		1342	lister	St. Neots
Ripton, John	1301		mason	Graveley (Cambs.)
Sawtry, Thomas	1308		miller	Sawtry
Sawtry, John	1308		miller	Sawtry
William, Richard		1328	pistor	Huntingdon

[b] Lawrence Tinctor also was noted as Lawrence le Lister.

Section c: 1349-1399

Surname	Date	Trade	Provenance
Ayshere, Roger	1366	shepherd	Hemingford Abbots
Baltoun, John	1365	carpenter	Quy (Cambs.)
Bernwelle, Henry	1366	mason	Barnwell (Northants.)
Beverle, William	1391	wright	Beverley (East Yorks.)
Bocher, Edmund	1361	butcher	Huntingdon
Bocher, John	1381	butcher	Huntingdon
Boltolf, Henry	1388	malter	Elsworth (Cambs.)
Bonde, John	1371	piscator	Huntingdon
Boterler, John senior	1390	bottle maker	Huntingdon
Chapman, John	1389	merchant	Hekelynton*
Cook, William son of Robert ye	1354	cook	Kingston (Cambs.)
Cook, John	1382	cook	Stukeley
Cook, John	1349	cook	Deopham (Norf.)
Cook, Alan	1393	cook	Ely (Cambs.)
Cook, William	1361	cook	Hemingford Abbots
Draper, John	1361	draper	Bassingbourn (Cambs.)
Draper, William	1380	draper	Swavesey
Faber, Godfrey	1385	faber	Houghton
Faber, Ralph	1349	faber	Huntingdon
Fauconner, Roger	1349	falconner	Toseland
Faukener, John	1385	falconner	Over (Cambs.)
Fisher, Andrew	1388	fisherman	Offord Cluny
Fisher, Simon	1388	fisherman	Huntingdon
Fuller, John	1379	fuller	Bluntisham
Fuller, Walter	1369	fuller	Offord Cluny
Gardener, Richard ye	1351	gardener	Hemingford Abbots
Goldsmith, John	1382	goldsmith	Hemingford Abbots
Hartford, John	1357	mason	Hartford
Herde, William le	1352	herde keeper	(Steeple) Bumpstead (Essex)
Kylpyn, Godfrey	1385	smith	Houghton
Lanne, John	1378	malter	Eynesbury
Leycester, Simon	1386	tyler	Leicester (Leics.)
Lister, Henry	1391	lister	Fen Stanton
Lister, John ye	1353	lister	St. Ives
Lister, Simon	1385	spicer	St. Ives
Malter, Henry	1382	malter	Huntingdon
Malter, William le	1354	malter	Offord Cluny
Mason, John	1357	mason	Hartford
Mason, Robert	1399	mason	Huntingdon
Mason, John	1357	mason	Hemingford
Mercer, William	1364	merchant	Offord Cluny
Michel, John	1388	malter	Eltisley (Cambs.)
Milner, Nicholas le	1349	miller	St. Ives
Milner, John	1374	miller	Eltisley (Cambs.)
Musterder, Henry ye	1354	mustard seller or maker	Barnwell (Northants.)

Surname	Date	Trade	Provenance
Outy, Reyner	1377	faber	London
Plowrighte, John	1361	plow maker	Offord Darcy
Plowrighte, Thomas	1360	plow maker	Stambourne (Essex)
Plowrighte, William	1373	plow maker	Hemingford Abbots
Plowrighte, Thomas	1361	plow maker	Offord Darcy
Poyser, Adam *ye*	1352	purse keeper	Conter Habirdayste*
Prycke, John	1375	roper	Wisbech (Cambs.)
Sadeler, John	1357	saddle maker	Huntingdon
Shepherd, William	1361	shepherd	Shengay (Cambs.)
Skinner, William	1399	skinner	St. Neots
Sonerdonne, Thomas	1351	draper	Sundon (Beds.)
Smith, Thomas	1392	smith	Huntingdon
Spicer, John	1366	spicer	Huntingdon
Tavener, Alan	1366	taverner	Huntingdon
Taylor, Robert	1369	taylor	Ellington Thorpe
Taylor, Robert	1380	taylor	Pittisle*
Taylor, Walter	1362	taylor	Papworth (Cambs.)
Taylor, William	1393	taylor	Fen Drayton (Cambs.)
Taylor, John	1364	fisher	Huntingdon
Thorpe, John	1356	merchant	Ellington Thorpe
Thressher, (Simon)	1349	thresher	Cornwall (Cambs.)
Turnour, William	1347	turner	Wennington
Ufton, John	1391	glover	Huntingdon
Webester, John	1391	webester	Huntingdon
Welewryte, John	1390	carpenter	Huntingdon
Wrighte, William	1393	carpenter	Hemingford

**

From the records at hand it seems possible to attempt a descriptive sketch of Godmanchester around 1300. With the 1279 Hundred Roll as the main backdrop, it would seem that one street (Post Street?) housed most of the wealthy townsmen, whether their wealth was in land or merchandise. Here, within a few yards of one another were those halls, houses and gardens where the court was held: Warenter, Grinde, Leyrstowe, *le* Masun. The remaining three streets housed a larger number of relatively modest townsmen, with some cluster of tenants who held little more than a low-cost (in farm terms) messuage. One might suggest that these less valuable clusters of holdings were on the fringes of the town reflecting expansion along the country roads.[21] Expansion towards

---

[21] See H. J. M. Green, *Godmanchester* (Cambridge, 1977), p. 32.

the river would be at the expense of valuable meadow and the messuages
in this area, such as those leased from Merton Priory (and in the vicinity
of the priory?) were held by some of the wealthiest men of the town!

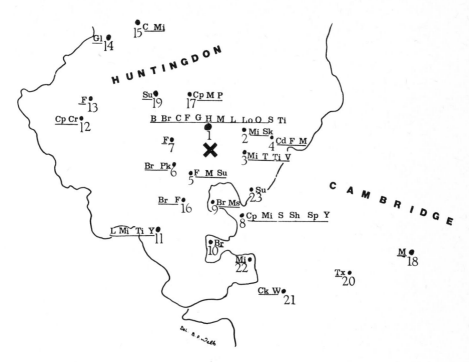

MAP 4. SOME REGIONAL SKILLED LABOUR RESOURCES DRAWN UPON BY
GODMANCHESTER, 1278-1348

Villages		Occupations	
× Godmanchester		B: Baker	Ms: Mason
		Br: Barker	O: Oylemaker
1 – Huntingdon	13 – Leighton	C: Carpenter	P: Ploughwrighte
2 – Houghton	14 – Gidding	Cd: Candelmaker	Pk: Parker
3 – Hemingford	15 – Sawtry	Ck: Cook	S: Smith
4 – St. Ives	16 – Gt. Paxton	Cp: Couper	Sh: Shepherd
5 – Offord Cluney	17 – Stukeley	Cr: Carter	Sk: Skinner
6 – Buckden	18 – Cambridge	F: Fisher	Sp: Spicer
7 – Brampton	19 – Alconbury	G: Goldsmith	Su: Sutor
8 – Papworth	20 – Comberton	Gl: Glover	T: Taylor
9 – Graveley	21 – Kingston	H: Horseman	Ti: Tinctor
10 – Croxton	22 – Eynesbury	L: Lister	Tx: Textor
11 – St. Neots	23 – Hilton	Lo: Lorimer	V: Vinur
12 – Catworth		M: Merchant	W: Wodeward
		Mi: Miller	Y: Yacher

Expansion appears to be a properly expressive term for conditions in the late thirteenth-century history of Godmanchester since the population of the town very likely was at one of the highest points of its history. In this respect, the 378 [22] messuages of the Hundred Roll are not at all indicative of the actual number of dwelling units. There is enough information in the court rolls to indicate that a messuage was only part of a complex unit including a courtyard (*curtilagium*) and several buildings. The courtyard was subdivided into units called "beddis"[23] or "cris"[24] presumably for garden and pasture. Houses, cottages and other buildings are described distinct from messuages.[25]

The great effort made to preserve rights of way in court roll conveyances attests further to this tangled subdividing of the messuage complexes. The following entry is typical of a score and more of references to right of way:

> Lawrence Julian takes seisin of a garden bought from John Grantesden and his wife Pellagia, with entry from the King's Road to that grange and the whole part of a wall bought from the same. While the said John and Pellagia hold the "capital" house they shall have right of way and whenever the said John and Pellagia should lease, sell or give their capital house that right of way shall be totally and completely reserved to the said Lawrence and not let to anyone else. (28 October 1316)[26]

For this smallish town at least, the late thirteenth century pattern appears to be rather different from the compact row houses of early industrial England or even the solid street fronts that have survived from Elizabethan times. One might better envisage the social living conditions as basically those of the modified estate — a household complex composed of several living units as well as subdivided properties and buildings. Servants,[27] relatives or others could be housed in rooms or separate residences. A tangle of paths and lanes facilitates access to buildings and separated the many subdivisions of the plots. In the variety of its component elements, although not necessarily in the quality of these, the messuage complex at Godmanchester resembled more the *curia* of the lord in a village than the villager's tenement.[28]

---

[22] If each messuage represented a commonable unit there were almost twice as many such units in 1279 as in 1514.

[23] See above, Chapter 1, p. 21.

[24] See above, Chapter 1, p. 22.

[25] See above, Chapter 1, pp. 21-23; see further on these points, Chapter 5, pp. 216-228.

[26] Box 7, bundle 1.

[27] See above, Chapter 1, pp. 29, 31.

[28] For an admirable description of these contrasting units, see P. D. A. Harvey, *A Medieval Oxfordshire Village* (Oxford, 1965), pp. 27 and 32 ff.

The "external" view of Godmanchester presented in Chapter 3 provides a useful corrective to the previous two chapters. One might think that the family laws of Godmanchester — necessarily studied as phenomena internal to the town in Chapter 1 — possibly generated a rather equalitarian society owing to the many titles to property from family membership alone. The settlement pattern depicted in Chapter 3 provides us with the best possible visual overview of the town until further mapping can become available with archaeological research. This overview leaves us in no doubt about the existence of widely divergent wealth patterns both within families as well as among different families. One might also conclude that the strong self-government machinery of Godmanchester described in Chapter 2 set the town apart from the world around it. But when Godmanchester has been seen in Chapter 3 from the point of view of outsiders involved in the town, it becomes clear that God-manchester is part of a much larger agrarian complex and for more sophisticated commercial and occupational purposes is part of a large regional entity.

Legal, social and economic structures as such — whether internal or external to the town — have taken us only so far in the effort to understand Godmanchester. It becomes obvious that the lives of the people themselves must inform us further. To the task of extracting this information we now turn.

Part Two

History Through the Family

4

Introducing the People of Godmanchester

A. DIFFERENT FAMILIES – DIFFERENT STORIES

Graphic representation of family trees has long been a convenient device for the ready identification of degrees of affinity and consanguinity. And yet, for the historian, the family tree can be misleading from the very fact of its linear simplicity. As the repository of most intimate human experiences as well as the locale in traditional society of those most elemental events called birth and death, the family more than any other social institution reflects the individuality and variety possible to the human condition. This point is manifested for Godmanchester by the manner in which even a prosaic court of land fines and entry fees introduces to us a wide variety and number of individuals and families. Social history is indeed only possible by isolation of common patterns which in this study are the common features of family identification, life cycle organization and economic roles. And yet, such common patterns blur the more individual features that are present in the full texts of God-manchester court rolls. For this reason, we introduce Chapter 4 by some samples of the variety of contexts in which individuals and families appear in these court rolls. The various texts employed throughout the volume are, of course, the most fully representative of details of family life to be found in the court rolls.

In the families illustrated below, some quite modest families draw considerable attention to themselves through litigation (Julian), other smallish families that are apparent newcomers to the town take greater care to register familial property conveyances (Dosyn, Gidding), while more affluent families (Garlop, Goni, Manipenny, Rede, Spruntyng) leave a record of themselves by the sheer bulk of their economic activity or of their wealth. On the other hand, families such as the Hopay are prominent in the record through a combination of litigation and at least sporadic affluence.

The bundle of Godmanchester court rolls for the year 1278-1279 begins with the court held in the feast of St. Dunstan the archbishop (19 May) in the 6th year of King Edward I (1278). In the first entry of this court we are told that "on the same day John Mason and his wife Lina appear with a royal writ against Mariota the daughter of Simon Julian regarding three rods of land and the court orders that she be summoned." The second entry of the court is similar: "On the same day Osbert the son of Gilbert and his wife Mariota appear with a royal writ against Simon the son of William the son of Julian about one half acre of land, and against Richard the son of William the son of Julian about a half acre of land and it is ordered that they be summoned." At the following court, on the Thursday before the feast of St. Barnabas the Apostle, brief entries state that the three Julians are summoned concerning a land plea and that this is the second summons. In the following court the third summons to the three parties was delivered. Notice of distraint upon the three Julians follows in the next three courts. The Julians were then essoined three times, the essoin of Mariota being a Robert Julian. Next the Julians pledge warranty. Then the Julians request an investigation (view of the land). During the period of this investigation the Julians continued to be essoined.

Why the Julians procrastinated is not clear to the historian since the jury of twelve townsmen finally came down with a verdict on the Thursday after the feast of the conversion of St. Paul (25 January 1279) in favour of the Julian title to these properties. Gradually, with the many entries the courts of this year drop "the son of" before Julian and simply adopt the latter as the surname. Indeed, while Simon becomes involved in another series of pleas later in 1279, reference to him in court changes from Simon the son of William Julian (May) to Simon Julian (August). Mariota Julian disappeared from the court records after 1279, perhaps owing to change of surname with marriage. However, a later entry in the courts of 1279 tells us that her apparent uncle Richard with his wife Isolda together sublet property. Richard and Isolda had a daughter Isabella who received property by bequest of her father in 1291. Perhaps they had a younger son Godfrey since Isolda and her son Godfrey sublet property together in 1279.

Both Richard and Robert Julian held property in the 1279 Hundred Roll lists for Godmanchester (a messuage, one croft, 7 acres of arable and 3 acres 2 rods of meadow; a messuage, 8 acres of arable, 1 and one half acres of meadow). This is undoubtedly the Robert who essoined for Mariota for later in 1279 he is identified as the son of William Julian when he sublet property. At the sale of property in 1302 we learn that the

wife of Robert was called Amicia. Robert's children are identified as Godfrey and Millicent in 1279. The families of Richard and Robert Julian disappear from Godmanchester by the early fourteenth century. Whether the Amicia conveying land in 1329 is the elderly widow of Robert one cannot be certain. Furthermore, a Simon son of Robert (1327) and Isabella daughter of Robert (1329) appear only in one isolated context so that their parentage remains uncertain.

Greater continuity at Godmanchester can be found for another Julian family, that of Alan and his wife Isolda who sublet property in 1279. We cannot determine whether Alan was a brother of William. However, Alan had a son Lawrence who bought a messuage in 1305 and two daughters, Leticia and Millicent, who conveyed property to their brother Lawrence in 1311. Lawrence is the only Julian taxed in the lay subsidy rolls of the early fourteenth century. In 1309 he was one of the poorer of those whose chattels have been listed, with only a total value of 12s. 5d. in taxable goods.[1] Lawrence married someone whose first name we know to be Isolda and Lawrence and Isolda were active in buyng an orchard and selling off bits of property over 1315-1317. By 1320, Isolda was widowed since executors sold off some of Lawrence's property and Isolda herself sold to Reginald Spruntyng and wife a house that she had formerly purchased from them. Lawrence and Isolda certainly had two daughters, Cristina and Elena, identified as the children of the former in land conveyances of 1327. Owing to the rather unusual first name of Lawrence, a Lawrence Julian who by the 1340s held land and had a son John, may have been the son of Lawrence who was dead by 1320 although the gap in time is considerable. In any case, the family name of Julian disappeared from Godmanchester with the Black Death.

Individuals taking their name from the central Huntingdonshire village of Gidding appear infrequently in the land market of Godmanchester (William, 1282; Alice, 1308; John son of Henry, 1353). A certain Henry *de* Gidding did establish a family in Godmanchester. Although the surname Gidding appears neither in the 1279 Hundred Roll, nor the lay subsidy taxation records of later decades, Henry was able to provide lands for a substantial family of five children — Godfrey, Hugh, Phillipa, Sabina and Margaret. We obtain considerable information about this family because the children of Henry except Sabina were either unwilling or unable to continue the family name in the town. Upon the death of Henry in 1307, his son Godfrey sold two acres three and one half rods of

---

[1] See Raftis and Hogan, *Lay Subsidy Rolls*, p. 122.

his inheritance; Godfrey bought land in 1309 but sold it shortly afterwards and over 1310-1311 sold three units of arable (3 acres, one half acre, one half acre). At his marriage to Elizabeth in 1297, Hugh *de* Gidding provided by dower that his unspecified land should go to Elizabeth and their possible children. In the following year Hugh released a messuage to the prior of Merton and sold a further acre of arable and 6 "cris" of meadow. If Hugh had any children these would appear to have been daughters only since Margaret and Joan, daughters of Hugh *de* Gidding, are mentioned in the land market from the 1320s.

Two of Henry *de* Gidding's daughters gave up their lands very quickly. Phillipa gave up all her lands to John Manipenny in 1294. The youngest daughter, Margaret, only seems to have come of age in 1312. In that year she received an unspecified bequest of land from her father Henry and immediately sold one half acre. Her name only appears again with the sale of land in 1315 and 1317. The other daughter, Sabina, received a substantial bequest of eight and one half acres of arable along with meadow from her father Henry in 1307. Sabina alone seems to have tried to maintain the family estate since she bought up properties from other members of her family (1309 from Godfrey, 1315 from Margaret, 1315 from Godfrey); in 1316 she sold one and one half rods of land to Margaret.

Striking economic success, as well as concern for security, could explain the survival of much information about numerically small families in the court records of Godmanchester. One such family had the distinctive surname of Garlop (Garloup). A certain Richard Garlop appeared in the 1279 Hundred Roll with the modest holding of one messuage, a croft, four acres of arable and one rod of meadow. Richard and his wife Phillipa sold off various parcels of this property over the following decades. During these same years it becomes apparent that Richard had two sons, Reyner and Robert. Reyner Garlop received some property (one half acre) from Richard in 1295 and purchased a further one half acre from his brother Robert in 1302. This was but a small part of Reyner's activities on the land market as he bought other properties in 1302, 1303 and 1304. By the time of the lay subsidy of 1309 Reyner was one of the more substantial inhabitants of Godmanchester with taxable property worth £6. 12s.

Reyner Garlop continued to purchase property (one half acre in 1311). He released one half of a messuage to his mother in 1317. Reyner was married to someone whose first name we know to have been Cristina when she received four acres and one rod by bequest of her brother in 1317. Cristina released a messuage and courtyard to the use of Reyner in

the same year. Both Cristina and Reyner are associated in the purchase of further properties until 1329. There do not seem to have been any children by this marriage and over 1329 Cristina sells much of her property. Now at an advanced age, Reyner very likely was doing the same, for he paid the smallish tax of 8d. and 3s. respectively in 1327 and 1332.

Robert Garlop does not seem to have prospered as well as his brother Reyner, although Robert and his wife Matilda did buy land in 1295 and 1297, and by 1307 had inherited one half acre from Reyner Vicory. In the year 1302 they sold land to Reyner, Robert's brother and in 1304 (one croft) to another townsman. Robert was not listed among those liable to taxation in 1309 and by 1319 he had the modest taxable goods to the value of 19s. 6d. (5 bushels of wheat 3s.; 1 quarter of barley 3s.; 1 quarter of peas 2s. 6d.; 1 affer 6s.; 2 sheep 4s.; and a vessel 12d.). However, he did not have enough to be taxed under the twentieth of 1327 and paid only 8d. to the tenth of 1332. Matilda apparently died and Robert remarried Isolda. Robert had children, by which wife we do not know. Robert's three daughters, Cristina, Phillipa and Pellagia were able to purchase small pieces of property over 1331-1332. Robert and Isolda let land to their children over this time and upon Robert's death in 1335 his son Reginald appears to receive the remaining land. Reginald's son John is mentioned in 1342 and it was John who carried the name through the difficult plague period.

The name Hopay embraced some of the largest concentrations of property in the 1279 Hundred Roll, a Richard Hopay having two messuages, one croft, 17½ acres, three acres of meadow (the farm tax being 13s. 8d.) and Amicia Hopay holding three messuage, one croft, five acres, three rods, two acres and one rod of meadow (the farm tax noted as 5s. 4d.). Amicia also held further one half rod, at a farm tax of 1d. The heirs of Henry Hopay are also noted as holding one hayhavedin (tax of 1d.). By 1293 Emma was the sole survivor of her generation. That year at the death of Thomas Hopay son of Amicia's brother Henry, Amicia laid claim to the seven and one half acres, one messuage and two acres of meadow held by Thomas.[2] Amicia's title was upheld by the Godmanchester court against the claim of John and William Hopay, sons of Amicia's brother Eustace.[3] Amicia's property was apparently absorbed into that of her husband, Richard le Rede. The Hopay family continued

---

[2] For the text of this claim, see above, p. 43.
[3] For the text of this claim, see above, Chapter, 1, p. 43.

on at Godmanchester throughout the fourteenth century; however, the relative affluence of 1279 never seems to have been regained and no Hopay gained mention in the lay subsidy lists between 1309 and 1332.

The purpose of these few illustrations has been to demonstrate that the families of Godmanchester, as with the individuals, have unique histories. For reasons of convenience, this volume concentrates upon elements that tend to be common to most villagers, that is, the life cycles presented in Chapter 1 and economic patterns outlined in Chapter 5. However, as we shall see, these Godmanchester court rolls did not pretend to be a complete register of life cycle property conveyances or of the land market of the town. Rather, this was a court of such conveyances and land trans-actions as were required by individual and familial exigencies, real or potential. Were space and publishing interest in family biographies to allow, this volume could be properly presented from court roll data as a series of family histories. However, the compromise is adopted of presenting the scale of family history data available in the tables in this chapter and in Part Three, along with illustrative case histories in Chapter 5.

B. THE METHOD OF NOMINAL IDENTIFICATION AT GODMANCHESTER

Alienation and anonymity are not generally thought to have been major social problems of pre-industrial society. As a result, there is an implicit methodological contradiction in approaching the question of nominal identification by "reading back" from the accepted evolution of modern identification processes — i.d. cards, social security cards, census data and so forth — to the evidence for identification in earlier periods of Western history. Less isolated from his social environment, pre-industrial man was accepted, acknowledged, recognized and identified in a great variety of ways. Paradoxically, therefore, there is no simple technique for our identification of pre-industrial man; we must approach him through that great variety of ways by which he was known in his own day and age. Otherwise one peasant of pre-industrial Europe will remain for us as like another as were the Australian Bushmen to the early European immigrants.

For the villagers of Huntingdonshire. a score of variant entry types in village court rolls indicate many aspects of the social relations of villagers. And so, many individuals may be identified from their patterns of involvement as officials, ale-brewers, tenants in the open fields, neigh-bours in frankpledge tithings and villeins owing service to the lord. The

land courts of Godmanchester obviously offer much less variety of information about social action than the less specialized village court roll. And yet the land courts do serve to reveal social relations in two important ways: first, from the necessity for identification of family rights in property, and secondly, from the sheer bulk of the land market recorded in these courts. From the specification of family rights in property emerges a good deal of information about the size as well as identity of nuclear or single family units. From the land market much is divulged about the cycles of economic success or failure of many inhabitants of Godmanchester.

The question of adequate surname development that so troubles many sceptics of the social history of pre-industrial man was taken for granted at Godmanchester. Chapter 28 of the Godmanchester customal of 1324 states: "That every one pleading in pleas shall answer and be called by that name and surname by which he is most commonly called without taking exception."[4] There is no reason to believe that this custom was new to Godmanchester of 1324 for from the earliest surviving court rolls of the town, that is, 1271, the inhabitants of Godmanchester were given distinctive Christian names and surnames in the same fashion as fifty years later.

The method by which people of Godmanchester were able to distinguish themselves is now familiar enough to historical demographers. Some 500 different surnames were required for the considerable population of Godmanchester between 1278 and 1348. About one sixth of these surnames were fashioned from place-names and about one tenth were clearly taken from occupational designations. Obvious patronymic and matronymic derivations formed something less than one tenth of the surnames, with patronymics outnumbering matronymics in the order of three to one. Remaining surnames were constructed from a wide variety of nicknames, toponymic and archaic forms that are not always easy to trace.

First names employed by residents of Godmanchester over this early period are found to be around 50 for men and 40 for women. The fact that there are almost as many female first names as those for males is significant in view of the survival of more than twice as many names for men as for women. That is to say, first names for men tended to concentrate about certain popular names (Edward, Godfrey, Henry, Hugh, John, Nicholas, Reginald, Richard, Robert, Simon, Thomas,

---

[4] Bateson, *Borough Customs*, p. 161.

Walter and William) whereas female first names were scattered more widely (Agnes, Alice, Amicia, Caterina, Cristina, Emma, Gunnilda, Helen [Elena], Isabella, Juliana, Mabel, Sabina and Sybil). As a glance through early thirteenth-century lay subsidy lists will show,[5] different first names were fashionable from place to place throughout the county. God-manchester seems to have given exceptional favour to the use of Bartholomew, Eusebius, Elias, Dionysia, Isolda, Albrida, Felicia, Millicent and Pellagia.

First names currently in use for males and females were adequate to the greater specification that might be required to avoid confusion with patronymic surnames or many branches of a well-established family. In this way at the end of the thirteenth century Augustine named his six sons Richard, William, Augustine, Godfrey, Nicholas and John; Edward named his six sons William, John, Godfrey, Simon, Nicholas and Roger; Eusebius' five sons were named John, Nicholas, Godfrey, Reginald and William. The substantial families of Goni had Edward first noted in 1278 who named his eight sons Reginald, Richard, John, Nicholas, William, Gilbert, Thomas and Robert; and the Manipenny family had noted in 1312 that John had three sons who were named Roger, John and Henry and six daughters who were named Agnes, Emma, Beatrice, Mabel, Matilda and Sybil; also in the Manipenny family there was a William in 1312 whose five sons and three daughters were called Reginald, John, William, Roger, Godfrey, Pellagia, Isabella and Agnes.

This complex of surnames and first names was capable of further refinement. Most patronymics became fixed and as with Edward, Nicholas and Simon this name was not repeated as a first name in succeeding generations. Where the first name was continued in both capacities as first and surname, identification becomes very complex. In this context, as with the surname John, one must usually be content with identification of one family unit at a time. It was still possible for the patronymic to be used again, without difficulty of identification, in multi-generational cycles. For example, in 1278 a Reginald son of Robert is noted in the court rolls. In 1284 and 1287 respectively, sons of this Reginald were noted as John son of Reginald son of Robert and Godfrey son of Reginald son of Robert. In short, the three generations were employed for purposes of identification. As a new generation came along the most senior generation patronymic would be dropped. And so, to continue with the same family, by the early fourteenth century Reginald

---

[5] See Raftis and Hogan, *Lay Subsidy Rolls.*

had become the patronymic for John and Godfrey. An entry for 1301 identifies Cristina as the daughter of John son of Reginald and Henry, Gilbert, Thomas and Walter as sons of John son of Reginald. By 1312 and 1316 we will find entries referring to Godfrey son of Reginald and John son of Reginald above. Occasionally, when greater clarification might be required, as at the time of a bequest, more detail is given on the family tree. With this same family again, in 1312 John the son of Godfrey the son of Reginald the son of Robert is recorded in the court as receiving a bequest of land from his father Godfrey and brother Godfrey.

Undoubtedly the hundreds of references to property in the court rolls provided another identity check upon the people of Godmanchester. It would be useful to know from a court entry of 1288, for instance, that Dionysia and Amicia, daughters of Simon Gildene, are women who held property in Cambridge Way. However, the very modern manner of identification by address was only employed when necessary. This necessity usually arose when individuals of two branches of a family had identical first names as well as surnames. There was a John Quenyng of London Street during the second and third decade of the fourteenth century. By 1330 at least he had a son John son of John Quenyng of London Street who was thereby clearly distinguished from John son of John Quenyng of West Street (1329). This numerous family found the address still useful by the 1340s when a John Quenyng senior of Mileslane and Philippa daughter of John *de* Mileslane were identified. Smaller families who still might have problems of identification because of a common occupational surname also found the address useful. There was a John Miller of Post Street and a John Miller of West Street in the early years of the fourteenth century. Over the 1320s a William Mason of Post Street and then a William son of William Mason of Post Street were recorded to distinguish from simply William Mason. In the same fashion a William Aylred of Arnyng Street and then a Roger son of William Ayled of Arnyng Street were recorded to distinguish between William Aylred and a Roger Aylred, although this was not because of the occupation of the family but because this family had many members. The Manipenny family, who were a large influential family at Godman-chester, found the address useful. A John son of John senior of West Street is noted in 1329, very likely to help distinguish between the numerous Johns that are found in this family. Even as late as 1373 they are using the address for this family when a John of West Street is noted. The Outy family used the address to distinguish from the many Johns that are found in this family. Outy of East Street in 1330 is noted as having a sister called Cristina Madecroft and also was married to Cecilia and their

son John lived in East Street. The occupational surname of Ploughwrighte had a Thomas noted in 1356 who was living at "ye mil cros," and there can be no question that this must be to differentiate between a Thomas Ploughwrighte *de* Stukeley (1340-1341) and Thomas Ploughwrighte at ye Stambourne (1360). Further examples of the address are: John Balle of West Street (1286); William *de* Borsworth junior of East Street (1382); William *de* Borsworth of Arnyng Street (1366); John Colowot junior of East Street whose daughter Agnes is noted in 1332; John Colowot junior of West Street (1338); John Goni of East Street (1347); Godfrey son of Reginald Seman of Arnyng Street (1330); Roger son of Reginald Spruntyng of Arnyng Street (1311) and his sister Isolda of Arnyng Street (1306); Thomas Taylor of London Street (1363); and William Waryn of West Street (1363).

Particularly for large families, the designation junior and senior could also be employed to compensate for the limited number of first names in that family tradition. This use of junior and senior appears to have been a regular feature in the villages of Huntingdonshire but rather infrequent at Godmanchester. Only some score of such cases are found in the court rolls. In many of these cases the designation does serve to isolate another family unit, but perhaps because of this very designation, less care is taken to indicate normal family relationships. John Balde named his two sons John senior (1295) and John junior (1295); John atte Barre named two of his four sons John, John senior (1309) and John junior (1316); Robert Batayle did not name his sons after himself but once again named them John senior (1306) and John junior (1307). The Colowot family had numerous Johns, and to confuse the issue further John Colowot named his two sons John, John junior (1322) who was dead by this date and a further John (1327), the father being noted as senior. Unfortunately we do not know the parentage of Phillip Cooperator Rotarum, his brother William (1311) and William the brother of Phillip and William (1317). Thomas Glewe by 1294 was noted as having two sons named John and the Le Longe family kept the tradition up as John senior named two of his three sons John (1303) and John brother of John (1312). There is only the one instance in the court rolls where two daughters were named the same, that is when John son of Reginald named his two daughters Cristina senior (1301) and Cristina junior (1301).

Identification of people at Godmanchester, then, easily falls under the general norms for acceptance or rejection of identification that have been developed by historical demographers.[6] Of course different records

---

[6] For a simple presentation of these norms see David Herlihy, "Record Linkages in

demand different modes of application of these norms and in turn elicit different data for the social historian. In the village court rolls of Huntingdonshire, identification was provided by the consistent use of names with various village economic, legal and social roles during the chronological period of maturity (active adult span). Since most of this information is about adult males, court rolls are less valuable for vital statistics than parish registers; on the other hand, court roll evidence can be much more rich in social and economic content than the fullest parish register series.[7]

Data from the Godmanchester court rolls fall somewhere between data obtainable from parish registers and court rolls. In the Godmanchester rolls over 90 percent of the names are given with some further specified familial relationship (lineal, conjugal and sibling) along with the common surname, although the occasion for the names appearing in the courts is property.[8] For this reason Table 26 "Family Data from Godmanchester Court Rolls" has been centred about this information on family relationships. The linkage is that of familial degree indicated by the court rolls.

In the context of Table 26, therefore, the main identification problems at Godmanchester are not those of changing or "underdeveloped" sur-name formulation; the main problems follow from lack of indicated family relationships. Concern for family relationship might not be great for a number of reasons. In some instances, this inadequate information

---

Tuscan Fiscal Records," in *Identifying People in the Past*, ed. E. A. Wrigley (London, 1973), p. 51.

[7] Cf. J. A. Raftis, *Warboys: Two Hundred Years in the Life of an English Mediaeval Village* (Toronto, 1974); E. J. Britton, *Broughton: 1288-1340. A Mediaeval Village Community* (Toronto, 1977). The most recent study of identification in village court rolls finds that a good series of courts rolls for a village (Iver, Bucks.) of a different geographical and manorial nature from the above villages of Huntingdonshire presents much the same advantages and problems of record linkage. Cf. J. M. Bennett, "Family Life and Village Society in a Fourteenth-Century Village" (unpublished licentiate research report, Toronto, 1977), chapter 1.

[8] See further, Chapters 1 and 5, upon the place of property in the family cycle and the village land market. Also it will be seen from the use of other records with court rolls in Chapter 3 that problems of record linkage for documents other than the court rolls are not many for the propertied people of Godmanchester. All records share in common problems issuing from the adequacy of the series, the conditions of the documents, the amount of population mobility and so on. For a good description of such problems in the context of parish registers, cf. E. A. Wrigley, ed., *An Introduction to English Historical Demography* (London, 1966), especially chapter 4. And for a more recent statement see R. S. Schofield, "The Representativeness of Family Reconstitution," *Local Population Studies*, no. 8 (Spring, 1972), pp. 13-17.

follows from the relatively brief involvement of individuals in the courts of Godmanchester, quite simply because of their less important economic role or because their family life would seem to centre beyond this town. For those whose family life centred beyond the town, the court was often content with reference to place rather than familial tie. Many of those with little involvement in property were practitioners of such trades as Faber, Aurifaber, Chapman, Ploughwrighte, Merchant, Carpenter, Taylor, Carnifex (Butcher) and Cook and the court found these occupational designations adequate alternatives to family ties.

Where there are given a number of individuals with the same surname, problems of identification follow from the nature and condition of the record. From the point of view of those who preserved the records of Godmanchester, our choice of 1278 would seem an arbitrary decision and the survival of records from the 1270s is a question of historical accident. Frequently, therefore, we know little about the parents prior to the 1280s whose name only survives in the context of a widow or children. For this reason, no dates are attached to many late thirteenth-century names.

At the other extreme, for larger families in most instances, the relationships seem to have been so obvious to the court that the scribe has not given the full familial relationship. That is to say, in a good many cases there is every indication from surname, first name and chronology that a certain individual may be the same person as the one indicated by a given familial tie, and yet this tie is not given in the records. Such individuals are treated separately in Table 26 but an asterisk is appended to their names to indicate that they are likely the same individual as appears on a previous line. For example:

Husband	Wife	Son(s)	Daughter(s)
QUENYNG [9]			
John	Matilda 1366 (d)	—	Matilda 1359
John*	unknown	Godfrey (c)	
Godfrey (c)	Amabilia 1361		

This Godfrey Quenyng son of John* whose wife Amabilia is noted in 1361 could be the son of John and Matilda, but the scribes do not indicate this relationship. Similarly:

RODE [10]			
Robert	Isolda 1280-1287	William 1286-1295 (c)	
William (c)	Mariota 1311		
William* 1289	unknown	William 1289	

---

[9] See below, p. 370, and p. 240 for the key to the abbreviations.
[10] See below, pp. 378-379.

Again this William* Rode could be the son of Robert. And again:

TODENHAM [11]

Richard 1300-1320	Beatrice 1295-1316 (d)	—	Joan 1316
Henry 1313-1317 (d)	unknown	—	Sybil 1325
Richard* 1329	Margaret 1329		

This Richard* Todenham very likely is the same Richard as the one married to Beatrice and Margaret is his second wife. Another indication of this is that the surname itself is not common and the only other family is Henry. Another possibility is that Richard* is the son of Richard and Beatrice. Further:

ACRY [12]

| Richard 1330-1342 | Agnes 1346 | Thomas 1345 | Margaret 1346 |
| Richard* 1351-1354 | Margaret 1350 | | |

Richard* Acry may be the same as the first Richard, with Margaret as his second wife.

Finally, for a considerable number of individuals with a common surname, the court has not given a family context for one reason or another. In some instances, as with the repeated reference to Julian noted at the beginning of this chapter, the scribe has shortened the names as part of the more economic recording of repeated cases pertaining to litigation. Where a few court rolls are missing, or damaged so as to be undecipherable, full identification may be lost with the full sequence of entries. More frequently, however, the court seems content to identify an outsider or a person engaged in a special occupation by such designations rather than by their relation to other villagers. In all such cases, for the purpose of Table 26 "Family Data from Godmanchester Court Rolls," such individuals are appended to the family list under the rubric, "probable kin."

C. THE PEOPLE OF GODMANCHESTER COURT ROLLS

A minimum of 5892 individuals may be identified from Godmanchester court rolls between 1278 and 1400. Of these individuals, some fifteen percent (896) do not appear in any family context (that is, with either a

---

[11] See below, p. 396.
[12] See below, p. 241.

surname common to someone else, or an indicated relationship) and are not included in Table 26. As was discussed in Chapter 3 above, many of these individuals were "outsiders" to Godmanchester, involved in debt pleas and increasingly in the later fourteenth century in seeking liberty of the town. The total (5892) remains a minimum figure since individuals indicated in Table 26 by an asterisk and as "probable kin" of the same first name as any contemporary are not included.

Those cited as individuals and not tabulated in Table 26 "Family Data from Godmanchester Court Rolls," were not all outsiders. Increasingly, too, as the fourteenth century wore on less family-related data are available so that a larger number of those with common surnames have to be relegated to the "probable kin" category or stand as one generation parent units without reference to parents or children. These characteristics of the surviving demographic data may not be employed to suggest a movement towards economic individualism in the later fourteenth century, nor, on the other hand, the survival of a more common family spirit to the early fourteenth century. These varying demographic characteristics simply reflect the changing recording practices of the court rolls. Taken over the long term, the total number of court roll entries (dealing with the land market) do not vary greatly between 1278 and 1400. The total number of references to families does vary considerably over the long run, as the following summary table (Table 20 "The Total Number of Family Surnames Referred to Each Year in the Court Rolls") indicates.

TABLE 20: THE TOTAL NUMBER OF FAMILY SURNAMES
REFERRED TO EACH YEAR IN THE COURT ROLLS

Year	Surnames	Year	Surnames	Year	Surnames	Year	Surnames
1278	46	1293	130	1308	152	1323	140
1279	62	1294	130	1309	144	1324	140
1280	88	1295	141	1310	150	1325	152
1281	96	1296	133	1311	157	1326	144
1282	97	1297	143	1312	158	1327	143
1283	105	1298	143	1313	161	1329	145
1284	100	1299	148	1314	163	1330	148
1285	107	1300	144	1315	164	1331	151
1286	113	1301	146	1316	171	1332	150
1287	118	1302	153	1317	154	1333	144
1288	117	1303	142	1318	152	1334	140
1289	114	1304	141	1319	147	1335	140
1290	123	1305	139	1320	149	1337	138
1291	127	1306	144	1321	156	1338	143
1292	120	1307	139	1322	155	1339	145

Year	Surnames	Year	Surnames	Year	Surnames	Year	Surnames
1340	149	1355	125	1370	117	1385	74
1341	150	1356	132	1371	122	1386	72
1342	138	1357	125	1372	118	1387	71
1343	138	1358	125	1373	116	1388	70
1344	147	1359	123	1374	109	1389	72
1345	144	1360	131	1375	111	1390	69
1346	147	1361	131	1376	105	1391	62
1347	137	1362	136	1377	107	1392	54
1348	135	1363	137	1378	101	1393	55
1349	136	1364	134	1379	95	1394	51
1350	152	1365	138	1380	99	1395	44
1351	144	1366	141	1381	85	1396	32
1352	133	1367	134	1382	83	1397	31
1353	139	1368	120	1383	77	1398	24
1354	131	1369	127	1384	74	1399	17

This long-run picture masks an important aspect of Godmanchester, that is the great number of families appearing and disappearing over the shorter run. Over the forty years between 1290 and 1330, 139 new families (surname) appeared and disappeared at Godmanchester; for the same period of time after 1360, 102 new families appeared and disappeared. Many of these families can clearly be identified as branches from neighbouring villages and towns (especially Huntingdon) who established a branch at Godmanchester for a generation or only a few years. In some instances, these short stayers were craftsmen or merchants from even more distant places who were attracted by the investment possibilities of properties at Godmanchester. For some families, as with the *de* Gidding family whose brief history is recorded in the first part of this chapter, younger members of the family seemed to lose interest in Godmanchester and no doubt disappeared by emigration. For a great many families, however, whether wealthy (e.g., Hopay, above p. 151) or poorer (as Julian, above pp. 148-149) inability to provide a male heir seemed to explain the disappearance of the name from the town records.

Family cycle data of Chapter 1 illustrate more fully families increasing gradually over the 1280s and 1290s to their highest level in the early half of the fourteenth century and then falling off only very gradually over the later century. Typical references are given in Chapter 1 and show that the data go beyond the merely numerical summary of Table 20. Fuller information is especially the case for the period prior to the Black Death.

Whereas there are relatively few references to children in court rolls after the mid-fourteenth century and hence little possibility of tracing family succession in the town (the bracketed "c" in Table 26 "Family Data from Godmanchester Court Rolls") such data are quite plentiful from the 1290s to the 1340s.

Table 22 below, "Godmanchester Family Units," lists in alphabetical order family names and the length of their period of survival ("Residence Span") at Godmanchester as indicated by the court rolls. The section of the table entitled "Number of Generations" summarizes more explicitly the actual number of nuclear family units (generations) to be found for each family. For example, the first family on the list, Acry, carried through from the 1290s to 1394 and the court rolls give us explicit reference to this family history by father to son to grandson to great grandson. However, for the next family on the list, Albon, there is only the one reference to a husband and wife holding property in the 1290s. On the other hand, we have information about the third family on the list, Albrid, beginning with the father, mother, son and doughter from 1280 and continuing with reference to the son and his wife in 1282, so that for the Albrid family we may dessignate a two generation family.

A rough indication of the ability of many families to establish more than one branch at Godmanchester may be seen by the number of families where more than one branch carries on for one, two or three generations. In most instances, court roll information is not sufficiently detailed to establish the link between the different branches. For example, our entries begin when there were already four families with the surname Alryth. One may assume common parentage, but how recently may not be establish. On the other hand, we do have explicit information about the marriage and settlement of five sons of Augustine around 1300. There is no evidence that the sixth son married and the sixth one generation unit comes from an isolated family with this surname living towards the mid-fourteenth century. One of the best documented families is the Aylred for whom we know the existence of 26 family units. When our period begins there were four branches of this family in Godmanchester. Two of these branches carried on for three generations; the other two branches and four children of various branches carried on for two generations; as street addresses begin to be employed towards the mid-fourteenth century, eight Aylred family units may be followed although only for one generation. Altogether, we have explicit information about the establishment of more than one branch at Godmanchester for 47 families over the 1280-1350 period.

The considerable data extant for the first half of the fourteenth century prompt some observations about family size and replacement.[13] A good number of sons would seem not to have married. This is suggested by the following statistics. To take only those families where continuity of more than one generation is usually indicated, many sons' names appear for a number of years without evidence for their having wives or children. For example, Eusebius the son of Aniz had the three sons Nicholas, Reginald and Godfrey. We know that Nicholas married Emma Parsons, but there survives a longer time span of references to Reginald and Godfrey without any mention of wives. Godfrey Alryth (1283-1326), Nicholas son of Augustine (1308-1315) and Henry son of Godfrey Aylred (1310-1329) are other illustrations of this phenomenon from names beginning with the letter A in Table 26. Indeed, parallel references to apparently unmarried daughters (Mariota Atenock [1282-1310], Millicent daughter of Martin Aylred [1302-1327], Alice daughter of John Aylred [1298-1316]) would not appear to be more frequent.

Much more significant in terms of replacement is the evidence for married sons who had no children. Excluding less well documented families for the second quarter of the century, families with surnames beginning with the letter A provide many illustrations: Robert Alryth, Richard Alryth, Nicholas Aniz, Stephen Atte Hall, John Aylred, Reginald Aylred and Bartholomew Aylward. The possibility of a family unit not replacing itself was very real indeed. For the whole of our period, 1278 to 1399, 653 of 1,366 families are recorded without any evidence for their having children. One cannot suggest that nearly one half of the families were childless because of the nature of family records for Godmanchester prior to 1300 and after the Black Death. Nevertheless, the phenomenon was obviously significant for the 1300-1348 period.

The difficulty families may have experienced in replacing themselves, owing no doubt to the hazards of childbirth and infancy in pre-industrial England, is further reflected by the very wide statistical scatter for children that did survive. Of the 1,888 children indicated between 1278 and 1399, two thirds fall within the better family documented period of 1300-1348. For this latter period we have 1,177 children noted for 600 families. The considerable variety in family size may be seen by the following tabulation:

---

[13] For additional demographic observations, see below, Chapter 5, pp. 201-229.

TABLE 21: GODMANCHESTER FAMILY STATISTICS BETWEEN 1300 AND 1348 [a]

Number of families		Number of children	
with children	603	sons	755
without children	285	daughters	424
Totals	888		1,179

1 son 224	2 sons 68 (136)[b]	3 sons 29 (87)	4 sons 4 (32)	6 sons 1 (6)
1 daughter 83	2 daughters 20 (40)	3 daughters 13 (39)	4 daughters 2 (8)	5 daughters 2 (10)
1 son + 1 daughter 51 (102)	1 son + 2 daughters 16 (48)	1 son + 3 daughters 8 (32)	1 son + 4 daughters 2 (10)	
2 sons + 1 daughter 24 (72)	2 sons + 2 daughters 15 (60)	2 sons + 3 daughters 6 (30)	2 sons + 4 daughters 2 (12)	
3 sons + 1 daughter 6 (24)	3 sons + 2 daughters 8 (40)	3 sons + 3 daughters 3 (18)	3 sons + 4 daughters 1 (7)	3 sons + 6 daughters 1 (9)
4 sons + 1 daughter 2 (10)	4 sons + 2 daughters 2 (12)	5 sons + 3 daughters 1 (8)	7 sons + 2 daughters 1 (9)	8 sons + 3 daughters 1 (11)

Grand total of children: 1,179

[a] Number of families with children		without children
1300-1348:	603	285
1348-1399:	212	273
Totals:	815	558
Grand total: 1,373		

[b] These figures in parentheses are the total number of children so described, i.e., the number of offspring times the number of families with that particular configuration of offspring.

What then was the population of Godmanchester? No certain figure can be established. The number of messuages are the most simple point of departure for a population estimate of the town. There were 387 messuages in the town in 1279. If one may judge from the size of families, Godmanchester participated in the general population growth of England of the late thirteenth century. One might well expect, therefore, that more messuages had spread along the lanes and roads from the town as described in Chapter 3 above and it may readily be assumed that there were more than 400 messuages by 1300. Some of this increase in numbers of messuages would be through the establishing of new family branches, already a common phenomenon in 1279 as has been noted in Chapter 3. Nevertheless, the bulk of evidence from the various sources does not point to the founding of new messuages, or homesteads, so much as the intensification of settlement upon the older and larger messuage complexes of the town. Some thirty instances of such settlement were noted in the 1279 Hundred Roll.

The number of properties settled upon various members of families and the number of marriages among children of families who would not inherit the homestead (or principal messuage) numbered well over 100 in the generation after 1300. It seems possible, therefore, to suggest a minimal figure of 500 family units as the population base of Godmanchester around 1300. With even the modest unitary replacement rate of two children to two parents, the population of the town would be some 2000. More than likely a larger multiplier should be employed and, as noted in Chapter 5 below, there were many single or non-propertied families in the town. As a final estimate then, one could readily envisage a population of 3000 as existing in Godmanchester around 1300.

TABLE 22: GODMANCHESTER FAMILY UNITS

Surname	Residence Span	Number of Generations				Total Families
		1	2	3	4	
Acry	1293-1394	—	—	—	1	4
Albon	1394	1	—	—	—	1
Albrid	1280-1301	—	1	—	—	2
Aldous	1295-1303, 1345-1349	2	—	—	—	2
Alewill	1293-1295	1	—	—	—	1
Alexander, son of	1278-1313	—	1	—	—	2
Aleyn	1331-1392	—	—	—	1	4
Alice, son of	1289, 1344-1346	1	1	—	—	3
Almayne	1377-1386	1	—	—	—	1
Alryth	1280-1372	4	1	—	—	6
Anfred	1322-1350	1	—	—	—	1

Surname	Residence Span	Number of Generations				Total Families
		1	2	3	4	
Aniz	1293-1318	—	—	1	—	3
Apparitor	1316	1	—	—	—	1
Aquam ad	1279-1283, 1327	2	—	—	—	2
Aspelon	1373-1382	1	—	—	—	1
Atebrut	1332-1340	1	—	—	—	1
Atelaneshende	1332	1	—	—	—	1
Atenock	1287-1310	1	—	—	—	1
Atemar	1321	—	1	—	—	2
Augustine, son of	1282-1348	6	—	—	1	10
Aula	1283-1349	3	—	—	—	3
Aurifaber	1315-1325, 1344	1	—	—	—	1
Ayle	1363	1	—	—	—	1
Aylred	1280-1395	8	6	2	—	26
Aylward	1285-1316	—	2	—	—	4
Ba	1285	1	—	—	—	1
Bachelor	1350	1	—	—	—	1
Baggele	1344-1345	1	—	—	—	1
Balde	1292-1378	1	—	1	—	4
Baldecote	1346	1	—	—	—	1
Baldock	1305	1	—	—	—	1
Baldry	1293	1	—	—	—	1
Balle	1278-1428	8	2	—	—	12
Banastre	1350-1380	1	—	—	—	1
Band	1343	1	—	—	—	1
Banna	1281-1286	2	—	—	—	2
Barbour	1314-1377	4	—	—	—	4
Bard	1280	1	—	—	—	1
Barefot	1315-1329	1	—	—	—	1
Barker	1304, 1346	2	—	—	—	2
Barman	1351	1	—	—	—	1
Baroun	1326-1395	2	1	—	—	4
Barre atte	1280-1441	6	2	1	—	13
Bartelot	1289-1423	3	2	—	—	7
Bartholomew, son of	1364-1365	1	—	—	—	1
Barton, de	1278-1316, 1349-1354	2	—	—	—	2
Basset	1380-1391	1	—	—	—	1
Batayle, de	1299-1348	—	2	—	—	4
Bate	1280-1399	4	2	—	—	8
Baxter	1297-1303	2	—	—	—	2
Beadle	1278-1287	2	—	—	—	2
Beatrix	1348-1356	1	—	—	—	1
Begenore	1311-1346	1	—	—	—	1
Bekyngham	1383	1	—	—	—	1
Bele	1287, 1389	3	—	—	—	3
Belysson	1395-1399	1	—	—	—	1
Benethebrok	1338	1	—	—	—	1
Bernard	1302-1327	1	—	—	—	1
Beverle, de	1329-1360	2	—	—	—	2

Surname	Residence Span	Number of Generations				Total Families
		1	*2*	*3*	*4*	
Bevewyk	1346	1	—	—	—	1
Bewschampe	1354	1	—	—	—	1
Bilneye, *de*	1322-1330	2	—	—	—	2
Bishop	1297	1	—	—	—	1
Blac	1316	1	—	—	—	1
Bluntisham, *de*	1318-1338	1	—	—	—	1
Bole	1281-1399	6	1	—	1	12
Bonde	1316-1393	4	1	—	—	6
Bonis	1281-1372	4	—	—	—	4
Boneville	1280-1322	—	2	—	—	4
Bore	1357	1	—	—	—	1
Borsworth, *de*	1353-1391	2	—	—	—	2
Boteler	1338-1350	1	—	—	—	1
Bourgos	1354	1	—	—	—	1
Bovetun	1278-1283	2	—	—	—	2
Boveyre	1348	1	—	—	—	1
Bowre, in ye	1351	1	—	—	—	1
Bradenham, *de*	1295-1329	1	1	—	—	3
Breton	1293-1299, 1360-1393	2	—	—	—	2
Brewer	1338	1	—	—	—	1
Broke, atte	1280, 1308-1341	2	—	—	—	2
Broughton, *de*	1330	1	—	—	—	1
Broun	1321-1394	2	1	—	—	4
Bryan	1362-1364	1	—	—	—	1
Bryd	1304-1322	1	—	—	—	1
Bryht	1381	1	—	—	—	1
Bucher	1358	1	—	—	—	1
Bulby	1338	1	—	—	—	1
Buldir	1278-1351	4	—	—	—	4
Bumstead, *de*	1351-1373	1	—	—	—	1
Burel	1331	1	—	—	—	1
Bury, *de*	1278-1279	1	—	—	—	1
Buxton	1277-1316, 1361	4	—	—	—	4
Byrlyngton	1371	1	—	—	—	1
Cage	1365-1373	1	—	—	—	1
Canne	1291	1	—	—	—	1
Cant' (Cambridge?), *de*	1338	1	—	—	—	1
Carnifex (Butcher)	1280, 1349-1380	2	—	—	—	2
Carpenter	1287-1313, 1330-1332	5	1	—	—	7
Carter	1298-1308, 1361-1378	4	—	—	—	4
Castelmp'lt	1307	—	1	—	—	2
Catelyne	1341-1391	1	1	—	—	3
Caterina, son of	1290-1301, 1326-1340	1	1	—	—	3
Catworth, *de*	1299-1302	1	—	—	—	1
Caunt	1350	1	—	—	—	1
Cementarius	1278-1324	3	—	—	—	3
Chadeslee	1369-1399	1	—	—	—	1
Cham, *de*	1325	1	—	—	—	1

Surname	Residence Span	Number of Generations					Total Families
		1	2	3	4	5	
Chaplain	1298-1348	1	2	—	—	—	5
Chapman	1278-1372	10	—	—	—	—	10
Chese	1281-1315, 1373-1398	1	1	—	—	—	3
Chesterfield, *de*	1309	1	—	—	—	—	1
Chorley	1326	1	—	—	—	—	1
Chyche' (Church), *de*	1315	1	—	—	—	—	1
Chyld	1360-1389	1	—	—	—	—	1
Cirpos, *ad*	1279-1348	5	—	1	—	—	8
Clare	1359	1	—	—	—	—	1
Clere	1315-1316	2	—	—	—	—	2
Clerk	1278-1373, 1380-1382, 1394	16	3	4	1	1	43
Clervaux	1297-1316, 1341-1354	3	—	—	—	—	3
Clopton	1321	1	—	—	—	—	1
Clubbe	1348	1	—	—	—	—	1
Cokayne	1308-1335	1	—	—	—	—	1
Cokyrmowe, *de*	1302	1	—	—	—	—	1
Colion	1308-1369	3	2	—	—	—	7
Colowot	1295-1354	6	1	—	—	—	8
Conerur	1291	1	—	—	—	—	1
Cook	1349-1390	8	—	—	—	—	8
Cooperator Rotarum	1311-1338	—	1	—	—	—	2
Cors	1286	1	—	—	—	—	1
Coteman	1390	1	—	—	—	—	1
Couper	1287-1375	9	—	—	—	—	9
Cowstone?	1348	1	—	—	—	—	1
Crane	1350-1366	1	—	—	—	—	1
Croxton	1311-1366	4	1	—	—	—	6
Crucem, *ad*	1278-1325	1	1	—	—	—	3
Currcaur	1345	1	—	—	—	—	1
Custaunce	1362	1	—	—	—	—	1
Dally	1341-1376	1	—	—	—	—	1
Dam	1333	1	—	—	—	—	1
Danewych	1371	1	—	—	—	—	1
Danlys	1315-1326	1	—	—	—	—	1
Das	1294-1327, 1352	1	1	—	—	—	3
Davy	1333	1	—	—	—	—	1
Dawson	1372	1	—	—	—	—	1
Defore	1329, 1349	1	—	—	—	—	1
Denne	1326-1393	1	1	—	—	—	3
Dereham, *de*	1314-1322, 1342	1	—	—	—	—	1
Derneford	1314	1	—	—	—	—	1
Dery	1344	1	—	—	—	—	1
Dewston	1348	1	—	—	—	—	1
Dicere	1350-1393	1	—	—	—	—	1
Dicoun	1351-1367	1	—	—	—	—	1
Doketon, *de*	1310-1333	1	—	—	—	—	1
Doraunt	1371	1	—	—	—	—	1

Surname	Residence Span	Number of Generations				Total Families
		1	*2*	*3*	*4*	
Dosyn	1281-1380	2	—	3	—	8
Douce	1367, 1369	1	—	—	—	1
Drew	1283-1316	1	1	—	—	3
Drury	1312, 1346-1362	2	—	—	—	2
Dulyn	1351	1	—	—	—	1
Dunnyng	1345	1	—	—	—	1
Dunstable, *de*	1319	1	—	—	—	1
Dunton, *de*	1293-1313	1	—	—	—	1
Ede	1295-1394	10	3	—	—	16
Edenham, *de*	1330	1	—	—	—	1
Edward, son of	1279-1323, 1340-1341	2	1	—	—	4
Edwyn	1291	1	—	—	—	1
Elias	1376	1	—	—	—	1
Elsworth, *de*	1334-1367	2	1	—	—	4
Ely	1278	1	—	—	—	1
Elys	1309-1348, 1382	4	—	—	—	4
Ese	1278-1369	1	2	1	—	8
Essex, *de*	1279-1397	2	2	—	—	6
Eton, *de*	1341	1	—	—	—	1
Eusebius, son of	1282-1331	—	1	—	—	2
Eustace	1349	1	—	—	—	1
Everard	1293-1325	2	—	—	—	2
Eynesbury, *de*	1357-1358	1	—	—	—	1
Faber	1278-1349	4	1	—	—	6
Fabyon	1339	1	—	—	—	1
Factorum	1325	1	—	—	—	1
Fanel	1283	1	—	—	—	1
Fanner	1313-1331	2	—	—	—	2
Fayrheved	1299-1316	1	—	—	—	1
Feltewell	1382	1	—	—	—	1
Fet	1331	1	—	—	—	1
Fing'	1309	1	—	—	—	1
Firmarius (Farmer)	1365	1	—	—	—	1
Fisher	1322-1428	4	—	—	—	4
Flaxmonger	1331	1	—	—	—	1
Flexwerer	1353	1	—	—	—	1
Focher	1331	1	—	—	—	1
Fole	1286-1327	2	—	—	—	2
Forthe (Forde), atte	1341-1377	1	—	—	—	1
Fouler	1357-1367	1	—	—	—	1
Fox	1313-1327	1	—	—	—	1
Freman	1373-1399	1	—	—	—	1
Frene	1380	1	—	—	—	1
Frere	1280-1392	5	1	1	—	10
Fressing	1289-1294	1	—	—	—	1
Freysol	1363-1388	1	—	—	—	1
Freyville	1283-1321	2	—	—	—	2

Surname	Residence Span	Number of Generations				Total Families
		1	2	3	4	
Fryday	1301	1	—	—	—	1
Fuller	1369	1	—	—	—	1
Fyn	1310	1	—	—	—	1
Gamelyn	1313	1	—	—	—	1
Garby	1360	1	—	—	—	1
Gardener	1354-1374	2	—	—	—	2
Garlop	1295-1383	1	—	—	1	5
Gate, atte	1338-1372	4	—	—	—	4
Gawesonne	1361	1	—	—	—	1
Gaylor	1361	1	—	—	—	1
George'	1299-1303	1	—	—	—	1
Gidding, de	1286-1353	1	1	—	—	3
Gilbert, son of	1278-1292	—	1	—	—	2
Gildersowe, de	1322-1340	1	—	—	—	1
Gildene	1283-1389, 1393	10	6	—	—	22
Gile	1278-1354	1	1	1	—	6
Gilekoc	1281-1329	1	—	—	—	1
Gille	1349	1	—	—	—	1
Glatton, de	1340-1341	1	—	—	—	1
Glewe	1279-1399	10	1	1	—	15
Glover	1349	1	—	—	—	1
Godard	1392	1	—	—	—	1
Godfrey, son of	1279-1361	—	1	1	—	5
Godman	1330-1389	2	2	—	—	6
Godoun	1324-1360	—	1	—	—	2
Godmanchester, de	1347	1	—	—	—	1
Godware	1283-1340	2	1	—	—	4
Godwyne	1345-1395	—	1	—	—	2
Gold	1348	1	—	—	—	1
Goni	1278-1379	15	4	2	—	29
Goodman	1321-1325	1	—	—	—	1
Gorne	1361	1	—	—	—	1
Grace	1372	1	—	—	—	1
Grafhan, de	1323-1373	1	—	—	—	1
Gransden, de	1298-1317	1	—	—	—	1
Graunt	1295-1334	1	—	—	—	1
Graveley, de	1278-1395	1	2	—	—	5
Grene, atte	1378-1381	1	—	—	—	1
Grigory	1291	1	—	—	—	1
Grinde	1282-1364	5	—	—	—	5
Grottyng	1363	1	—	—	—	1
Grove, atte	1285	1	—	—	—	1
Gryt	1353	1	—	—	—	1
Gyleman	1311-1332	1	—	—	—	1
Haddenham, de	1313-1322	1	—	—	—	1
Haldows	1372	1	—	—	—	1
Halupetyr	1281-1301	1	—	—	—	1

Surname	Residence Span	Number of Generations				Total Families
		1	2	3	4	
Hamerton, *de*	1278-1349	2	1	—	—	4
Hamyoht	1292	1	—	—	—	1
Hardley, *de*	1288-1335	1	—	—	—	1
Hardy	1289-1345	1	1	—	—	3
Hardwick, *de*	1278	1	—	—	—	1
Hare	1361	1	—	—	—	1
Hartford, *de*	1280-1308, 1361-1376	5	1	—	—	7
Haveley, *de*	1293-1298	—	1	—	—	2
Havenok	1287	1	—	—	—	1
Haythewolf	1299-1302	1	—	—	—	1
Hdewy, *de*	1278	1	—	—	—	1
Hekedoun	1366	1	—	—	—	1
Helen, son of	1280	—	1	—	—	2
Hemingford, *de*	1327-1372	2	1	—	—	4
Hemington, *de*	1286	1	—	—	—	1
Henry, son of	1278-1316, 1351-1372	—	2	—	—	4
Henyham	1378	1	—	—	—	1
Hercy	1340	1	—	—	—	1
Heringmonger	1298-1307	1	—	—	—	1
Herle	1378	1	—	—	—	1
Herlishevid	1280-1284	2	—	—	—	2
Herny	1369-1386	1	—	—	—	1
Hert	1366	1	—	—	—	1
Hertesturp, in	1340	1	—	—	—	1
Higney, *de*	1302	1	—	—	—	1
Hildegar	1311-1334	—	1	—	—	2
Hildemar	1298-1395	4	2	1	—	11
Hirne, in le	1299	1	—	—	—	1
Hitchin, *de*	1299-1341	—	—	1	—	3
Hobbis	1280	1	—	—	—	1
Hockerill	1295-1346	—	1	—	—	2
Hogan	1341	1	—	—	—	1
Holland, *de*	1281	1	—	—	—	1
Holiw	1332-1340	1	—	—	—	1
Homan	1350-1394	1	—	—	—	1
Hon	1298-1303	2	—	—	—	2
Honewyn	1351	1	—	—	—	1
Hopay	1278-1393	1	2	1	—	8
Hore, *le*	1335	1	—	—	—	1
Horold	1304-1325, 1348-1360	2	1	—	—	4
Horseman, *le*	1318	1	—	—	—	1
Hot	1278-1291	1	—	—	—	1
Houlot	1320	1	—	—	—	1
Houghton, *de*	1288-1311, 1321-1339	1	1	—	—	3
Hougos	1366	1	—	—	—	1
Houtere	1377	1	—	—	—	1
Howe	1310-1322, 1349-1379	4	—	—	—	4
Howefyl	1351	1	—	—	—	1
Howelond	1371	1	—	—	—	1

Surname	Residence Span	Number of Generations				Total Families
		1	2	3	4	
Howman	1323-1391	1	1	—	—	3
Hugh, son of	1290-1366	—	1	1	—	5
Huntingdon, de	1279, 1298, 1304, 1348	3	—	—	—	3
Ilster	1349-1389	1	—	—	—	1
Ingelond	1278-1339, 1356	4	1	—	—	6
Ingleys	1312-1313, 1346-1376	3	—	—	—	3
Inhewyn	1279-1378	4	1	—	—	6
Ironmonger	1295-1315	—	1	—	—	2
Isabella	1297-1303	1	—	—	—	1
Isham, de	1325-1329, 1355-1396	2	—	—	—	2
Isleham, de	1322-1334	1	—	—	—	1
Isolda, son of	1278	1	—	—	—	1
Ivel	1331-1350	—	1	—	—	2
Ives	1323-1347	1	—	—	—	1
Ivete	1302	1	—	—	—	1
Ivettson	1367	1	—	—	—	1
Ivo	1361	1	—	—	—	1
Jemys	1380	1	—	—	—	1
Jelekoc	1314	1	—	—	—	1
John, son of	1278-1394	8	8	3	—	33
Jowot	1375	1	—	—	—	1
Juel	1320-1324	1	—	—	—	1
Julian	1278-1351	2	2	—	—	6
Juys	1301	1	—	—	—	1
Kele	1393	1	—	—	—	1
Kem	1321	1	—	—	—	1
Keyston, de	1356	1	—	—	—	1
King	1329-1380	6	—	—	—	6
Kingston, de	1329-1372	1	—	—	—	1
Knytte	1377	1	—	—	—	1
Kokkil	1280	1	—	—	—	1
Kombere	1280	1	—	—	—	1
Kors	1278-1291, 1297	1	—	—	—	1
Kutere	1280-1353	2	2	1	—	9
Kylpyn	1387	1	—	—	—	1
Kyne	1287-1334, 1348-1388	3	—	—	—	3
Lache	1293	1	—	—	—	1
Lamberd	1338-1361	1	—	—	—	1
Lane, in the	1279-1394	11	3	—	—	17
Langeley, de	1335-1378	2	—	—	—	2
Langlane	1361	1	—	—	—	1
Larke	1332-1350	1	—	—	—	1
Lavendar	1341	1	—	—	—	1
Lawman	1381	1	—	—	—	1
Lawrence, son of	1347-1349	1	—	—	—	1

Surname	Residence Span	Number of Generations				Total Families
		1	2	3	4	
Leberd	1390	1	—	—	—	1
Leffeyn	1291-1360	1	—	—	—	1
Legat	1344-1380	2	1	—	—	4
Legge	1281-1348	8	1	—	—	10
Leicester, *de*	1382	1	—	—	—	1
Leighton, *de*	1308	1	—	—	—	1
Leirstowe, atte	1271-1333, 1351-1367, 1390	7	—	1	—	10
Lenman	1313	1	—	—	—	1
Lewe, atte	1282-1316	—	1	—	—	2
Lincoln, *de*	1293-1361	1	1	—	—	3
Lister	1320-1346, 1361-1367	1	—	1	—	4
Locksmyth	1280-1394	6	—	—	—	6
Lockyngton	1367-1394	1	—	—	—	1
Lodelowe	1344-1346	1	—	—	—	1
Londoneys	1316	1	—	—	—	1
Long, *le*	1303-1393	4	3	—	—	10
Looseworth	1375	1	—	—	—	1
Lorimer	1330-1353	—	1	—	—	2
Loxunt	1329-1359	4	—	—	—	4
Lucas	1299	1	—	—	—	1
Lucy	1291	1	—	—	—	1
Luton, *de*	1295-1363	3	—	—	—	3
Mabel	1287	1	—	—	—	1
Machoun	1351	1	—	—	—	1
Maddermonger (Warenter)	1280-1357	3	—	3	—	12
Maddermonger	1329-1357	—	1	—	—	2
Man	1351-1363	1	—	—	—	1
Manipenny	1278-1386	12	2	1	—	19
Manyhays	1377-1389	1	—	—	—	1
Marewele	1315-1327	1	—	—	—	1
Mariot	1346-1356	2	—	—	—	2
Marshall	1279-1363	13	1	—	—	15
Martin, son of	1286-1346	1	3	—	—	7
Masoun	1280-1379	9	2	—	—	13
Matilda, son of	1279-1322, 1356-1367	1	4	—	—	9
Mattishall, *de*	1280-1376	5	1	—	—	7
Mayse	1349	1	—	—	—	1
Merton, *de*	1279-1371	2	2	—	—	6
Messager	1310-1316	1	—	—	—	1
Messor	1317	1	—	—	—	1
Michel	1389-1395	2	—	—	—	2
Mildenhall, *de*	1350-1351	1	—	—	—	1
Mileward	1278-1377	2	3	—	—	8
Millicent	1285-1363	4	1	—	—	6
Miller	1286-1333, 1348	9	2	—	—	13
Molesworth, *de*	1317	1	—	—	—	1

Surname	Residence Span	Number of Generations				Total Families
		1	2	3	4	
Montem, super	1280-1368	4	—	—	—	4
Moore, of the	1356-1378	1	—	—	—	1
Morgrove	1298-1346, 1365	1	—	—	—	1
Moulton	1310-1349	2	—	—	—	2
Mun	1291-1295	2	—	—	—	2
Mundford, *de*	1314-1383	1	1	—	—	3
Muram, super	1280-1351	5	1	—	—	7
Nem	1280-1308	1	—	—	—	1
Newman	1316-1392	4	—	—	—	4
Nicholas, son of	1280-1360, 1371	5	2	—	—	9
Nicol	1348-1372	—	2	—	—	4
Nocemo	1350-1388	1	—	—	—	1
Nolly	1350	1	—	—	—	1
Nook	1342	1	—	—	—	1
Norborwhigam	1378	1	—	—	—	1
Norfolk, *de*	1317-1334	1	—	—	—	1
Norreys	1327-1348	1	—	—	—	1
Notting	1279-1394	4	—	1	—	7
Nunne	1281-1393	1	—	—	—	1
Offord, *de*	1310, 1330, 1351	3	—	—	—	3
Oliver	1308-1383	2	—	—	—	2
Ol the Thorpe, *de*	1388-1395	1	—	—	—	1
On ye, *de*	1377-1396	1	—	—	—	1
Opar'	1316	1	—	—	—	1
Ortun	1286	1	—	—	—	1
Osteler	1365-1366	1	—	—	—	1
Ostipil	1350	1	—	—	—	1
Oundle, *de*	1306-1369	1	1	—	—	3
Outy	1278-1398	7	2	1	—	14
Over, *de*	1308-1393	2	—	1	—	5
Overton	1361-1377	1	—	—	—	1
Oxford, *de*	1358-1380	1	—	—	—	1
Pademor, *de*	1280-1391	2	1	—	—	4
Page (Pays, Pelliparius)	1299-1344	1	1	—	—	3
Page (Pays)	1280-1387	6	1	1	—	11
Pagot	1329	1	—	—	—	1
Pakaret	1349	1	—	—	—	1
Palmer	1312, 1372-1382	2	—	—	—	2
Papworth, *de*	1308-1353	5	—	—	—	5
Parlor	1281	1	—	—	—	1
Parminter	1306	1	—	—	—	1
Parson	1280-1389	5	1	—	1	11
Parvaunt	1350	1	—	—	—	1
Parvus	1278-1366	2	1	—	—	4
Paternoster	1387-1390	2	—	—	—	2

Surname	Residence Span	Number of Generations				Total Families
		1	2	3	4	
Paxton, de	1279	3	—	—	—	3
Peek	1295, 1386-1387	2	—	—	—	2
Pedder	1342	1	—	—	—	1
Pekenot	1347	1	—	—	—	1
Pellage	1278-1349	1	—	1	—	4
Peneman	1290-1373	3	2	—	—	7
Pent'	1298	1	—	—	—	1
Pernel	1310-1399	2	1	1	—	7
Peter	1344	1	—	—	—	1
Peyntour	1333-1343	1	—	—	—	1
Peysel	1324-1361	—	1	—	—	2
Phinte	1281	1	—	—	—	1
Picard	1352	1	—	—	—	1
Pick	1298	1	—	—	—	1
Pikiring	1282-1356	2	—	—	—	2
Pistor	1282-1321	3	1	—	—	5
Plomer	1364-1394	1	—	—	—	1
Ploughwrighte	1330, 1361-1367	2	—	—	—	2
Plumbe	1349-1350	1	—	—	—	1
Plumpton	1380-1432	1	—	—	—	1
P'not	1305	1	—	—	—	1
Pope	1278-1378	2	—	1	—	5
Porter	1282, 1335-1347	2	—	—	—	2
Porthos	1340, 1380-1381	2	—	—	—	2
Prechetere	1363-1365	1	—	—	—	1
Prentys	1391-1393	1	—	—	—	1
Presbyter	1281, 1299, 1348	2	—	—	—	2
Psalse	1281	—	1	—	—	2
Puttock	1280, 1316-1326, 1354-1360	2	1	—	—	4
Pykenot	1308, 1324	2	—	—	—	2
Pysford	1377-1386	1	—	—	—	1
Quenyng	1279-1397	7	5	1	—	20
Quenyng (Thorley)	1288-1347	—	—	2	—	6
Quy, de	1391	1	—	—	—	1
Rabat	1351-1372	1	—	—	—	1
Radwell, de	1357	1	—	—	—	1
Rag	1297	1	—	—	—	1
Ralph, son of	1351-1377	—	—	1	—	3
Randolph	1342-1356	1	—	—	—	1
Raveley, de	1291-1320, 1342	2	—	—	—	2
Raven	1281-1327	—	1	—	—	2
Ray	1280	1	—	—	—	1
Red	1281-1360	1	1	—	—	3
Rede	1281-1389	6	1	2	—	14
Redelyster	1302-1322	1	—	—	—	1
Reder	1327-1347	1	—	—	—	1

Surname	Residence Span	Number of Generations				Total Families
		1	2	3	4	
Reginald	1278-1347	1	3	—	1	11
Reginald, son of	1316, 1329, 1349,					
	1360-1377	1	2	—	—	5
Reins	1286-1301	1	—	—	—	1
Remer	1356	1	—	—	—	1
Reve	1311, 1334	2	—	—	—	2
Reynold	1317-1322, 1349-1399	2	—	—	—	2
Richard, son of	1278-1348	1	—	—	—	1
Richer	1302-1320	1	—	—	—	1
Ripam, ad	1320-1326	1	—	—	—	1
Ripton, de	1314-1315	1	—	—	—	1
Rissle	1340-1348	2	—	—	—	2
Ro	1351-1380	—	1	—	—	2
Robert, son of	1308-1376	2	—	1	—	5
Robyn	1347, 1362-1382	3	—	—	—	3
Rode	1278-1378	6	—	1	1	13
Roger, son of	1280-1340, 1353-1376	4	—	—	—	4
Rokyston	1375	1	—	—	—	1
Rome	1294-1391	1	1	—	—	3
Rote	1361-1363	1	—	—	—	1
Rowusor	1373	1	—	—	—	1
Roysis, at ye	1351-1354	2	—	—	—	2
Russel	1297, 1302-1360	2	1	—	—	4
Rynis	1280	1	—	—	—	1
Saly	1308-1332	1	—	—	—	1
Sandone	1369	1	—	—	—	1
Saundresson	1366	1	—	—	—	1
Savage	1291-1313	1	—	—	—	1
Schalam						
Ecclesia, ad	1281-1282	—	1	—	—	2
Scholar	1380	1	—	—	—	1
Scot	1280-1389	5	3	—	—	11
Seges	1353, 1362	1	—	—	—	1
Selde	1372-1397	1	—	—	—	1
Seman	1278-1397	7	3	—	—	13
Serwyks	1347	1	—	—	—	1
Sewstere	1393-1395	1	—	—	—	1
Shepherd	1332-1347	1	—	—	—	1
Shyrford, de	1302-1309	2	—	—	—	2
Simon, son of	1279-1423	—	2	—	1	8
Skriven	1344-1350	1	—	—	—	1
Skinner	1287, 1350, 1369	2	—	—	—	2
Slaiurire	1280	1	—	—	—	1
Sly	1362-1387	1	—	—	—	1
Sofyn	1340	1	—	—	—	1
Somayster	1354-1371	1	—	—	—	1
Somersham, de	1325	1	—	—	—	1
Sommenour	1297-1325	—	1	—	—	2

Surname	Residence Span	Number of Generations				Total Families
		1	2	3	4	
Somyrton	1381-1399	1	—	—	—	1
Southoe, *de*	1372-1379	1	—	—	—	1
Spaldwick, *de*	1307, 1394	1	—	—	—	1
Spalding, *de*	1285, 1302	1	—	—	—	1
Sparwe	1350-1361	1	—	—	—	1
Spicer	1283-1340	—	1	—	—	2
Sprag	1352	1	—	—	—	1
Spruntyng	1295-1367	4	1	1	—	9
Stalum	1311	1	—	—	—	1
Stamford, *de*	1380	1	—	—	—	1
Stanton, *de*	1351-1352	1	—	—	—	1
Startle	1280-1394	6	2	—	—	10
Stircup	1315-1329, 1349	1	—	—	—	1
Stephen, son of	1287-1321	—	1	—	—	2
Stirtloe, *de*	1307-1379	1	1	—	—	3
Stoke	1362-1372	1	—	—	—	1
Stondon	1335-1340	1	—	—	—	1
Strateshill, *de*	1310-1332	1	—	—	—	1
Strut	1326, 1334	1	—	—	—	1
Stukeley, *de*	1288-1387	3	1	—	—	5
Sturpayn	1340	1	—	—	—	1
Stygeneye	1346	1	—	—	—	1
Stykedet	1316	1	—	—	—	1
Sutor	1280-1366	2	1	1	—	7
Swetman	1353	1	—	—	—	1
Swineshead, *de*	1278-1279	1	—	—	—	1
Swon	1295-1358	4	1	—	—	6
Swynford	1389	1	—	—	—	1
Syer	1333	1	—	—	—	1
Syle	1353	1	—	—	—	1
Tabbe	1325-1359	—	1	—	—	2
Tanner	1278	1	—	—	—	1
Tavener	1349-1366	1	—	—	—	1
Taylor	1325-1372	4	2	—	—	8
Teband	1306	—	1	—	—	2
Tesard	1279-1303	1	—	—	—	1
Textor	1283-1295	1	—	—	—	1
Teye	1366-1367	1	—	—	—	1
Thame, *de*	1380	1	—	—	—	1
Thomas, son of	1306	1	—	—	—	1
Thome	1342-1374	—	1	—	—	2
Thresshere	1361	1	—	—	—	1
Thrumbolt	1315-1345	1	1	—	—	3
Thurlby	1377-1393	1	—	—	—	1
Thykthorn	1372-1396	1	—	—	—	1
Tinctor	1279-1330	5	—	—	—	5
Tinker	1327	1	—	—	—	1
Todenham, *de*	1300-1329	3	—	—	—	3

Surname	Residence Span	Number of Generations				Total Families
		1	2	3	4	
Togod	1285-1301	1	—	—	—	1
Trappe	1373-1393	1	—	—	—	1
Trippe	1293	1	—	—	—	1
Trumpeston	1302	1	—	—	—	1
Turnour	1350-1351	1	—	—	—	1
Ulf	1309-1313, 1364, 1372	2	—	—	—	2
Underne	1308, 1314	—	1	—	—	2
Underlespitel	1316-1349	1	—	—	—	1
Underwode	1302-1371	2	1	—	—	4
Upton, de	1286	1	—	—	—	1
Uteband	1307	1	—	—	—	1
Utting	1340-1348	1	—	—	—	1
Valey	1329-1373	1	—	—	—	1
Vecheram	1287-1297	1	—	—	—	1
Vicar	1298, 1350	2	—	—	—	2
Ville, ad capud	1294-1340	2	1	—	—	4
Viceloy	1351	1	—	—	—	1
Vincent	1285-1321	1	—	—	—	1
Viting	1299	1	—	—	—	1
Wake	1307	1	—	—	—	1
Wakefield	1392-1398	1	—	—	—	1
Walcot, de	1348	1	—	—	—	1
Wale	1341	1	—	—	—	1
Waleys	1298-1390	3	1	—	—	5
Walfrom	1360	1	—	—	—	1
Walgate	1391	1	—	—	—	1
Walshe	1300-1306, 1332, 1390	3	—	—	—	3
Walter, son of	1280-1303	1	1	—	—	3
Warde	1313-1327, 1340-1364	2	—	—	—	2
Waresley, de	1331-1341	1	—	—	—	1
Warmington, de	1291-1332	1	1	—	—	3
Waryn	1339	1	—	—	—	1
Wat'	1315	1	—	—	—	1
Waterledere	1280-1291	1	—	—	—	1
Webester	1315, 1329, 1345	3	—	—	—	3
Welle, atte (Fontem, ad)	1283, 1293-1348	—	1	—	—	2
Wennington, de	1314-1316	1	—	—	—	1
Wenent'	1308	1	—	—	—	1
West	1362-1398	2	—	—	—	2
Weston, de	1330-1367	1	1	—	—	3
Wethyng	1369-1399	1	—	—	—	1
Wiggenhall, de	1332	1	—	—	—	1
Wilde	1282-1320	—	1	—	—	2
Wille	1298-1302	1	—	—	—	1
William, son of	1283-1397	1	5	1	1	18

Surname	Residence Span	Number of Generations				Total Families
		1	*2*	*3*	*4*	
William, Little	1297, 1311	1	—	—	—	1
Wimblington, *de*	1295-1298	1	—	—	—	1
Wistow, *de*	1300-1333, 1382	2	—	—	—	2
Witman	1283-1390	1	1	—	—	3
Wollaston, *de*	1341-1399	1	—	—	—	1
Wolle	1349	1	—	—	—	1
Woodstone, *de*	1281-1325	—	1	—	—	2
Wright	1300, 1329, 1350, 1399	5	—	—	—	5
Wulleman	1386-1391	1	—	—	—	1
Wyce	1316	1	—	—	—	1
Wyldebryd	1311-1312	1	—	—	—	1
Wygon	1361-1362	1	—	—	—	1
Wyke	1387-1395	1	—	—	—	1
Wymer	1333-1348	1	—	—	—	1
Wyn	1291-1316	3	—	—	—	3
Wynier	1341-1382	—	1	—	—	2
Wynot	1346	1	—	—	—	1
Wysdom	1339-1346	1	—	—	—	1
Wytyng	1301-1315	—	1	—	—	2
Yacher	1302	1	—	—	—	1
Yelling, *de*	1325	1	—	—	—	1
Yonge	1313, 1324	—	2	—	—	4

5

Resources and Their Utilization
at Godmanchester

A. PRIMARY RESOURCES

Various perspectives may add to our understanding of a town — the surprising detail of aerial photography, the patient reconstruction of archaeology, the particular views of personal memoirs and the specialized framework of institutional records. Each perspective is selective and given the limited resources available to the student of society, past or present, it may be fairly presumed that the student's approach will always remain selective. That the fortunes of history should have imposed a selective approach through the records allowed to survive for Godmanchester, therefore, must not be construed as an unusual deterrent to our understanding of the town. Indeed, Godmanchester is extraordinarily well served by records and this fact must spur the historians on to more interpretation.

A more severe limitation, that of a too sharp distinction between city and countryside, was examined in the Introduction. Was Godmanchester town or country — a sort of frustrated urban development or merely a larger rural settlement? The findings of this study suggest that such questions are irrelevant. However badly these may fit the neat categories of students of society, it is apparently within the capacity of man to create almost endless variations of human institutions. Actually, this statement should elicit no surprise since the *mentalité*, psychological desire or sheer will for such creativity is a well known phenomenon in the history of differing types of patriotism.

The history of the town of Godmanchester does not seem to fit the classical model of institutional development. Whether this model is expressed in the liberal economic terms of division of labour — arriving at sufficient wealth to be able to support more sophisticated institutions — or in the marxist doctrine of exploitation of surplus labour, really does not

matter. Both theories suggest an inevitability of institutional organization that is not to be found at Godmanchester. There seem to have been the resources for more institutional development. The revenues of the Priory of Merton were not a heavy drain on the town. In the local tax assessment of 1309, the priory was on the "second level" of those with taxable resources.[1] As we have seen, the town carefully protected itself from further property control by religious houses. The royal farm of £120 must have been a rather horrendous burden when first imposed by King John — an increase of almost two and one half times over the farm previously paid to the king. However, despite the great increases in productivity and inflation over the thirteenth century, the farm payment was not raised again. By 1300, this payment could not have been a heavy drain upon the total revenues of the town.[2] According to the Hundred Roll of 1279, commercial interests from across the river were making heavy inroads on Godmanchester property. Again, however, the town seems to have successfully prevented these outsiders from obtaining long-term control over resources of Godmanchester. One is left with the conclusion that the disposition of Godmanchester resources remained largely in the hands of the townsmen. Before further analysis of this disposition can be made, we must attempt an assessment of just what these resources were.

The farm total that can be calculated from the surviving 1279 Hundred Roll manuscript for Godmanchester comes so close (within four shillings) to the £120 farm owed that it must have been considered by the hundred roll commissioners to be a complete survey of the town. In an entry following a listing of the total property owned by the Prior of Merton[3] it is stated that such property (both arable, meadow and pasture) pay eight pence per acre to the farm. From the total arable, meadow and pasture of the town (some eight acres less than 3,000) the farm payments at eight pence per acre would amount to £96 9s. 4d. An additional £15 were paid to the farm from the mills "cum hulmo," and another 14s. from fisheries, bringing the total to £112 3s. 4d. This left nearly eight pounds to be collected from crofts, messuages, shops and small pieces of land. One cannot generalize about the farm owed by these units of property since they are usually combined with each other, and where this is not the case, the separate units vary so much in farm valuation that one may suspect these are not really comparable crofts and messuages. Nevertheless, an

[1] See Raftis and Hogan, *Lay Subsidy Rolls*, p. 127.
[2] See further below, p. 184.
[3] *1279 Hundred Roll*, p. 591.

effort must be made to assess the significance of the £120 farm in the economy of Godmanchester.

Property conveyances at Godmanchester were usually concluded by the formula "paying the accustomed farm."[4] However, there is considerable evidence that townsmen had introduced a "beneficial" assessment for their own personal purposes. When Cristina Drewe received two acres and one rod of land from her father Nicholas, the assessment was only that for one acre plus a penny.[5] The four acres that John, son of Simon le Masun, received by bequest of his father in an undated roll of ca. 1300 was said to pay (defend) as only two acres to the farm. This discounting of farm payments also extended beyond family conveyances to ordinary sales. Among the dozens of examples that could be cited is the purchase of one half acre by Adam Grinde in 1288, a property to pay farm as only one rod. Since we know nothing of the economic condition, or relative sale price, of such discounted properties, it would be hazardous to suggest that such discounting was a policy. All that may be said from surviving records is the fact that, where farm amounts are indicated, discounting was the common practice. As such, these discounts indicate the ease with which the farm obligations could be more thinly spread on property by the late thirteenth century.

There is practically no information available on the sale price of land at Godmanchester. In an entry quoted in Chapter 1[6] the two Paxton daughters each paid 20 marks for the purchase of six acres of arable from their father. There undoubtedly was an element of gift in this intra-familial purchase of 12 acres at something over £2 to the acre. On the other hand, the same Paxton family was involved in a considerable land sale that came to less than £2 to the acre, if the following entry fully accounts for purchase considerations:

> William Colion took seisin of 20 acres of land bought from Nicholas Paxton and Cristina his wife, lying in various parts of the fields of Godmanchester, to defend for the farm that is due. Also, this William is seised of one half of a capital messuage of the said Nicholas and Cristina, together with one half of the curtilage appurtenant to that messuage, and as well, 16 acres one rod of arable, three acres of meadow and three rods of leyes along with

---

[4] See texts in Chapter 1, above, passim. In short, the actual farm tax assessed according to the court rolls was one half that assessed in the 1279 Hundred Roll. This reduction cannot be simply attributed to sown acres in the field system since meadow is reduced in the same fashion.

[5] See the text above, p. 25.

[6] See above, Chapter 1, p. 36.

the half of that messuage noted above together with the appurtenant curtilage to be received after the death of the said Nicholas Paxton and Cristina his wife and to defend for the due amount. The terms of this agreement were that the above William Colion should pay for having those tenements as given above the amount of 49 pounds and 15 shillings sterling to the said Nicholas and Cristina his wife or their assignees. (Fine: 2s.)[7]

When Albrida Godware paid off the debts of her husband the rate seems to have been more in the order of £5 to the acre. The debt was £10 and the property given for its redemption was one and one half acres of arable and a swath of meadow:

> Albrida Godware, widow of Alexander the reeve, delivered into the hands of the bailiffs to the use of Godfrey Quenyne three one half acres of land and one swath of meadow, defending as one acre, from the land that the above Alexander gave to the said Albrida while he was alive. And the court adjudged it proper for her to sell that land to acquit herself and her son and heir of ten pounds of silver before the itinerant justices at Huntington. Her son and heir agreed to this sale to quit his father's debt. And [Godfrey Quenyne] had seisin.[8]

This prices of five pounds per acre is probable nearer to the market value of land.[9] While the purchase period was not specified for the

---

[7] Box 5, bundle 1. 8 August 1325.

Willelmus Colion cepit sesinam de xx[ti] acris terre emptis de Nicholao Paxton' et Christine uxore eius, iacentibus in campis de Gumecestr' divisim, ad defendendum pro firma debita. Dictus Willelmus sesitus est de medietate capitalis mesuagii dicti Nicholai et Christine uxoris eius cum medietate curtilagii eidem mesuagio pertinente et de xvi acris terre arabilis et una roda et de tribus acris prati et de tribus rodis lays emptis de predicto Nicholao et Christina uxore eius iacentibus divisim in campis predictis. Et predictus Willelmus Colion predictas xvi acras terre et unam rodam et tres acras prati et tres rodas lays cum medietate predicta mesuagii predicti et curtilagio eidem pertinente recipiet post obitum dictorum Nicholai Paxton et Christine uxoris eius ad defendendum pro firma debita, sub hac forma quod predictus Willelmus Colion pro predictis tenementis habendis in forma predicta solvat eisdem Nicholao et Christine uxori eius vel eorum assignatis quadraginta et novem libras et quindecim solidos sterlingorum.

[8] Box 5, bundle 1. Ca. 1280.

Albrida Godware que fuit uxor Alexandri prepositi reddidit in manu ballivorum tres dimidias acras terre et 1 swat prati de ipsa terra quam predictus Alexander donavit predicte Albrede in vita sua ad opus Galfridi Queyne ad defendendum pro una acra. Et consideratum fuit per curiam quod bene posset predictam terram vendere acquietandam ipsam et filium suum et heredem de decem libris argenti predictis coram iusticiariis intinerantibus apud Huntedon' et ad istam venditionem consensit filius suus et heres pro debito patris sui acquietandam et habuit seysinam.

[9] Further evidence for the value of Godmanchester land comes from the establishing of a chantry by William Millicent junior and colleagues whereby rents were pro-rated as high as 16s. a year from meadow and 8s. from arable. For the text of this chantry foundation, see above, pp. 47-48.

properties noted above, Roger Notting paid seven marks over four years to the executors of Robert Whyn for a place in Longlane.[10] This place was town property but there is no indication that it included buildings. The St. Ives fair court of 20 May 1300 informs us that John Spicer repaid a debt owed to Peter Mercator with a messuage at Godmanchester worth 40 shillings.[11] This messuage has not been identified in Godmanchester records, but the average messuage farm in the list given above[12] was only threepence.

The three thousand acres specified in the Hundred Roll of Godmanchester, then, may have had a market value of between £6,000 and £15,000. What multiple should be applied to other sources of revenue, such as the mills and fisheries, it is impossible to even speculate about. In any case, there was farm of nearly £100 directly assessed upon arable and meadow. If one takes £10,000 as an average figure for the market value of Godmanchester arable and pasture and assumes this to be of ten-year purchase, the annual value would be in the order of £1,000. The £100 payable to the royal farm would, therefore, be some ten percent of the annual market value of these properties.

The agrarian basis of this value of Godmanchester land can be seen in broad terms from the sowing and sheep lists drawn up for assessment of the 1334 lay subsidy. Since the first sowing and sheep list (Table 12) had only one third of those paying the tax in 1332, one may multiply the amounts sown and the number of sheep by three as a possible estimate of total resources in these categories. In this fashion, the 1,157 sown acres of this first list may be tripled to suggest that some 3,471 acres were actually sown in a year around 1334; one may expect to find five or six hundred acres at fallow in the same year.[13] Tripling the 1,328 fleeces and 361

---

[10] Box 4, bundle 3. 22 January 1327.

Rogerus Notting cepit sesinam de una placea iacente in Le Longlane empta de executoribus Roberti Whyn ad defendendum pro firma debita. Et si contingat dictum Rogerum in perte vel in toto solutionis septem marcarum infra quatuor annos solvendarum dictis executoribus defecerit videlicet quolibet anno trium annorum propinqorum duas marcas et quarte anno unam marcam de inde dictus Rogerus omnino iure suo dicte placee carebit sine recuperatione denariorum ac dicti executores predictam placeam cum predictis denariis sine conditione alicui recuperabunt nisi meliore gratia predictorum executorum fuerit. (2d.)

[11] See below, p. 198.

[12] See above, pp. 117-118. If this were an average, nearly 400 messuages of Godmanchester would be worth £800!

[13] In general terms, that is to say, not with respect to each furlong, a maximum of one quarter of the arable might be expected to lie fallow in the grain cycle of Godmanchester by this time; the one-third fallow system may still have obtained in 1279.

lambs gives a flock of 3,984 sheep and 1,083 lambs for the same time. This figure of some 4,000 acres of arable, 1,000 acres remaining for pasture, meadow and crofts does come close to the modern acreage (approximately 5,000). While the 3,471 acres derived from the calculations we have used cannot be taken with any great precision, it does draw our attention to the fact that the acreage indicated as such in 1279 is vastly understated. Indeed, this sown figure does suggest that the modest 1279 Hundred Roll acreage figure (ca. 2,500, above, p. 94) also indicates sown acres only. One could note that no acreage figures are given in 1279 for land within the four streets or for those numerous plots and closes extending beyond the town as partial explanation of this under-statement. However, the sown acre resolution would seem much more plausible.

The 1,328 fleeces would comprise five and one half sacks (at 240 fells to the sack) and, from some data from around this time,[14] may be taken to be worth six to seven pounds per sack. Taking the lower price, one can estimate that the wool noted in the list of ca. 1340 (Table 13) would be worth something more than £30. It is difficult to evaluate the lambs, but a minimum figure might be a shilling each, giving a total of £13 for the 361 lambs. It should be noted that the value of the fleeces is exclusive of the sheep themselves. Sheep would be worth more than lambs so that a flock of more than 1,300 sheep may have been evaluated at something near £100. The total market value of the partially recorded sheep at Godman-chester may have been closer to £150, and with a multiplier of three, well over £400.

The soil of Godmanchester lent itself admirably to the methods of pre-modern agriculture. In the words of the seventeenth-century observer Godmanchester was spoken of as having "a great name for tillage; situate in an open ground, of a light mould, and bending in ye sun."[15] By the time of the first sowing list (1334 – Table 12) Godmanchester had already moved into the concentration upon legumes and barley that was to become the pattern for the late medieval and early modern farming of the region. If one includes the bracketed data in the 1334 sowing list (on the premise that bracketed data are a minimal figure)[16] the total sown acreage indicated by this fragment is 1,187 acres and 3 rods. Of this acreage, slightly more than one third was in barley (34% – : 402 acres, 1 rod),

---

[14] See T. H. Lloyd, *The English Wool Trade in the Middle Ages* (Cambridge, 1977), Chapter 9, passim.

[15] See vcH, p. 286.

[16] See above, pp. 102-116.

more than one third in peas (36% +: 435 acres, 2½ rods), and the
remainder divided among wheat (less than 15% of the total: 154 acres,
2½ rods), oats (less than 10% of the total: 109 acres, 3 rods), rye (only
some 5%: 61 acres, 3½ rods) and dredge (only some 2%: 23 acres 2½
rods).[17]

There are no specific data for crop yields or sowing rates at Godmanchester at this time. No estimate, therefore, can be more than broadly
suggestive. If one takes the gross yield per acre as slightly above the
average for the best source available for cropping in thirteenth and
fourteenth-century England[18] and supplies peas and dredge data from
neighbouring villages,[19] a modest gross yield for Godmanchester might be
suggested as 10 bushels per acre for wheat, 15 bushels per acre for barley,
10 for oats, 10 for peas, 10 for rye and 12 bushels per acre for dredge
(barley and oats). In figures rounded to the nearest hundred, the 1334
sown acres of Godmanchester would then have produced 1,500 bushels
of wheat, 6,000 bushels of barley, 4,300 bushels of peas, 1,100 bushels of
oats, 600 bushels of rye and 300 bushels of dredge. Converting bushels to
quarters and multiplying by prices to be expected in England at this time[20]
(wheat, 5s.; barley, 4s.; peas, 4s.; oats, 2s.; rye, 4s.; dredge, 3s.) the value
of this grain would become: wheat, £47; barley, £155 8s.; peas, £107 8s.;
oats, £13 14s.; rye, £15 8s.; dredge, £5 11s. — for a total of £344 9s.
Again, employing a multiplier of three, the value of standing grain at Godmanchester would be in excess of £1,000.

Behind the sowing of crops in a mixed farming economy such as that of
Godmanchester lay a great amount of "operational" capital in stock and
equipment. The first surviving local tax list for Godmanchester (1309)
calculated more of the surplus of such capital than later local lists. The 120
individuals in this 1309 list had taxable stock evaluated as follows: 105
affers (£19 15s. 5d.), 7 horses (£2 11s. 4d.), 108 cows (£38 3s. 7d.), 6
calves (11s.), 21 pigs (£2 5s.), 22 piglets (14s. 8d.), 29 oxen (£14 10s.), 34
young oxen (£9 3s.), 35 mares (£6 14s. 3d.), 24 carts (£5 4s. 10d.), fen
(£23 0s. 5d.), and straw (£6 19s. 1d.). The total value of these items of
farm capital comes to £129 12s. 7d. This figure far exceeded the sheep and
lambs taxable in 1309 (sheep: £37 14s. 10d.; lambs: £3 14s. 6d.). Indeed,

---

[17] The percentage is almost the same in the 1340 sowing and sheep list (Table 13).
[18] See J. Z. Titow, *Winchester Yields: A Study in Medieval Agricultural Productivity*
(Cambridge, 1972).
[19] See J. A. Raftis, *The Estates of Ramsey Abbey* (Toronto, 1957), pp. 264 ff.
[20] See the chapters by David Farmer in the forthcoming volume of *The Agrarian
History of England and Wales* (Cambridge, in press).

these items that have here been termed "capital" were valued at more than one half of the taxable grain (which amounted to £222 3d. ob.q.).

If this amount of capital was surplus in 1309, what was the actual non-taxed capital required for normal operation of the town's agrarian economy? The 120 individuals taxed represented only some 25 percent of those holding land in the hundred roll of 1279. But these were the more wealthy individuals of the town so that it would be meaningless to use any sort of multiplier simply based upon numbers of tenants. However, it would seem useful to "re-convert" the surplus grain of 1309 to the acreage that must have been required to produce this amount. By employing the same productivity quotas per acre for each type of grain as was done above for 1334 the following acreages are derived: wheat, 146 + ; barley, 117 + ; rye, 116; peas, 168 + ; dredge, 118 − for a total of 665 acres.

If one employs the arable acreage from the Hundred Roll (2,511 acres) and assumes that five to six hundred acres may have lain fallow in one year, then this 665 acres would represent less than one third of the arable sown at Godmanchester around 1309. Employing the larger figure suggested by sowing data of 1334 (3,471 acres) with proportionate fallow, the 665 acres would represent less than one quarter of the total arable sown. In consideration of the fact that produce from the 665 acres was taxable surplus, and arable was so widely held, the latter figure appears more plausible. This emphasis is also supported by meadow "produce" from the two periods. Only 549 sheep and lambs were taxed in 1309 yet the sowing and sheep list of 1334 (Table 12) gives 1,689 (fleeces and lambs) and the multiplier, 5,067. In short, the taxable sheep of 1309 may have been little more than one tenth of the total number of sheep and lambs at Godmanchester at that time.[21] In any case, it would seem that a minimum figure for the "operational" capital at Godmanchester (horses, cattle, pigs, carts) would be indicated by a multiplier of four, that is, a sum around £500.

From arable produce alone, then, one may estimate the gross product of Godmanchester to have been about £1,000 per annum. Sheep added another £400 and other animals (and carts) a further £500, although not all these animals were annual products. On the other hand, as occupational names have already suggested, a great many commercial

---

[21] It is clear from the land market indicated in the court rolls, as well as lists such as the subletting lists given in Chapter 3 above, that meadow was as widely dispersed as arable among the people of Godmanchester.

products must have been produced and changed hands yearly at Godman-chester.

There were 16 items variously designated as cauldrons in the 1309 local assessment list. These pots varied in value from that of Eusebius Clerk, worth only 12d., to that of William Manipenny worth 6s. 8d. Altogether these pots (including a measure and some undecipherable item called "vag't") were valued at £7 9s. 8d. in 1309. Since such items bear no particular reference to the amount of wealth of those taxed at this time, or whether their wealth was in farm produce or merchandise, it may be assumed that such pots or vessels were utensils for ordinary domestic use. This being the case, every house might be expected to have a cauldron of some sort[22] so that the total number of cauldrons (in terms of messuages) would be at least 350 more than those listed in 1309. Even at a minimum value of one shilling, these would be worth a further £17 or more.

These pots, along with carts that have been included in the operational capital above, were only two of some twenty items considered worthy of special mention when not specifically bequeathed:

> It is decided and ordered by the full court of Godmanchester that every chief heir shall receive, as it were by inheritance, all the movables hereafter mentioned after the death of his kinsmen, if they be not specifically bequeathed, saving to the wife her dower if she survive her husband; and that nevertheless (he shall have) his portion of all the remaining utensils; to wit, the best pot of the whole house, with the best pan, a laver and basin, a mortar and pestle, a trivet, a gridiron, a spade, a shovel, a fork, a chest, a cup, a table with tressels, an axe, a bed, a table-cloth, a towel, the best cart, the plough with the irons belonging thereto, a bushel measure, a sledge, a barrow. And if the wife shall have received a part of the aforesaid things to be for her own use, she shall deposit the price out of her receipts, and shall pay to the heir, if she does any damage therein. Further, the wife shall receive her portion of all the remaining vessels and utensils except the aforesaid things belonging to the heir, doing her will therewith (with power) to assign them to whomsoever she will.[23]

It seems reasonable to assume that such utensils for the whole town, inclusive of pots but excluding carts, would be worth a minimum of £100.

In summary, then, by such crude calculations as the above, one can easily come to a figure of more than £2,000 of gross new capital per year

---

[22]   There is incidental information in court rolls that identifies having a cauldron with establishing a ménage.

[23]   Bateson, *Borough Customs*, pp. 141-142.

as produced at Godmanchester around 1300. Such a figure does not include data from peasant efforts on the subsistence level — economics of space in sharing living quarters, intensive cultivation of small domestic plots of land, the maintenance on refuse of animals such as pigs, the availability of seasonal "surpluses" (fish, fruit, nuts, rabbits, wood) and so on. Studies of developing economies today indicate the subsistence importance of such resources but these resources are virtually impossible to measure and, in any case, do not provide a capital base for economic growth. Furthermore, the gross new capital figure for Godmanchester does not give an adequate index to capital availability. The velocity of property turnover, as indicated generally by all the land data of the court rolls, and in more startling fashion by the surviving fragments of lists of short-term leases, attest to a ready pool of liquid capital. Finally, it must be noted again that this gross capital figure is calculated largely from primary resources. An effort must now be made to discover whether these considerable resources in agrarian capital at Godmanchester made possible independent commercial endeavours by the townsmen and even secondary industry.

B. SECONDARY RESOURCES

Quantities of material resources are but one aspect of a town life; the availability of such resources is another matter. Unquestionably there were great economic inequalities at Godmanchester and it will be part of the purpose of the following pages to draw attention to those who never seemed to acquire property and those who always seemed to hold a disproportionate amount of the town's wealth. Nevertheless, it is all too easy in the study of an economy about which we have such little knowledge to allow our investigations to be straight-jacketed by such hidebound heritages of nineteenth-century thought as theories of exploitation. The continual development of flexible forms of wealth today is causing some historians to question whether the distinction between ownership of private property and its use have not been overdrawn in the past. For Godmanchester, a striking feature of the preceding chapters has been the mobility of property and skills. Some attempt must now be made to give further interpretation to this phenomenon.

While, as we have seen in Chapter 4 above, there can be only an uncertain estimate of the total population of Godmanchester from local records, an estimate of the total labour resources available to the town cannot even be attempted. Traditional societies had a considerable mobile

and transient population. The numbers of these non-landed people cannot be assessed for Godmanchester, but one can be certain that they were not negligible. In a frankpledge court for Godmanchester prior to the fifteenth century, that entered with the regular court for 1294,[24] 24 householders of Godmanchester were fined for giving hospitality to outsiders (*extranei*) "against the assize." Who and how many these outsiders were, we are not told.[25] The Eyre Roll of 1286[26] reports that an unknown man was found killed by the road in Godmanchester. And the same roll recorded that three natives of Godmanchester were exculpated in the death of William Page by a jury that accused "unknown malefactors" of his murder. Apparently neither local nor royal courts were surprised to find many unknown strangers wandering through the town of Godmanchester.

This lack of information about names of outsiders must not be simply construed as a lack of concern, for many were in fact identified. In the same court of 1293 an apparent outsider, John Soreweles, was charged with drawing blood from Godfrey Bedel. A further entry in the same court notes that William Hardy was to be amerced for having received Elena Soreweles who had been "prohibited the vill." The Eyre Roll of 1286 found that Thomas Postel of Godmanchester accidentally killed John son of Osbert with a stone he was throwing at a dog. Although Thomas Postel was in tithing, he had no chattels and there is no record of his having held property. John son of Osbert is similarly not mentioned among property holders of the town. The same eyre recorded that Warin *le* Beggar, who was an outsider from Northampton "and so neither in tithing nor having chattels," had murdered John *le* Leman of Godman-chester and escaped from the prison. The same court charged Thomas *de* Suthoe from Toseland, William Startle of Godmanchester and William Turgh of Swavesey with being a gang (?) of thieves. While the three were acquitted of this charge, Thomas *de* Suthoe was found guilty of vagabondage.

It has been established from references to fines for bad work per-formance, that villagers of Huntingdonshire often hired outsiders, more or

[24] Box 6, bundle 1. 25 March 1294. This is the only extant instance prior to the fifteenth century where some entries from a frankpledge court have been entered with a court of fines and entry fines.

[25] English society in general, and one may presume at Godmanchester in particular, had changed so much between the thirteenth and fifteenth centuries that it has not seemed useful to "read back" from the many extant fifteenth-century frankpledge rolls on this point.

[26] See Anne and Edwin DeWindt, *Royal Justice and the Medieval English Countryside* (in press).

less "known," as casual labour.[27] The same practice would no doubt have been followed at Godmanchester. The royal Eyre Roll of 1286 reported that William Wylde and Robert Rode, haywards of Godmanchester, and William *le* Waleys, hayward of the Prior of Merton killed and robbed three outsiders, two men and a woman. Robert Rode and William *le* Waleys fled and were outlawed; neither had any chattels, nor had they been in tithing since they were vagabonds. William Wylde, who with his wife held property in Godmanchester, was acquitted of the murder charge. These haywards (*messarii*) were not the important officials by the same name whose role was spelled out by Walter *de* Henley.[28] Rather, these may be taken to be labour hired for the large meadow harvest at Godmanchester. If one may judge from the numbers of workmen to be found at the bees, or boon work, seasons in neighbouring Ramsey villages,[29] peak seasonal employment demands could have been in the hundreds at Godmanchester.

One has only to glance at the Lay Subsidy rolls for Godmanchester to realize why shepherds, haywards, pigmen and carters need not have required chattels of their own. There were plenty of carts, rich hay fields, herds of pigs and flocks of sheep to require their attention. If one were to take only the "surplus" carts and animals of the 1309 local assessment list, there would be horses and carts for a score of carters, numerous shepherds and ploughmen. The fact that such humble tasks gave surnames to practitioners is not merely significant for our understanding of the division of labour possible to this period of history. Surnames were recognition of social as well as economic roles and, however modest the pecking order, it has been frequently observed in rural areas of modern England that identification with an expertise lends relative prestige and authority to working men.

It is only from incidental information, therefore, that these least wealthy specialists come to our attention. Among the probable farming specialists, John *de* Catworth, carter and John *de* Barnwell, carter, were involved in lawsuits in 1299 and 1316 respectively. A Richard Carter was noted in 1279, a Robert Carter in 1300 and his son John over the next decade. Alan the Carter acquired a smallholding in 1344 and Thomas the Carter was charged with failing to appear at court to answer a plea between 1345 and 1348. As probable pigmen were Robert *le* Swon and

---

[27] See Raftis, *Tenure and Mobility*, Chapter 6.

[28] See *Walter of Henley and other Treatises on Estate Management and Accounting*, ed. Dorothea Oschinsky (Oxford, 1971), s.v. hayward.

[29] For example Raftis, *Warboys*, p. 210.

Simon *le* Swon mentioned before 1300, Richard son of Simon *le* Swon in 1302, William *le* Swon acquiring a smallholding in 1332 and Reginald *le* Swon involved in a lawsuit over 1343-1344. No beadles were noted on the court rolls after Godfrey (1279), Robert (1281) and Reginald (1278-1287). Apparently of this same occupational level were Walter *le* Horseman of Huntingdon and his son John, both appearing in Godmanchester court rolls in 1318.

Our sources are no better with respect to other smallish occupations. There are fewer references in court rolls to tailors than one finds in rural villages of Huntingdonshire one quarter the size of Godmanchester. Earliest references to tailors very likely only occur because these were outsiders to the town: in 1295 a certain Jordan of Hemingford, tailor, purchased a toft and in 1298 the same Jordan sold one half acre of arable; in 1311, a William *de* Scorham, tailor, was involved in a lawsuit at Huntingdon. One could conclude that tailoring at Godmanchester was a part time occupation and not sufficiently unique to cause the identification of its practitioners by this surname. On the other hand, tailoring may very likely have become distinct from surnames for Godmanchester people as with the two outsiders noted above. However, only from the mid-century does the specification of occupations permit a more complete picture of the tailors of the town: Richard *le* Cissor, 1320; Godfrey Aylred, 1361; Robert Bartholomew, 1363; Roger Gardener, 1393; Simon Ilster, 1349; Thomas son of John Kele, 1393; Simon King, 1376; William Legge, 1352; William Longe, 1349; John Swetecok, 1350; Isolda Seuster, 1344; Henry *le* Taylor, 1348; and John son of Walter *le* Taylor, 1327.

Fishing at Godmanchester was a professional monopoly of the town and must have engaged many people. From the fact that the Godmanchester fishing industry paid 14 shillings to the royal farm, one might expect that the industry brought in a net product worth at least ten times this amount. And yet the court rolls mention only modest "little" individuals Emma *le* Fisher (1301) and John *le* Fisher (1312-1315) as apparently of Godmanchester. Undoubtedly, fish was a basic staple for the diet of Godmanchester people and not sufficiently full time as an occupation to attract family surnames. The significance of the wealth of the fisheries only comes through from the fact that numerous outsiders, apparently professional fishermen, were involved in Godmanchester and even sought liberty of the town: John *de* Brampton, 1322; William Boy *de* Hunts, 1327; Henry *de* Hunts, 1322; John *de* Offord Cluny, 1321; Robert *de* Broughton, of St. Ives, 1316; Ralph *de* Offord, 1330 (liberty); Richard son of Dany *de* Paxton, 1327 (liberty); Adam son of Dany *de* Paxton, 1327 (liberty); Andrew *de* Offord Cluny, 1388; Simon *de* Hunts, 1388;

John Aleyn, 1391; John Bonde *de* Hunts, 1371; John Falconer, 1386; William Scot, 1379; and John *de* Hunts, 1364.

This pattern of information about tailors and fishermen is repeated for many other trades. That is, for workers in wood, metal and leather that one might expect in any town or village of this size, most of the information is incidental to outsiders. Enough information has been given on these in the previous chapter so that it need not be repeated here.

It is extraordinarily difficult to extract from the records an adequate gauge of the extent of commercial activities at Godmanchester. In the 1279 Hundred Roll there is mention only of one smithy and a modest factory (*domus fabricationis*). By contrast with the thousands of references to other properties, court roll references to shops are even more exceptional than those in the Hundred Roll:

> Henry, the son of John Pellage took seisin of a certain bakeshop that came to him in gift from his mother, which shop he is to defend as for one half acre. And it was testified before the court at that time that Phillippa, the mother of the above Henry, lawfully during her life gave the said shop to that Henry her son.[30]

> Reginald in the Lane came into full court and placed into the hands of the bailiffs for the use of his daughter Catherine all his rights to a messuage that is the bakeshop pertaining to the Hemmings that lies from the king's road to the bank. This is to be defended for 8d. at the term (for such payments). (Fine: 4d.)[31]

> Henry, son of Henry Spruntyng, is seised of a building called a workshop in gift of his father Henry, to be received after his father's death and for which a penny is paid at the usual time. (One penny fine.)[32]

> Henry de Brunne, weaver, was seised of a built-up place that Richard Lacy had held and delivered into the hands of the community to the use of that Henry. And the whole community allows seisin to Henry of this

---

[30] Box 6, bundle 1. 31 December 1298.

Henricus filius Johannis Pellage cepit sesinam de quodam pistrino quod ei accidit ex dono matris sue ad deffenddendum pro dimidia acra et testatur curie ex illa hora quod Phillipa mater predicti Henrici in legitima vita sua dedit predictum pistrinum dicto Henrico filio suo. (Fine: ?)

[31] Box 7, bundle 1. 22 April 1311.

Reginaldus in the Lane venit in plena curia et reddidit sursum in manus ballivorum totum ius suum uno messuagio quod est pistor' pertinens ale hemminges a via regia usque ad ripam ad usum Katerine filie sue ad deffendendum pro viii.d. ad terminum. (4d.)

[32] Box 7, bundle 1. 13 December 1312.

Henricus filius Henrici Spruntyng sesitus est de una domo que dicta fabrica de dono Henrici patris sui ad deffendendum pro uno denario ad terminum, recipiendum post obitum dicti patris sui. (1d.)

property and invests him with the same that pays a halfpenny at the term. Pledges for this act (are) William the son of Reginald Clerk, Godfrey Clerk the son of Godfrey, Edward Gony, Thomas ad Cirpos.[33]

Robert, son of John Balle, took seisin of a building for baking and a half acre of land coming to him as heir after the death of his father and defending for the farm payment that is owed. (He also obtains seisin) to right of way for the entry of carts between the said bakehouse and the house of his sister Isabella by agreement of that Isabella, saving to Isabella the same right of entry. This right of entry is given on condition that Robert does not alienate this right at any time to anyone. (Fine: 2d.)[34]

John Godman took seisin of a piece of land four feet in width extending from the house of John Fox to the kiln of William Masoun. John Godman placed one side of a room upon this property that he had bought from the above William Masoun and he defends this property for the usual farm obligation.[35]

Cristina, daughter of Godfrey Cokayn, took seisin of a building right at the gate of the grange, together with access by cart, to defend for the farm that is due and to be received after the death of that Emma. (Fine: 2d.)[36]

[33] Box 5, bundle 8: 18 November 1283.

Henricus de Brunne tixtor seysitus fuit de una area edificata quam Ricardus Lacy tenuit et in manibus communitatis renunciavit ad opus predicti Henrici. Et tota communitas seysinam predicte aree predicto Henrico concessit et de eadem eundem Henricum investivit reddendum inde annuatim obolum ad terminum. Huius rei fideiussores Willelmus filius Reginaldi Clerici, Galfridus Clericus filius Galfridi, Edwardus Gony, Thomas ad cirpos.

Within the year Henry added to this property by purchasing part of an adjoining messuage and, at another date, buying an acre and one half of arable.

[34] Box 7, bundle 1. 9 May 1324.

Robertus filius Johannis Balde cepit seysinam de una domo pistera et una dimidia acra terre sibi accidenti [ut] heres post decessum patris sui defenddendum pro firma debita et cum ingressu ventioni carectarum inter dictam pisteram et domum Isabelle sororis sue de conssessione dicte Isabella salvo dicte Isabelle ingressu sicut dicto Roberto. Ita quod dictus Robertus dictum ingressum non alienari faciat aliquo tempore alicui alio. (2d.)

[35] Box 4, bundle 3. 24 May 1330.

Johannes Godman cepit sesinam de una pecia terre habente in longitudine a domo Johannis Fox usque ad ustrenam Willelmi Masoun et habente in latitudine quatuor pedes super quam peciam terre Johannes Godman superposuit parietem unius camere quam dictam peciam Johannes dictus emit de Willelmo Masoun antedicto ad defendendum pro firma debita et onerata. (No fine entered.)

[36] Box 7, bundle 1. 11 April 1325.

Christiana filia Galfridi Cokayn cepit sesinam de una domo usque ad ostium grangie cum ingressu carecte ad defendendum pro firma debita et ad recipiendum post obitum dicte Emma. (2d.)

In a previous entry John Pelliparius took seisin of a place bought from Cristina, daughter of Godfrey Cokayn and Emma her mother, that is, to defend for the farm that is due.

William Swavesey took seisin of a grange as well as the foundation of that grange that abuts on the messuage of the said William. This property William bought from Richard Cokayn and it is to come to him after the death of Emma Cokayn along with a waterfall belonging to that grange, defending for a farthing at the proper time. (Fine: 1d.)[37]

Emma Cokayn took seisin of a piece of curtilage lying behind her baskeshop and of an oven (?) bought from her son Richard Cokayn that Richard had been seised of in previous courts in gift of Emma his mother, to defend for a farthing at the term. (Fine: 1d.)[38]

Richard Cokayn took seisin of a piece of curtilage and a certain oven in gift of his mother Emma to defend for a farthing at the term to be paid to Cristina, daughter of Godfrey Cokayn, or whoever holds the capital messuage formerly belonging to Godfrey Cokayn. Accordingly, the said Richard has quit claimed to the above Emma Cokayn the entire rights that he has, or had, or was able to have in properties or in mobile or immobile goods formerly belonging to his father that may come to him under title of inheritance, except for a brass pot with basin along with a rod of land abutting on hodopolhavenden. The said Richard may not sell or let for any period of time that piece unless this be done, namely that one half of the moneys so obtained be distributed within the vill of Godmanchester in various alms for the souls of Godfrey Cokayn and Emma his wife and for the souls of all the departed. (Fine: 1d.)[39]

[37] Box 7, bundle 1. 12 June 1326.
Willelmus Swanvesle cepit sesinam de una grangia cum fundamento eiusdem iacenti abuttanti super mesuagium dicti Willelmi empta de Ricardo Cokayn recipiendum post decessum Emme Cokayn et cum casu aque pertinenti predicte grangie ad defendendum pro quadrante ad terminum. (1d.)

[38] Box 7, bundle 1. 18 April 1325.
Emma Cokayn cepit sesinam de una pecia curtilagii iacenti retro pistrinam suam et de uno fimario [sic] [funario ?] empto de Ricardo Cokayn filio suo unde predictus Ricardus pre sesitus fuit ad presedendas curias de dono Emma matris sue ad defendendum pro quadrante ad terminum. (1d.)

[39] Box 7, bundle 1. 17 October 1325.
Ricardus Cokayn cepit sesinam de una pecia curtilagii et de quodam Fimario de dono Emme matris sue ad defendendum pro quadrante ad terminum reddendum Christine filie Galfridi Cokayn vel cuicumque capitale messuagio quondam Galfridi Cokayn tenenti. Ita dictus Ricardus quietus clamaret predicte Emme Cokayn omnimoda iura sua que habet vel habuit vel habere potuit in tenementis vel in bonis mobilibus et immobilibus quondam Galfridi patris sui sibi accidentibus iure hereditario salvis quadam olla enea cum pelve et una roda terre abuttante super hodopolhavenden nec non dictus Ricardus predictam peciam vendere non liceat aliquo tempore vite sue vel si faciat videlicet medietas pecunie inde sumpta fiat infra villatam de Gumecestr' in diversis elemosinariis pro animabus Galfridi Cokayn et Emme uxoris eius et pro animabus omnium defunctorum. (1d.)

William Longe took seisin of a shop lying at the end of Longlane between Agnes Fleyshewer and the watercourse of William Gyle to supply candles for the use of the Guild of Blessed Mary. This same shop had been given to that fraternity by John, son of Nicholas Fleshewer and it defends for the customary farm obligation.[40]

Early fourteenth-century lay subsidy rolls at Godmanchester give a dramatically different, if somewhat confused, picture of commercial wealth than the court rolls. One may suspect that the confusion was a deliberate attempt to conceal town resources from the view of the "foreign" eye of the royal taxation authorities. As has been noted in the introduction to the edition of these local records, some important farm products were omitted from the detailed assessments after 1309.[41] On the other hand, no real attempt was made in any of the surviving local rolls to detail commercial items so that this picture remains cryptic indeed and very uneven. In the local assessment of 1309, five townsmen were reported as holding merchandise, three with goods *in camera*, three with goods in the hall (*in aula*) and two with timber. In the first local assessment of 1319, eight individuals were reported as having chattels (*in catallis*) and 51 (of a total of 115) as having goods (*in bonis*). The second list of 1319 noted 33 individuals with goods and only one with chattels.

If one takes the somewhat extreme position that "goods" in these local records could be farm produce, there still remain identifiable in the first two decades of the fourteenth century more than twenty individuals apparently holding commercial capital:

Reginald *de* Alconbury, *sutor* 18s.
Reginald Aylred, *mercator* 36s.
Godfrey Aylred, in the hall 3s.
John Baroun, in the hall, 6s. 8d.
Godfrey ad Cirpos, 1 quarter of malt 3s. 4d.
Reyner Garlop, (*in camera*), 2s.
William *de* Graveley, timber 6s.
Adam Grinde, *in camera* 6s. 8d., timber 6s., merchandise 86s. 8d.
Roger *de* Histon, chaplain, in the hall 2s.
Godfrey in ye Lane (in Venella), 1 quarter of malt 6s. 8d., 2 quarters of malt 6s., in the hall 2s.

---

[40] Box 4, bundle 3. 10 September 1366.

Willelmus Longe cepit seisinam de una shoppa iacente ad finem de Longlane iuxta Agnetam Fleyshewere et iuxta ledam Willelmi Gyle ad usum Gylde beate Marie in dandello de Gumecestre que quidam shoppa Johannes filius Nicholai Fleshewere dedit predicte fraternitati ad defendendum pro firma debita et consueta. (No fine entered.)

[41] Raftis and Hogan, *Lay Subsidy Rolls*, p. 105.

John son of Gilbert Manipenny, merchandise 40s.
William Manipenny, *in camera* 6s.
Alan Miller, in the hall 4s.
John Millicent, in the hall 6s. 8d.
John son of Thomas Outy, 2 quarters of malt 6s.
Richard Pernel, in the hall 2s. 6d., malt 10s.
John Peysel, *in camera* 6s. 2d.
John Quenyng, merchandise 10s.
John Quenyng, butcher, 16s.
John son of Alexander Balle, chattels 24s.
John Glewe, chattels 32s. 6d.
Alan Leirstowe, chattels 14s. 10d.
John super Murum, chattels 18s.

This evidence from the detailed local lay subsidy rolls is confirmed by the sowing and sheep lists.[42] On the first list (Table 12) a good number of individuals paid tax (indicated by an asterisk) who did not have the sowing or sheep to warrant such an obligation:

John Baroun; John atte Broke; John Gilling (Yelling); Richard Howman; William son of John; John Marny (Mariner); William Mason; John son of Nicholas; Godfrey Outy; Simon Parson; the widow of Robert Rede; John Scot; Reginald Seman and William Swavesey.

Several others very likely could be added to this category but the record is too fragmentary to be totally confident on this point. In parallel fashion, it may be noted that the vast majority of people from Huntingdon paid to the lay subsidy through the Huntingdon lists despite the fact their sowings at Godmanchester were very small.

Incidental information obtainable from outside the town about God-manchester commercial personnel adds further to this picture. Of the six individuals specified to be from Godmanchester who appeared in the fair court of St. Ives,[43] only one is in the above list from lay subsidy rolls. This is John Baroun (or Barun) who had farm goods assessed at nearly 100 shillings in the local lay subsidy list of 1309 together with the modest amount of 6s. 8d. "in the hall." Yet, in the St. Ives fair court of 9 May 1315, John Baroun is found to be a cloth merchant at that fair, for he was distrained by 11½ rayed cloths until he should reply to a debt demand of 31 marks. One of the important officials at the fair was the alnager for canvas and a Richard Bromholm of Godmanchester performed this

---

[42] See above, Chapter 3, pp. 102-116.
[43] Mrs. Ellen Moore who is currently completing a study of this fair has kindly made these references available.

function on 28 April 1287, 24 April 1288 and 12 May 1291. Richard
Bromholm may have moved from Godmanchester by the time of our
period of study for no reference is found to this name in the hundred roll
or courts of the town. Another substantial merchant type from Godmanchester to appear at the fair was John Spicer. John Spicer had obtained a
loan of 60 shillings from Peter Mercator of St. Ives on 28 January 1296
while at Huntingdon. This loan had been received in order to finance the
travel of John Spicer to Scotland to sell porret seed there. On 20 May 1300
John Spicer repaid Peter's debt by a messuage at Godmanchester given in
perpetuity along with two horses worth 20 shillings each.

The other three entries from St. Ives fair records give evidence to the
movement of less important people from Godmanchester for various
economic reasons. At the fair court of 8 May 1293 it was reported that
John *le* Couper of Godmanchester had failed to appear at the inquest
about a suit between Michael *de* Gaunt, a taverner, and John *de* Deping
and his wife Alice, cooks. John was pardoned the sixpence fine for non-
appearance because of poverty. There was no reference to a couper in the
1279 Hundred Roll and a John Couper only appears with a modest
property transaction in 1287, so John would indeed appear to be one of
those poor craftsmen who ranged over a wide region in search of
specialized employment. The Gony (Goni) family at Godmanchester were
numerous and of medium wealth. A Thomas Gony of Godmanchester
appeared as a plaintiff in an unspecified suit of the St. Ives fair court on 31
May 1302. Which one of the several Thomas Gonys to be found in the
Godmanchester court rolls of this time was at St. Ives cannot be
ascertained. However, all Thomas Gonys were of less substantial
branches and we likely have here another example of an artisan of modest
means moving throughout the region. Finally, the John *le* Longe of Godmanchester who was the defendant for an unspecified debt in the St. Ives
court of 13 May 1317 has a clearly traceable family line in Godmanchester records. But the *le* Longe family never made much of an entry to
the land market of the town. In the 1279 Hundred Roll John *le* Longe
senior held a messuage and John *le* Longe junior another messuage along
with two acres of arable and one half rod of meadow. Since there is no
evidence that family fortunes changed over the next forty years, the John
le Longe at St. Ives must have been another artisan moving about the
region.

Entries in the Patent Rolls[44] throw further light upon how local records
fail to indicate the commercial range of Godmanchester people. On 25

---

[44] The following five references are to the relevant volumes of the edited Patent Rolls.

November 1318 Godfrey (or Geoffrey) Pademor and Andrew Bovis (or Bonis) of Godmanchester were given safe conduct until the following Easter to go with corn and victuals to the north for the sustenance of the king's forces.[45] To be responsible for a wagon train carrying hundreds of quarters of grain — if one may judge by other royal purveyance orders to the county where amounts were specified — was no small task. And yet, Andrew Bonis only occurs in the two local lay subsidy rolls for 1319 with taxable farm produce of 35s. 2d. and 34s. 6d. Godfrey Pademor had 90s. in taxable produce in the 1309 subsidy list but only 12s. 3d. in "chattels" in the first list of 1319 and 13s. 4d. in "goods" in the second list of that year. Clearly, both men were mainly merchants rather than farmers. This is further exemplified in a Patent Roll entry of 4 May 1322 when Godfrey Pademor was given the standard merchant protection for a ship.[46] On 3 June of the same year Reyner Garlop had been given this same protection[47] and this is the first clear evidence to be found that this prominent landholder was also a merchant.

This same pattern simply repeats itself with more scattered evidence. Poorer craftsmen surface under less respectable conditions. There is no evidence from court records that Elias le Barker held land at Godmanchester. On 20 November 1346 Elias le Barker of Godmanchester was pardoned for homicides and outlawry because of his good service with the king's army in France.[48] Nicholas de Paxton came from an established propertied family. Under 23 March 1324 the Patent Rolls tell us that Nicholas de Paxton of Godmanchester was given royal protection.[49] Nicholas was clearly a merchant, although his taxable wealth in 1319 was simply stated to be 20s. 6d. in "goods." Indeed, the local assessors performed their task so skillfully that in the second local assessment of 1319[50] none of the assessors — Henry Rode, John Baroun, Nicholas Paxton and William, son of Simon were found to have taxable wealth!

There is no reason to believe that such protection implied that Godmanchester merchants moved throughout the region only. No doubt they did flourish in the region and the map of merchants appearing in Godmanchester[51] may be taken as equally indicative of the range of interest of

---

[45] III: 219.
[46] IV: 110.
[47] IV: 118.
[48] VII: 509.
[49] IV: 397.
[50] See Raftis and Hogan, *Lay Subsidy Rolls*, pp. 136 ff.
[51] Above, p. 141.

native Godmanchester merchants. But some would also range more widely, and if Godfrey Pademor and Andrew Bonis were considered to be familiar with the Midlands grain commerce of the early fourteenth century, there would be others to respond to the East Anglian commercial vitality of a century later as the following text indicates:

> The King granted to the men of the Manor of Gumecester, commonly called Gurnouneschestre, which is old demesne of the crown, that they may be quit of toll of goods, 28 March, 4 Richd. iii (1381), and Thos. Gunyene of Gurnounschestre demands to be quit of toll demanded in 6 April, Richd. ii, for "Walnotebark."[52]

An exceptionally detailed series of borough court rolls for Huntingdon[53] in the late fourteenth century offers further corroboration for the commercial practices of Godmanchester people. The provenance of individuals appearing in this series of rolls is not reported with consistency and only after a thorough study of these records will a more definitive list of Godmanchester people become possible. However, the readily available evidence falls into obvious categories. Debt pleas reveal Godmanchester people were trading among themselves: Godfrey Fisher of Godmanchester with Simon Pennyman of the same town, Thomas Wolman of Godmanchester with Godfrey Fisher and Richard Attewodesend (of Godmancester?), Richard Ludde of Godmanchester with Robert Dally of the same town, Henry *de* Over of Godmanchester with Richard Attewodesend, Robert Dally with Edward Bocher of Godmanchester, William Mileward of Godmanchester with Simon Wymer of Godmanchester. Debt pleas also indicate the scope of regional trade: from St. Ives, Simon Legge had been trading with Godfrey Fisher and Lazetta Forster with Bartholomew Chapman of Godmanchester; the same Bartholomew Chapman had a suit against John Morice of Wood Weston (Alconbury Weston); the above-mentioned Henry *de* Over was attached to reply to John Belle (of Huntingdon?); Robert Bocher of Godmanchester was charged with debt by William Wareton of Bulwick, Reginald King of Godmanchester claimed a debt from John Kent of Wood Weston (Alconbury Weston); John Quynhyne, senior, of Godmanchester entered a claim against John Barker (of Huntingdon?), Adam Gissyng of Godmanchester charged Richard *de* Swinford with debt and Richard Ludde of

[52] *Court Rolls of the Borough of Colchester*, eds. I. H. Jeaynes and W. G. Benthem (Colchester, 1921), 4: 1383. I am grateful to Dr. Elaine Clarke for drawing this reference to my attention.

[53] Huntingdon Borough Court Rolls, County Record Office, Huntingdon.

Salisbury claimed that he was owed money by Robert Dally of Godmanchester. Some of these transactions involved such farm produce as grain, cattle and horses but in most instances money was still owed from some unspecified agreement (*conventio*).

In summary, what might be described as the commercial resources of Godmanchester fall into several categories. On the most modest level were those with special skills who apparently developed these at Godmanchester and, during the earlier years of this study at least, took their surnames from their occupation. However, in order to sell their skills these practitioners would seem to have been required to move about a wide region. The scope of their movements was no doubt much the same as those with similar occupations who surfaced from time to time in Godmanchester from outside.[54] That this group were required to move for a living and rarely acquired property at Godmanchester are indices of their poverty. Somewhat better off were a modest "shopkeeper" category who were able to maintain a foothold in the Godmanchester property market and establish families.

Commercially involved individuals at Godmanchester with a capital base for their activities also appear in two categories. One of these categories did not seem to invest heavily in property of the town and carefully concealed from the tax assessors, and the historian (!) what capital resources were at their disposal. We must probe further to know whether such individuals found their capital base among others of their type either at Godmanchester or beyond. The second category of those with capital involved scions of families with a well-established agrarian base of wealth. Since most of the surviving data cluster about such families an effort must be made in the following section to establish a more detailed picture of the distinction, if any, between the agrarian and commercial activities of these families.

C. MOBILIZING WEALTH THROUGH THE FAMILY

From the scope of the data presented in this volume, it would seem to be an obvious conclusion that the social structure of Godmanchester may be described in terms of families. And yet, to show such a conclusion is not to take us very far, for in the present state of historical demography the definition of the family in pre-industrial, and particularly medieval

---

[54] See above, p. 141, Map 4: "Some Regional Skilled Labour Resources Drawn upon by Godmanchester, 1278-1348."

Europe, is still *sub judice*. Scholars reject the use of the concept of a median household[55] or of extended versus nuclear families,[56] to mention but a few points. In order to avoid this issue of definition in the following pages, the first emphasis will be upon description of the degree to which families tend to be revealed by the records as the social structure of Godmanchester whatever "family" might mean.

With respect to families, then, during the continual probing of the records of Godmanchester a single factor emerges again and again as dominant in the life of the town. This factor is the whimsical pattern of family replacement rates. Modern demographic studies, very understandably, have taken their point of departure from the human decisions involved in family replacement, above all the greater possibilities of family planning in recent decades and the Malthusian spectre that has so influenced social programmes since the early industrial revolution. It may be questioned whether human decisions are the proper point of departure for the demographic study of pre-industrial Europe. Human decisions did influence family lives at Godmanchester in many ways, as may be seen throughout this volume. But the over-riding conclusions from available data point to patterns of family disappearance, or survival, arising from causes beyond the control of human decisions. Non-human elements are, of course, the major causal consideration with the onslaught of the Black Death bacteria. But the pattern of forces beyond control was wider and earlier.

Information in our records about family survival is most certain for wealthier families since there is the likelihood that reference to such families will occur in lay subsidy and court rolls as well as the hundred roll. From this information it is clear that a goodly number of families simply terminated by inability to produce male heirs. Wealthier individuals in the 1279 Hundred Roll whose names do not appear thereafter were Henry Arneborn (1 messuage, 1 croft, 16 acres of arable, one half acre of meadow), Thomas Chichely (2 messuages, 17½ acres arable, 2 acres meadow), Simon Chichely (with one messuage and one half acre meadow) who also failed to continue, and John Hazewl (1 messuage, 11 acres 3 rods arable). When some of this wealthier group are referred to in court rolls after 1279, the reason for the subsequent disappearance of their names becomes obvious. Lawrence Nem held 1

---

[55] See, for example, Jack Goody, "The Evolution of the Family," in *Household and Family in Past Time*, ed. Peter Laslett (Cambridge, 1972), p. 170.
[56] See Britton, *The Community of the Vill*, Chapter 1.

messuage, 2 crofts, 8 acres 1 rod of arable and 1 acre 1 rod of meadow according to the Hundred Roll. The court roll tells us that Lawrence was married to Juliana and Lawrence was mentioned in the court rolls until 1308. There is no mention of children and the family name disappears after 1308. Similarly, John Tesard (with 1 messuage, 8 acres of arable, and 1 acre of meadow in the 1279 Hundred Roll) was married to Emma according to court rolls, but there were no children. One can pursue this list further by including John Vecharem who had 1 messuage, 1 croft, 21 acres 3 rods of arable and $3^1/_2$ acres of meadow in 1279. The court roll tells us that John was married with children, John and Joan. This son John in turn was married to a Felicia by the 1280s but no children were reported and the name disappears before 1300. The disappearance of these families alone would have thrown 6 messuages, 4 crofts, 83 acres 1 rod of arable and 9 acres 1 rod of meadow back into the Godmanchester land market.

Although the lay subsidy rolls are less comprehensive than the Hundred Roll of 1279 the same pattern may be found. Among the five wealthiest men of the town according to the local roll of 1309, one was the Prior of Merton and two of the remaining four were Robert Danlys (with taxable goods valued at 173s. 6d.) and Adam Grinde (with taxable goods valued at 377s.). Neither Adam Grinde nor Robert Danlys had sons to continue their name in the village. According to the court rolls, each of these individuals had one daughter only.

If the total disappearance of a family name is one of the most striking of demographic phenomena, the ability of families to maintain several branches is even more common. As is noted with respect to the family data (Table 26), these multi-branched families are frequently characterized by the survival of a large number of children. This is not to argue that there was a simple equation between large families and the continuation of several branches. Several large families did not establish many branches, or at least branches that continued for long. Owing to the paucity of direct evidence about the number of children inheriting property in specific families, the point can only be made that the genetic factors of survival that produced several branches very likely continued in many instances to guarantee the survival of several branches.

However independent of each other family branches or individuals remained at various periods of their lives, it is significant that branched families did not tend to belong to the opposite ends of the economic ladder. The family support system has already been described in Chapter 1. Despite the residual nature of such information, comparative data from the lay subsidy rolls present an interesting visual picture of the degree to

which wealth remained in families (see Table 23). These rolls show a two-generational overlap, at one time concentrated in one branch and at others spread fairly evenly among several branches despite re-allocations to be made because of the termination of some branches. Since the bases for taxation varied from year to year, the comparative position of individuals in one year would seem to be more significant than comparisons of economic wealth between taxable years.

When the lay subsidy information is extended into the 1330s and 1340s to include records of sown acres and sheep, further understanding can be obtained about "family" properties (see Table 24). Where numbers of the family remained much the same, as with the Balle and Lane families, acres sown and sheep pastured remained much the same. Whether of greater or lesser families the amount of holdings tended to increase with numbers of family members '(Dosyn, Ede, Elys, Gildene, Manipenny, Quenyng) or decline with family numbers (Aylred, Goni, Rede, Seman). Of course, individuals could flourish or decline as other examples here illustrate. (See Tables 23 and 24.)

Shifts in the personnel of families to be taxed and assessed as having so much sown or so many sheep are in part a reflection of varying stages in the life cycle of families. For instance, several women of considerable taxable wealth in lay subsidy assessments were widows. The considerable taxable wealth of Robert *le* Rede and John Glewe in the 1332 lay subsidy list was represented by the large amounts sown under the widow's name in the 1334 sowing and sheep list. But shifts in family property holding were also attributable to a flexible inheritance pattern. If one were to take the inheritance system of Godmanchester strictly in isolation, that is land devolving to the youngest son, it might be expected that town family properties were frozen by the necessity of handing on family properties to one individual. *De facto*, however, the main heir seems to have acquired a prior right to the principal messuage but often to have been treated rather equitably with other members of the family for the properties remaining. Indeed, it may be significant that the various surveys spoke of "heirs" rather than "the heir" when the occasion arose. For example, the 1279 Hundred Roll listed 44 acres of arable, along with related properties, as belonging to the heirs of Page.[57]

The most detailed disposition of family properties in our period was the 1312 will of John Manipenny leaving a messuage, 6 acres and some meadow to his son John, a croft, 6 acres and some meadow to his son

---

[57] See above, p. 122, for further examples.

TABLE 23: TAXABLE WEALTH OF SOME FAMILIES IN THE LAY SUBSIDY ROLLS

Surname	First Name	1309	1319A	1319B	1327	1332
AYLRED	Dionysia	33s. 6d.	—	—	22s. 1d.	36s. 8d.
	Elena	42s.	—	—	—	—
	Godfrey	122s.	69s. 2d.	79s. 2d.	54s. 2d.	—
	Godfrey	91s. 10d.	(45s.)	37s. 8d.	—	—
	Henry	—	(14s. 3d.)	13s. 4d.	17s. 1d.	14s. 2d.
	Joan	—	—	—	—	25s.
	John	—	8s. 11d.	8s. 9d.	—	20s.
	Mabel	28s. 9d.	—	—	—	—
	Reginald	—	10s. 6d.	10s. 6d.	—	10s.
	Reginald	—	31s.	28s. 6d.	—	—
	Simon	32s. 3d.	—	—	—	—
	William	25s.	?	25s. 4d.	11s. 8d.	23s. 4d.
	William, mercator	—	36s.	36s.	—	—
Total		£18 15s. 4d.	£10 14s. 10d.	£11 19s. 3d.	£5 5s. 0d.	£6 9s. 2d.
BALLE	William	(45s.)	—	—	16s. 8d.	30s.
	William, chaplain	—	35s. 2d.	—	—	—
	John son of Alexander	—	24s.	14s.	—	16s. 8d.
	John	—	—	—	—	—
	Alexander	31s. 9d.	—	—	—	15s.
	Thomas	106s.	—	—	—	—
	Roger	53s. 1d.	—	—	16s. 8d.	—
Total		£11 15s. 10d.	£2 19s. 2d.	14s.	16s. 8d.	£3 1s. 8d.
CLERK	Eusebius	61s. 2d.	52s. 6d.	41s. 6d.	37s. 1d.	29s. 2d.
	Henry	15s.	13s. 6d.	13s. 3d.	—	20s.
	Henry	—	—	—	—	8s. 4d.
	Reyner	—	16s. 6d.	16s. 6d.	17s. 6d.	—
	Stephen	82s.	17s. 3d.	15s. 1d.	10s.	16s. 8d.
	William son of Simon	25s. 4d.	—	—	—	20s.
Total		£9 3s. 6d.	£4 19s. 9d.	£4 6s. 4d.	£3 4s. 7d.	£4 14s. 2d.

Surname	First Name	1309	1319A	1319B	1327	1332
COLOWOT	Cristina	—	?	8s. 5d.	—	6s. 10d.
	John	41s. 8d.	16s. 6d.	15s. 8d.	—	—
	John	89s. 6d.	—	—	—	—
	Godfrey	—	—	—	—	10s.
	Mariota	—	23s. 8d.	23s. 3d.	—	—
Total		£6 11s. 2d.	£2 0s. 2d.	£2 7s. 4d.	—	16s. 10d.
GRAVELEY	John	72s.	10s.	10s.	22s. 1d.	15s.
	William	32s.	—	—	—	—
	John	—	22s.	—	—	—
Total		£5 4s. 0d.	£1 12s. 0d.	10s.	£1 2s. 1d.	15s.
GLEWE	John	50s. 4d.	32s. 6d.	32s.	40s.	22s. 6d.
	John, copt'	—	—	—	—	10s.
	Matilda	—	—	—	—	6s. 10d.
	Millicent	72s.	—	—	—	—
	Sarra and Godfrey her son	23s. 3d.	—	—	—	—
Total		£7 5s. 7d.	£1 12s. 6d.	£1 12s. 0d.	£2	£1 19s. 4d.
GONI	Alexander	32s.	—	—	10s. 5d.	10s. 10d.
	Godfrey	—	13s. 3d.	(14s.) 3d.	—	—
	John	—	14s.	12s. 7d.	—	—
	John	—	13s. 11d.	—	—	—
	John son of Alexander	—	—	—	—	6s. 8d.
	John son of Godfrey	—	—	—	11s. 8d.	—
	John son of Nicholas	—	—	—	14s. 2d.	—
	Reginald	69s. 9d.	10s.	9s.	—	—
	William	25s. 6d.	?	18s. 4d.	—	—
	William	50s.	—	—	—	—
Total		£8 17s. 3d.	£2 11s. 2d.	£2 14s. 2d.	£1 16s. 3d.	17s. 6d.

Surname	First Name	1309	1319A	1319B	1327	1332
GILDENE	Cristina	106s. 9d.	—	—	—	—
	Emma		16s. 6d.	?	—	12s. 6d.
	Godfrey	65s.	—	—	—	—
	John	22s. 7d.	—	—	—	—
	Matilda		36s. 4d.	34s. 10d.	26s. 8d.	—
	Richard		—	—	30s. 10d.	—
	Roger		13s. 2d.	( ) 9d.	25s. 10d.	25s.
	Thomas		—	—	—	—
Total		£9 14s. 4d.	£3 6s. 0d.	£1 15s. 7d.	£4 3s. 4d.	£1 17s. 6d.
JOHN, son of	Gilbert	77s. 8d.	—	—	15s.	10s. 10d.
	Reginald		?	—	—	—
	Robert	43s.	27s.	26s.	30s. 5d.	25s.
	William		—	—	25s. 5d.	14s. 2d.
Total		£6 0s. 8d.	£1 7s. 0d.	£1 6s. 0d.	£3 10s. 10d.	£2 10s. 0d.
LANE (VENELLA in the)	Eusebius	38s. 10d.	—	—	—	—
	Gilbert		(24s.) 4d.	22s. 4d.	25s. 10d.	—
	Godfrey	64s. 10 q.	64s. 8d.	62s.	41s. 10d.	60s.
	John		14s. 6d.	13s. 6d.	—	—
	Reginald		—	13s. 6d.	—	—
	Richard		12s.	13s. 6d.	—	10s.
	Roger		13s. 6d.	10s.	—	—
	William	?				
Total		£5 3s. 8d. q.	£6 9s. 0d.	£6 1s. 4d.	£3 7s. 8d.	£3 10s. 0d.
LINCOLN	Richard	67s. 8d.	—	—	21s. 8d.	—
	Robert	80s.	—	—	—	—
Total		£7 7s. 8d.			£1 1s. 8d.	

Surname	*First Name*	1309	1319ᴀ	1319ʙ	1327	1332
LEIRSTOWE, atte	Alan	—	14s. 10d.	14s. 1d.	—	—
	John	27s. 4d.	—	—	—	—
	Roger	—	—	—	—	—
	William	25s. 6d.	—	—	15s.	—
Total		£2 12s. 10d.	14s. 10d.	14s. 1d.	15s.	—
MASON	William le	28s. 6d.	—	—	—	—
	William	85s.	—	—	—	—
	John	—	—	—	—	7s. 6d.
	John	—	—	—	—	13s. 4d.
Total		£5 13s. 6d.				£1 0s. 10d.
MILLICENT	John	375s. 4d.	72s. 6d.	58s. 4d.	40s.	50s.
	Matilda mother of John	—	36s.	33s. 4d.	—	—
	William	66s.	32s. 8d.	28s. 2d.	20s.	16s. 8d.
Total		£22 1s. 4d.	£7 1s. 2d.	£5 19s. 10d.	£3	£3 6s. 8d.
MANIPENNY	Alice	—	—	—	66s. 8d.	—
	Agnes	—	31s. 4d.	29s. 10d.	20s. 10d.	66s. 8d.
	Amicia	—	90s. 6d.	85s. 6d.	—	—
	Godfrey	—	—	—	17s. 6d.	33s. 4d.
	Henry	—	24s. 10d.	22s. 2d.	20s. 10d.	20s.
	John	99s.	36s. 10d.	36s. 2d.	26s. 8d.	20s.
	John	—	—	—	—	—
	John son of Gilbert	66s.	—	?	—	11s. 8d.
	Reginald, chaplain	—	53s. 8d.	33s. 5d.	—	25s.
	Roger	—	41s. 2d.	—	70s.	50s.
	William	408s. 4d.	—	—	25s. 10d.	32s. 6d.
Total		£28 13s. 4d.	£13 18s. 4d.	£10 7s. 1d.	£12 8s. 4d.	£12 19s. 2d.

Surname	First Name	1309	1319A	1319B	1327	1332
MURUM super (WAL. le)	Godfrey	(14s.) 9d.	—	—	11s. 8d.	10s.
	John	—	25s. 8d.	18s.	34s. 2d.	25s.
Total		(14s.) 9d.	£1 5s. 8d.	18s.	£2 5s. 10d.	£1 15s. 0d.
QUENYNG	Isolda	—	12s.	12s.	—	—
	John	20s. 2d. ob.	—	19s. 7d.	—	—
	John	50s.	—	—	—	—
	John	111s.	—	—	—	—
	Godfrey	100s.	17s.	17s. 4d.	—	—
Total		£14 1s. 2d. ob.	£1 9s. 0d.	£2 8s. 11d.	—	—
REDE	Agnes le	—	—	—	—	66s. 8d.
	Cristina le	—	36s. 10d.	34s. 8d.	36s. 3d.	20s.
	Robert le	—	—	—	—	25s.
	Robert le	—	—	—	—	30s.
	Simon	85s. 2d.	35s. 6d.	29s. 3d.	25s. 5d.	30s.
	William	111s. 6d.	—	—	30s. 5d.	16s. 8d.
	William de Hunts	120s. 6d.	—	36s. 5d.	—	—
Total		£15 17s. 2d.	£3 12s. 4d.	£5 0s. 4d.	£4 12s. 1d.	£9 8s. 4d.
RODE	Henry	112s. 6d.	24s. 6d.	—	13s. 4d.	30s.
	Robert	(14s.) 6d.	—	—	—	10s.
Total		£6 7s. 0d.	£1 4s. 6d.	—	13s. 4d.	£2
SEMAN	Felicia	53s. 9d.	10s. 6d.	8s.	—	—
	John	56s. 2d.	—	—	—	—
	Pellagia	51s.	13s. 4d.	13s.	—	—
	Reginald	—	?	14s.	26s. 8d.	20s.
	Roger	80s.	—	—	—	—
Total		£12 0s. 11d.	£1 3s. 10d.	£1 15s. 0d.	£1 16s. 8d.	£1

TABLE 24: TAXABLE WEALTH OF SOME FAMILIES IN THE SOWING LISTS

Surname	Taxable Wealth[a] 1327	Taxable Wealth 1332	Sown Acreage and Sheep ca. 1334	Number of Individuals ca. 1334	Sown Acreage and Sheep ca. 1340	Number of Individuals ca. 1340
AYLRED	£4 12s. 6d.	£6 0s. 10d.	52 acres 1 rod; 168 sheep	8 male, 2 female (10)	5 acres 1½ rods; 4 sheep	2 male (2)
BALLE[b]	16s. 8d.	£3 4s. 4d.	25 acres 1 rod; 20 sheep	2 male, 3 female (5)	21½ acres 3 rods; 30 sheep	4 male, 1 female (5)
COOK	None	None	5½ acres 1 rod	2 male, 3 female (5)	12½ acres ½ rod	1 male
DENNE	None	(£1 3s. 4d.)	19½ acres 1 rod; 38 sheep	1 male	9½ acres 2½ rods	1 male
DESORE (DEFORE)	None	10s.	1 rod	1 male	1 acre 3 rods; (15) sheep	1 male
DOSYN	None	6s. 8d.	1 acre 1 rod	1 male	18½ acres 3 rods; 13 sheep	4 male, 1 female (5)
EDE	£1 11s. 3d.	16s. 8d.	7 acres ½ rod	1 male	11 acres 2½ rods; 7 sheep	2 male (2)
ELYS	None	£1 5s. 0d.	4½ acres 3 rods	1 male	10½ acres 3½ rods; 7 sheep	1 male, 2 female (3)
ESE	None	None	3 acre 2 rods	1 male	4½ acres 2½ rods; (12) sheep	1 male
GILDENE	£3 19s. 2d.	£3 7s. 6d.	19 acres 3½ rods; 43 sheep	2 male (2)	27½ acres 2½ rods	1 male, 2 female (3)

[a] The taxable wealth shown is the accumulated amount for the whole family both for the 1327 and 1334 lay subsidies.
[b] In the 1340 sowing list the name Bole is written, but actually it should be Balle; this has been checked out in the court rolls, which clarify the identification of these individuals.

Surname	Taxable Wealth 1327	Taxable Wealth 1332	Sown Acreage and Sheep ca. 1334	Number of Individuals ca. 1334	Sown Acreage and Sheep ca. 1340	Number of Individuals ca. 1340
GLEWE	£2 0s. 5d.	£3 7s. 6d.	11 acres ½ rod	1 male, 1 female (2)	41 acres 3 rods; 32 sheep	2 male, 1 female (3)
GONI	£1 16s. 3d.	£1 5s. 10d.	63½ acres 2 rods; 56 sheep	8 male (8)	9½ acres 3½ rods; 4 sheep	1 male, 1 female (2)
GRINDE	None	None	2 acres 3½ rods	1 male	4 acres ½ rod	1 male
HILDEMAR	£4 1s. 8d.	£2 6s. 8d.	9½ acres 3 rods; 14 sheep	1 male	10 acres 3½ rods; (18) sheep	1 male
INHEWYN	None	None	1 acre	1 male	5 acres 2 rods; 3 sheep	1 male
LANE (VENELLA)	£3 17s. 11d.	£2 15s. 0d.	26½ acres 2½ rods; (17) sheep	3 male (3)	28 acres 2 rods; 36 sheep	3 male (3)
MANIPENNY	£12 7s. 6d.	£12 19s. 2d.	21½ acres; 12 sheep	1 male, 1 female (2)	33½ acres 2½ rods; 56 sheep	3 male, 1 female (4)
PARSON	None	£2 5s. 0d.	2½ acres 2 rods; 15 sheep (?)	1 male, 1 female (2)	12½ acres 1½ rods; (7) sheep	2 male (2)
PENNYMAN	None	None		1 male	6½ acres; (20) sheep	4 male (4)
QUENYNG	None	£2	2½ acres 2 rods	2 male (2)	28 acres 1 rod; 27 sheep	3 male (3)
REDE	£4 8s. 4d.	£8 18s. 4d.	80½ acres 1½ rods; 112 sheep	3 male, 2 female (5)	21½ acres 3 rods; 23 sheep	1 male
SCOT	£3 17s. 11d.	£2 10s. 0d.	6½ acres ½ rod	1 male	3½ acres 3½ rods; 13 sheep	2 male (2)
SEMAN	£1 6s. 8d.	£1	15½ acres 2½ rods; 17 sheep	2 male, 1 female (3)	2 acres; 2 sheep	1 male
WARDE	None	None	2 rod; 4 sheep	1 male	1 rod	1 female

Henry, 6 acres and some meadow to his son Roger, a messuage and $3^1/_2$ acres to his daughter Agnes, a plot and $3^1/_2$ acres to his daughter Emma, while 14 acres were to be divided equally among his other daughters Beatrice, Mabel, Sybil and Matilda.

Another example, suggesting that these bequests gave more equitable family sharing by being put into operation before the death of the testator, comes from the Clerk family.[58]

While the court rolls, unlike the hundred roll or lay subsidy lists, do not provide an index to the wealth of individuals, these rolls are indicators of family concerns. In Chapter 1 above, the same point has been presented in more detail. The marginal quality of this family concern is illustrated by the fact that nearly all court roll transfers, over the period of the hundred roll and lay subsidy rolls, were dealing with small units of property. It is interesting, therefore, to present in Table 25 the purchase and release of properties by family groups in the courts of Godmanchester as a reflection of the property "market management" dictated by family needs.

TABLE 25: SOME FAMILY LAND MARKETING [a]

Surname	Date	Units of Land Bought	Units of Land Sold
BALLE	1278-1300	14	33
	1301-1314	24	13
	1314-1326	10	8
atte BARRE	1278-1300	3	8
	1301-1314	9	6
	1315-1326	10	11
CLERK	1278-1300	31	44
	1301-1314	38	14
	1315-1326	17	21
GONI	1278-1300	25	26
	1301-1314	45	54
	1315-1326	30	47

[a] It should be noted that these figures are only the number of transactions that took place in the above stated years, and not the number of acres that were bought or sold.

[58] Reynerus filius Willelmi Clerici seysitus fuit de uno mesuagio integro sicut jacet et medietate unius virgate terre.... Item Reginaldus Stephanus et Johannes et Helena pueri dicti Willelmi seysiti fuerunt de octodecim acris terre .. cum ad legitimam etatem per-venerint....

Box 6, bundle 1. 9 October 1287. The parchment is somewhat damaged at this point.

Surname	Date	Units of Land Bought	Units of Land Sold
MANIPENNY	1278-1300	20	1
	1301-1314	40	4
	1315-1326	27	10
SCOT	1278-1300	8	16
	1301-1314	16	21
	1315-1326	8	8
SEMAN	1278-1300	10	16
	1301-1314	7	7
	1315-1326	4	20
OUNDLE (UNDELE)	1278-1300	1	—
	1301-1314	3	2
	1315-1326	11	4
TINCTOR	1278-1300	29	6
	1301-1314	—	—
	1315-1326	1	3
WARENTER	1278-1300	10	4
	1301-1314	1	14
	1315-1326	—	7

Some paragraphs in the previous section of this chapter have already noted the fact of considerable commercial activity among Godmanchester people and yet the difficulty in obtaining any degree of comparatively complete information about such activities. Nevertheless, we do have enough information to know that commercial activity was not simply one facet of the life of certain substantial agrarian property holders, but also the specialized interest of branches of wealthier families, such as the Glewe and the Gildene. In short, lucrative occupations and trades were practised by these families as perquisites, as sectors of diversified family economic involvement. However successful John Baroun may have been as a merchant, John Glewe as a master (?) baker and Thomas Gildene as a faber and Henry Gildene as a merchant — and their property interests indicate success — there is no evidence that such family branches showed any inclination to change their names. Whether these branches functioned only at Godmanchester or throughout the region they were careful to maintain identity with their traditional family dynasty.

Evidence for marriages provides important supplementary information about the economy of family management at Godmanchester. The fact

that we know the family names of relatively few wives must not be construed as a sign of female inferiority in the family contract. Quite to the contrary, it would seem that dower and dowry arrangements along with the right to bestow property on children gave the wife an adequately defined area of rights so that it was usually enough to identify her by her first name only. In any case, the maiden names of wives can be obtained for some eighty couples and these data form an interesting three-fold pattern.

First, information about marriages points overwhelmingly to inter-marriage among the wealthier families of Godmanchester. Furthermore, such intermarriage predominated over the whole chronological period under consideration here. Of the nine marriages for which we have information before 1300, five were already in the more wealthy category: Joan Fayrheved married Augustine (of the Canons), Matilda atte Lewe married Edward Glewe, Helen daughter of Roger Goni married Thomas Witman, Amicia Hopay married Richard *le* Rede, and Emma daughter of Richard Millicent married John Tesard. The remaining four marriages recorded for this period fall into the other two categories of "occupational" and "outsider" marriages: Muriel Bele married John Carpenter, Sarra Winborn married Simon *de* Merton, Matilda Hus Hog married Godfrey son of Henry Russel of Hemingford, and Emma Amiont married William Page Startle. Very possibly these four marriages were among more wealthy people also, although information is lacking about their families from the 1279 Hundred Roll and pre-1300 court rolls.

For the period after 1300 information about intermarriage among wealthier families abounds: Elena Balle – Godfrey Bate; Amicia Bole – John Pellage; Pellagia daughter of John Mason – Walter Merchant; Cristina ad Fontem – Henry Clerk; Agnes Clerk – Reginald Godwar; Alice Clerk – Simon Miller; Juliana daughter of John Miller – Reyner *de* Doketon; Cristina daughter of Thomas Gildene – Godfrey Ede; Juliana daughter of Emma and Richard Scot – Gilbert Loxunt (Locksmith); Agnes daughter of John and Isolda Quenyng – John son of William Manipenny; Cecilia daughter of Robert and Matilda Aula – William junior, son of William Manipenny; Albrida daughter of Nicholas, son of Ma-tilda – Roger Spruntyng (his second wife); Isabella daughter of Robert Scot – Godfrey son of Eusebius Aylred; Masceline daughter of Thomas Hildemar – Roger Spruntyng (his first wife); Sybil atte Cros – Henry Spruntyng.

Second with the more detailed knowledge from records of this time it also becomes clear that Godmanchester people were intermarrying with

substantial commercial families from beyond the town: Amicia Baroun – Thomas *de* Merton; Isolda daughter of Godfrey Glewe – Richard *le* Mercator of Little Stukeley; Emma daughter of John *de* Graveley – Robert *le* Small; Cristina daughter of Adam Grinde – Nicholas *de* Paxton; Margaret *de* Hemingford Abbots – ? Ingleys; Joan daughter of Lawrence *le* Lister *de* Hunts – Henry Mileward; Margaret daughter of Richard Scot – John *de* Haveley; Emma *de* Papworth – John Seman.

Third marriage among prominent commercial interests, whether originally from Godmanchester or outside, was again obviously desirable: Joan daughter of John *de* Hamerton – Roger Barbour *de* Hunts; Helen daughter of Kyne – Adam *de* Henlow, carpenter; Joan daughter of Nicholas *de* Hardley – Henry *le* Hore *de* Hunts; Cristina daughter of John Richardyn – William *de* Hemingford; Cristina *de* Yelling – ? Horold; Margaret *de* Stukeley – Thomas *de* Lincoln; Emma daughter of Roger *de* Mattishall – John *de* Thomeston; Agnes daughter of William *de* Mattishall – John *de* Over, clerk; Matilda daughter of William *de* Raveley – William Maddermonger; Cristina Atenok – Roger *de* Spaldwick; Agnes daughter of Alan Lutgate (Ludgate) – Reginald Spicer; Margaret Luicda – Thomas *de* Stukeley; Mariota Freman (*de* Weston?) – Roger Tinctor; Sabina *de* Hunts – Henry Underlespitel.

After the Black Death these marriage patterns continued: Emma daughter of Reginald Denne – Thomas Clerk *de* Offord Cluny; Elena daughter of Reginald Denne – Richard West *de* Graveley; Cristina daughter of Reginald Denne – Henry Acry; Pellagia Dosyn – Godfrey son of Hugh; Alice daughter of Nicholas Quenyng – John Ede; Joan daughter of Hugh *de* Gidding – John Smith *de* Polebrok; Cecilia Waleys – John Glewe, pattissar'; Isabella daughter of John Glewe, cooperator – John *de* Graveley; Cristina daughter of John Glewe, cooperator – William Nottyng; Cristina daughter of John son of Henry – John Quenyng; Emma daughter of William Colier – William Scot.

Available information about second marriages in all instances of widows, further substantiates the patterns found above: Ivetta widow of William Bartelot – Augustine Turk; Amicia widow of Robert *de* Bluntisham – Simon *le* Stone; Emma widow of Gilbert *de* Strateshylle – John son of William Clerk; Sybil widow of William Colion – John Lodelowe; Margaret widow of Reginald Goni (and maiden name Lane) – Roger son of William Manipenny; Agnes widow of Roger Manipenny – John Plomer; Isolda widow of John Quenyng – Eustace *de* Thorley.

The remaining marriage data are less complete, although there is evidence that at least one of the parties was from wealthier families (and)

or an outsider: Sybil Colowot – Stephen Syle; the mother of Thomas *de* Hartford married to someone from (*de*) Luton; Matilda daughter of Roger Manipenny is referred to as Matilda *de* Doncaster 1332, very likely married someone from there. Cristina the sister of John, son of Outy is noted as Cristina Madecroft, very likely her married name.

*
**

More flesh and blood can be given to the previous pages of this chapter by a few family stories. More than 95 percent of the property transactions in the Godmanchester court rolls were in the nature of isolated bits and pieces of property, usually a messuage or "place" or half acre of arable or rod or two of meadow. During the first fifty years of the extant court rolls more concentrated property transactions tended to be reported only on the occasion of some possibly litigious title. In nearly all cases this involved outsiders and merchants or clerks, as has been noted in previous chapters. In short, the great majority of larger property transfers are not reported in our earlier records. Typical of this lack of detail in earlier entries is a memo from a court as late as 26 September 1325: "Be it noted that Godfrey Glewe took seisin of a place, along with the buildings and curtilages appurtenant to it, and of all other tenements of Margaret daughter of John Couper, in gift of that Margaret to defend for the farm that is owed." (No farm amount or fine are given.)

On the other hand, from the second quarter of the fourteenth century bulk property transfers of a more "normal" nature began to be noted. This was not a major change in court roll reporting, but simply the fact of specifying property amounts whereas earlier one was merely said to have received property in gift, or by bequest, and so on. Nor did this reporting in detail become a consistent part of the recording procedure. However, enough cases can be found to help us visualize in more detail the movement of properties within families.

For traditional Christian society in Europe the family was not broken by death. Belief in the immortality of the soul implied the continuation of life. A support for this extension of family life after death was expressed in various liturgical ways. Both this belief in the continued existence of the ancestors and the material requisites for their liturgical support modified considerably a possible tendency to absolute rights under the title of primogeniture or ultimogeniture. As a recent study of a traditional society has graphically described,[59] the heir or heirs lived on with a vital sense of

---

[59] See Emmanuel Le Roy Ladurie, *Montaillou, village occitan de 1294 à 1324* (Paris, 1975).

their ancestors still about them. In turn, the powerful theological and ecclesiastical thrust that lay behind the development of the last will and testament[60] made the will an admirable instrument for the continued influence over property of the invisible hand of the ancestor.

In the example of this control by an ancestor that follows here it should be noted that, as far as our evidence allows, Thomas seems to be the only surviving son of John Pentel. As principal heir, Thomas is clearly expected to take over the traditional family home and properties. Yet, the conditional control that John is able to maintain over these properties is formidable:

> Be it noted about a certain matrimonial gift that John Pentel gave to his son Thomas in free marriage, namely, in the first place that John gave to the said Thomas seven acres of arable to be held during the life of John and one acre to be received after John's death. It is understood that the said John shall have the care of the whole household and of all the goods of the said Thomas and his wife during the life time of that John and according to whatever arrangements they are able to agree upon among themselves. And if it should happen that some disagreement should arise between John and his son Thomas, though may this not come to pass, then it shall be permitted to John to assign the seven acres of land to his son Thomas from his own land and to allow the same Thomas, his wife and all the family of that Thomas to live beyond the household or home of that John until the death of the same John. Furthermore, the same John gave to the above Thomas his son the capital messuage to be received after the death of that John upon condition, namely that the same Thomas the son of John, his heirs and assignees, should pay or have paid each year for ever on the anniversary day of that John 20d. for the maintenance of one wax candle before the image of Blessed Mary in the chapel of the church of Godmanchester and 4d. for masses and prayers for the soul of John and his wife Agnes and of all their benefactors. This is to be carried out with the view and direction of the vicar and two bailiffs of Godmanchester of the time. And if the above Thomas, his heirs or assignees, should fail in the payment of the above 2s. on the above noted day in any year then it is my wish that anyone closest to me in blood should have that messuage and its appurtenance for the performance of the above annual service. And should anyone holding that messuage after the death of the said Thomas fraudulently fail in the above service then that messuage is to be sold and disposed for the soul of that John and for the soul of his wife and of all the

---

[60] See M. M. Sheehan, *The Will in Medieval England*.

faithful departed by the direction of the said vicar and two bailiffs of God-manchester in the best manner that they should deem fitting.[61]

In contrast with the drain upon family resources by the dead hand of the ancestors, events could contrive to bring peculiar advantages to the resourceful principal heir. Godfrey Manipenny may be cited as a striking instance of such success. Of the three Manipenny branches in the 1279 Hundred Roll — Herbert, John and William — the last had thrived considerably by the end of the century. William was also a prolific family man in begetting eight children who survived to adulthood. Three of these — sons John, William and Roger — can be found accumulating property and marrying (at least John and Roger) by the early fourteenth century. The remaining five children would appear to have been under age in 1312 when their mother Amicia arranged for the gift of properties that Amicia had just received by the death of her sister Cristina: Pelagia daughter of Amicia and William gift of 1 croft plus one half acre one rod of arable; Isabella daughter of Amicia and William gift of one rod or arable; Agnes daughter of Amicia and William gift of one and one half rod of arable; Godfrey son of William and Amicia gift of one acre of arable and

---

[61] Box 4, bundle 3. 3 August 1340.

Notandum de quadam donacione matrimoniali quam Johannes Pentel dedit Thome filio suo in libero matrimonio videlicet primo dabit dictus Johannes predicto Thome vii acras terre arabilis habendas in vita dicti Johannis et unam acram terre recipiendam post obitum dicti Johannis. Ita quod dictus Johannes habeat tutelam tocius domus ac omnium bonorum dicti Thome et uxoris eius ad terminum vite dicti Johannis suo ordine et secundum ordinacionem suam gubernandam dum ad invicem concordare poterint. Et si contingat dictos Johannem et Thomam filium suum in aliquam discensionem accidere quod absit deinde liceat dicto Johanni predicto Thome filio suo vii acras terre de terra propria tribuere et eundem Thomam et uxorem eius et totam familiam d cti Thome extra domum seu mansionem dicti Johannis ad libitum eius continue fugare quousque post mortem dicti Johannis. Etiam idem Johannes dedit Thome filio suo predicto capitale mesuagium suum percipiendum post obitum dicti Johannis sub hac condicione quod idem Thomas filius dicti Johannis heredes et assignati sui annuatim et imperpetuum die anniversarii dicti Johannis solvat seu solvant ad sustentacionem unius cerei sustinendi coram ymagine beate Marie in cancello ecclesie de Gumecestre xx d. et in missis ministrantibus iiiid. pro animabus dicti Johannis et Agnetis uxoris eius et omnium benefactorum suorum, et hoc fiat per visum et ordinacionem vicarii et duorum ballivorum de Gumecestre qui pro tempore fuerint. Et si predictus Thomas heredes vel assignati sui aliquo anno ad dictam prenotificationem in solucionem supradictorum duorum solidorum ut supradictum est, defecerit seu defecerint, deinde volo quod aliquis de proximiori consanguinitate mea dictum mesuagium cum suis pertinenciis habeat pro supradicto servicio annuali faciendo. Et si aliquis post obitum dicti Thome dictum mesuagium tenens de servicio supradicto fraudulenter defecerit deinde vendatur dictum mesuagium et fiat pro anima dicti Johannis et pro anima uxoris eius ac omnium fidelium defunctorum per ordinacionem dictorum vicarii et duorum ballivorum de Gumecestre meliori modo quo ordinare poterint.

Reginald the son of William and Amicia one acre of arable. Since Amicia first appears in the records at this time and continues as widow for nearly two more decades — that is, for some twenty years after the death of her husband William — Amicia may have been the second wife of William. Some other woman, whose name we are not given in the less personal records of earlier decades, may have been William's first wife and the mother of the three older sons.

In any case, by the 1320s Godfrey is clearly of age and involved in the land market. There is incidental information to suggest that Godfrey, like his father William, had commercial interests. In 1321 Godfrey, along with a Richard Mercator, purchased a messuage that would no doubt supply commercial frontage. In 1329, Godfrey was involved in a lawsuit with John Gamboun of St. Ives. The latter may have been a merchant attracted to the land of Godmanchester. Land was a consistent interest of Godfrey. From the court records one can see him keeping a sharp eye out for bits and pieces of property that become available. The list of his acquisitions gradually grows: 1321 – one rod + one rod; 1315-16 – cris of meadow; 1326 – one half acre + four headlands + one rod; 1327 – one half acre + one headland + one curtilage; 1329 – one curtilage. This policy of piecemeal property accumulation would continue for another twenty years. Godfrey survived the Black Death to live on into the mid-1350s.

Godfrey Manipenny held the post of bailiff intermittently over a twenty-year period. Around 1330 Godfrey held this post almost continuously for some three years. It was during this time that Godfrey had his inherited lands "registered" on the court roll. No reason is given for this registration and no fine is indicated. Those bequeathing the lands — Godfrey's father and "uncle" — were long since dead. Furthermore, there is no evidence that Godfrey was married and had children at this time.

From the date of Godfrey's appearance in the court rolls it would seem likely that he was the youngest surviving son of William and Amicia. It is not surprising, therefore, in the text Godfrey had entered on the court roll of 22 March 1330, to find that Godfrey is said to hold the principal messuage by bequest of his father. The remaining lands specified as coming from the father's will were less than four acres, that is, a small amount of land to guarantee the sustenance of Godfrey should there be difficulties with his obtaining his regular family "portion." The second category of land that Godfrey had entered upon the court roll were from Herbert Manipenny. Herbert was a contemporary of Godfrey's father William. Herbert had a son William who was mentioned in court rolls around 1300 but then disappears very shortly after the beginning of the

century. Godfrey was obviously the closest surviving heir to Herbert's properties, very likely Herbert's nephew, although surviving records do not say so and Godfrey would likely have recovered Herbert's lands through his own father. In any case, it is interesting that the properties Godfrey held from Herbert's land in 1330 almost exactly approximate the total held by Herbert in 1279 Hundred Roll (13 acres, 1 rod) in so far as there is no evidence from court rolls of further property acquisitions by Herbert over the 1280s and 1290s. Among the slightly more than ten acres that Godfrey noted as his as portion of the properties remaining (after the willed estate!) from his father there appear to be three categories. Slightly more than one half of these lands were simply identified as to place and would appear to have been part of the family patrimony. Several units were identified as "from" someone else: one half acre from Godfrey Onty, one rod from Stephen atte Hall, one rod from Wylde, one and one half rods from Stephen atte Hall, one rod formerly belonging to William in ye Lane from Alexander on ye Wal. Whether such properties were acquired by purchase, gift or bequest we do not know. A third category of lands does specify two purchases, of three rods and three one half acre units, from Robert *le* Plouwrighte and Martin *le* Rede respectively. These purchases would be by Godfrey's father rather than the above-mentioned purchases by Godfrey himself from the 1320s.

From the will of his father, inheritance from a terminated branch of the family along with his own customary portion of the family estate Godfrey was given nearly thirty acres of land. From this property base Godfrey was an obvious choice as bailiff and had the capital resources to add again and again to the family property heritage. Since the entry concerning Godfrey is largely a list of properties, it does not seem necessary to translate the Latin of the following text:

> Galfridus Manipeny sesitus est de tenementis sibi legatis specialiter in testamento patris sui videlicet de una acra super Themelond. de dimidia acra in lose iuxta Adam grynde. de una roda et dimidia super blakelond. de principale mesuagio. de prestesgoren. de una roda ibidem. de una dimidia acra terre abuttante super m[urum] Willelmi le rede. de uno swat prati iuxta Johannem filium Ricardi Tyngtor. de terra Herberti Manipeny videlicet de dimidia acra super le thorefurlong iuxta Robertum de aula. de una roda apud Wrxyswelle. de tribus dimidiis acris in le mor. de una roda apud le hayhaveden. de una dimidia acra in Gorinscroft iuxta Johannem de Thorleye. de una acra apud le spitel. de dimidia acra apud midlichehaveden iuxta divisam. de una roda super [shi] torsile coniuncta cum una roda de terra Bartholomeum Gony. de una dimidia acra super stonylond. de una dimidia acra apud henngfordemar unde unum capud est forera. de dimidia

acra apud shepdentñnge iuxta priorem. de una roda abuttante super foreram Godchild. de dimidia acra apud hertistorp. de le gores apud le dedeman. de dimidia acra ad capud predictarum gores. de una roda apud foreram quondam Walteri Spencer. de tribus dimidiis acris abuttantibus super predictam foreram ex alia perte. de dimidia acra abuttante super foreram parvi Willelmi ex alia perte. de una roda super dictam foreram ex illa perte. de dimidia acra apud le onerewellis abuttante super decwelbroc. de una apud Wyburwong iuxta Willelmum Gony. de dimidia acra ibidem iuxta Reginaldum filium Johannis. de una roda apud semaneswong. de dimidia acra abuttante super foreram Roberti de aula. de una roda prati in le damgars iuxta Hugonem de matesale et Willelmus ate Leystowe. de una roda in le damgars iuxta Galfridum in ye Lane. de dimidia acra apud Londonweye iuxta domum Willelmi Balle. de tribus rodis apud Wyboldesdick. de dimidia acra in depden' iuxta Willelmus filium Willelmi Manipenny. Item dictus Galfridus sesitus est de portione sua tenementorum residuorum quondam patris sui videlicet de dimidia acra super annohowebroc proximum ex perte propinquiore. de dimidia acra in longelose de Galfrido Onty. de dimidia acra super dodeshil. de una roda apud hemmisgoren proximum. de dimidia acra apud potteresmade proximum le goren. de una roda apud foreram Henrici rode ex parte offordeweye. de una roda apud Wyburwong. de dimidia acra apud le mar' unde unum capud est forera. de dimidia acra apud Shitsillebroc ex parte shepden. de una roda super Estbiriwang de Stephano ad Aulam. de una roda et dimidia super Estbiriwong de terra Wylde proximum crucem. de dimidia acra abuttante super foreram Walteri Spencer in lose. de una roda et dimidia apud Estbiriwong de Stephano ad aulam. de dimidia acra super blakelond iuxta Ricardum Tyngtorem. de dimidia acra abuttante super foreram Galfridi filii Reginaldi apud Riggeweys iuxta Johannem Tyngtorem. de una forera apud Futwelehaveden. de dimidia acra apud Londoñ weye iuxta Galfridum in ye Lane. de una forera apud potteresmade cum roda ibidem. de una roda apud foreram quondam Willelmi in Ye lane. de terra Alexandri super murum. de una forera de tribus super dotwelebroc de media de tribus continentibus unam acram apud foreram Willelmi in ye Lane. Item dictus Galfridus sesitus est de tribus rodis terre empte de Henrico filio Roberti le Plowrihte unde due rode iacent apud Londoneston et una roda super Kokkeshep. Item sesitus est de tribus dimidiis acris abuttantibus super todalisbroc emptis de Martino le rede ad defendendum pro firma debita. Item dictus Galfridus sesitus est de tribus dimidiis acris lays iacentibus super refurlong de residuo terrarum patris ad defendendum omnia predicta tenementa iuxta consuetudinem villate de Gumcestre. (No fine.)[62]

[62] Box 4, bundle 3. 22 March 1330.

Despite the clear designation in Godmanchester customary law of a principal heir, there was a strong egalitarian thrust to these customs. In the above paragraphs the family gifts from their mother to Godfrey Manipenny, a brother and three sisters have been noted. Where evidence is available, there is the same obvious concern for equality in the descent of property from fathers. For example, the court of 8 June 1332 records the seisin of lands by Reginald, Thomas, Joan and Emma Maddermonger coming to them after the death of their father John:

> Reginald – 3 acres 1 rod land and meadow, ⅓ curtilages and herbage (by hereditary right: *iure hereditario*) (8d.);
>
> Thomas – 3 acres land and meadow, ½ swat meadow, ⅓ curtilages and herbage (by hereditary right: *iure hereditario*) (8d.);
>
> Joan – 1 acre arable, 1 swat meadow, ¼ curtilage (bought formerly from William Maddermonger), ½ of a garscroft (formerly John Canne) which tenements John Maddermonger bequeathed to the said Joan his daughter as may be found in the will of John (quod dictum tenementum Johannes Madirmonger legavit predicte Johanne filie eius prout patet in testamento dicti Johannis) (4d.);
>
> Emma – 1 rod + 1 rod + 1 rod + 1 rod + 1 rod (all arable with separate location), 1 swat meadow, a part of one croft and its herbage which tenements she had in gift from her father as may be found in his will (que dicta tenementa de dono habuit patris sui prout patet in testamento patris eiusdem) (3d.).

In the above, as other entries of this kind, sons are favoured over daughters in the "value" of two to one, if one may employ the fines as indicators. However, there is an obvious effort to treat the sons and daughters equally within their sexes. Furthermore, the will (and the attendant gift form) were clearly employed to arrange support for the more needy daughters. This was a lifetime concern of parents. John had purchased land for his daughter Joan and both entries for daughters betray much more concern for the careful identification of properties both as to source and location in order to protect the rights of women.

The equal sharing of property among sons could involve much greater amounts of land than that given in the above text for the Maddermonger family. In the court of 29 November 1341 there is this entry:

> Henry and Thomas, sons of Lawrence Rode, took seisin together of 40 acres of arable and meadow lying in the fields and meadows of Godmanchester. These 40 acres had formerly been given in free marriage by Henry Rode to Lawrence his son, his wife Cristina and heirs legitimately procreated by them. These 40 acres were to be received upon the death of Lawrence, father of the said Henry and Thomas to defend for the

customary farm that is owed. Thomas, son of Lawrence Rode, took seisin of a built up place called Fressyngesplace with appurtenances which place Henry his father had conceded and given to him to be received after the death of the said Lawrence and to defend for the customary farm that is owed. (Fine: 40d.)[63]

Since the name Thomas follows that of Henry he was very likely the younger son. As such, Thomas would be the principal heir according to the customs of Godmanchester and the "built-up place" that he received was very likely the Rode "homestead" or traditional family messuage residence. A complementary entry in the court rolls confirms this interpretation. On 8 August 1342, Lord Robert Denne and John son of Godfrey took seisin in their own name and in the name of John *de* Godesfeld and Lord Roger of Mildenhall, chaplains, of all lands formerly belonging to Henry Rode in Godmanchester "except a messuage formerly called Fressyngesplace and 40 acres of land, meadow and pasture that the said Henry Rode formerly gave to Lawrence his son and Cristina his wife and their children in free marriage."

It would be incorrect to deduce from the above instances that daughters were always discriminated against in all categories of bequest. Whatever custom might have been, it was clearly within the power of parents to purchase property and alienate it in whatever fashion they saw fit. An example of greater equality of treatment among sexes may be found in the Spicer family. Spicers diligently bought up small units of land in the two generations after the 1279 Hundred Roll although the only family member (Henry) noted as holding property in 1279 had but one acre. The family reasons for this property accumulation are well illustrated by court roll entries of 17 November 1334:

> Matilda, daughter of Reginald Spicer, took seisin of her portion, seven acres and one rod of land. This same land that Matilda had and it came to her as was noted in the seisin by purchase of her father [quam dictam terram dicta Matilda habuit et accidit eidem prout continetur in sesina de

---

[63] Box 5, bundle 9.

Henricus et Thomas filii Laurentii Rode ceperunt coniunctim sesinam de xl acris terre et prati iacentibus in campis et pratis de Gumecestre quas dictas xl acras quondam Henricus Rode dedit in libero maritagio Laurentio filio suo et Christine uxori sue et eorum heredibus inter eos legitime procreatis percipiendas post obitum Laurentii patris dictorum Henrici et Thome ad defendendum pro firma debita et consueta. Thomas filius Laurentii Rode cepit sesinam de una placea edificata cum pertinentiis que vocatur Fressyngesplace quam dictam placeam Laurentius pater eius sibi concessit et dedit percipiendam post obitum dicti Laurentii ad defendendum pro firma debita et consueta.

perquisitione patris sui] to defend for the farm owed saving rights claimed by anyone. (Fine: 5d.)

Richard, son of Reginald Spicer, took seisin of his portion, seven acres and one rod of land lying in the fields of Godmanchester, which said portion of land came to the same Richard as was noted in the seisin by purchase of his father, to defend for the farm owed saving rights claimed by anyone. (Fine: 5d.)

Cristina, wife of Adam *de* Blaysworth, took seisin of her portion and right [de portione sua et iure suo], seven acres and one rod of land, lying separately [divisim] among the fields of Godmanchester, which said portion of land came to the same Cristina as was noted in the seisin by purchase of her father, saving the rights claimed by anyone, to defend for the farm owed. (Fine: 5d.)[64]

However free parents might have felt in allocating purchased properties to children as they wished, it would still be expected that the principal heir had priority. It is not surprising, therefore, to find a court entry a few weeks after the above entries, bestowing the family messuage and considerably more property upon Richard Spicer:

Richard, son of Reginald Spicer, took seisin of a place in Post Street formerly belonging to John Spicer, that had at one time been Whitawer's, and of 18 acres of land and meadow lying separately in the fields and meadows of Godmanchester and of three and one half rods of land and meadow. The above tenements came to the same Richard by hereditary right after the death of that Reginald father of the same Richard. For the said Reginald Spicer formerly and in turn purchased the said tenements, as may be found in the court rolls, to have and to hold for himself and Agnes Ludgate his wife and their heirs. The said Richard recovered seisin of these same tenements before the full court, saving rights of others, to defend for the customary farm owed. (Fine: 3s. 3d.)[65]

---

[64] Box 6, bundle 2 for all three entries.

[65] Box 6, bundle 2. 29 December 1334.

Ricardus filius Reginaldi Spicer cepit seysinam de placea quondam Johannis Spicer in Postrate que quondam fuit Whitawer de octodecim acris terre et prati divisim iacentibus in campis et pratis de Gumecestre et tribus rodis terre et prati et dimidie. Que supradicta tenementa acciderunt eidem Ricardo iure hereditario post obitum predicti Reginaldi patris eiusdem Ricardi. Quia dictus Reginaldus Spicer quondam et per vices perquisivit dicta tenementa ut invenitur per rotulos curie habendum et tenendum sibi et Agneti Ludgate uxori sue et heredibus eorum. De quibus predictis tenementis dictus Ricardus in plena curie presenti recuperavit seysinam salvo iure cuiuslibet ad defendendum pro firma debita et consueta.

Although the Godmanchester court rolls may have been employed to register with more or less care the details of parents' concern for their children, one must carefully keep in mind that the court record in no way pretended to be complete. A consequence of this fact is the rather disjointed record of family action in court rolls. A newcomer to the town might acquire a residence and other properties immediately or over months, or even years. Property activity at the marriage or death of the family member may be concentrated in a flurry over a few weeks or spread over several years. Among the above entries for the Spicer family, for example, the reference to Cristina, wife of Adam *de* Blaysworth comes in the same court as the references to her sister Matilda and brother Richard, but after another entry that had nothing to do with the family. Perhaps Cristina, apparently living outside Godmanchester with her husband, simply arrived at the court later in the day! The entry about Richard's principal inheritance came six weeks later.[66]

Six months later, 6 July 1335, occurs an entry that records the portion and inheritance received by Richard's brother John. The Spicer family appeared to have had some interest in the cloth industry in early fourteenth century and to have been identified occasionally as Thrumbolt. John may have made this his main profession for the name was uniquely applied to him at this time. In addition, there is evidence that John lived in Godmanchester. Henry, the first Spicer to appear in Godmanchester records, had a residence (messuage) in Huntingdon.[67] John, very likely a great-grandson of Henry, may have continued the family presence in Huntingdon, adopted a name more suitable to the main industry of that town and been unable to be present with his brother and sisters six months earlier. It is interesting in this context that the entry for John alone of the children employs a phrase to be expected of outsiders, that is, the land is specified as "within the 'liberty'." The 1335 entry shows John receiving almost exactly the same portion (seven acres) as each of his sisters and his brother as well as exactly the same amount of inheritance as Richard:

> John, son of Reginald Thrumbolt, took seisin of his portion, seven acres of land and meadow coming to the same John from purchases by his father and mother. Furthermore, he was seised of 18 acres, $3\frac{1}{2}$ rods of land and meadow as his own property coming to that same John by hereditary right

---

[66] Box 6, bundle 2. 29 December 1334.
[67] See Anne and Edwin DeWindt, *Royal Justice and the Medieval English Countryside* (in press).

after the death of Reginald his father. These said holdings lie separately within the liberty of Godmanchester defending for the farm owed. (Fine: 1d.)[68]

The continued listing of women as tenants with considerable holdings at Godmanchester attests to the disappearance of male heirs, but also to the fact that women were considered as eligible as men to continue the family blood lines with the attendant title to property. An example of this phenomenon may be taken from the Euseby family. Eusebius was one of those exotic first names that occasionally could be found among a few of the wealthier families in the late thirteenth century. By the time of the 1279 Hundred Roll one family had already begun to employ the first name — often as Euseby — as surname and perhaps this led to decline of interest in the name by others of the town.[69] Furthermore, the surname Euseby would appear to have quickly become sufficiently distinctive by this time to allow the dropping of the one or two generational specifications of the father's first name.

William, son of Robert Euseby was one of the wealthier townsmen of 1279 with two messuages, 3 crofts, 28 acres of arable and four acres three rods of meadow under one entry and a further one and one half acres of arable and forland added towards the end of the roll. By 1282 the court rolls simply refer to a Euseby with a wife Isolda and over the next two decades five sons (John, Nicholas, Godfrey, Reginald and William) appear in the same records, with a daughter Cristina, as their children.

Of the five sons, it would appear that only John, Nicholas and William married. And of these marriages a son of John, Gilbert, was the only male issue. William had modest taxable wealth in 1309 but none of the family are mentioned by the surname of Eusebius in later lay subsidy records. The Gilbert son of John, who had modest taxable wealth goods in 1319, 1327 and 1332 may have been of the family. In any case, the disposition of family property in the court rolls of 1325 are of interest. In the court

---

[68] Box 6, bundle 2. 6 July 1335.

Johannes filius Reginaldi Thrumbolt cepit sesinam de porcione sua. septem acrarum terre et prati accidente eidem Johanni de perquisitione patris et matris eiusdem. Item sesitus est de proprietate sua octodecim acrarum et trium rodarum et dimidie terre et prati accidente eidem Johanni iure hereditarie post obitum Reginaldi patris sui que dicta tenementa iacent divisim infra libertatem de Gumecestre ad defendendum pro firma debita.

[69] The name was taken up again by at least one family in the second quarter of the fourteenth century after the disappearance of these Eusebies. However, these later Eusebies were apparently derived from a William, son of Eusebius, clerk.

before the feast of Michaelmas, 1325, occurs the brief entry: "Gilbert, son of John, took seisin of 42 acres of land and meadow, and of one messuage, lying in the liberty of Godmanchester in gift [*de dono*] of Cristina daughter of William Euseby to defend according to the customs of the same vill." Clearly, the 42 acres indicated that William had prospered, perhaps because he was the youngest son but more certainly because he was the longest lived and inherited from his unmarried brothers and the married who left no children. Nicholas appears to have died shortly after 1300; there is a record of John bequeathing property to Reginald in 1315; Godfrey and Reginald drop out of the court records in 1321 and 1322 respectively.

This gift of the 42 acres to Gilbert, the son of John, is suspiciously brief and vague. Furthermore, it is followed by an entry whereby a Henry, the son of William (no relation to the Eusebius family) purchased one half acre from Agnes Euseby, Cristina her daughter and Gilbert the son of John. Whether this was part of the 42 acres, we are not told, but it is clear that Cristina and her mother wanted their first cousin Gilbert to be associated with the transaction. It is only from a memo at the end of this court that we can fully understand the gift of the 42 acres to Gilbert. This gift is one part of a legal fiction in order to avoid counterclaims by the sole remaining male grandchild of Eusebius. The really significant portion of the gift is the re-grant by Gilbert to Cristina and her mother, given in great detail:

> Memo that Agnes formerly the wife of William Euseby and Cristina her daughter together took seisin of one messuage with the appurtenant curtilages lying in East Street between the messuage of William *le* Couter senior to the east and the place of John *de* Graveley to the west and of 42 acres of arable and meadow lying in various places throughout the liberty of Godmanchester. These tenements the above Agnes and Cristina have in gift of Gilbert the son of John, to have and to hold by Agnes and Cristina and heirs of the body of that Cristina with the right of inheritance [et heredibus de corpore dicte Cristine procreatis et iure hereditario]. And if the said Cristina should die before her mother Agnes without leaving heirs of her body, then that Agnes may sell all the above tenements whenever and to whomsoever she wishes during her life or have them sold for her after death, saving only rights customarily belonging to the husband of that Cristina. The money thus obtained is to be distributed in various alms within the vill of Godmanchester according to the will of the said Agnes for the souls of William Euseby and his ancestors and for the souls of the above Agnes, Cristina and their benefactors. And should the above Cristina outlive Agnes her mother, she may sell or have sold these tenements in the

same manner [and] she is to defend all the above tenements according to the customs of the vill.[70]

The types and amounts of property holding cited in the previous few pages — Cristina Euseby (who outlived her mother) with 42 acres, the Spicers with more than 67 acres, the two Rode sons with 40 acres, Godfrey Manipenny with 30 acres by inheritance (and possibly close to 30 acres by purchase), four Maddermonger children with less than 10 acres, John Pentel with 7 acres — were familiar to the Godmanchester scene. There is no reason to believe that the property spread of 50 years earlier had altered by the mid-fourteenth, or indeed later fourteenth century. In 1279 the property spread given by the Hundred Roll was:

number of tenants with holdings of 60 acres or over	1
between 50 and 59 acres	1
between 30 and 39 acres	2
between 20 and 29 acres	28
between 15 and 19 acres	23
between 10 and 14 acres	42
between 5 and 9 acres	29
under 5 acres	215

This pyramid form of property holding has long been recognized by studies of manorial surveys as well as the classical analysis of landholding in the 1279 Hundred Rolls.[71] However, such studies have failed to isolate the dynamics still possible to such a tenurial structure. First, the possibility for considerable entrepreneurial activity is obvious in the records of God-manchester. Each generation saw several individuals forge ahead. Some of these were merchants, some outsiders and some — like Godfrey Manipenny — quite simply more fortunate and talented townsmen. The "age of the individual" may have been earlier than conventional historical wisdom has led us to believe! Secondly, the limit to the exceptional accomplishments of individuals was dictated by the time span of their lives. There was no obvious egalitarian thrust to the society of Godman-chester. Death was the great leveller, bringing to a term the talents of exceptional individuals and, at the same time, forcing some dispersal of the fruits of their success. Again, one might question whether the dispersal effect of modern succession duties is such an entirely new phenomenon in western society as we may have been lead to believe.

[70] Box 7, bundle 1. 26 September 1325.
[71] See E. A. Kosminsky, *Studies in the Agrarian History of England in the Thirteenth Century* (New York, 1956).

Thirdly, the "welfare" effect[72] of family property arrangements was not considered to conflict with maintenance of the family's social and economic role. Dependent as we are upon property records only, and not having the record of moveables that could be entirely disposable by will,[73] no doubt the disposition of all resources considered necessary to maintain the principal family "business" does not come within our purview. Nevertheless, it is clearly demonstrable from the property records of God-manchester that those wealthier families, such as the Aylreds or Manipennys, who "increased and multiplied" at a prolific pace, did not lose their prominent role in the town. The rare, important family of the town who had only a replacement rate of children — such as the Millicent — does not manifest a consistently greater concentration of wealth than the Manipennys or Spicers described above.

No doubt the latter families benefited from the failure to survive of other families that brought land on to the market, and well-established families had a tradition of diversified interests in shops, and crafts as well as husbandry. But the over-riding reason for the success of such families was the corporate support that could be generated for each new nucleus by purchased portions, properly selected marriage partners and the mutual gifts of dower and dowry. Only very slowly have historians come to realize the degree to which the family has supplied the corporate base for economic development.[74]

---

[72] In this context it would be interesting to push back further the brilliant thesis of Joan Thirsk developed in her *Economic Policy and Projects: The Development of a Consumer Society in Early Modern England* (Oxford, 1978).

[73] This is, of course, the main theme in Sheehan, *The Will in Medieval England*.

[74] See, for example, N. McKendrick, "Josiah Wedgwood: An Eighteenth-Century Entrepreneur in Salesmanship and Marketing Techniques," *The Economic History Review*, 2nd series, 12 (1960), 408-433.

6

Godmanchester:
Historical Model of a Small Town

Records surviving for thirteenth and fourteenth-century Godmanchester tell us much about the formal organization of the small town, from family customs through town government to actual settlement patterns. However, it is inevitable that from the thousands of entries for various acts of individuals in these records the historian derives stories of people of the town rather than impersonal institutional history as such. Furthermore, throughout this volume it has been repeatedly stated that Godmanchester did not evolve according to the criteria traditionally assigned to the town. How, then, is its development to be described?

It will be proposed in the following paragraphs that Godmanchester does indeed represent a "small town" model that is distinct from both the village and the town proper. One might expect that this small town model was not unique to Godmanchester and, in fact, that the organizational characteristics of this model were so flexible that the model may have been widely represented throughout both medieval society and in modern society until quite recently. However, the records of Godmanchester are rather too distinctive to allow comparison with other small towns. At least such would appear to be the current state of scholarship in so far as this writer has been able to assess the matter.

There exists a large body of analytical literature that could be called upon to describe Godmanchester as a traditional community. Nevertheless, to apply analytical tools to social and economic materials of a provenance totally distinct from sources employed for the development of such tools can too readily "shape" the evidence. For example, the concept of "embeddedness" brilliantly described by Karl Polanyi[1] and now further

---

[1] Karl Polanyi, et al., *Trade and Market in the Early Empires: Economics in History and Theory* (Glencoe, Ill., 1957).

developed by his equally brilliant successor, George Dalton,[2] may well be an apt formulation of the small town complex at fourteenth-century God-manchester. But for the historian of a town at even this early period the concept of "embeddedness" is too negative in so far as it does not allow for the co-existence of the traditional community with considerable social and economic articulation. To make this point is not to criticize the concept within the anthropological framework that has led to its development but rather to admit that medieval historiography is currently incapable of adapting the term along the lines that Polanyi and Dalton might expect. In short, "embeddedness" for the medieval historian evokes the traditional image of archaic customary societies as impenetrable to the historian because of the "inarticulated and irrational web" of social relations.

The distinct feature of Godmanchester as a small town may be described simply as the availability of social resources. Economic historians are familiar enough with the need of a certain level of capital accumulation and related "know-how" before an industrial "take-off" may become possible. In the case of Godmanchester, it is useful to envisage the accumulated heritage of social resources in the town as making possible, if not an industrial take-off, at least that easy ambience for the commercial, legal and political life of the time that we have seen in the records of the period.

The expression "social resources" has been employed here to underline the fact that the people played a very elemental social role in the functioning of Godmanchester as a small town. Again and again, the town called upon some group of people to support various economic and legal actions rather than appealing to a "higher court" of institutions and officials external to the local community. People provided the social "capital" required by the level of life the town had arrived at. The terms "resources" and "capital" are employed here advisedly because an essential aspect of this phenomenon was the capacity Godmanchester had for mobilizing such resources. This capacity had its base in the flexibility of the physical resources of the town, that is to say, the continuing activity of dividing, subdividing and concentrating a multitude of small units that went to make up the arable fields, meadows and even town properties. But this capacity was pre-eminently an organizational capacity upon every level of life.

[2] For a recent example see his "Peasant Markets," *Journal of Peasant Studies*, 1 (1974), 240-243.

As has been seen in Chapter 1, above, the vastly complex questions to which the modern welfare state addresses itself were administered by family custom. Whereas welfare costs today threaten the state with an impossible financial burden, Godmanchester people were able to absorb these costs within the immediate circle of those involved. Godmanchester people became loathe to employ their own court to register various arrangements of the family cycle.

Recourse did have to be made to the courts for lawsuits. One might expect this to have been a costly procedure at the time as the various cases went through their tedious stages of three summons, three distraints and three essoins. However, the summons and distraint were formal notices only and did not carry penalties if they were acknowledged in person. As the cases became more complex, the social base of the response was widened. For example, in a court of November 1278, Simon, the son of Alexander, entered a claim for two and one half acres against Ranulph the son of Gilbert (one acre), William Sutor (three rods), Godfrey de Hamerton (one rod), Eusebius son of Richard (one rod) and Reginald the son of Isolda (one rod). Simon the son of Alexander had initiated his suit with a writ from the king. Nevertheless, the case continued through the courts for some eight months. When the stage for essoins was arrived at, Ranulph the son of Gilbert was essoined in turn by William the son of Simon, Elias Faber and Godfrey Engelond senior. William Sutor was essoined four times through Roger Ray, Robert Fraunceys, Godfrey son of Godfrey *le* Bedel and John Kimme. Godfrey *de* Hamerton was also essoined four times by Robert Fraunceys, Thomas Goni, Thomas *de* Hamerton and John *de* Hamerton. The three essoins for Eusebius son of Richard were presented by John Goni, William the son of Simon and Reginald in the Lane. Reginald the son of Isolda had the four essoins by Godfrey Ese, Thomas Sali, Robert Fraunceys and John Page. Simon the son of Alexander finally won his case and the land was seized by the bailiffs for Simon on the technical charge of non-appearance of the defendants. In the meantime, however, 15 men of the town had provided a buffer for the defendants.

It would be misleading to give the impression that the social capital of Godmanchester derived from some primitive good fellowship or reservoir of euphoria. Godmanchester people had this great resourcefulness because the economic and social realities of their environment demanded this of them. Involvement in administration was inevitable to every level of life. Although there were many changes in Godmanchester from the thirteenth to the fifteenth centuries, surviving customs seemed to indicate that the administrative organization of the town remained much the same.

It is important, therefore, to note that the bailiffs, powerful though their role might have been in administration of town property, were but one part of the Godmanchester officialdom. From the first surviving frankpledge roll, that of 1422, it is clear that the twelve jurors of Godmanchester exerted a powerful influence over peace and order in the town comparable to such frankpledge juries in the neighbouring manors of Ramsey. That is to say, these jurors were the prominent men of the town and it was before them that various officials reported. In turn, these other officials were too numerous to allow any one to concentrate power. At the end of the frankpledge roll, headed by the name of the jurors, were listed the bailiffs, the constable, two collectors of the royal farm, from each of the four streets, four custodians of the mills, two custodians of the church, one collector of fines from each street, two collectors of tolls (John Bate and William Manipenny), clerk of the court, collector of the farm from outsiders (foreigners) and a collector of the farm from Remyng'.

The apparent plethora of officials at Godmanchester does not mean that the town was over governed. Rather, in this medieval town surrounded by meadows liable to floods and an open-field system of arable, the political economy was necessarily very complex. In a previous chapter, the great amount of petty property movement has been indicated. This detail may also be found for other interactions among villagers. In that same frankpledge roll of 1422, there are more than 100 fines for petty offences, especially failure to maintain ditches and trespass upon the property of others. A fine was assessed to Roger Ledder under the assize of bread. Under the assize of ale were fined the following (*pandoxatores*): Joan Smith, Margaret Lee, Joan Sly, Margaret Page, Mariota Bate, Emma Fisher, Isabella Cole, John Bron, Margaret Prior, Alice Rasin, Emma Chamber, Amicia Portos, Agnes Ledder, Joan Baker, Alice Gray. Margaret Cole, Emma Wafrer, Joan Bayng'ton, William Lancuham, Agnes Porter, Thomas Wt'lyng, Richard Cabe, Cristina Cook. Fined simply as retailer (*auxiatores*) were Agnes Chese, Isabella Ive, Isabella Fuller, Alice Scot, Alice Ferrour and Margaret Glover.

While writing this volume the author has been engaged in a consultative capacity for a development project in Africa. It might seem tempting, therefore, to epitomize the "Godmanchester experience" in some of the catchy contemporary phrases such as "intermediate technology" or "small is beautiful." To do so would be misleading. There is nothing in the Godmanchester experience as such to suggest a model for the devolution of contemporary centralization. What the story of Godmanchester does tell us is that there is a third category of social

organization intermediate to the village and town and that this category may demonstrate better than the full-blown institutions of urban life the variety of life possible to a well-socialized people.

The magnitude of the detail about individuals and families at Godmanchester serves as a critique for an over-ready tendency to typologize towns. For example, the Godmanchester experience would suggest that the concept of "region" has been employed in too static a fashion.[3] For Godmanchester we have seen that there are several regions: agrarian, occupational, commercial and political. Some of these regions are more interlocking than others, for example, the agrarian and occupational. In turn, some of these "regions" interlocked in a very ad hoc fashion, for example, royal purveyance and commerce in times of war. In as much as the linkage pattern of the regions was affected by families and/or common occupational ties, it may further be questioned whether the famous thesis[4] about the movement of industry from town to country in the late thirteenth century must not be posed in fresh terms. Industrial personnel from the cloth borough of Huntingdon "went to the country" indeed by investing in land at Godmanchester. Families with the surname Tinctor are interesting in this respect. But this was evidently a diversification of family investment rather than the shifting of the industry base as such. By the same token, landbased families at Godmanchester developed commercial ties through towns rather than more extensive rural investments.

The experience of Godmanchester people also challenges some traditional generalizations about town social structures as such. It is undoubtedly true that the town was proud of its privileges and that the local government system seemed to function efficiently. Nevertheless, satisfaction with privileges does not mean the development of more egalitarian structures in royal towns than in rural manors. The customary laws might have made possible a great amount of property circulation but they were no guarantee that an individual or family would acquire property. Indeed, it is amazing how closely the pyramided social structure at Godmanchester paralleled that of Ramsey manors in the County.[5] In the Ramsey manors, a veritable "class" structure developed despite the common demands placed upon villeins by the lord. Et Godmanchester an

---

[3] Postan, *Medieval Economy and Society*.

[4] For a useful review of the literature on this subject see E. Miller, "The Fortunes of the English Textile Industry in the Thirteenth Century," *The Economic History Review*, 2nd series, 18 (1965), 64-82.

[5] See Britton, *Community of the Vill*.

equally wide gap was maintained between the wealthier people of the town and those with little or no property despite the common privileges of the freemen of the royal manor. There is much here that requires further explanation by the social historian. On the whole, however, Godmanchester evidence suggests that there is a broader base of information available for economic and social analyses rather than at this time for simply replacing one generalization by another. For example, it is to be hoped that the ability of women to acquire considerable property by customary inheritance as well as purchase, and the relatively greater use of purchase or short-term leasing of small units of property by poorer (or younger) individuals can be substantiated by studies of other small towns.

Part Three

The People of the Court Roll

7

The Families of Godmanchester

For the presentation of Table 26 it may be useful to repeat some of the points developed above in Chapter 4. The data obtainable from the God-manchester court rolls fall somewhere between the data from parish registers and normal court rolls. In the Godmanchester records, over 90 percent of the names are given with some further specified familial relationship along with the common surname. Therefore, the following table (Table 26) has been centred about this information on family relationships. The linkage is that of familial degree indicated by the court rolls.

In this context, therefore, the main problems of identification are not those of changing or "underdeveloped" surname formulation but simply the lack of information about familial relationships. In some instances this inadequate information follows from the relatively brief involvement of certain individuals in the courts of Godmanchester quite simply because of their small involvement in matters of property — such as the practitioners of certain trades — or because their family life would seem to centre beyond the town — in which cases the court often settled for a reference to place only.

Where there are given a number of individuals with the same surname, problems of identification follow from the nature and condition of the record. Survival of records from the 1270s is a question of historical accident and frequently, therefore, we know little about parents prior to the 1280s whose names survive only in the context of widows or children. For this reason no dates are attached to many late thirteenth-century names.

At the other extreme, especially for larger families, the relationships seem to have been so obvious to the court that full familial relationship is not given. Even though there is every indication from surname, first name and chronology that a certain individual may be the same as one indicated elsewhere by a given familial tie, this tie is not given in the court records.

Such individuals are treated separately in the table, but an asterisk is appended to their names to indicate that they are likely the same individual as appears on a previous line.[1]

Finally, for a considerable number of individuals with a common surname, the court has not given a family context for one reason or another. For instance subsequent records of continued court appearances in particular cases may abbreviate the identification for the sake of economy; where a few rolls are missing or damaged, the initial full identification and the sequence may be lost. More frequently, however, the court seems content to identify an outsider or a person engaged in a special occupation by such designation rather than by their relationship to other villagers. In all such cases these individuals are appended to the family list under the rubric, "probable kin."

In Table 26 families are listed alphabetically by surname, but first names, where possible, are in chronological order. An asterisk indicates an individual who may already be listed (see above); "(d)" indicates dead; "(c)" after a name indicates that this individual married and therefore appears below as a head of another family — "(c1)," "(c2)," etc. distinguish persons of the same name; "(2nd)" indicates a second wife; "sen" means senior; "jun" means junior; and "dau" means daughter.

---

[1] See above, Chapter 4, p. 158 for a discussion of some particular examples.

TABLE 26: FAMILY DATA FROM GODMANCHESTER COURT ROLLS

Family Name and Husband	Wife	Son(s)	Daughter(s)
ABOVETOWN *see* BOVETOWN			
ACRY			
Richard 1293-1316 (d)	Cristina[a] 1312 (d)		
	(2nd) Mabel 1316-1322		
Richard 1330-1342	Agnes 1346	Thomas 1345	Margaret 1346
Richard* 1351-1354	Margaret 1350		
Thomas jun 1351-1358	Amicia 1365-1375		
Henry 1371-1394	Cristina dau of Reginald Denne 1372-1380		
ALBON			
William *de* Hunts 1394	Joan 1394		
ALBRID (ALBRIT)			
Eusebius 1280-1301	Isolda 1280-1301	John 1281-1282 (c)	Alice 1282
John (c)	Emma 1282		
probable kin: Richard 1282			
ALDOUS			
Thomas 1295-1303	Isabella 1295-1298	John *de* Hunts 1348	
Robert 1345-1348 (d)	unknown		
probable kin: Thomas *de* Hunts 1302			

[a] Cristina is the sister of Phillipa wife of William Aylred.

Family Name and Husband	Wife	Son(s)	Daughter(s)
ALEWILL			
Richard 1293-1295	Isolda 1293-1295		
probable kin: Margaret de Papworth 1303			
SON OF ALEXANDER			
Alexander	unknown	Simon 1278-1280	Agnes 1313
		Hugh (c)[b]	
Hugh (c)	unknown		
ALEYN			
John de Weston 1331-1335	Pellagia 1331-1335		
John* 1337-1350 (d)	unknown		
Thomas 1352	Margaret 1352	Thomas 1337	
Thomas* 1354-1388	Cristina 1356-1388		
John 1358-1389	Cristina 1358-1389	John 1382-1387	
John*	unknown		
John 1392	Isabella 1392	Reginald 1354-1374	
probable kin: William 1340-1348			
Roger 1341, 1376			
William, chaplain 1354			
Thomas jun 1387			
John, piscator 1391			
ALICE			
unknown	Alice	John 1289 (c)	
		Richard 1289	

b See above, p. 240.

Name	Wife	Children
John (c)	unknown	
Godfrey (c)	Millicent 1346	Godfrey 1344 (c)
		Alice 1282
ALMAYNE		
Robert 1377-1386	Joan 1382	
ALRED see **AYLRED**		
ALRYTH (**ALRICH**)		
Eusebius 1280	unknown	Godfrey 1283-1326, dead by 1331
		Reginald 1311-1325, dead by 1348 (c)
Reginald (c)	unknown	William 1359-1372
John 1281	unknown	Godfrey 1281-1313 (d)
unknown	unknown	John 1282
		William 1282
Robert 1306-1322	Isolda 1306-1317	
Richard 1329-1344	Cristina 1329	
probable kin: Richard 1280		
Alice 1281 (*see* SCOT)		
Henry 1349 (d)		
ANFRED (**AUFRED**, **AVERED**)		
John *de* Hunts 1322	Matilda 1328	John *de* Hunts 1349-1350
probable kin: John 1280-1281		
ANIZ		
Aniz	unknown	Eusebius 1293-1318 (c)
Eusebius (c)	unknown	Nicholas 1295-1298 (c)
		Reginald 1298-1314
		Godfrey 1301-1307
Nicholas (c)	Emma Parsons 1297	

Family Name and Husband	Wife	Son(s)	Daughter(s)
APOTEKARIUS *see* SPICER			
APPARITOR			
Godfrey 1316	unknown	Thomas 1316	
AD AQUAM			
Ivo 1279-1283	unknown		Egace 1283
unknown	Edith	Richard 1327	
probable kin: Robert 1298			
ASPELON			
Richard 1373-1382	Margaret 1373-1382		
ATEBRUT			
John 1332-1340	Joan 1332-1340		
ATELANESHENDE			
John *de* Hunts 1332	unknown	John 1332	
ATENOCK			
Simon 1287-1289	unknown		Mariota 1282-1310
probable kin: Cristina 1309-1323			
ATEMAR			
Peter *de* Bumstead	unknown		
John (c)	Alice 1321	John 1321 (c)	
AUFRED *see* ANFRED			
AUGUSTINE (AUSTYN TURK)c			
Augustine of the Canons	unknown	Augustine 1303 (d) (c)	

c This surname is unique in so far as it ranges from over the period of the 1280s to the 1340s with two name changes. It starts off as "Augustine of the Canons, who has a son called Augustine"; by the 1300s the surname of "Turk" is incorporated and one finds entries under both "Augustine son of Augustine Turk" (1309) and "Augustine son of Augustine" (1301 to 1307). By the 1340s "Turk" has been dropped and the surname of "Austyn" is used. This applies to the last generations of the family — Simon son of Augustine (Austyn) 1335, Robert son of Simon son of Augustine (Austyn) 1335, and John son of Richard son of Augustine (Austyn) 1340-1348. From the court rolls this family does not continue on into the 1390s and 1400s.

Augustine (c)

Joan Fayrheved
dead before 1301
(2nd) Margaret widow 1303

Richard 1282-1317 (d) (c)
William 1299-1302 (c)
Augustine 1307-1313 (d) (c)
Godfrey 1293-1307 (d) (c)
Nicholas 1308-1315
John 1316-1317 (c)
John 1327-1338

Isabella 1327-1330
Joan 1327
Matilda 1299
Ivetta 1326

Richard (c)   Alice 1327-1329   Richard 1329-1330 (c)   Emma 1317 (d)
                                                Simon 1335 (c)
                                                John 1340
                                                Walter 1317 (d)

William (c)   Aldosia 1299

Augustine (c)   Ivetta Bartelot 1306-1311   John 1340-1348
                                                     Robert 1335-1340

Godfrey (c)   unknown
John (c)   Isabella 1316-1317
Richard (c)   unknown
Simon (c)   unknown
William 1341-1345   Beatrix 1348   Godfrey 1295, 1307   Millicent 1307

AULA (ATTE HALL)
Robert 1283-1310   Agnes 1283-1310
Stephen 1291-1292 (d) Alice 1291
Robert 1320-1325   Matilda 1320   John 1332   Cecily 1338 married to William
                                                                                Manipenny
                                                                             Sybil 1349

probable kin: Isabella 1283
               Walter 1286
               Robert de Brampton 1325
               Simon 1338-1349

Family Name and Husband	Wife	Son(s)	Daughter(s)
AURIFABER (GOLDSMITH)			
William *de* Hunts 1315-1321	unknown	John *de* Hunts, 1315-1325, 1344	
probable kin: John *de* Hunts 1280-1302			
Nicholas *de* Hunts 1315-1316			
Nicholas 1279			
Helen 1325			
AUSTYN TURK *see* AUGUSTINE			
AVERED *see* ANFRED			
AYLE			
John *de* Buckworth 1363 (d)	unknown		Agnes 1363
			Joan 1363
AYLRED (ALRED)			
Eusebius 1280	Isolda 1280	Godfrey 1303-1326 (c)	
Godfrey (c)	Isabella dau of	Henry 1310-1329	
	Robert Scot 1303		
		John 1310	
		Reginald 1329-1335 (c)	
		Richard 1329-1348 (c)	
Reginald (c)	Cristina 1344	Gilbert 1348	Margaret 1344
		William 1337-1348	Cristina 1344
			Amicia 1344 (d)
Richard (c)	Caterina 1344	William 1348	Cristina 1348
		Godfrey 1348	
Martin	unknown	Simon 1299-1316 (c)	Cristina 1300-1302
		John 1307-1312 (d)	Millicent 1302-1327

	Wife	Sons	Daughters
Simon (c)	unknown	Roger 1327	
Walter 1289	unknown	Walter 1308-1309 (c)	Elena 1302
		John 1300-1329 (c)	
Walter (c)	unknown	Reginald 1319-1324 (c)	Isolda 1342-1345 (d)
		John 1345	
John (c)	Dionysia Bulgon 1316-1324		
Reginald (c)	Cristina 1324	William 1299-1326 (c)	Margaret 1304-1310
William 1280-1298 (d)	Phillipa 1303		Cristina 1304-1310
			Emma 1310
			Matilda 1310
			Sybil 1327
William (c)	wife of 1327	William 1306, 1327	
		Reginald 1306, 1327-1348	
Robert 1303-1316	unknown	Richard 1317	
William	Agnes 1306-1312 (d)	Richard 1312	
		Godfrey 1317-1321	
William de Arnyng St	unknown	Roger 1327-1348 (c)	
		Henry 1329-1348	
Roger de Arnyng St (c)	unknown	William 1334	
Godfrey	unknown	Alan 1343-1371 (d)(c)	Cristina 1345
Alan (c)	Agnes 1371	John 1349-1350	
		Thomas 1370-1395	
John	unknown	William 1348	
Simon 1345-1349	unknown	Roger 1345-1361	Emma 1348
Henry 1350-1367	Sybil 1351	John 1351-1376 (c)	
John (c)	Phillipa 1365		
William 1354	Emma 1354	Godfrey 1351-1373 (d)(c)	
Godfrey (c)	Amicia 1351-1354		
	(2nd) Joan 1367-1373		

Family Name and Husband	Wife	Son(s)	Daughter(s)
Godfrey 1373-1380	Matilda 1373-1380		
John 1382	Matilda 1382		
probable kin: Master John and brother 1323			
Bartholomew 1348			
Mabel 1361			
Julian 1367			
William 1390-1443			
AYLWARD			
Aylward	unknown	Bartholomew 1285-1305 (d)	
		Roger 1290	
		John 1297-1316 (c)	Alice 1298-1316
			Mariota 1298-1310
John 1295 (d)	unknown		
John (c)	Amicia 1304		
BA			
Godfrey le 1285	Agnes 1285		
BACHELOR			
Thomas 1350 (d)	unknown		Emma 1350
BAGGLE			
John de Hemingford Grey	Beatrix 1344-1345		
BAKER see PISTOR			
BALDE			
John 1294	Cristina 1294	John jun 1295-1297	Cristina 1293
		John sen 1295-1297, dead by 1321	Emma 1292-1294

Member	Spouse		
John* [d]	unknown	Richard 1321 (c)	
Richard (c)	Emma 1338	Robert 1324-1326	
Alexander	unknown	Gilbert 1327	
		Godfrey 1361-1362	
		Alexander 1331	
BALDECOTE			
John *de* Hunts 1346	Joan 1346		
probable kin: Robert *de* Hunts 1346			
BALDOCK			
Stephen 1305	Joan 1305	Godfrey 1293	
BALDRY			
Baldry	unknown		
probable kin: Edward 1291-1308			
BALLE			
Godfrey 1278-1291	unknown	Lord Robert, chaplain, 1283-1297	Agnes 1300
John 1278-1283	unknown	Ralph 1282	Matilda 1278-1289
Thomas 1278-1311	unknown	Lord William, chaplain, 1304-1330	Isolda 1289
unknown	Pellagia (c)	Thomas 1308	Pellagia 1308 (d)(c)
William 1291-1303	unknown	Reginald 1308-1316	Cristina 1308-1325
Reginald (c)	Gunnilda 1317	Reginald 1293-1310 (c)(d)	Cristina 1308 (d)
			Emma 1303-1309
			Agnes 1307-1318
			Amabilia 1307-1318

[d] This John could be either John jun or John sen, both sons of John (1294).

Family Name and Husband	Wife	Son(s)	Daughter(s)
Alexander 1297-1302	Pellagia 1297	John 1309-1320 Robert 1312 Thomas 1324-1325	Isolda 1307-1318 Helen 1307-1318 Cristina 1307-1318 Matilda 1308-1316 Helen 1308-1316
Walter 1291	Albrida 1291		Agnes 1316 Cristina 1302 Matilda 1304-1308
Elias	unknown		Agnes 1307 Juliana 1307 Isabella 1307, 1325
unknown	Matilda	John 1331	
John 1349	Agnes 1349	Thomas 1362-1375	
William 1350-1361	Pellagia 1361		
Henry 1374-1377	unknown	Nicholas 1372 Thomas 1385-1394 (c) John 1394-1428	
Thomas (c)	Emma 1394		

probable kin: Emma 1281
Felicia 1286
John *de* West St 1286
Nicholas 1325
Cristina 1338
Lord Robert, chaplain 1343-1346
Lord William, chaplain 1366
Thomas *de* Offord Cluny 1360-1363

BANASTRE
John, clerk 1350-1380   Isabella 1350

BAND
William 1343   Beatrix 1343
probable kin: Henry 1343
Nicholas *de* Hunts 1343

BANNA
Hugh   unknown   William 1281
Thomas 1286   Alice 1286

BARBOUR
Roger *de* Hunts 1314   Joan 1314 dau of John   Nicholas 1314
de Hamerton   John 1333
Elias 1342-1377   Phillipa 1342   William 1341-1375
Henry 1340   unknown   Henry 1340-1374
John 1356-1360   Questel 1356
probable kin: Gilbert *le*, merchant, *de* Sudbury 1325
Thomas 1361 (d)
John, farmer, *de* Cambridge 1378
John, chaplain, of St John *de* Gt Paxton 1378
Robert *de* Hunts 1392

BARD
Robert   unknown   Simon 1280

BAREFOT
Godfrey 1315-1316   Isabella 1315-1316

BARKER
Roger   Cristina widow 1304   Sybil 1329

Family Name and Husband	Wife	Son(s)	Daughter(s)
Thomas			
probable kin: John *le, de* Hunts 1326	Agnes widow 1346		
Thomas *de* Hunts 1330			
Robert *de* Gt Paxton 1342			
Thomas 1361			
BARMAN			
John 1351	Sybil 1351		
BAROUN			
Thomas *de* Merton 1326	Amicia Baroun 1326	John, mercator 1326-1345 (d) (c)	Emma 1361
John, mercator (c)	Agnes 1326-1331		
John 1352-1354	Sybil 1356		
John*	unknown	Thomas *de* Hemingford Abbots 1361	Margaret 1385
John, carpenter 1385-1395	Cristina 1385		
probable kin: Richard *de* Graveley 1346			
Matilda *de* Hemingford Abbots 1366			
John, mercator 1368			
John 1372-1376			
John *de* Hemingford 1377			
ATTE **BARRE**			
Phillip 1280	Isolda 1280	Godfrey 1287-1327 (c)	Sarra 1316
		John 1309, 1320	
		Henry 1327 (c)	
Godfrey (c)	unknown		
Henry (c)	Matilda 1329-1340		

	Wife	Sons	Daughters
Robert 1288, 1301 (d) John 1307	Albrida 1288 Cristina 1325 (d)	John 1288 John sen 1309-1330 John jun 1316 (c) Walter 1316-1340 (c) William 1316-1332	Caterina 1338 Emma 1307 (d)
John jun (c) Walter (c) Reginald John *de* Post St Ralph *de* Hemingford Abbots 1339 Roger 1342-1357	Isolda 1316 Cristina widow by 1347 unknown unknown Cristina 1339 Cristina 1343-1348 (2nd) Beatrix 1351-1366	John 1338 John 1330 Henry 1341-1365 (c)	
Henry (c) William 1351-1361	Matilda 1349 Cristina 1351	Godfrey 1363 Henry 1363-1388	Agnes 1428
Adam 1388-1441 probable kin: Gilbert 1287 Matilda 1304 (d) John, pelliparius 1312 Simon 1349-1393 Richard 1360 Reginald 1361-1367	unknown		

BARTELOT

	Wife	Sons	Daughters
William dead by 1300	Ivetta widow 1300; re-marries Augustine Turk; widow by 1313	John 1289, 1308	Helen 1298-1313 Millicent 1298-1319
Robert 1316-1332 Nicholas 1345	Cristina 1319 unknown	John 1339-1343 (c) Godfrey 1339-1376 (c)	Agnes 1316

Family Name and Husband	Wife	Son(s)	Daughter(s)
John (c)	Agnes 1345		
Godfrey (c)	Agnes 1361-1367	William 1347-1354 (c)	
Robert*	unknown	Godfrey 1377-1399	
William (c)	Isolda 1348-1362		
John 1375-1423	Sybil 1375		
probable kin: Isolda 1316			
John 1351 (d)			
SON OF BARTHOLOMEW			
Bartholomew	unknown	Thomas 1364-1365	
probable kin: Roger 1326			
Robert, taylor 1363			
DE BARTON (BERTON)			
Walter 1278-1316 (d)	unknown	William 1295	Joan 1278-1295
		Simon 1316	
		William 1349 (c)	
Simon*	unknown		
William (c)	Denise 1350-1354		
probable kin: Simon, chaplain 1344-1348			
William de Papworth 1353-1362			
William jun 1358			
BASSET			
John 1380-1391	Emma 1380		
probable kin: John sen 1387-1388			
BATAYLE (BETELE)			
Robert 1299	unknown	John sen 1306-1348	Emma 1302
		John jun 1307-1323 (c)	Madda 1302-1309

John (jun or sen) (c)   Margaret 1323
probable kin: John 1349-1350
               Isabella 1358

BATE
John 1280-1302 (d)   unknown   Isolda 1302
                           Cristina 1302

Henry 1320   unknown

Henry (c)   Elena 1345   Henry 1326 (c)
John 1326-1345   Isabella 1326   Thomas 1326
Godfrey 1329-1348 Elena Balle 1348 William 1327-1340 (d)
unknown   Amicia 1302   Henry 1356-1399
unknown   unknown

                                 Phillipa 1302

William (c)   Matilda 1380-1399 William 1363-1399 (c)
probable kin: John de Hilton 1313   Robert 1367-1398
               Robert 1340
               John de Hunts 1361 (d)
               Henry, lockyer 1390
               John de Bassingbourne 1382
               William, servant of Robert Lockyer 1360

BAXTER
John 1297   unknown   Edith 1297
                           Caterina 1297
                           Cristina 1299-1303

Richard 1298   unknown   William 1303
probable kin: Godfrey and Emma see COKAYN
               Godfrey 1372

Family Name and Husband	Wife	Son(s)	Daughter(s)
BEADLE			
Robert 1278	unknown	Reginald 1278-1287	
Godfrey 1279	unknown	Godfrey 1279	
probable kin: John 1343-1380			
John sen 1360			
BEATRIX			
unknown	Beatrix	John 1348-1356	
BEAUCHAMP see BEWSCHAMPE			
BEGENORE			
William de Hunts 1311, 1314 (d)	Mariota 1314	Peter de Hunts 1314-1322 (d)	
		Paul de Hunts 1314-1346	
BEKYNGHAM			
Robert 1383	Alice 1383		
BELE			
John	unknown		Muriel 1287 married to John Carpenter
Godfrey 1389	Alice 1389		
probable kin: John 1350-1351			
BELYSSON			
John 1395-1399	Margaret 1395-1399		
BENETHEBROK			
Thomas 1338	unknown	Henry 1338	
probable kin: Elias de Hunts 1298			
BERNARD			
William 1302-1327	Agnes 1302		
BERTON see DE BARTON			

BETELE *see* **BATAYLE**

DE BEVERLE (BEVERLEY)
Richard *de* Hunts 1329   Agnes 1329
John *de* Hunts 1333-1351   Joan 1333-1348   Agnes 1333
                                 (2nd) Sarra 1356-1360

    probable kin: Robert *de* 1282
               John *de* 1309
               William, wryght 1391

BEVEWYK
John 1346   Margeria 1346

BEWSCHAMPE (BEAUCHAMP)
Walter *de* Hunts 1354   Beatrix 1354
    probable kin: William Lord, chaplain, canon *de* Hunts 1349, 1361

DE BILNEYE
John *de* Hunts 1322 (d)   Agnes 1322
father of Hugh 1329   unknown   Hugh 1329-1330
    probable kin: John 1288-1310, 1330

BISHOP
Henry *de* Broughton 1297 (d)   unknown   Albrit 1297
                                                         Walter 1297

BLAC
Phillip 1316   unknown   Phillip 1316

DE BLUNTISHAM
Robert 1318-1338 (d)   Amicia 1338 re-marries
                                 Simon *le* Stone 1340

BOLE
unknown   unknown   John 1281-1307 (d) (c1)   Cristina 1307 (d)
John (c1)   Isolda 1308   Godfrey 1302-1348 (d) (c)
                                                         John 1304-1315 (c2)
                                                         Thomas 1312-1341

Family Name and Husband	Wife	Son(s)	Daughter(s)
Godfrey (c)	Elena 1338 (d)	Lawrence 1338 Thomas 1349-1386 (c)	
Thomas (c)	Elena 1353-1356	John 1354-1399	Isolda 1349 Pellagia 1353
John (c2)	Cristina 1303	John 1332	Amicia 1303 married to John Pellage 1316 Juliana 1316 Cristina 1326
Martin 1299-1306 (d)	Isabella 1297	William 1303-1315 (c) William jun 1303-1311	Cristina 1311 husband called Simon Cristina 1322
William (c)	Gunnilda Mendy 1304 and wife 1318		
Richard 1318	Cristina 1350-1357		
William 1350-1357	Isabella 1351		
John 1351	Amicia 1351		
Robert 1357	Sybil 1366		
John, cooperator 1361-1372	Sybil 1389		
Godfrey 1389			
probable kin: Henry de Offord Cluny 1340			
Godfrey 1352-1375			
John, butcher 1353			
Henry 1362			
Nicholas de Yelling 1377-1394			
Walter de Yelling 1377-1394			
Hugh de Hartford 1380			
John sen 1394			

BONDE
Simon 1316 unknown
Hugh 1317-1320 Emma 1317   Sarra 1316
                   Sarra 1317
Hugh 1340 unknown
Henry (c) Helen 1350-1358 (d) Henry 1343-1372 (c) Cristina 1343
Richard *de* Lt. Stukeley 1348 Isolda 1348
John 1354-1393 Joan 1354
probable kin: Nicholas 1338
      John 1343
      Richard 1350-1381
      Peter *de* Brampton 1361
      John, piscator *de* Hunts 1371-1392
      William *de* Graveley 1374
      John *de* Hemingford Abbots 1393

BONES *see* BONIS
BONEVILLE
William 1280-1310 unknown
Richard (c) Agnes, widow 1322 Richard 1310 (c) Cristina 1311
BONIS (BONES, BONYS)
John 1281-1295 Agnes 1281-1295 Richard 1303-1304 (d)
William 1287-1333 unknown   John 1325-1348

unknown mother of Ivetta 1356   Ivetta 1356
Jowett unknown   Hugh 1372
probable kin: Godfrey 1282-1286
      Richard 1283-1284
      Robert 1287
      Alexander 1311, 1345 (d)
      Alditha 1333-1342 (d)
      Edward 1340-1365
      Thomas jun 1399

Family Name and Husband	Wife	Son(s)	Daughter(s)
BORE			
John	unknown	William 1357	
BOREL see BUREL			
DE BORSWORTH			
William sen 1353-1367	Felicia 1364-1391		
William jun *de* East St 1382	Amicia 1382		
probable kin: Lord Roger 1347, 1364-1376			
William *de* Arnyng St 1366			
BOTELER			
Thomas 1338-1350 (d)	Agnes 1350		
probable kin: Peter 1350 (d)			
Robert 1350			
John 1367			
John sen *de* Hunts 1390			
BOURGOS			
Thomas 1354	Margaret 1354		
BOVETUN (ABOVETOWN)			
William 1278	unknown		Cristina 1278
Henry 1280-1282	unknown	William 1280-1283	
probable kin: Dionysia 1278, 1282			
Mabel 1280-1294			
BOVEYRE			
unknown	Millicent 1348	Godfrey 1348	
IN YE BOWRE			
John 1351	Cristina 1351		

DE BRADENHAM			
Alexander 1295-1304	unknown	Simon 1318-1329 (c)	Alice 1329
Simon (c)	Catherine 1318-1319		
Elias 1329	Cristina 1329		
BRETON (BRETOUN)			
unknown	unknown	Godfrey 1293-1299	
		William 1293-1299	
William 1360-1393	Cristina 1361		
probable kin: William 1341			
BREWER			
Humphrey 1338	Phillipa 1338		
ATTE BROKE			
Walter	wife of 1280		
John 1308-1341	Cristina 1338		
probable kin: John, butcher, *de* Hunts 1371-1372			
DE BROUGHTON			
Hankinus 1330	Alice 1330		
probable kin: Robert *de*, piscator *de* St Ives 1316			
BROUN (BROWN)			
John 1321-1323	unknown	William 1323	
William	unknown	John 1360	Cristina 1360
		Godfrey 1360	
John 1389-1394	Sybil 1389-1394		
probable kin: John jun 1381, 1394			
John sen 1394			
Thomas 1394			
BRYAN			
Hugh 1362-1364	Agnes 1362-1364		
probable kin: Thomas 1363-1394			

Family Name and Husband	Wife	Son(s)	Daughter(s)
BRYD			
John 1304-1322	Amicia 1304		
probable kin: Alice 1364			
John de Eltisley 1398			
BRYHT			
Simon	unknown	William 1381	
BUCHER			
Thomas	unknown		Isabella 1358
BULBY			
Richard 1338	unknown	John 1338	
BULDIR			
William 1278-1288 (d)	Agnes 1278		Helen 1278-1280
Robert de Hunts 1329-1341	unknown	Robert 1330, 1341	
John de Hunts 1335-1351	Margaret 1335-1346		
Henry de Hunts 1338	Matilda 1338		
probable kin: Alan 1279			
Henry 1279			
DE BUMSTEAD			
William de Godmanchester, le shepherd 1351-1373	Cristina 1354-1373		
BUREL (BOREL)			
Simon de Hemingford 1331	unknown	John 1331	Alice 1331
		William 1331	Gunnilda 1331
DE BURY (BYR)			
Henry de Hunts	unknown	Henry 1279	

Stephen *de* Dunstable
brother of Henry 1278-1279

John 1281-1282	Sarra 1281
Godfrey 1310	Mabel 1288
	Ivetta 1308
	Sabina 1308
	Joan 1306 married to Peter
	Wyldegrys
	Alice 1316

probable kin: William atte 1347-1354
    Hugh 1358

BUTCHER *see* **CARNIFEX**
BUXTON (**BUXSTON**)

Andrew 1277	Alice 1277
Benedict 1278-1301	Joan 1278-1301
unknown	Emma 1316
William 1361	Beatrix 1361
probable kin: John 1304	
Margaret 1316	

BYR *see* **DE BURY**
BYRLYNGTON

Richard 1371	Agnes 1371

CAGE

Robert 1365-1373	Alice 1368-1373

probable kin: Reginald 1350 (d)
CAMBRIDGE *see* **DE CANT'**
CANNE

John 1291	Alice 1291

probable kin: Godfrey 1312
    John 1333

Family Name and Husband	Wife	Son(s)	Daughter(s)
DE CANT' (CAMBRIDGE?)			
John 1338	Matilda 1338		
probable kin: Walter *de* 1291			
Fulco 1327			
CAPELLANUS *see* CHAPLAIN			
CARNIFEX (BUTCHER, FLESHEWERER)			
Andrew 1280	Nichola 1280		
Nicholas 1349-1368	Sybil 1362-1377	John 1362-1380	
Nicholas*	Elena 1377		
probable kin: Roger 1350			
John *de* Weston 1353			
CARPENTER			
Nicholas 1287	unknown	John 1287 (c)	
John (c)	Muriel dau of John Bele 1287		
Richard *de* Sawtry 1301	unknown	Thomas 1301	
Robert 1302	unknown	John jun 1302, 1312	
Adam *de* Henlow 1313	Helen dau of Kyne 1313		
Robert*	unknown	Henry 1330	
Roger 1331-1332	Sybil 1331-1332		
John 1380	unknown	John 1380	
probable kin: Roger *de* Hunts 1302			
John 1351			
CARTER			
Robert 1300 (d)	Cristina 1300	John 1298-1308	
William 1361-1367	Emma 1362-1367	Stephen 1362	

John 1371-1375   Juliana 1371-1375
John 1378   Emma 1378
probable kin: Richard *le* 1278-1280
Emma 1342
Alan 1344
Thomas 1345-1348
John *de* Hartford 1375

CASTELMP'LT
Gilbert 1307   unknown
Hugh (c)   Mariota 1307   Hugh 1307 (c)

CATELYNE
William 1341-1342   unknown
John (c)   Imama widow 1354   John 1344-1354 (d) (c)   Joan 1341-1342
John 1352-1367   Agnes 1352   Thomas 1351-1391   Sybil 1354
probable kin: Godfrey 1341-1347 (d)
Felicia 1350-1373
John *de* Fen Drayton 1366
Cristina 1341 (d)

SON OF CATERINA
unknown   Caterina

John (c)   unknown   John 1290 (c)   Emma 1292
Godfrey (c)   Matilda 1301   Godfrey 1301 (c)
unknown   Caterina

DE CATWORTH (CATTEWORTH)
John, carter, 1299, 1302   Mariota 1302   John 1326-1340
probable kin: Robert *de* 1315   William 1332-1340

Family Name and Husband	Wife	Son(s)	Daughter(s)
CAUNT			
Richard 1350	Catherine 1350		
CEMENTARIUS (CIMITERO)			
Stephen of Hunts	unknown	James 1278-1281 (d)	
John 1287	unknown	Pellage 1287	
William	unknown	John 1318	
		William 1324	
probable kin: Simon 1303			
Master John 1324			
CHADESLEE			
John 1369-1371	Pellagia 1374-1399		
DE CHAM			
Robert 1325	Sabina 1325		
CHAPLAIN (CAPELLANUS)			
Simon 1298-1307	unknown	John 1307 (c)	
		William 1312 (c)	
John (c)	unknown	Henry 1307	Sybil 1307
			Helen 1307
William (c)	unknown		Felicia 1312
			Agnes 1312, 1322
Chaplain	unknown	Richard son of, de	
		Altherhethe 1295-1301 (c)	
Richard de Altherhethe (c)	Felicia 1301		
Elias, tannator de Hunts 1332	unknown	John 1332, 1348	

probable kin: Martin the chaplain 1279-1307
Walter *de* Elsworth 1279-1299
Roger 1317-1346
Lord Peter, *de* Eton 1329-1331
William, *de* Burtonsteye 1327
Lord Walter, *de* Stukeley 1331
William 1353

CHAPMAN (MERCATOR, MERCHANT, MERCER)ᵉ

Richard 1278-1303 (d) — Emma 1295-1303
Mercator — unknown
Walter 1302-1306 — Pellagia dau of John Mason 1302-1306 — Thomas 1304 — John 1304 — Matilda 1303-1316, daus of 1299

Wymer — unknown
Henry 1310 — Isolda 1318
Reginald *de* Wood Newton 1331 — Agnes 1331
Richard *de* Lt. Stukeley 1333 — Isolda dau of Godfrey Glewe 1333-1348 — Pellagia 1366
 (Richard 1334-1348)
Thomas 1329-1346 — unknown — Agnes 1344, Sybil 1344-1346

John 1335-1342 — unknown — John 1351, Richard 1351, 1361
John 1350-1356 — unknown — William 1352-1372

ᵉ Chapman, Mercator, Merchant and Mercer all indicate the same occupational surname of "merchant."

Family Name and Husband	Wife	Son(s)	Daughter(s)
probable kin: John le, de Hunts 1281-1294			
Ralph 1282-1302			
Hugh 1284-1310			
Robert 1285			
Reginald, de Norfolk 1298			
Ralph, de Offord 1303			
William sen 1315			
John, de Hunts 1327-1329			
William 1341-1348			
Robert 1346			
Idona 1350			
Henry le 1354			
Thomas 1352			
William, de Offord Cluny 1365			
Alan 1366			
Bartholomew 1372, 1390			
William, bailiff 1388 (d)			
John, de Hekelynton 1389			
CHESE			
John 1281-1299	Mariota 1281-1299		
John (c)	unknown	John 1308 (c)	Isolda 1308
			Cristina 1309-1315
			Felicia 1312
			Sarra 1312
Reyner 1373-1398	unknown	Thomas murdered 1372	

probable kin: Millicent 1315
Agatha 1356-1366
John 1380-1396

DE CHESTERFIELD
John 1309   Mariota 1309   Thomas 1326

CHORLEY
Eusebius   unknown
probable kin: John 1330 (d)

DE CHYCHE (CHURCH?)
William 1315   unknown   Sare' 1315

CHYLD
Henry 1356-1389   Agnes 1389
probable kin: Thomas 1380
CIMITERO see CEMENTARIUS
AD CIRPOS (AD RISSIS)

Thomas 1279-1281   Cristina 1295   John 1291-1312
                             widow 1303   Walter 1291-1322
                                                        William 1291-1303
                                                        Augustine 1291-1304 (d) (c)
                                                        Nicholas 1304-1326 (d) (c)
                                                        Augustine 1308
                                                        Godfrey 1315-1348
                                                        William 1329   Sybil 1303, 1313-1314

Martin   unknown
Augustine (c)   Juliana 1291-1300   John sen 1298
                                                        John jun 1298, 1308
                                                        William 1299
                                                        Godfrey 1303-1310
                                                        Richard 1303-1308 (d)

Nicholas (c)   Juliana 1326-1329
unknown   unknown

John 1299-1303 (d)   unknown

Family Name and Husband	Wife	Son(s)	Daughter(s)
Thomas jun	unknown	John 1300	
Thomas	unknown	John 1332	
probable kin: Robert 1287			
Gunnilda 1303 (d)			
William 1361-1366			
CLARE			
Robert	Sybil widow 1359		
CLERE			
John 1315	unknown	William 1315	
Simon 1316	unknown	William 1316	
probable kin: William de West St 1323			
CLERK			
unknown	unknown	Godfrey 1278-1312 (d) (c1)	
		Simon 1278 (c2)	
Godfrey (c1)	unknown	Eusebius 1311-1340 (d) (c3)	Felicia 1302
			Pellagia 1301
Eusebius (c3)	Cristina 1345-1348	Godfrey 1340-1348 (c4)	Cristina 1340
		Dennis 1348	Caterina 1340-1343
			Dionysia 1340
			Agnes 1340
Godfrey (c4)	Cristina 1340-1348, 1361 (d)	William 1279-1319 (c5)	
Simon (c2)	unknown	John 1278-1306 (c6)	
		Robert 1291	

William (c5)	Helen 1302-1329	Stephen 1279-1326 (c7) Reginald 1281-1312 (d) John 1300-1337 (c8) Henry 1311-1344 (c9) Reyner 1312-1345 (c10) (d 1349) William 1325-1329 (c11) Robert 1334 (c12)	Helen 1287, 1308 Isabella 1281

Stephen (c7)
John (c8)
	Cristina 1325-1333
	Emma Goni 1320-1322,
	  widow of Gilbert
	  Strateshyll
	Cristina 1332-1333
		John 1324	a daughter 1344

Henry (c9)		William 1331-1354 (c13) Stephen 1332-1340 (c14) Nicholas 1341-1361	Cristina 1332 Sybil 1341
William (c13) Stephen (c14) Reyner (c10)	Elena 1354 unknown unknown	Reginald 1353 Thomas 1348 Godfrey 1348	Alice 1367
William (c11)	Cristina 1325		Agnes 1331, married to Reginald Godmar
Robert (c12)f John (c6) John*	Matilda 1334 unknown unknown	Richard 1278-1288 Martin 1282	Emma 1316

f Although of late date, this is in the manuscript as "Robert son of William son of Simon 1334."

Family Name and Husband	Wife	Son(s)	Daughter(s)
Robert 1281-1292 (d)	unknown		Phillipa 1292 Isolda 1292
Reginald (the clerk)	unknown	Henry 1291 John 1291 (c15)	
John (c15)	unknown	Henry 1301-1315 (c16) John 1304-1308	
Henry (c16)	Cristina ad Fontem 1315		
John de Hemingford 1302	unknown	John jun, de Hemingford 1329-1330 (c17)	Alice 1330, wife of simon Miller Matilda 1330
John jun. de Hemingford (c17)	unknown	William de Houghton 1329	
John de Houghton	unknown	Gilbert de Warboys 1334	
John de Warboys	unknown	John (c18)	
Roger 1348	unknown	John 1350-1351 (c19)	Agnes 1340
John (c18)	Cristina 1341 (d)		
John (c19)	Sybil 1352	William 1331, 1341 Reginald 1346-1354 (d) (c20)	
Simon	unknown	Godfrey 1348-1349	
Reginald (c20)	unknown	Thomas 1351-1373 (c21)	
Richard de Godmanchester	unknown		
Thomas de Godmanchester (c21)	Emma 1354 (d) (2nd) Sybil 1360-1366		
Henry* de Godmanchester 1356-1366	Amicia 1356-1366	Reyner*	Agnes, wife of William and sister of Reyner 1345
unknown	unknown		

William*	unknown	Henry 1363
William *de* Hunts	Margaret 1364	
Thomas *de* Offord Cluny	Emma dau of Reginald Denne and sister of Elena West, 1380-1382	
Reyner sen	unknown	John 1394

probable kin:

Thomas 1278-1292
John *de* Brampton 1279
William *de* Broughton 1279
Thomas *de* Hunts 1280-1282, 1286 (d)
John *de* St. Ives 1285
William of the church 1285
Robert *de* Brampton 1295
William *de* Hemingford 1329-1330
John *de* Hunts 1329
William *de* Hunts 1329
Gilbert *de* Godmanchester 1327-1333
Reginald* 1346-1348
John* 1346-1376
Peter 1349 (d)
Margaret 1350 (d)
Henry *de* Olney 1356
(*manet* in West St.)
John sen* 1362
Thomas, vicar of Godmanchester 1362
William, butcher 1366-1394
William sen* of Godmanchester 1371-1372
Robert *de* Hopwood 1380
William 1389-1397

Family Name and Husband	Wife	Son(s)	Daughter(s)
CLERVAUX			
Ralph 1297	Cristina 1297		
John 1297	Isolda 1297 (d)	Ralph 1316	
William 1341-1354	Elizabeth 1354	Henry 1316	
		John 1316	
		William 1316	
CLOPTON			
John *de* Houghton 1321	Amicia 1321		
CLUBBE			
Reginald 1348	Agnes 1348		
COKAYNE			
Godfrey (also known as *le* Baxter) 1308-1320	Emma 1308-1320	Richard 1326-1335	Cristina 1325
DE COKYRMOWE			
Peter 1302	Agnes 1302		
COLION (COLYON)			
unknown	unknown		Mabel 1316-1333 (c)
			Elena 1308
			Margaret 1325-1333
unknown	Mabel (c)		
William 1315-1342 (d)	Sybil 1342; re-marries John Lodelowe 1344		
William 1327-1361	Amicia 1340	John 1341-1348 (c)	Emma 1347-1350
John (c)	Emma 1348		

Name	Spouse	Sons	Daughters
Reginald	unknown	Andrew 1340 / John 1340	Cristina 1366
John 1350-1366 probable kin: Roger 1291 John 1295-1311 Godfrey 1325 g Michael 1326 Agnes 1331-1351 (d) John* 1399 (d)	Cristina 1366		

COLOWOT

Name	Spouse	Sons	Daughters
unknown John de West St 1313	Dionysia unknown	John 1295-1298	Felicia 1313 Cristina 1313 Agnes 1323
John 1325 (d)	Cristina 1323, 1340	John 1316-1338 Henry 1323-1340 (d) Godfrey 1327 (d) John jun 1322 (d) John 1327	Cristina 1322 Sybil 1319-1322 married to Stephen Syle by 1353 Sarra 1322, 1340 Felicia 1327, 1334
John sen	unknown		
John sen* h	unknown	John jun 1327, 1334 Godfrey 1327, 1354 (c)	Helen 1354 Agnes 1332
Godfrey (c) John jun de East St.i Henry 1338-1354	unknown unknown Margaret 1338		

g Godfrey is very likely the grandfather of Margaret daughter of Mabel since the court rolls state "anus in 'free marriage' from him."
h This John sen could be the son of John sen, as he had a brother called John jun who died by 1322. The courts would indicate junior and senior when two sons were given the same Christian name.
i John jun de East St. could be the son of John sen in 1327, 1334 and just lived in East St.

Family Name and Husband	Wife	Son(s)	Daughter(s)
probable kin: Edward 1294			
Mariota 1327			
John jun *de* West Street 1338			
COLYON *see* COLION			
COMBERE *see* KOMBERE			
CONERUR			
Reginald 1291	unknown		Felicia 1291
COOK			
Nicholas 1349	Cassandra 1349		
John 1349-1377	Margaret 1349-1377		
Simon 1350-1377	Agnes 1361		
John, butcher 1351-1361	Emma 1351-1357		
Godfrey 1352-1372	Juliana 1361-1367		
Robert ye, *de* Kingston	unknown	William 1354	
unknown	Isolda		Cristina 1354, 1361
probable kin: John *de* Depenham (Deopenham) 1349			
Elena 1351			
William *de* Hemingford Abbots 1361-1378			
John jun 1362-1366			
Thomas, vicar of church of Godmanchester 1363-1365, 1380			
Thomas, rector *de* Broughton 1366			
Richard 1367-1371			
Roger 1375			
William sen 1379			
John *de* Stukeley 1382			
William, faber 1386-1389			
Thomas jun 1391			

COOPERATOR ROTARUM (THACHER, DE PAPWORTH)ʲ

unknown	unknown	Phillip 1311, 1330-1332 (c)
		William 1311-1316, 1330-1332 (c)
		William 1317-1318, 1327-1330
Phillip (c)	Emma 1311, 1338	Alice 1309
William (c)	Cristina 1311, 1316	
CORS		
Roger 1286	Sarra 1286	
COTEMAN		
William 1390	Matilda 1390	
COUPER (THACHER)		Agnes 1325
Nicholas le 1287-1311	unknown	
Simon 1311	Agnes 1311	
William 1317	Helen 1317	
Robert de Catworth 1321	Alice 1321	Hammond 1321
John de Kingbury	unknown	Thomas 1347
Roger de Gt Stukeley 1340-1347	unknown	
John 1363	Joan 1363	
John 1372	Elena 1372-1375	
William 1372-1375	Sybil 1372	

ʲ Which one of the brothers called William married a Cristina by 1311 is difficult to determine. I have taken the William who continued on to 1332, since his brother William abjured the realm in 1330 because of homicide. In 1338 it is only Emma who is noted as acquiring land, and not her husband Phillip, who could be dead. These three brothers came from Papworth, and sometimes the court entry would indicate *de* Papworth, or Phillip *le* Cooperator Rotarum *de* Papworth, or William *le* Thacher *de* Papworth.

Family Name and Husband	Wife	Son(s)	Daughter(s)
probable kin: John 1287			
Godfrey *le* 1322			
Thomas *le, de* Sibthorpe 1331			
Andrew 1341-1377			
Thomas *de* Hunts 1346			
John 1348			
Reginald 1348			
Roger 1354			
Richard 1378			
John sen 1380			
COUTERE *see* KUTERE			
COWSTONE?			
unknown	unknown		Juliana 1348
			Amicia 1348
COWTER *see* KUTERE			
CRANE			
John 1350-1366 (d)	Margaret 1366		
probable kin: John 1375-1378 (d)			
Agnes 1392-1395			
DE CROXTON			
John *de* Hunts 1311 (d)	unknown	John, tannator 1311	
John	unknown	Reginald 1311	
		John 1315	
John sen 1316-1320	Isolda 1316 (d)	Roger 1316-1349 (c)	
Roger (c)	Emma 1329-1349		

John sen* 1329-1340   Amicia 1329 [k]
John 1344-1366   Sybil 1344
probable kin: John jun 1308, 1340-1341
              John* 1349 (d)
              William 1354 (d)
              Godfrey 1356-1366 (d)
              John de Godmanchester 1366-1397

                                                  Mabel 1308

AD CRUCEM
Walter 1278-1289   unknown
Michael de Hartford 1281-1310   Alice 1310   Roger 1310
unknown   unknown   Robert 1287
                                                  Simon 1291-1325 (c)

Simon (c)   Cristina 1312, 1316 (d)
probable kin: Pellagia 1284
              John de Hartford 1313
              Henry 1325

CURRCAUR
unknown   Isabella 1345   Thomas 1345

CUSTAUNCE
Robert 1362-1382   Emma 1362

DALLY
Robert 1341-1376   Margaret 1341, 1366
probable kin: Roger 1363

[k] Amicia's parents are noted in 1329 as being John and his wife Matilda; the surname is not given. This Amicia could also be the second wife of John sen (1316-1320) who was married to Isolda.

Family Name and Husband	Wife	Son(s)	Daughter(s)
DAM			
Adam 1333	Cristina 1333		
DANEWYCH (DANEWICH)			
John *de* Godmanchester 1362-1399	Elena 1371-1372		Catherine 1322
DANLYS			
Robert 1315-1316	Matilda 1315-1326		
DANWICH *see* DANEWYCH			
DAS			
Richard 1294	unknown	Simon 1294-1327 (c)	Cristina 1326
Simon (c)	Margaret 1308-1326		
Roger 1352	Emma 1352		
DAVY			
unknown	unknown	Adam 1333	
		Richard 1333	
DAWSON			
Henry	unknown		Matilda 1372
probable kin: Thomas Dawesson 1395-1399			
DEFORE			
Roger 1329	Masceline 1329	Roger 1331	
		Henry 1349	
DEGOUN, DEGUN, DEKONE *see* DICOUN			
DENNE			
unknown	unknown	Robert, chaplain	
		1326-1350 (d) (c)	
		Reginald 1326-1366 (c)	

Robert (c)	Cristina Garlop 1349[1]	Margaret 1349
		Cristina 1349
		Amicia 1349
Reginald (c)	Caterina 1347-1393	Elena 1380 married to Richard West *de* Graveley
		Emma 1380 married to Thomas Clerk *de* Offord Cluny
		Cristina 1372 married to Henry Acry
Roger 1333	Catherine 1333	
probable kin: Henry 1308		
John 1331-1333 (d)ᵐ		
Lord Robert 1332-1356		
John 1363		
Nicholas 1367		
Reyner 1375		
DE DEREHAM (DERHAM)		
Peter	unknown	Peter *de* St. Ives 1314-1322
		Peter of Hunts 1342
DERNEFORD		
Thomas 1314	Joan 1314	
DERY (DERRY)		
Richard 1344	unknown	Thomas 1344

[1] Cristina Garlop is not the wife of Robert Denne, but she is the mother of his three daughters — Margaret, Cristina and Amicia. See above, p. 34.

ᵐ This could be the father of Robert and Reginald: he made a bequest to Reginald in reference to a dowry in "free marriage" arrangement.

Family Name and Husband	Wife	Son(s)	Daughter(s)
DESOUN *see* DICOUN			
DEWSTON			
Reginald 1348	unknown	unknown	Matilda 1348
DICERE			
Thomas 1350-1393, chaplain	Isabella 1353-1358		
probable kin: Simon 1350-1390			
Henry *de* Hunts 1353			
Henry 1356-1391			
Hugh 1375			
William 1399			
DICOUN (DEGUN, DESOUN, DEKONE, DEGOUN)			
Walter 1351-1367	Isolda 1350-1360		Amicia 1351 (d)
probable kin: John 1354			
Richard 1386			
DE DOKETON			
Reyner 1310-1333	Juliana dau of John Miller 1310-1316		
DORAUNT			
Thomas	unknown		Idonia 1371
probable kin: Ralph 1378			
DOSYN			
Thomas 1281	unknown	Robert 1281-1324 (c)	
		Godfrey 1281-1315 (d) (c)	
		John 1297	

Robert (c)	unknown	John 1326 Simon 1333-1366 (d) (c) also known as LEGAT	Alice 1325 Pellagia 1325, 1366 wife of Godfrey son of Hugh Sybil 1325-1340 (d)
Simon (c) (also known as LEGAT) Godfrey (c)	Emma 1350-1366 Cristina 1289-1310	William 1315-1326 (c) Roger 1315-1366 (c)	
William (c) Roger (c) William 1338 Thomas 1366-1372 probable kin: Henry 1349 (d)	Matilda 1320 Emma 1334 Amicia 1338 Sybil 1371-1372	Godfrey 1378-1380	

DOUCE

William, butcher 1367, 1369	unknown	John 1367

DREW

unknown John (c) Nicholas 1297	Isabella 1283 Dionysia 1301-1316 unknown	John 1283-1316 (c) William 1302	Mabel 1297-1302 Cristina 1301-1316

DRURY

Andrew 1312 John 1346-1362	unknown Isolda 1352-1373 (d)	John 1312

DULYN

Henry	unknown	Thomas 1351

DUNNYNG

Robert de Cambridge 1345	Agnes 1345

Family Name and Husband	Wife	Son(s)	Daughter(s)
DE DUNSTABLE			
William 1319	Joan 1319		
DE DUNTON			
Vincent 1293	Isolda 1293		Millicent 1311-1313 Leticia 1311
EDE			
unknown	unknown	Godfrey 1295[n] Reginald 1295	
Elias	unknown	Walter 1295-1324	Cristina 1295 Agnes 1299 Amicia 1303
Ede	unknown	Roger 1292 John 1316 (c)	
John (c)	unknown	Godfrey 1343-1357[o]	
John	unknown	Godfrey 1303-1326 Reginald 1321-1325	
Simon	unknown	Reginald 1304 (d) (c) Godfrey 1325	
Reginald (c)	unknown		Margaret 1304
Thomas 1303-1317	Alice 1315-1317		
Reginald 1306	Helen 1306		
the Chaplain	unknown		Joan 1310-1317

[n] These could be the sons of either John or Simon.
[o] The court rolls state "Godfrey son of John son of Ede" 1357.

Richard 1325	unknown	
Godfrey 1325	Cristina 1325 (d) dau of Thomas Gildene	Agnes 1325
	Constance 1329	
Godfrey* 1329	Isolda 1353	
Walter 1331-1354		Sybil 1354
		Godfrey 1342-1383 (d) (c)
		Roger 1347-1348
Godfrey (c)	Emma 1354-1369	Stephen 1347
Reginald 1333-1345	unknown	Robert 1356
John 1352-1365 (d)	Alice 1365-1394 dau of Nicholas Quenyng	John 1346
		Pellagia 1350
probable kin:	John 1285, 1311	
	Lina 1311	
	Bartholomew 1342-1348	
	Henry 1372-1393	
	John sen 1378	
	John, *de* Staunton 1375	
	John jun 1395	

DE EDENHAM
Alan   unknown   Simon 1330
SON OF EDWARD
Edward   unknown   William 1279-1303 (c)
                                                                             John 1279 (c)
                                                                             Godfrey 1284-1323 (c)
                                                                             Simon 1298 (d) (c)
                                                                             Nicholas 1309, 1312 (d) (c)
                                                                             Roger 1310 (d) (c)
                                                                             Nicholas 1279

William (c)   unknown

Family Name and Husband	Wife	Son(s)	Daughter(s)
John (c)	Mariota 1279		
Godfrey (c)	unknown	William 1317	Sybil 1327
Simon (c)	unknown		Felicia 1298
Nicholas (c)	Pellagia 1309	William 1309	
Roger (c)	unknown		Alice 1312 and married to Thomas
			Pellagia 1311
Edward* ᵖ	Caterina 1298-1299	Godfrey 1298	
Godfrey	unknown	John 1340	
		William 1341	
probable kin: Godfrey jun 1279			
John de Ely 1389			
EDWYN			
Edwyn	unknown	Robert son of 1291	
ELIAS			
Elias	unknown	William son of 1376	
DE ELSWORTH			
Adam 1334	Cristina 1334	Reginald 1350-1361	
Henry 1347	and wife 1347	Godfrey 1353-1367 (c)	
unknown	unknown		

ᵖ This Edward could be the same Edward who had six sons, above, but he is put separately owing to the fact that only Godfrey son of Edward and Caterina is noted in 1298.

Godfrey (c)
probable kin: William *de*, chaplain 1297   and wife 1358   John 1361
               Walter *de* 1322-1323
               John 1338
               Ralph 1351-1352

ELY
William 1278 (d)   Alice 1278   Isolda 1278

ELYS
Richard 1309   Matilda 1309-1313 (d)   Emma 1314
                                                        Isolda 1314-1348
                                                        Cristina 1314-1325

William 1322-1349   Cristina 1322-1349
William 1339-1348   Matilda 1339-1348
Thomas 1382   Alice 1382
probable kin: John 1316-1342, 1365 (d)
               Thomas 1327-1366
               William *de* Hilton 1371
               John, parson of church *de* Haverhill 1351-1365

ENGLE *see* INGLEYS
ESE
Eustace 1278-1280   unknown   Robert 1278
                                               Godfrey 1279-1281 (c)
                                               John 1304
                                               Alexander 1299-1302 (c)
                                               Reginald 1294-1320 (c)
                                               William 1306

Godfrey (c)   Cristina 1291-1301

Alexander (c)   Emma 1321-1325   Felicia 1325

Family Name and Husband	Wife	Son(s)	Daughter(s)
Reginald (c)	Helen 1313	John 1318-1331 Richard 1317-1341 William 1278-1302	Agnes 1298-1324
Richard 1278-1287	unknown		Helen 1280-1313 (c)
Roger	unknown	Peter 1316	
unknown	Helen (c)	Thomas 1327-1347 (c) William 1329-1357 (d) (c)	
Reginald 1332	unknown	Robert 1344-1347	
Thomas (c)	Emma 1345-1361 [q]	John 1366-1369	
Thomas*	Margaret 1345		
William (c)	and wife 1349		
probable kin: Godfrey 1354			
DE ESSEX			
Nicholas 1279-1299 (d)	Agnes 1299-1312	John 1298-1302 (d) (c)[r]	Cristina 1288-1299 Margaret 1282 Isolda 1298 Cristina 1304-1319 Agnes 1304-1313 Helen 1325
John (c)	Matilda 1300-1315 [s]	Thomas 1297 John 1313-1315	
unknown	Cristina	John 1353-1357 (c)	
unknown	unknown	Henry 1359-1382	

[q] Emma wife of Thomas; her parents' names are Elena and Thomas.
[r] John was hung for the crime of burglary in 1302.
[s] Matilda, the widow of John, had a sister called Cristina in 1303.

John (c)		
John *de* Hunts 1397	Margaret 1362-1372	
	Alice 1397 (d)	
DE ETON		
Richard 1341	Margaret 1341	
SON OF EUSEBIUS		
Eusebius of Post St. 1282	Isolda 1282	Cristina 1285
John (c)	unknown	John 1288-1303 (c)
Nicholas (c)	Emma 1295	Nicholas 1295 (c)
William (c)	Agnes 1325	Godfrey 1298-1321
		Reginald 1308-1322
		William 1309-1325 (d) (c)
		Gilbert 1325
probable kin: Robert 1287		Cristina 1309-1325
Alan 1344		Mabel 1331
Agnes 1351		
William 1351		
EUSTACE		
Eustace	unknown	John son of 1349
probable kin: Robert 1375		
EVERARD		
William 1293-1295	unknown	Agnes 1312
Nicholas	unknown	John 1312
		William 1312-1325
		William *de* Hemingford 1324
DE EYNSBURY		
Lawrence	unknown	John 1357-1358

Family Name and Husband	Wife	Son(s)	Daughter(s)
FABER (SMITH)			
Richard de Hunts 1278	unknown	Roger 1278-1322 (d) (c)	
Roger (c)ᵗ	Amicia 1317-1322	John 1322	
Robert 1280-1311	Lucy 1280		
Ivo de Papworth 1290	unknown	John 1290	
Robert 1304 (d)	Isabella 1304		Pellagia 1304
Ralph de Hunts 1349	Beatrix 1349		
probable kin: Cristina 1279			
Elias 1279			
Thomas 1279			
John de Leyton Bromswold 1279			
William 1284			
John, marshall de Hunts 1285			
Walter 1341			
Henry 1350			
William 1351			
William, malter 1372-1378			
John 1374			
Margaret 1381, 1391			
Robert 1382			
Godfrey de Houghton and Wyton 1385			
Thomas de Hunts 1392			
Edmund 1399			

ᵗ The court roll states that Roger and Amicia had more children but they are not named.

FABYON		
Richard	unknown	Joan 1339
probable kin: John 1348		
FACTORUM		
unknown	unknown	John 1325[u]
		William 1325
probable kin: Alexander 1331-1332		
FANEL		
William 1283	Agnes 1283	
probable kin: Thomas 1283		
FANNER		
Roger	unknown	Robert 1313-1320
	unknown	Gilbert 1325-1330
		Robert 1331
Clarice *le* 1331		
probable kin: Agnes *le* 1291		
FARMER *see* **FIRMARIUS**		
FAYRHEVED		
William 1299	unknown	Cristina 1299
		Felicia 1316
		Helen 1316
probable kin: Joan *see* **AUGUSTINE**		
FELTEWELLE (FOLTEWELLE)		
John 1382	unknown	John 1382
probable kin: Adam 1376		

[u] These could be the children of either Phillip or William Cooperator *de* Papworth Deneys, but the court rolls do not add "*de* Papworth," nor give the children's parents; the rolls just state that they are brothers.

Family Name and Husband	Wife	Son(s)	Daughter(s)
FET			
Roger 1331	Pellagia 1331	Godfrey 1331	
FING'			
Robert de Washingley 1309	Alice 1309		
FIRMARIUS (FARMER)			
John 1365	Pellagia 1365		
FISHER (PISCATOR)			
John de Brampton 1322	Caterina 1322		
Dany de Paxton	unknown	Richard 1327	
		Adam 1327	
John 1388-1399 (d)	Sybil 1399, 1428		
Godfrey 1388-1391	Caterina 1388-1391		
probable kin: Emma le 1301			
John le 1312-1315			
John de Offord Cluny 1321, 1332			
Henry de Hunts 1322			
Ralph de Offord 1330			
Andrew de Offord Cluny 1388			
Simon de Hunts 1388			
Simon 1390			
FLAXMONGER			
John 1331	unknown		Elena 1331
probable kin: Hugh de Erle 1332			
FLESHEWERER see CARNIFEX			

FLEXWERER
John, ye cook 1353 — Emma 1353

FOCHER
John 1331 — Caterina 1331

FOLE
Reginald 1286
Simon 1286-1295 — unknown / unknown — Hugh 1300 / John 1300-1332 / Roger 1300 / William 1300 — Mariota 1303-1327

FOLTEWELLE see **FELTEWELLE**
ad FONTEM see **ATTE WELL**
atte FORTHE (FORDE)
William 1341-1377 — Imama 1341-1377

FOULER
John 1357-1367 — Sybil 1357, 1361

FOX
John 1313-1314 — Cristina, widow by 1345 — Hugh 1327

FREMAN
Thomas 1373-1399 — Elena 1399 — Thomas 1380 — Margaret 1380
probable kin: William 1357
John *de* Northampton 1390

FRENE
unknown — unknown

FRERE
Richard 1280 (d) — unknown — Godfrey 1280-1307 (d) (c) / John 1280-1322 / Reginald 1295-1327 (d) (c)

Family Name and Husband	Wife	Son(s)	Daughter(s)
Godfrey (c)	Matilda 1324	William 1307-1324 Robert 1316 John 1326-1332	
Reginald (c)	unknown		Cristina 1316-1329 Amicia 1316-1329 Isolda 1291-1302
Eustace *le*, dead before 1288	unknown	Roger 1291-1316 John 1308-1311	
Simon	unknown		
John *de* Hunts 1310	Matilda 1310		
William 1333-1348	Pellagia 1345-1348	John 1346-1361 (d) (c)	
John (c)	Elena widow 1361	John 1345-1361 (c)	
John son of John (c)	Matilda 1351-1392		
John*ᵛ	unknown	Henry 1348	Cristina 1337 Elena 1347
unknown	unknown		Cristina 1348*
Nicholas	unknown	John 1361-1372	
probable kin: Mabel 1318 William jun 1335-1348 Elias 1338			
FRESSING Simon 1289	unknown		Matilda 1289-1294
probable kin: Reginald 1298 Matilda 1332			

ᵛ John could be one of the two Johns listed above.

FREVILLE *see* **FREVILLE**

FREYSOL
John *de* Long Stanton 1363-1388   Margaret 1364-1377

FREVILLE (**FREVILLE**)
Richard 1283-1316   Matilda 1315
William 1321   Matilda 1321

FRYDAY
John *de* Offord 1301   unknown   Juliana 1299
    Alice 1301; her husband is called
    William

FULLER
Water *de* Offord Cluny 1369-1397   Margaret 1369
probable kin: John *de* Bluntisham 1379

FYN
Robert 1310   Sarra 1310

GAMELYN
Henry 1313   Ivetta 1313

GARBY
Richard   unknown   John 1360

GARDENER
Richard 1354-1374   Agnes 1354-1374
Roger, taylor 1393   Elena 1393
probable kin: Pellage *le* 1285-1292
Richard *ye, de* Hemingford Grey 1351, 1373

GARLOP
Richard *de* Warboys 1295   Phillipa 1295   Reyner 1295-1332 (c) 1335 (d)
    chaplain 1308, 1311
    Robert 1295-1317 (c)
Reyner (c)   Cristina 1317-1329

Family Name and Husband	Wife	Son(s)	Daughter(s)
Robert (c)			
Robert* 1332 [w]	Matilda 1303 Isolda 1332	Reginald 1335-1364 (c)	Cristina 1331-1335 Phillipa 1331 Pellagia 1332
Reginald (c)			
John (c)	unknown Sybil 1361-1372	John 1342-1383 (c)	
Reginald sen	unknown	John 1381-1383	
probable kin: Hugh 1345-1369			
Henry 1348			
Hugh, chaplain 1350-1354			
ATTE GATE			
Reginald 1338-1348	Cristina 1338-1348 [x]		
Ralph de Hemingford Abbots 1339-1350 (d)	Cristina 1339-1348		
Roger at ye	Cristina 1353		
John 1372	Cristina 1372		
GAWESSONE			
Henry	unknown	William 1361	Matilda 1361
GAYLOR			
William 1361	Sybil 1361		
GEORGE'			
George'	unknown	John 1299-1303	

[w] This could be the same Robert as "Robert son of Richard *de* Warboys" in which case Isolda would be his second wife.

[x] This is as the manuscript — all the wives are called "Cristina."

DE GIDDING			
Henry 1286-1307 (d)	unknown	Hugh 1297-1335 (c) Godfrey 1307-1316	Phillipa 1294 Sabina 1307-1316 Margaret 1309-1317 Joan 1348, married to John Smith *de* Polebrok Margaret 1329-1348
Hugh (c)	Elizabeth 1297		
Henry probable kin: William 1282 Ralph *de* Hunts 1359-1361 Ralph 1372	unknown	John 1353	
SON OF GILBERT			
Gilbert	unknown	Ralph 1278 Osbert 1278 (c) Eusebius 1278 (c) Walter 1278	Isolda 1292
Osbert (c) Eusebius (c)	Mariota 1278 Mariota 1278		
DE GILDERSOWE			
John 1322-1340 probable kin: Robert 1348	Rose 1335-1340		
GILDENE			
Thomas 1283-1309 (d)	Cristina 1309	Thomas 1303-1346 Richard 1303-1327 John 1303-1348 Reginald 1313-1316 (c) Richard 1314	Cristina 1307-1325 (d) married to Godfrey Ede
John 1283-1306	unknown		

Family Name and Husband	Wife	Son(s)	Daughter(s)
Reginald (c)			
Simon 1288	Isolda 1313	Gilbert 1314-1327 John sen 1314-1316 John jun 1315-1317	
Godfrey 1293-1317 (d)	unknown	John 1288-1311	Amicia 1288 Dionysia 1288
unknown	unknown	John 1311-1325	Amicia 1317 Agnes 1317
Gosceline 1308-1321	Emma 1322	Godfrey 1317 John 1317	
John (c)	Phillipa 1350-1361	John 1321-1350 (d) (c) Godfrey 1333	Agnes 1322-1329 Amicia 1325 (d)
John de West St.	unknown		
Richard*	unknown	John 1329-1347 Thomas 1329-1353 Godfrey 1329-1338 (d) Henry 1340-1349	Elena 1330 Cristina 1347
Thomas*	unknown	John 1334 (c)	
John (c)	Cristina 1334		
Reginald	unknown	John 1340	
Godfrey*	Felicia widow 1343-1344	Godfrey 1349-1375 Henry, chapman 1350-1356 (c) John, chapman 1349 (c)	Emma 1340 (d) Alice 1353
John*	unknown		

Henry, chapman (c)	Matilda 1350-1356 and wife 1351		
John chapman (c)	Phillipa 1350-1361	John 1355	Sybil 1353
John	Cecily	Henry, mercer 1349-1361, 1389 (c) (d)	
unknown		Thomas 1353 (c)	
Richard* 1351-1362	Amicia 1378 (d)		

Henry* (c)	Cristina 1349-1359	
Thomas* (c)	unknown	
Gosceline	unknown	John 1361 (c)
John (c)	Matilda 1361	
Thomas sen 1375-1377	Agnes 1376-1377	
Henry*	Sybil 1378	
John 1393	Amicia 1393	

probable kin: Matilda 1322
Thomas, faber 1348-1357
John, carpenter 1349-1367
William 1354, 1381-1382

GILE

Adam	unknown	John 1278-1310 (c)	Albrida 1280
John (c)	unknown	William 1316-1348, dead by 1354 (c)	Hawysia 1316-1349

William (c)	Agnes 1354	Dunstan 1353	Emma 1333
Robert 1291-1312	unknown	Hugh 1321-1351 (d) (c)	
Hugh (c)	unknown	Reyner 1362	
Stephen 1338-1354 (d)	Sybil 1351-1354 (d)		

probable kin: Amicia 1329

Family Name and Husband	Wife	Son(s)	Daughter(s)
GILEKOC			
John 1281-1329	unknown	John 1318 (d)	Helen 1281 Agnes 1281-1325
probable kin: Cecilia 1287 Ivetta 1287 (d)			
GILLE			
Nicholas 1349	and wife 1349		
DE GLATTON			
William 1340-1341	unknown	John 1340-1341	
GLEWE			
Thomas 1279-1294 (d)	unknown	John 1294-1341 John 1294-1311	
Simon 1281-1292	Amicia 1277-1279 (2nd) Cecilia 1292	Godfrey 1295-1317 (d) (c)	Phillipa 1283
Godfrey (c)	unknown	Walter 1312-1332 (c) John 1314	
Walter (c)	Sybil 1325-1344		
Roger 1281-1296	Sarra 1283		
Edward 1299-1302 (d)	Matilda Lewe 1299	John 1306-1353 Godfrey 1314 William 1311 (d) John 1307	Cristina 1306
Reginald	unknown		
Godfrey 1324-1327 (d)	Matilda 1348 (d)	John 1331-1345 (c)	Matilda 1330 Cristina 1330 Isabella 1330 Isolda 1335

John (c)
Godfrey *le* Maddermonger 1333-1351 — Felicia 1331-1348 — John 1333-1354, William 1347-1358, John 1349 — Isabella 1350, married to John *de* Graveley; Cristina 1350, married to William Nottyng; Cristina 1356; Agnes 1356
Simon — unknown
John, cooperator 1351 (d) — Emma 1351

John, Patissarius 1354 (d) — Cesseline Waleys 1354-1356
John 1362 — Agnes 1362
Robert 1346-1388 — Margaret 1399
probable kin: William 1289
John, butcher 1357-1365 (d)
Isolda 1365

GLOVER
Walter — unknown — Godfrey 1349
probable kin: Robert *de* Gidding 1348
Thomas 1372, 1388

GODARD
Thomas 1392 — Pellagia 1392
SON OF GODFREY
Godfrey — unknown — John 1279 (c), Walter 1278, Robert 1321-1331 (c), Roger 1329 (c), John 1321-1345 (d) — Amicia 1325

Godfrey — unknown — John 1279, John 1349-1361 (c)

John (c) — unknown
Robert (c) — unknown
John (c) — Margaret 1360-1361

Family Name and Husband	Wife	Son(s)	Daughter(s)
Roger (c)	unknown	Simon 1329 Godfrey 1337	
GODMAN			
Godfrey 1330	unknown	John 1330-1349 (d) (c)	
John (c)	Elena 1349 widow		
Thomas de Hunts	Agnes 1351, 1389		
Walter	unknown	John 1349-1356 (d) (c)	
John (c)	Matilda 1350		
William 1360-1384	Agnes 1364		
probable kin: Henry 1331-1349			
GODOUN			
Reginald 1324 (d)	Mabel 1324-1330	Thomas de Hunts 1330-1345 (c)	
Thomas de Hunts (c)	unknown	John de Hunts 1360	
DE GODMANCHESTER			
Roger 1347	unknown	Godfrey 1347	
GODWARE			
Simon 1283-1332	Alice 1299-1314	Bartholomew 1308-1313 (d) (c)	
Bartholomew (c)	unknown	Roger 1329-1340	Albrida 1310-1314 Isolda 1310-1314 Matilda 1313
William 1293-1314	unknown	Nicholas 1293	
Reginald 1332	Agnes 1332 dau of William *le* Clerk		
probable kin: Reginald 1287-1316 Margaret 1321			

GODWYNE
Richard 1345-1368
Richard jun (c)
probable kin: Thomas 1391-1394

GOLD
John *de* Eton 1348
GOLDSMITH *see* AURIFABER

GONI
Edward 1278-1301 (d)

Reginald (c)

Richard (c)
Robert (c)
John son of Robert (c)
Gilbert Strateshylle 1321 (d)

John

Ivetta 1363-1367
Emma 1392-1395

Joan 1348

Sabina 1284-1292
(2nd) Isolda 1301

Margaret Lane, widow 1316
and re-marries Roger
son of William Manipenny
1323

unknown
unknown
Agnes 1346
Emma Goni (c) and
re-marries John
unknown

Richard jun 1391-1395 (c)

Reginald 1292-1316 (d) (c)
Richard 1300-1313 (d) (c)
John 1300-1302
Nicholas 1300-1324 (d)
William 1301-1308
Gilbert 1312-1345
Thomas 1312-1313
Robert 1312-1325 (c)

John 1311
John 1346 (c)

William 1286-1327 (d)
Thomas 1286-1299
Roger 1286-1318

Cristina 1292
Emma 1294-1327 (c)
Margaret 1301

Cristina 1321-1327

Family Name and Husband	Wife	Son(s)	Daughter(s)
Reginald 1282-1297	Agnes 1293		
Thomas* [y]	unknown	Thomas 1306	Cristina 1309, 1311
Thomas 1307-1313 [z]	Joan 1307, 1313	John 1313-1316	
John 1289	Mabel 1289-1312		Felicia 1310-1311 (d)
			Cristina 1311
Roger 1309-1315 (d) [a]	Margaret 1315 re-marries John		Helen 1287-1317 married to Thomas Witman
			Felicia 1308-1315 (d)
			Sybil 1308-1315 (d)
Godfrey 1304 (d)	unknown	John 1288-1327	Agnes 1304-1312
William	unknown	Alexander 1307-1315 (sen by 1344) (c)	Amicia 1306
		William 1312-1317 (c)	
		John 1325-1349 (d) (c)	
Alexander sen (c)	Mariota 1345		Agnes 1345
John son of Alexander (c)	Margaret 1345		
William son of William (c)	Agnes 1314		
Nicholas 1307-1310 (d)	Cristina 1307	John 1309-1326	Joan 1307, husband called John
		Reginald 1309-1326 (c)	Amicia 1307
		Godfrey 1312-1317	Catherine 1307
Reginald son of Nicholas (c)	Emma 1317		

[y] This Thomas is very likely the son of Thomas son of John (1286-1299).

[z] This Thomas is very likely the Thomas son of Thomas (1306).

[a] This Roger is very likely the son of Roger son of John (1286-1318).

Thomas 1315 (d)	Cristina 1321	John 1310	Agnes 1321
		Nicholas 1316-1340	Margaret 1315
			Margretta 1315
			Mariota 1315
Reginald	Cristina 1322	Roger 1329, 1352 (c)	Amicia 1347
William* [b]	unknown	Thomas 1329-1344	
		Godfrey 1349	
John	unknown	John 1332-1367 (c)	
		Thomas 1340, 1375	
Roger son of John (c)	unknown		
Nicholas* [c]	unknown		
John son of Nicholas (c)	Isolda 1351	William de Godmanchester 1340-1376	Cristina 1348
William	Isolda 1341	John 1348	Sybil 1345
Thomas [d]	unknown		Elena 1347, 1375
			Sybil 1347
Reginald* [e]	unknown		
Alexander jun	unknown	John 1345-1363 (c)	Cristina 1361
		Robert 1351-1377	
		Godfrey 1361	
John son of Alexander jun (c)	Agnes 1347-1360	John 1361	
		Godfrey 1361	
		William 1361	

[b] This William is very likely William the son of William (1312-1317).
[c] Nicholas is very likely the son of Thomas (1315-1340).
[d] Thomas could be the son of Nicholas 1340, 1376.
[e] This Reginald must be either Reginald jun or Reginald sen.

Family Name and Husband	Wife	Son(s)	Daughter(s)
Reginald jun	unknown	John 1345-1348	
Reginald sen	unknown	John 1346	
William	Cristina 1378-1379		Isabella 1366
Thomas *de* Offord 1357	Amicia 1357		
probable kin: Bartholomew 1283			
Andrew 1321			
Reginald 1345			
Lord Robert, chaplain 1345			
John *de* East St. 1347			
John sen of Post St. 1349-1380			
Peter 1352-1399			
John jun 1360-1376			
John 1363-1376			
John sen 1363-1376			
GOODMAN			
John 1321-1325	Margaret 1321-1325		
GORNE			
Richard 1361	Cristina 1361		
GRACE			
John 1372	Amicia 1375		
DE GRAFHAM (GRAUNHAM)			
John sen 1332-1373	Joan 1358, 1360		
probable kin: John jun 1360			
Thomas *de* 1369			
Robert *de* 1373			

DE GRANSDEN (GRANTESDENE)
William 1301-1316 (d) — Isolda 1301-1317 — John 1298
Reyner 1304-1317

probable kin: Reginald 1345
GRAUNHAM see DE GRAFHAM
GRAUNT
Robert 1295-1334 — unknown — Elias 1295
Cristina 1282
Sarra 1309
Emma 1312 married to Robert le Small
DE GRAVELEY
William 1278-1289 — unknown — John 1317
Simon 1287-1309 (d) — unknown — John 1287-1304 (c)
John (c) — unknown

John 1351-1362 (d) — Isabella dau of John Glewe, cooperator 1360-1367 — William 1366-1395 (c)
William (c) — Alice 1371-1377
probable kin: Lord John, rector of church de Graveley 1300
Master William 1308
John jun 1335-1341
John sen 1341
John* 1340 (d)
Matilda 1342
Nicholas 1349
John parson of church de Graveley 1356

ATTE GRENE
John 1378-1381 — Matilda 1378-1381
probable kin: Reginald 1363

Family Name and Husband	Wife	Son(s)	Daughter(s)
GRIGORY			
Alexander 1291 (d)	unknown		Margaret 1291
probable kin: Felicia 1299-1308			
GRINDE			
Adam 1282-1319 (d)	unknown		Cristina 1318-1341 married to Nicholas *de* Paxton
			Isolda 1287-1318
Eustace 1286-1309	Matilda 1290-1316	John 1320-1321	
Simon 1316-1348	Amicia 1322		
Henry 1341-1356	Catherine 1356, 1392		
John 1362-1364	Catherine 1362-1364		
probable kin: Godfrey 1287-1311			
Thomas 1381-1390 (d)			
GROTTYNG			
Thomas 1363	Pepina? 1363		
ATTE GROVE			
Richard 1285	unknown	Aubtus? 1285	
GRYT			
John 1353	Salda? 1353		
GYLEMAN			
unknown	Helen 1311-1330		Cristina 1330-1332
probable kin: Mariota 1311-1326			
Felicia 1315-1317			
Agnes 1329			
DE HADDENHAM			
Eustace 1313	Cristina 1313		Felicia 1308

HALDOWS
John *de* Hunts   unknown   Amicia 1313-1321
                                                     Isabella 1317-1322

ATTE HALL *see* AULA

HALUPETYR
William 1281-1301   Edith 1298

DE HAMERTON
Godfrey 1278-1291   and wife 1278, 1291
John 1279-1314 (d)   Phillipa 1296-1313 (d)   Thomas 1314
                                                      John 1314-1326 (c)

                                                      Joan 1306, married to Reginald
                                                        le Barbour 1314

John (c)   Helen 1316-1326   Agnes 1349
Nicholas   unknown
probable kin: William *de* 1278
               John *de* Hunts 1306-1326, 1362
               Richard 1349-1379
               John 1351 (d)

HAMYOHT
unknown   unknown   Isabella 1292
                                                      Ivetta 1292

DE HARDLEY
Nicholas 1288-1335 (d)   Elena 1288-1295   John 1313-1326
                            (2nd) Matilda 1298
probable kin: Richard *de* 1295
               Nicholas *de* Hunts 1327

                                                      Joan 1335 married to Henry *le*
                                                        Hore, *de* Hunts

HARDY
William 1289-1298   Leticia 1298-1304

Family Name and Husband	Wife	Son(s)	Daughter(s)
William	unknown		
John (c)	Beatrix 1337-1340	John 1330-1345 (c)	
probable kin: Robert 1279			
Simon 1298-1333			
John 1315			
Thomas 1333-1335			
Reginald *de* Hemington 1338			
DE HARDWICK			
Nicholas 1278-1286	and wife 1278		
probable kin: Simon 1280			
Robert 1282			
HARE			
John 1361	Constance 1361		
DE HARTFORD (HEREFORD, HERFORD)			
William 1280-1296	Isolda 1280		
Edward	unknown		
Roger (c)	Matilda 1280	Roger 1280 (c)	
Richard 1292-1297	and wife 1292		
Godfrey 1308	Agnes 1308		
unknown	Emma	William 1361-1376	
probable kin: Oliver *de* 1308, 1313			
Phillip *de* 1326			
Robert 1330			
vicar of 1350			
John *de* 1351, 1380			
Walter 1378			

DE HAVELEY
William
John (c)   Agnes 1298 (d)   John 1293-1295 (c)
                            Margaret Scot 1293-1298,   Robert 1295
                            1302-1329

probable kin: Mariota 1308

HAVENOK
Simon 1287   unknown   Mariota 1287

HAYETHEWOLF (HAYEWOLF)
Henry 1299-1302   Isolda 1299-1302
probable kin: John 1295
              Roger 1339-1354 (d)

DE H'DEWY
unknown   unknown   Robert 1278, 1287
                                                        Richard 1278, 1287
                                                        Edward 1287

HEKEDOUN
Sayerus 1366   unknown   John 1366
SON OF HELEN
unknown
Thomas (c)   Helen
                            Emma 1280   Thomas 1280 (c)

DE HEMINGFORD
John 1327   Catherine 1327
William 1329-1345   Cristina dau of John
                            Richardyn 1329-1345

William de Hunts 1338-1344 unknown   William 1354-1372 (c)
William (c)   Margaret 1372   Beatrix 1363

Family Name and Husband	Wife	Son(s)	Daughter(s)
probable kin: Ralph 1295			
Peter 1309			
John de, de Hunts 1350			
Walter de 1361			
Joan de Grafham 1399			
DE HEMINGTON			
Henry	unknown	William 1286	
probable kin: John 1313			
Lord Phillip 1326-1329			
John de Hunts 1345			
SON OF HENRY			
Henry	unknown	John 1278-1316	
		William 1278 (c)	
William (c)	Helen 1278		
Henry	unknown	John 1351-1357 (c)	
		William 1351-1372 (c)	
John (c)	Felicia 1354		Cristina 1351 married to John Quenyng
William (c)	unknown	Ralph 1372	
HENYHAM			
William jun 1378 (d)	unknown	John 1378	
HERCY			
Thomas 1340	Amabilia 1340		
HERINGMONGER			
John 1298-1307	Felicia 1298		

HEREFORD, HERFORD *see* DE HARTFORD

HERLE
John 1378 — Joan 1378

HERLISHEVID
Edward 1280 — unknown — Simon 1280-1284
unknown — unknown — Godfrey 1284
Richard 1284

probable kin: Roger 1282-1295
HERNE *see* IN LE HIRNE
HERNY (HIRNI)
Richard 1369-1386 — Sybil 1372
probable kin: John *de* Gt Paxton 1377

HERT
John 1366 — unknown — William 1366
IN HERTESTURP
John — unknown — Gilbert 1340

HICHIN *see* DE HITCHIN
DE HIGNEY (HIGENEYE)
unknown — Alice — Agnes 1302
Alice 1302

HILDEGAR
Hildegar — unknown — John 1311-1332 (c) — Millicent 1316-1321 (d)
Leticia 1316
Helen 1311, 1316
Emma 1316

John (c) — Emma 1334
probable kin: Robert *de* Compton 1337
Thomas, chaplain 1394

Family Name and Husband	Wife	Son(s)	Daughter(s)
HILDEMAR			
Nicholas 1298-1308	Amicia 1298	Eusebius 1298	Emma 1309-1316
			Cristina 1309-1312 (d)
Bartholomew (c)	Matilda 1309	Bartholomew 1308-1348	
	(2nd) Agnes^f	dead by 1354 (c)	
		Simon 1309-1327	
		Roger 1326	
		Simon 1345-1385 (d) (c)	
		Robert 1348-1349 (c)	
		William 1348	
Simon (c)	unknown	John 1385	Amicia 1364 (c)
Robert (c)	Sybil 1348-1349		Emma 1364
unknown	Amicia (c)		Elena 1302-1327 (d)
Thomas 1303 (d)	unknown	John 1303-1314	Masceline 1303-1311 (d)
		Robert 1303-1311	
Hildemar	unknown	John son of 1311	Isolda 1331-1334
John* 1315-1329	Cristina 1326-1331		Agnes 1331
			Cristina 1344 (d)
Nicholas 1333	Alice 1333		
John 1344	Emma 1344		

f The court rolls state, "John [1385] land as heir of his father Simon who had it after the death of Agnes wife of Bartholomew"; the date of Agnes' death is not known. She also must be the second wife of Bartholomew since there is no other Bartholomew noted in this family.

John*
Thomas (c)
Thomas sen 1391-1395   unknown
probable kin: Simon 1280   Alice 1361-1362   Thomas 1352-1376 (c)
               John 1295   Margaret 1391-1395
               Hugh 1357
               Henry 1383
               John sen 1391
               Thomas* 1391 (d)

ON YE/SUPER LE HILL *see* SUPER MONTEM

IN LE HIRNE (HERNE)
Hugh *de* King's Ripton   unknown
probable kin: William in ye, *de* Elsworth 1340
               Henry *de* King's Ripton 1360-1367   Ivo 1299
               Henry 1361-1363
               John *de* Buckden 1365
               John *de* King's Ripton 1375
               John *de* Papworth 1380
               John *le* 1381
               Henry *de* Papworth 1381

HIRNI *see* HERNY
DE HITCHIN (HICHIN)
Robert 1299-1326   Isabella 1295-1299   Robert 1299-1341 (c)   Sarra 1316
                                                      John 1325-1332
Robert (c)   unknown   Nicholas 1303-1325 (c)
Nicholas (c)   Margaret 1317

Family Name and Husband	Wife	Son(s)	Daughter(s)
probable kin: John 1322 (d)			
Emma *de* Hunts 1347 (d)			
Robert 1354			
Nicholas *de* Hunts 1354			
Peter *de* 1356 (d)			
HOBBIS			
unknown	Agnes		Cristina 1280
HOCKERILL (HOKERYLLE, HOG)			
Roger 1295-1315 (d)	unknown	John *de* Papworth 1315-1327 (d) (c)	Cristina 1326
John (c)	unknown	John *de* Papworth 1346	
probable kin: Walter 1280			
John 1280			
John 1369 (d)			
HOGAN			
Thomas *de* Papworth 1341	Cristina 1341		
HOKERYLLE *see* HOCKERILL			
DE HOLLAND			
Peter 1281	and wife 1281		
HOLIW			
John	unknown	John 1340	Matilda 1332
			Agnes 1339 (d)
HOMAN			
John *de* Godmanchester 1350-1394	Agnes 1350-1394		
probable kin: Robert 1361-1364			

Hon
Eustace 1298-1303
John 1298 (d)   Sarra 1303   John 1303
probable kin: Thomas 1278-1281   Matilda 1303 (d)
              William 1278-1281   Amicia 1280-1310 married to
              Pellagia 1303   Richard *le* Rede
              Cristina 1307

Honewyn
William 1351   Emma 1351

Hopay
unknown   unknown   Henry dead by 1279 (c)
                                                       Eustace 1293 (c)

Henry (c)   unknown   Thomas 1293 (d)
Eustace (c)   John 1299-1304, 1308 (d)
                                                       William 1310-1346 (c)
William (c)   unknown   Godfrey 1332-1352
                                                       Simon 1332
                                                       John 1339-1353

Thomas 1312-1351 (d)   unknown   John 1351-1361 (d) (c)   Alice 1351-1359
William* 1351 (d)   Elena 1351   Nicholas 1350-1393
unknown   unknown

John (c)   Felicia 1361   John 1351
probable kin: Thomas 1354-1356
              Peter 1369 (d)

Le Hore
Henry *de* Hunts 1335   Joan 1335 dau of Nicholas *de*
                                      Hardeley

Family Name and Husband	Wife	Son(s)	Daughter(s)
HOROLD			
John	unknown		
William (c)	Agnes 1307-1310	William 1304-1325 (c)	
	(2nd) Matilda 1317		
unknown	Cristina *de* Yelling 1348-1364	Godfrey 1348	Agnes 1350
John *de* Yelling	unknown		
probable kin: Henry *de* Yelling 1353			
John 1353-1388			
Richard *de* Yelling 1383			
LE HORSEMAN			
Walter *de* Hunts	unknown	John 1318	
HOT			
Godfrey 1278-1291	Ivetta 1283-1291		
probable kin: Walter 1278-1288			
William 1278			
Beatrix 1278			
Caterina 1286			
DE HOUGHTON			
William 1288	Ivetta 1298	William 1298	Iona 1291
		Richard 1311	
John	Helen 1324		
John (c)	Amicia 1321	John 1321-1339 (c)	
probable kin: Edward *de* 1291			
John 1361-1399			
HOULOT			
Thomas *de* Lt. Stukeley	unknown	Simon 1320	

HOURGES
Thomas 1366 — Margaret 1366
probable kin: John 1374

HOUTERE
William — Emma 1377

HOWE
Eustace 1310-1316 — Sarra 1310-1316
John 1321 — Amicia 1321 — Agnes 1339
unknown — Helen — Godfrey 1322 / Simon 1322 / William 1322

John 1349-1379 — Alice 1349
probable kin: Roger 1295
John 1321 (d)

HOWEFYL
John — unknown — John 1351

HOWELOND
John *de* Yelling 1371 — Elena 1371

HOWMAN
Henry *de* Offord Cluny — unknown — Robert *de* Offord Cluny (c) 1323-1345

Robert *de* Offord Cluny (c) — Elena 1340 (d)
Robert 1338-1369 — Cristina 1338-1356 — John 1353-1391
probable kin: Richard 1325-1340 (d)
Richard 1345-1349
John sen 1375

Family Name and Husband	Wife	Son(s)	Daughter(s)
SON OF HUGH			
Hugh	unknown	John 1289-1317 (c) Simon 1299-1326 (d) Godfrey 1308-1316 (d) (c)	
John (c)	Emma 1317	John 1289 Godfrey 1297-1326 Robert 1322	Amicia 1316
Godfrey (c)	unknown	Thomas de Chatteris 1321 Godfrey 1329-1374 (d) (c) Robert 1329-1348 (c) William 1343-1345 (d) (c)	
Hugh	unknown		
Hugh	unknown		
Godfrey (c)	Pellagia 1365-1366 nee Dosyn	Robert 1351	
Robert (c)	Cristina 1335		
William (c)	Agnes 1342-1348		
DE HUNTINGDON			
Richard 1279, 1304 (d)	unknown	John 1304	
Lawrence	unknown	Henry 1348	
Benedict	unknown	Michael 1298	Isabella 1298
probable kin: Ralph 1291-1306			
ILSTER			
Simon, taylor 1349-1389	Cristina 1356-1389		Matilda 1356
INGEL see INGLEYS			

INGELOND

Godfrey 1278-1310 (d)	unknown	John 1311-1318	Sybil 1310
			Agnes 1310-1311 (d)
John* 1317-1320	Cristina 1317	Godfrey 1322-1324 (c)	
Simon jun	unknown	John 1325-1332	
		William 1325-1339	
Godfrey (c)	Matilda 1324	Godfrey 1356	
John* 1338	Agnes 1338		
unknown	Cristina 1356		

probable kin: Godfrey jun 1278-1282
Simon 1278
Godfrey 1387 (d)

INGLEYS (INGEL, ENGLE)

Reginald 1312-1313 (d)	unknown	Eustace 1312-1313	
unknown	Margaret de Hemingford Abbots 1346, 1376 (d)	Thomas de Hemingford Abbots 1346	
		William 1363-1368	

John de Hemingford Abbots | unknown
probable kin: John de Hemingford Abbots 1299-1312
John jun de Hemingford Abbots 1324

INHEWYN

unknown	Sybil 1279	William 1304-1339 (c)	
William (c)	Cristina 1339 g		
Hugh 1291-1313 (d)	Agnes 1291-1321	John 1316 (d)	3 daus of Hugh 1317-1320
John	unknown		Cristina 1320-1322

g Cristina's mother's name is Pellagia.

Family Name and Husband	Wife	Son(s)	Daughter(s)
William			
William 1371-1378 (d)	Emma widow 1350	Henry 1378	
probable kin: John 1282-1298	unknown		
Bartholomew 1279-1280			
Isabella 1313			
Thomas 1331-1340			
John 1351-1387			
IRONMONGER			
Robert 1295	unknown	John *le* 1295-1315 (c)	
		Nicholas 1295-1304 (d)	
John (c)	Felicia 1304		
	(2nd) Joan 1306-1315		
SON OF ISABELLA			
unknown	Isabella 1297	John 1303	
DE ISHAM			
John 1325-1329	Cristina 1325-1329		
John 1355-1386	Albrida 1394	John jun 1394-1396	
DE ISLEHAM (ISLHAM)			
unknown	unknown	Adam 1322-1325	
		Roger 1315-1334 (Lord,	
		chaplain 1315-1322)	
probable kin: Simon 1327-1351			
SON OF ISOLDA			
unknown	Isolda	Roger son of 1278	

Family / Person	Spouse		
IVEL			
William	unknown		
John (c)	Agnes 1350	John 1331-1350 (c)	
probable kin: Isabella 1329			
Godfrey 1346			
IVES (YVES)			
William 1323-1347	Catherine dau of Reginald in the Lane 1323		
IVETE			
William	Matilda widow 1302		
IVETTSON			
John 1367	Felicia 1367		
probable kin: Thomas 1367			
IVO			
Ivo	unknown	Henry *de* King's Ripton 1361	
JEMYS			
Richard 1380	unknown	Phillipa 1380	
JELEKOC			
William 1314	Agnes 1314		
SON OF JOHN [h]			
Richard	unknown	John 1278	
John	unknown	John 1278 (c)	
John son of John (c)	Philippa widow 1297-1311	Robert 1297-1312	Isolda 1301-1311
		William 1297-1308	Agnes 1311
			Margaret 1311

[h] Owing to the commonness of this patronymic, relationships are difficult to define. Where the relationships are known the family is traced out; the latter part of the chart just shows the "son of John" listings.

Family Name and Husband	Wife	Son(s)	Daughter(s)
John			
Reginald (c)	unknown	Reginald 1278-1320 (d) (c)	Joan 1316
	Agnes 1320 widow	John 1309, 1317	Helen 1318-1326
		John 1317	
		Henry brother of John and John 1317-1348	
John	unknown	William 1312-1316	
		Robert 1315-1334 (c)	
		Nicholas brother of William and Robert 1316 (d)	
		William 1363 (c)	
Robert (c)	unknown		
William (c)	Agnes 1363		
John*	unknown		
Reginald (c)	Cristina 1322	Reginald 1314 (d) (c)	Cristina 1326
John*	unknown	Roger (c)	
Roger (c)	unknown	Henry 1329	
John*	unknown	Hugh (c)	
Hugh (c)	unknown	John 1334	
		Godfrey 1335 carter	
John*	unknown	William (c)	
William (c)	Matilda 1335-1342	John 1335	Matilda 1342
John*	unknown	Reginald 1326-1348 (c)	
Reginald (c)	unknown	Gilbert 1337-1342	
John	unknown	Robert 1351-1362 (d) (c)	

Robert (c)	Emma 1351-1362	William 1361-1362 (c)
William (c)	Margaret 1363	Reginald (c)
John*	unknown	Reyner (c)
Reginald* (c)	unknown	Godfrey 1354-1367 [i]
Reyner (c)	unknown	William (c)
John de Godmanchester	Agnes 1363	Henry son of 1295
John	unknown	John son of 1298 (d)
William (c)	Sybil 1373	John son of 1316, 1327
John	unknown	Gilbert son of 1316-1345
		William son of 1329-1340 (d)
		John son of, de St. Ives 1349
		John son of 1356
		William son of 1354-1361
		Roger son of 1376
		Godfrey son of 1390-1394

probable kin: Hugh, servant of John, de Wolle 1316

JOWOT

Thomas 1375	Felicia 1375	

JUEL

unknown	unknown	William 1320-1324
		Isabella 1320

[i] An example of the relationship shown: Godfrey son of Reyner son of Reginald son of John 1354-1367.

Family Name and Husband	Wife	Son(s)	Daughter(s)
probable kin: Simon 1278-1287			
Godfrey 1278-1291			
Edward 1280-1297			
Robert 1280			
William 1291-1324			
Matilda 1295			
John 1342-1346			
JULIAN (JULIEN)			
William	unknown	Simon 1278-1312 (c)	Mariota 1278-1279
		Richard 1278-1291 (d) (c)	Isabella 1291
		Robert 1278-1302 (c)	
Simon (c)	unknown	Godfrey 1297	Millicent 1299
Richard (c)	Isolda 1291	Godfrey 1299	Isabella 1329
Robert (c)	Amicia 1303, 1329	Simon 1327	Leticia 1311
Alan	Isolda 1279	Lawrence 1305-1320 (d) (c)	Millicent 1311
Lawrence (c)	Isolda 1315-1331 dead by 1351		Cristina 1327-1332
			Elena 1327-1329
Lawrence 1344, 1351	unknown	John 1331-1347	
		William 1340-1347	
John de St. Ives	unknown	John 1349	
JURYS			
unknown	Emma	William 1301	

KELE			
Thomas 1393	unknown	Thomas, taylor 1393	
KEM			
Walter *de* Papworth	unknown	Robert 1321	
DE KEYSTON (KEYSTYNNE)			
Richard 1356	and wife 1356		
KING			
Ralph *de* Broughton 1329-1344	Alice 1331-1344	Thomas 1348-1349	
John *de* Lt. Stukeley	unknown	John 1349	
unknown	unknown	Reyner 1341-1392	
		Simon 1350-1376	Catherine 1380
John sen 1356-1374	Cristina 1356-1372		
John jun 1356-1363	Sybil 1358		
Simon 1376-1380	Cristina 1380		
probable kin: Edward 1329			
Godfrey 1349			
DE KINGSTON			
Roger *le* Wodeward 1329-1372	Amicia 1329-1372		
probable kin: John 1356			
Robert 1399			
KNYTTE			
John 1377	Margaret 1377	John 1377	
KOKKIL			
Gregory 1280-1282	unknown		
KOMBERE (COMBERE)			
Robert 1280	and wife 1280		
KORS			
Roger 1278-1291	Isabella 1281	Henry 1297	Cristina 1281-1283

Family Name and Husband	Wife	Son(s)	Daughter(s)
KUTERE (COUTERE, COWTER)			
Simon 1280-1333	Cristina 1283-1302[j] dead by 1347	Godfrey 1307 (d) Simon 1309-1329 (c)	
Simon (c)	unknown	William 1317-1349 Henry 1319-1349 (d)	
John (c)	unknown	John 1330 (c)	
Nicholas 1295 (d)	unknown	William 1332-1341	
William 1316-1324	Leticia 1322	Godfrey 1295-1302	Matilda 1295 Caterina 1322
unknown	unknown	William jun 1347-1351 Godfrey 1347 (d)(c)	
Godfrey (c)	Cristina 1347 (d)	John 1340-1353 (c)	
William*	unknown		
John (c)	wife 1353		
probable kin: Godfrey le jun 1291-1322 (d)			
William 1299			
Godfrey sen 1303			
KYLPYN			
Godfrey de Houghton, smith 1385	Matilda 1387		
KYNE			
Edward 1287-1318	Isolda 1318		

[j] Cristina had a sister called Matilda 1303.

Godfrey 1327-1349   Margaret 1327-1334
John, chaplain 1349-1385   Agnes 1349-1385
probable kin: Lawrence 1281
         Roger 1287

LACHE
John *le* 1293   unknown   Cristina 1293
probable kin: Ivetta *le* 1295
         Richard *le* 1298

LAMBERD (LAMBERT)
John 1338-1361   Mabel 1338-1346
probable kin: Emma 1281
         Alice 1286-1292
         John 1399
         John sen 1380-1382

IN THE LANE (VENELLA)
Ivo 1279-1312   Matilda 1279-1311   John 1296-1332   Emma 1284-1288 (c)
unknown   Emma (c)   a son 1284
Thomas 1282-1306   unknown   John 1304 (d)   Amicia 1304
Richard 1282   unknown   Godfrey 1284-1311 (c)   Margaret 1301-1306 widow of
     Richard 1306-1349 (c)   Reginald Goni and re-married
     Roger son of William Mani-
     penny 1315
     Pellagia 1301-1315

Godfrey (c)   Isolda 1284-1316 [k]   Gilbert 1316
     John 1316

[k] Isolda's mother's name was Juliana 1284.

Family Name and Husband	Wife	Son(s)	Daughter(s)
Richard (c)			
Reginald 1282-1311	Mariota 1320	Reginald 1310-1325	Catherine 1311-1347 married to
	Margaret 1306		William Ives 1323-1347
			Juliana 1311-1333
			Isolda 1311-1316
Eusebius 1288-1320	Matilda 1317 (d)	Gilbert 1313-1317	
William 1291	unknown	Godfrey 1304-1313	
		Walter 1298-1316 (c)	
Walter (c)	unknown	John 1332 (d)	
Reginald 1297 (d)	Matilda 1294	Godfrey 1297-1327	Matilda 1283
		John 1297 (d)	Isolda 1297
		Reginald 1297 (the eldest brother)	
Godfrey 1312 (d)	wife of, dead by 1312	John 1312-1320	Joan 1319-1322
		Gilbert 1312-1321	
Ivo*	unknown	John 1326-1330	Cristina 1324
		Roger 1330 (c)	
Roger (c)	Alice 1330	Roger 1330	
John*	unknown	Godfrey 1338-1348	Emma 1335-1345
		Henry 1340-1348	
Gilbert	unknown	William 1343-1394	
Godfrey*	wife of, dead by 1344	Henry 1344 (d)	
		John 1350	
unknown	Isolda	Reginald 1345-1375	

Alexander 1360-1390   Emma 1366-1378   John 1430
probable kin: Agnes 1351-1360
            Gilbert 1358

DE LANGLEY
Richard 1335-1378   Joan 1335-1346
               (2nd) Margaret 1378
John *de* Papworth 1357-1363 (d)   Margaret 1363

LANGLANE
John, hayward 1361   Agnes 1361

LARKE
William 1332-1350 (d)   Sybil 1332
probable kin: Robert 1356-1383
            Agnes 1361
            Cristina 1361
            John jun 1373

LAVENDAR
Roger 1341   Emma 1341
probable kin: Reginald 1341

LAWMAN
John 1381   Agnes 1381
probable kin: Richard, foster 1365

SON OF LAWRENCE
Lawrence   unknown   John 1347-1349
                               William 1349 (d)

LEBERD
Peter 1390   Amicia 1390

LEFFEYN
Robert 1291-1332   unknown   Emma 1315-1364 (d)

Family Name and Husband	Wife	Son(s)	Daughter(s)
probable kin: Walter 1308			
Agnes 1341			
Godfrey 1380			
LEGAT			
unknown			
Robert	Cristina 1344	John 1363-1380 (c)	Cristina 1344
John (c)	unknown		
Simon 1366 *see* DOSYN	Margaret 1363		
probable kin: John 1351 (d)	Emma 1362-1366 *see* DOSYN		
John, miller 1352-1358			
Simon 1380			
LEGGE			
unknown	Isabella 1281	John 1298	Alice 1302
		William 1298	Juliana 1282-1285
			Mabel 1311
			Cristina 1311-1333 (d)
			Sybil 1318-1335 (d)
Roger 1281-1294 (d)	Matilda 1283-1294	Roger 1287-1319 (c)	
Roger (c)	Helen 1317	John 1333	
Nicholas 1287-1291	unknown		
Simon 1291-1316 (d)	Mabel 1297-1314	William 1307	
		Godfrey 1307-1337	
		John 1324-1333	
		Simon 1313-1325	
		Godfrey 1325-1330	
		William 1325-1330	
Godfrey 1291-1320 (d)	Helen 1316-1320		
Martin	unknown		Emma 1292

Simon 1304
Simon jun
Simon sen
probable kin: William ᵧe taylor 1352   Matilda 1304   William 1325-1348
              Simon 1358-1388 (d)   unknown   William 1333
              Cristina 1364   unknown

DE LEICESTER
John 1382
probable kin: John 1313   Emma 1382

DE LEIGHTON
Robert 1308
probable kin: John 1295   Cristina 1308
              Roger, burgess of Hunts 1329
              John, faber 1338-1341
              Robert 1354
              John 1351-1361

ATTE LEIRSTOWE
William 1271   and wife   John 1271[1]
                            William 1271[1]
                            Thomas 1271[1]

Richard 1279-1287   unknown   John 1299-1302   Isolda 1305-1308
William*   Matilda 1301-1309 ᵐ   William 1281-1316   Agnes 1302-1314
                             John 1299-1302   Matilda 1331
                             Roger 1315-1316
                             Alan 1316-1330

[1] All three are of age.
ᵐ Matilda's father's name is Edward.

Family Name and Husband	Wife	Son(s)	Daughter(s)
John* 1326 (d)	unknown	John (c)	Cristina 1309
John (c)	unknown	William 1304	Sarra 1309
		John 1306-1318 (c)	
John (c)	Helen 1318		
John	Matilda 1329	Simon 1329-1353 (d)	Matilda 1326-1334
William 1331-1333	Cristina 1331-1333		
Simon 1351-1363	Matilda 1362-1367 (d)		
John 1390	Emma 1390		
probable kin: Simon 1279-1292			
Roger 1379 (d)			
Agnes 1350 (d)			
LENMAN			
Simon 1313	Margaret 1313		
ATTE LEWE			
Thomas 1282-1310	Emma 1299[n]	William 1298-1316 (c) (noted as Hayl 1300)	Matilda 1299, married Edward Glewe
William (c)	Mabel 1302		
probable kin: Pellagia 1285			
LEXAUNT see LOXUNT			
DE LINCOLN			
Richard 1293-1310 (d)	Emma 1310 and re-marries a John 1314-1325	John 1318-1331	Margaret 1321
		Reginald 1318	

[n] Emma has a brother called William 1299.

Robert 1322-1362   unknown

Thomas (c)   Margaret de Stukeley 1327   John son of John 1325°
probable kin: Nicholas 1298-1299   Roger son of John 1322°
John, sutor 1312   Godfrey 1322-1361 (d)
Agnes 1361-1375   Thomas 1327 (c)
the chaplain of church de Gt Paxton 1378

LISTER
William le   unknown   Lawrence le de Hunts 1320-1347 (c)

Lawrence (c)p   Amicia 1326 (d)   Henry de Hunts 1326-1347 (c)
(2nd) Beatrix 1326   John de Hunts 1326

Joan 1333 married to Henry Mileward
Matilda 1338
Sybil de Hunts 1340-1342
Margaret de Hunts 1340-1346

Henry (c)   Cristina 1320-1339   Thomas 1361-1367
Alan de Hunts 1351 (d)   Margaret 1351
probable kin: John ye, de St. Ives 1353
Simon, spicer, de St. Ives 1386
Henry de Stanton 1391

LOCKSMYTH (LOCSMYTH)
Robert 1280-1298   wife of 1294   Gilbert 1310-1316
unknown   Emma 1316q

° John and Roger de Lincoln are the sons of John; whether Emma is their mother is not certain.
p Lawrence le Lister and his sons Henry and John are also noted as le Tinctor.
q Emma had a sister called Pellagia 1316.

Family Name and Husband	Wife	Son(s)	Daughter(s)
Gilbert 1344-1348	Joan 1346-1347 (d)		Cristina 1349
unknown	Cristina 1345-1346	John 1345-1348	
Richard 1346-1381	Alice widow 1388	Godfrey 1368-1394	
John 1349	Agnes widow by 1374		
probable kin: Isabella 1303-1309 (d)			
Emma 1349			
LOCKYNGTON			
Richard 1367-1380	Sybil 1394		
probable kin: Agnes 1367			
Alred 1367			
Walter 1382			
LODELOWE			
John 1344-1346	Sybil widow of William Colyer 1344-1346		
LONDONEYS			
Hugh 1316	Matilda 1316 (d)	John 1316	Sarra 1316 Agnes 1316 (d)
LE LONG			
John sen	unknown	John 1303-1325 John brother of John 1312 Simon 1308	
John*	unknown	John 1306-1309 (c) William 1309	
John (c)	Agnes 1306, 1333	John 1321	Cristina 1333
John*, faber 1321-1327	unknown	John brother of John 1322	

Roger sen 1332-1338   Cristina 1333-1348   Thomas 1346-1371   Emma 1346

Henry (c)   Cristina widow 1366   Henry 1355 (d) (c)
Simon *de* Papworth   Mabel 1342   Agnes 1342
                                           Margaret 1342
                                           Joan 1342

John 1351-1357   unknown   Roger 1340-1343
                                William 1343-1356
                                Godfrey 1354-1388 (c)

Godfrey (c)   Mabel 1367-1372   John 1387
William, taylor *de*   unknown   John 1363, 1393
Godmanchester 1354
probable kin[r]: John jun 1283-1286
                 Roger 1313
                 John, faber jun 1333
                 John sen, carpenter 1331-1344
                 Thomas de Earith 1331
                 William 1337-1349
                 William, clerk 1353-1389
                 John sen 1360-1390
                 Isolda 1372
                 Henry 1375
                 Simon sen 1376
                 Godfrey sen 1394

[r] There is no question that most of these Johns should be in the above family charts, but to which family they belong cannot be determined. It is also true that this surname is a "nickname surname" and some of these probable kin could indeed be unrelated to the other Longs.

Family Name and Husband	Wife	Son(s)	Daughter(s)
LOOSEWORTH			
William 1375	Felicia 1375		
LORIMER			
John *de* Hunts 1330	unknown	John *de* Hunts 1330-1353 (c)	Mabel 1333
		William 1330	
John (c)	Cristina 1330-1338		
probable kin: Thomas *de* Hunts 1279			
John *de* Hunts 1319-1326			
John jun 1378			
LOXUNT (LEXAUNT)[s]			
Gilbert 1329-1340	Juliana 1333-1340 dau of Emma Scot		
Richard	unknown		
Roger 1359	Sybil 1359		Juliana 1351
John	Agnes widow 1349-1350		
LUCAS			
Nicholas *de* Abbots Ripton 1299	unknown		Margeria 1299
LUCY			
Thomas 1391	Beatrix 1391		
DE LUTON			
John 1295-1304 (d)	Joan 1304	Thomas 1309-1346	Juliana 1309
		John 1310-1350 (d)	Caterina 1319
Thomas *de* Hunts 1322	unknown	Henry *de* Hunts 1343-1346	

[s] This family is very likely a branch of "Locksmyth" family as the name is a variant form of "locksmith."

LOOSEWORTH (continued)

unknown		Thomas 1363
probable kin: Elias Lord, *de* 1310	mother of Thomas *de* Hartford 1363	
William 1350		
William *de* Hunts 1380		

MABEL

unknown	Mabel	Godfrey son of 1287

MACHOUN

Ralph	unknown	Henry 1351
probable kin: John 1349-1353		
William 1349		

MADDERMONGER (WARENTER)[1]

Henry *le*	Cristina Godchild 1280-1296	Robert *le* 1280-1304 (d) (c)
		John 1295-1311 (c1) (parson 1298)
		Roger 1302-1322 (c)
		John 1295-1327 (c2)
		William 1309-1316 (c)
Robert (c)	unknown	Agnes 1280
		Cristina 1280
John (c2)	Matilda 1311	Robert 1313-1318
William (c)	unknown	William 1318
John (c1)	Emma 1295-1326	John 1332-1357
Roger (c)	Cristina 1310-1322	Cristina 1325 married to Richard Taylor

[1] *Le* Maddermonger and *le* Warenter indicate the same trade name of "dyer." After 1326 the *le* Warenter is dropped and only Maddermonger (next entry) is found.

Family Name and Husband	Wife	Son(s)	Daughter(s)
probable kin: Henry *le* Warenter[u]			
William Maddermonger 1332			
Richard Maddermonger 1357			
John Maddermonger 1375			
MADDERMONGER			
John[v]	unknown	Reginald 1329-1350 Thomas 1332-1354 (d) (c)	Joan 1332 Cristina 1332
Thomas (c)	unknown	Thomas 1350-1357	
MAN			
Richard *de* Hartford 1351-1363 (d)	unknown		Alice 1363 Helen 1363
probable kin: John *de* Godmanchester 1386-1388			
MANIPENNY			
John 1278-1312 (d)	unknown	Roger 1308-1312 John 1312-1315 Henry 1312-1348 (d) (c)	Agnes 1312 Emma 1312 Beatrix 1312 Mabel 1312 Matilda 1312 Sybil 1312
Henry (c)	Hawysia widow 1349		

[u] Henry *le* Warenter (1288) could be the son of Henry *le* Maddermonger, but as no further entries are noted this could be a scribal error and meant to read "1280."

[v] John Maddermonger is very likely one of the Maddermonger/Warenter sons mentioned above, but which one is not certain.

William 1278-1312 (d) — Amicia 1312-1331 (d)[w]

- Reginald 1296-1314
- John 1302-1334 (c)
- William 1302-1316
- Roger 1307-1316 (c1)
- Godfrey 1312-1357
  - Pellagia 1312
  - Isabella 1312
  - Agnes 1312

John (c) — Agnes 1315-1334 dau of John and Isolda Quenyng

- Roger 1327-1344 (c2)
- John 1329
- Reginald 1329-1346 (c) 1332-1338 chaplain
  - Agnes 1323-1332
  - Amabilia 1340

Roger (c1) — Margaret 1315-1330 (d) widow of Reginald Goni, nee Lane

Roger (c2) — (2nd) Matilda *de* Doncaster 1332[x]
Cristina 1347-1348

- John 1339
  - Cristina 1332

Reginald, chaplain (c) — Margaret 1338
Herbert — unknown
William — Cecilia 1316 (d)
John sen, *de* West St. — unknown
William — unknown

- William 1296-1313
- John 1316
- John 1329-1346
- William 1330-1348 jun (c)
- Lawrence 1341-1361 (c)
  - Cristina 1354, 1371
  - Agnes 1335-1350 (d)

William jun (c) — Cecilia 1338 dau of Robert and Matilda Aula
Agnes 1371

Lawrence (c) — Cristina 1345-1351 (d)
Godfrey

- John 1396-1397
  - Margaret 1371, 1399

[w] Amicia had a sister named Cristina who died and bequeathed her land to Amicia in 1312.
[x] As in manuscript.

Family Name and Husband	Wife	Son(s)	Daughter(s)
Roger			
John atte Grene	Cecilia 1351 (d)		
John 1361-1363	unknown	Reginald 1354-1359	
William	Agnes 1361-1363		
Richard 1363	Sybil widow 1363, 1380		Sybil 1349-1394
	Sybil 1363		Helen 1363
Roger*	Agnes,y re-married to John Plomer 1364		
Thomas	Agnes 1375		
Reginald	Agnes 1386		
probable kin:z William jun 1309			
William sen 1309			
Agnes 1329 (d)			
John jun 1350			
Agnes 1354			
John 1354 (d)			
John 1360-1376			
Henry 1364-1376			
John de West St. 1373			
Roger 1375			
Isabella 1381			

y Which Roger who had a wife Agnes is difficult to know, especially since any of the Rogers could have re-married. In the court roll it states only that she was the former wife of Roger Manipenny, so that when the marriage was is not known. It could be "Roger the son of William Manipenny," whose first wife Margaret Goni died around 1330.

z It is apparent that some of these probable kin appear in the chart above, but which William, Roger or John is difficult to establish.

MANYHAYS (MANYHASH)

John 1377-1389	Emma 1377	William (son of Emma) 1377
	(2nd) Agnes 1389	Thomas (son of Emma) 1377

MAREWELE

Godfrey 1315-1327 (d)	unknown	Amicia 1315
probable kin: Matilda 1306		
Joan 1317		
Cristina 1327		

MARIOT

Thomas 1346-1356	Emma 1346-1355
	Cristina 1349
probable kin: John 1295	
Thomas de St. Ives 1309	
John de Hilton 1387	

MARSHALL

John 1279-1310 (d)	Isabella 1310-1311 [a]	Matilda 1309-1311
William 1279	unknown	William 1315
Godfrey le 1280-1291	unknown	Syward 1295
John de Hunts 1282-1330, 1349	unknown	Simon 1349
Robert 1290	Cristina 1290	Elena 1333
John 1325	Beatrix 1325	Cristina 1290-1302
Godfrey	unknown	Agnes 1340
Stephen 1330	and wife 1330	Henry 1327
William 1354 (d)	unknown	Margaret 1338
		Reyner 1340-1346

[a] Isabella left the town 1311.

Family Name and Husband	Wife	Son(s)	Daughter(s)
Thomas de Hemingford Abbots 1346	unknown	John 1346 (12 years old), 1361	Agnes 1359
Roger 1348	and wife 1348		
unknown	Agnes	Richard 1346	
John 1359	Sarra 1359		
Rober de Hunts 1350-1356	unknown		
Ralph (c)	Lucy 1361	Ralph 1361-1363 (c)	
probable kin: Hugh 1277-1283			
Thomas de Hunts 1279-1289			
Godfrey de Hartford 1282-1283			
William de Hunts 1283			
Roger 1285			
Robert 1337			
Margaret 1348			
John, chaplain 1349			
John 1352			
Hugh de Melbourne 1360			
Margaret de Hemingford Abbots 1369			
SON OF MARTIN			
Martin de Hunts	unknown	Ralph de Hunts 1286-1291	
Martin	unknown	Richard son of 1278-1287	
		Thomas son of 1298-1315 (c)	
Thomas (c)	Matilda 1315		Emma 1317
Martin	unknown	John son of 1325-1346 (c)	
John (c)	and wife 1325		

Martin	unknown	Nicholas son of (c)	
Nicholas (c)	Margaret 1335		
probable kin: Cristina 1333, 1345			
Phillip 1338			
David 1345			
MASOUN (MASON)			
Simon *le* 1280-1309	Agnes 1295	John 1294-1316 (c)	
John (c)	and wife 1316	and sons 1316	
Roger	unknown	Eustace 1278-1299 (c)	
Eustace (c)	Isolda 1298		Isolda 1282
Reginald	unknown	Eusebius 1288-1299	
		William 1288	
John *le* 1285-1286	unknown	William 1299	Pellagia 1299-1304 married to Walter Marchant 1302
John 1280-1284 (d)	Lucy 1284-1285		
John 1326	unknown		Isabella 1326
William* 1324 (d)	Agnes 1325	Reginald 1316	Matilda 1325-1326
		John 1322-1324	Agnes 1325-1326
William 1325-1348	Matilda 1335	Thomas 1325-1349	Margaret 1349
		Godfrey 1331	
		Henry 1344	
William *de* Post St. 1329	unknown	William 1329	
John 1362-1379	Beatrix 1363, 1373	Henry 1353	
Ralph	Isolda 1350	Henry 1350-1352	Felicia 1350 (d)
			Agnes 1350 (d)
			Matilda 1350 (d)

Family Name and Husband	Wife	Son(s)	Daughter(s)
probable kin: Godfrey 1279-1287			
William le, de Godmanchester 1299-1300			
William le jun 1300			
William de East St. 1306			
Reginald dead by 1349			
Agnes ye, de Hartford 1354			
John de Hartford 1357			
John de Hemingford Abbots 1357			
Robert de Hunts 1399			
John sen 1392			
SON OF MATILDA			
unknown	Matilda	Reginald 1279-1322 (d) (c)	Cecilia 1295
		Roger 1288	
Reginald (c)	Millicent 1322	William 1309	
		Simon 1309	
		Godfrey 1322	
unknown	Matilda	Nicholas 1291-1309 (d) (c)	
		Godfrey 1291-1299 (c)	
Nicholas (c)	unknown	Reginald 1302	Phillipa 1302
		John jun 1309	Cristina 1309
		William 1312	Matilda 1309
			Albrida 1311 married to Roger Spruntyng, his second wife
Godfrey (c)	Felicia 1299	Roger 1304-1321	Matilda 1304 (c)
	(2nd) Cristina 1309	Robert 1321-1331	Amicia 1309 (c)

unknown   Matilda (c)
unknown   Amicia (c)
unknown   Matilda   Robert 1299 (c)   Cristina 1304-1309
Robert (c)   unknown   John 1299   Cristina 1309
               Godfrey 1299
               Reginald (c)

unknown   Matilda
Reginald (c)   Agnes 1339   Elena 1333
unknown   Matilda   Reginald 1356-1367

DE MATTISHALL (MATTISHALE)
Roger 1280-1308   Cristina 1280-1289
John 1298   Matilda Mustarder widow 1326

William 1306-1332 (d)   Matilda 1324   Emma 1322 married to John de Thompson (Thomostan)
             Agnes 1324 married to John de Over, Clerk

Hugh de Hunts   Agnes former wife of Hugh 1329-1332

unknown   unknown   William 1347
           John 1347

William   unknown   Godfrey 1349-1376 (c)
Godfrey (c)   Matilda 1351
probable kin: William de 1277-1287
          Amicia 1295
          Hugh 1295-1298
          Alice 1315
          Thomas 1332
          John de Hunts 1347

MAYSE
Thomas 1349   Cristina 1349
probable kin: Ingrid 1365

Family Name and Husband	Wife	Son(s)	Daughter(s)
MERCATOR, MERCER, MERCHANT *see* **CHAPMAN**			
DE MERTON			
Thomas 1279-1322 bailiff of Prior *de* Merton	wife 1313	John 1327-1344	
Simon 1291	Sarra Winborn 1291		
Thomas *de* Godmanchester	unknown	John 1349-1371 (c)	
John(c)	Isolda 1361-1371		
MESSAGER			
Richard 1310-1316	Sybil 1310-1316	Gilbert 1310-1316	Pellagia 1310-1316
			Cristina 1310-1316
probable kin: Richard 1341			
MESSER			
Roger 1317	wife 1317		
MICHEL			
John *de* Eltisley, malter 1389-1395	Elena 1395		
John *de* Hartford probable kin: William 1389-1399	unknown	Adam, chaplain 1394	
DE MILDENHALL			
William 1350-1351	Cristina 1350-1351		
MILEWARD			
John 1278-1280	Pellagia 1278-1280	Godfrey 1280-1309 (c)	
		Simon 1300	
Godfrey (c)	and wife 1280		

John			
Henry (c)	unknown	Henry 1335-1357 (d) (c)	Emma 1339
		Henry 1361	
		John 1364-1391	
		William 1340-1353 (d) (c)	
		John 1347-1363 (d)	
Thomas 1340-1347 (d)	Joan 1335 dau of Lawrence Lister *de* Hunts		
	Isolda 1350		
William (c)			
Alan 1343-1348	Emma 1340	William 1340-1348	
	Cristina 1344-1347 (d)	John 1344-1348	
Hugh 1349-1377	Agnes 1365-1377		
John*	Emma 1361-1363		
William* 1350-1374	Matilda 1354		
probable kin: Ingrid 1366			
MILLER (MOLENDARIUS)			
John *le* 1286-1315	unknown		Juliana 1310-1316 married to Reyner Doketon
Alan 1298-1333	Emma 1311	John 1319-1327	
		William 1330-1332	
John *de* West St. 1298	Pellagia 1298	John 1307	Emma 1308-1325, husband called John
		Simon 1309-1326 (c)	Pellagia 1316
Simon (c)	Alice Clerk, the sister of John Clerk *de* Hemingford 1330		
John sen	unknown	John 1307	Cristina 1327
John jun	unknown	John 1308-1309	
Thomas 1313-1327	Isolda 1331	a son 1323	
Nicholas *de* Papworth 1323 (d)	unknown		
Godfrey *de* Hemingford 1323	Cristina 1323		

Family Name and Husband	Wife	Son(s)	Daughter(s)
Hugh de Houghton 1310	unknown	Godfrey de Houghton 1310, 1329 (c)	
Godfrey de Houghton (c)	unknown		Amicia 1329
John	unknown	Henry 1332	
Nicholas de St. Ives 1349	Margaret 1349		
probable kin: Simon 1287			
John de Post St. 1298-1329			
John de Hemingford Grey 1310			
John 1315-1325			
John de Eltisley 1374			
William 1378, 1394			
Thomas 1383			
MILLICENT			
Richard 1285-1294	unknown		Agnes 1283
			Emma 1279 married to John Tesard
			Amicia 1308, dead by 1321
Simon 1292-1308 (d)	Cristina 1292-1321	John 1321	
William sen 1295-1311 (d)	Matilda 1295-1327 (d)b	John 1311	
John 1312-1340 (d)	Mabel widow 1340	Godfrey 1334-1361 (d) (c)	
		William 1337-1344	
Godfrey (c)	Agnes 1361-1363		
William 1330-1350 (d)	Cristina 1347-1363		

b Matilda had a sister, Agnes.

Helen 1335-1349   Cristina 1338-1342

Mabel 1280
Matilda 1280

William 1324-1349
Walter 1327-1331

John 1317

probable kin: John 1286-1306 (d)
               Thomas 1308
               Richard 1338
               Isabella 1347

DE MOLESWORTH
   Robert   unknown
MOLENDARIUS see MILLER
SUPER MONTEM (SUPER LE HILL, ON YE HILL)
   Walter 1280-1326   unknown

   William 1322   Cristina 1324-1332

   William de Riseley 1348-1349   Matilda 1348
   John 1345-1361 (d)   Cecilia 1359-1368
   probable kin: Isabella 1287
                  Seginius de Hartford 1320-1326
                  Reginald de Brampton, living at Godmanchester, de East St. 1329-1331
                  Walter 1333
                  Roger 1335
                  Lord Thomas 1345
                  Richard 1351
                  Thomas 1365-1366 (de Hartford 1365)
                  William of ye, de Spaldwick 1380

OF THE MOORE
   John 1356-1378   Cristina 1361-1375
   probable kin: Simon, chaplain 1391
MORGROVE
   Albric' 1298-1346   Isolda 1299

Family Name and Husband	Wife	Son(s)	Daughter(s)
Nicholas 1346	unknown	John 1365-1375 Nicholas 1365	Sybil 1366 (d)
probable kin: Richard 1278-1280 Reginald 1345-1364 (d)			
DE MOULTON (MULTON)			
Lambert 1310-1340	Felicia 1348	John 1340	Isabella 1348-1349 Elena 1346
Alan	unknown		
MUN (MUNER)			
John le 1291-1297	Pellagia 1292	John 1291-1294	
Alan 1295	Emma 1295		
probable kin: Cristina 1292			
DE MUNDFORD (MUNDEFORD)			
Eusebius 1314-1340	unknown	Robert 1346-1366 (c) Godfrey 1378-1383	Elena 1346 Margaret 1375-1379
Robert (c)	unknown		
John de Offord 1322, 1348	Emma 1322		
probable kin: Elena 1297			
John 1351-1391 (d)			
Agnes 1376			
MUNER see MUN			
SUPER MURAM (SUPER LE WAL)			
Alexander 1280-1330	unknown	William 1315 John 1321 Godfrey 1322-1349 (d) (c) John 1348-1349 Henry 1349	Matilda 1320
Godfrey (c)	unknown		

Reginald 1283	unknown		
Godfrey* 1288-1316	Sybil 1316	Robert 1290-1298	
Martin 1295-1318 (d)	Emma 1301-1318	Godfrey 1327-1330	
John	unknown	Godfrey 1318	Emma 1318
Richard 1341-1348	Sarra 1341	John 1318-1340 (d)	
		John 1331-1351	
		William 1342	

probable kin: Amicia 1295
　　　　　　　　John sen 1363-1389
　　　　　　　　Thomas 1375
　　　　　　　　John jun 1377-1391

NEM

Lawrence 1280-1308	Juliana 1281

NEWMAN

Richard	unknown	Eusebius 1316-1333	
Nicholas	unknown	William 1331	Agnes 1331
Henry de Hemingford Abbots 1331	Dionysia 1331		Agnes 1331
John 1350-1387	Agnes 1354-1392		Agnes 1392

probable kin: Robert de Hemingford 1295
　　　　　　　　Robert 1298-1302
　　　　　　　　Margaret le 1316
　　　　　　　　William de Waresley 1330
　　　　　　　　John de Sowthe 1349-1350
　　　　　　　　Simon de Hemingford Abbots 1350, 1363
　　　　　　　　John 1366-1369
　　　　　　　　John de Hilton 1389
　　　　　　　　William de Fen Stanton 1399

Family Name and Husband	Wife	Son(s)	Daughter(s)
SON OF NICHOLAS			
Nicholas	unknown	Walter 1280-1281 (c)	
Walter (c)	unknown	Simon 1286	
Nicholas	Pellagia 1315-1321	John 1310-1340 (c) William 1310-1331, 1348	Matilda 1315-1319 Helen 1321 Sybil 1321
John (c)	Elena 1340	Reginald 1345-1348 (d) Godfrey 1339-1355 John 1340	
William*	unknown	Edward 1343-1347	
Reginald*	Agnes 1329-1348		Agnes 1348
John de Godmanchester 1357 (d)	unknown	Reginald 1354-1360	
Nicholas	unknown	John de Hemingford Grey 1371	
Nicholas	unknown	Simon son of 1285-1299 Reginald son of 1316-1325	
NICOL (NICHOLE) (NICHOLAS?)			
William 1349	unknown	Edward 1348-1349	
Godfrey (c)	unknown	Godfrey 1350-1372 (c)	Caterina 1350-1363, husband called Thomas
John	unknown		
Reginald (c)	Isolda 1361	Reginald 1354-1361 (c)	
probable kin: Roger 1341-1376 Reginald 1391 William 1391-1399			

NOCEMO (NOCENNO, NOCENIO)
Roger 1350-1388 (d)   Margaret 1353-1367
probable kin: Reginald 1363

NOLLY
unknown

probable kin: Robert *de* Brampton 1378-1380

NOOK
unknown   Cristina, dead by 1350   William 1350
                                     John 1350

NORBORWHIGAM
William, sutor 1378   Cristina 1342   John 1342

DE NORFOLK
Stephen 1317-1334   Mabel 1378

NORREYS
unknown   Joan 1330

probable kin: William 1295   Margeria 1327   Simon 1327-1348

NOTTING
Roger 1279-1330   Isolda 1279   Cristina 1312

Robert (c)   Emma 1309   Robert 1303-1315 (c)
Roger (c)   Dulce 1315   Roger 1311 (c)
John (c)   unknown   John 1321-1346 (d) (c)

William 1347-1375 (c)   Ivetta 1330
John 1347   Margaret 1347
Thomas 1347-1394 (c)   Matilda 1365

William (c)   Cristina 1354-1387[c] dau of
               John Glewe, cooperator

[c] Cristina had a sister called Isabella, the wife of John *de* Graveley 1360.

Family Name and Husband	Wife	Son(s)	Daughter(s)
Thomas (c)	Cristina 1365-1392		
Simon	unknown	Richard 1282	
probable kin: Agnes 1322			
John sen 1344			
NUNNE			
Godfrey 1281-1291	unknown		
DE OFFORD			
John 1310	Emma 1310	John 1293	
unknown	Isabella		
John	unknown	John 1351	Matilda 1330
probable kin: Edeline 1279			
Andrew 1317			
Ralph, merchant 1322			
OLIVER			
unknown	Matilda 1308	Thomas de Hartford 1308-1331	
John de Hartford	unknown	Thomas 1342-1383	
DE OL. THE THORPE			
John 1388-1395	Amicia 1388-1395		
probable kin: Edmund 1386			
DE ON YE			
John 1377-1396	Caterina 1377-1396		
ONTY see OUTY			
OPAR'			
William 1316	Helen 1316		

ORTUN		
Roger 1286	Cristina 1286	
OSTERLER		
John 1365-1366	Joan 1365-1366	
probable kin: John *de* Hunts 1378		
OSTIPIL		
John 1350	Agnes 1350	
DE OUNDLE (UNDELE)		
William	unknown	Godfrey 1306-1341 (c)
		Thomas 1369 (d)
Godfrey (c)	unknown	
Walter	Agnes, former wife of, 1329	
OUTY (ONTY)		
Godfrey 1278-1279	Phillipa 1317 (d)	
Simon 1279-1332 (d)	unknown	John 1310-1332 (d)
		Robert 1310-1323 (c)
		William 1313-1317 (c)
		Godfrey 1333-1351 (d)
		a daughter 1313 (d), sister of William son of Simon
Robert (c)	Matilda 1310, 1323	Richard 1316 (c)
Richard (c)	Albrida 1319	
William (c)	unknown	William 1317 (c)
William (c)	Helen 1317	
John* 1313	Matilda 1313	Walter 1319-1334
		William 1325-1337
		Robert 1333
William sen*	unknown	
unknown	unknown	Outy *de* East St. 1330 (c)
		John *de* East St. 1330
Outy *de* East St. (c)	Cecilia 1330	Cristina Madecroft 1333

Family Name and Husband	Wife	Son(s)	Daughter(s)
William 1323	Agnes 1323	Reyner 1338-1359	
William 1337	Cristina 1337	Reginald 1351-1357	
John 1340	Pellagia 1340	Reyner 1385 (c)	
William*	unknown		
John	unknown		
Reyner (c)	Cristina 1398		
probable kin: William, chaplain 1359			
Godfrey 1361			
Reyner, faber de London 1377			
John, priest de Brampton 1378			
DE OVER			
Robert	unknown	Nicholas 1308	
Walter	unknown	John, clerk 1325 (c)	
John, clerk (c)	Agnes Matishall 1325	Henry 1351-1393 (c)	Cristina 1353
		John 1354-1356	
Henry (c)	Cristina 1356-1393		
John 1360-1388	Alice 1361-1388		
probable kin: Thomas 1351-1353			
John jun, clerk 1353-1372			
Robert 1376			
Richard 1391			
OVERTON			
Robert de Brampton 1361-1377	Cristina 1361-1377		
probable kin: Nicholas de Brampton 1397			

DE OXFORD (OXENFORDE)

Richard de Godmanchester — Sybil 1361-1380
1358-1372

DE PADEMOR

William 1279-1280 — Alice 1280
           (2nd) Isabella 1285

Godfrey 1291 — Amicia 1291   William 1325
Henry 1343-1363 (d) — Amicia 1361, 1372   William 1363-1364
                           Thomas 1382-1391 (d) (c)

Thomas (c) — Agnes 1391
probable kin: Godfrey 1341

PAGE (PAYS, PELLIPARIUS)d

Nicholas 1299, 1304 (d) — unknown   Lawrence 1299-1312 de
                                     Houghton (c)

Lawrence (c) de Houghton — Pellagia 1312   Godfrey 1294-1344
Lawrence* e — unknown   John 1335-1344   Phillipa 1333

PAGE (PAYS)

unknown — Alice   Henry 1280-1308 (d) (c)
                     Simon 1280 (c)
                     John 1280-1307 (c)

Henry (c) — Mariota 1280-1308   John 1332-1378   Beatrix 1325
Simon (c) — Joan 1282
John (c) — Emma 1307   William 1309 (c)
Richard 1283 — unknown

---

d Since only this "Lawrence" family is noted with these three surnames, and of Houghton, it is obvious that they had the occupation of *pelliparius* (skinner). "Page" and "Pays" could be the dialect form of the surname.

e This could be the same Lawrence as above, but the dating of the son and daughter is much later. John, however, is also known as *Pelliparius*.

Family Name and Husband	Wife	Son(s)	Daughter(s)
William (c)	Juliana 1309-1345	John 1309 (c)	
John (c)	Cristina 1309		
William, clerk 1346	Elizabeth 1346		Emma 1346
Reginald 1350-1387	Emma 1350-1387		
Lawrence 1351-1376	Cristina 1361, 1373		Sybil 1351-1363
Robert	unknown		
Reyner 1360-1389	Matilda 1396		
William 1390-1438	Beatrix 1422		
probable kin: Walter 1280-1283			
Clemens 1350			
John 1361			
PAGE *see also* STARTLE			
PAGOT			
Robert 1329-1347	Alice 1329		
probable kin: John 1329			
PAKARET			
John	unknown	Thomas 1349	
probable kin: John 1377			
PALMER			
John *de* Hunts 1312	Matilda 1312		
Richard 1372-1397	Emma 1372-1382		
probable kin: William *de* Offord 1278			
Ralph 1298			
John *de* Offord 1322-1324			
John 1367			
Peter 1376			

PAPE *see* POPE

DE PAPWORTH

Simon 1291	unknown	Simon 1291	
Reginald, sutor 1308-1324	Helen 1325		
Gilbert 1306	Joan 1306		
William 1308	Matilda 1308		
John jun 1353	Agnes 1353		
probable kin: Roger 1295			

DE PAPWORTH *see also* COOPERATOR ROTARUM

PARLOR (PARLUR)

Eustace 1281	Dionysia 1281		

PARMINTER

Phillip 1306	unknown	Godfrey 1306	
probable kin: Lawrence *le* 1302-1314			

PARSON (PERSON)

unknown	unknown	William 1280	Agnes 1280
unknown	Juliana 1284	John 1284 (c)	
John (c)	Cristina 1284		
unknown	unknown		
		John 1285-1306 (c)	
John (c)	Emma 1295	Simon 1285-1322 (c)	
		John 1318	
Simon (c)	Matilda 1285-1322 dau of William *de* Raveley	Nicholas 1303-1309, 1312 (d) (c)	
		William 1310-1315 (c)	
		John 1315-1322 (c)	
		William 1325-1349	
Nicholas (c)	unknown		
William (c)	Cristina 1310-1313		
John (c)	Sabina 1325-1326		Amicia 1326

Family Name and Husband	Wife	Son(s)	Daughter(s)
Richard			
William 1350-1379 (d)	Beatrix 1349		
John de Hunts	Sybil 1350-1390 (d)		
John 1377-1389	Matilda 1363		
	Alice 1377-1389		
probable kin: William de Trinity 1279			
Master John de Graveley 1298			
John de Holy Trinity 1308			
Isolda 1325, 1335 (d)			
Reginald 1350-1367			
Robert 1350-1363			
John de Weye 1351			
PARVAUNT			
John 1350	Alice 1350		
PARVUS (SMALL, LITTLE)			
Robert 1278-1280	Margaret 1278-1280		
Robert (c)	Emma 1325-1326	Robert 1297-1326 (d) (c)	Sybil 1325-1331
John 1351 (d)	unknown	John 1337-1343	Joan 1354
		John 1351-1356	
		Henry 1354	
William de Hunts 1354	Matilda 1362	John de Hunts 1363	
		William de Hunts 1362-1366	
probable kin: William 1327-1347			
John 1340			
Emma 1363			
PATERNOSTER			
John jun 1387-1388	Margaret 1387-1388		
John sen 1390	Cristina 1390		

DE PAXTON
William 1279-1302   Agnes 1279-1302   John *de* St. Ives 1325, 1348   Agnes 1326-1341
Nicholas *de* Hunts 1308-1329   Cristina 1318-1341 dau   Cristina 1326
                            of Adam Grinde
                            Amicia wife of 1308

Paxton [only]
probable kin: Walter *de* 1281
               Cristina *de* 1284

PAYS *see* PAGE

PEDDER
Richard 1342   Isolda 1342

PEEK (PECK)
unknown   Elena 1295   John 1295   Cristina 1282-1303
Thomas 1366-1387   Emma 1386-1387   Agnes 1282
probable kin: Godfrey 1290   Elena 1283-1299
               Alan 1295   Dionysia 1340-1349
               Richard 1295
               William 1365-1399

PEKENOT
John   unknown   Godfrey 1347

PELLAGE
unknown   Pellagia 1293   John 1278-1313 (c)
John (c)   Phillipa 1297-1313   Henry 1292-1335 (c)
                                                       William 1299-1347 (c)
Henry (c)   unknown   Godfrey 1325-1345 (d)
William (c)   Cristina 1331
John   Amicia Bole 1316-1324
probable kin: Matilda 1344

Family Name and Husband	Wife	Son(s)	Daughter(s)
PELLIPARIUS see PAGE and SKINNER			
PENEMAN (PENNYMAN)			
Godfrey sen 1290-1325	unknown	Godfrey 1322-1348 / Robert 1331 / Robert 1317 / William 1317-1332 (c)	Anabel 1329
unknown	Juliana 1292	William 1293-1304 (c)	Mabel 1306
William (c)	Emma 1331		
Seman 1292	unknown		
William (c)	Isolda 1304		
Simon 1348-1391 (d)	Ivetta 1348		
Godfrey jun 1362-1373	Cristina 1362		
probable kin: Richard 1299			
Cristina 1349 (d)			
Godfrey sen 1352-1372			
PENT'			
Henry de Hunts	unknown	Roger 1298-1299	
PENTIL see PEYSEL			
PERNEL			
Richard 1310-1322 (d)	Emma 1310-1315 (2nd) Albrida 1322-1344		
William de West St. 1283-1317 (d)	Emma 1327 (d)	William 1310-1332 (c) / Walter 1318-1332 (c) / Robert 1329-1345 (c) / John 1332	
William (c)	Agnes 1325		
Walter (c)	Agnes 1341		

Robert (c)	Cristina 1345	Thomas 1350-1376 (c)	Emma 1356
John* 1351	unknown	William 1351-1386 (c)	Emma 1355
		John 1363-1375 (d) (c)	
		William 1353-1390	
		Simon 1353 (d)	
Thomas (c)	unknown		
William (c)	unknown		
John (c)	Agnes 1375		
William 1386-1399	Sybil 1399		
probable kin: William *de* Arnyng St. 1360-1361 (d)			
Godfrey 1358-1372			
Thomas jun 1387-1388			

PERSON *see* PARSON

PETER

Lawrence 1344	Felicia 1344	Henry 1341-1343	Agnes 1333-1341

PEYNTOUR

Godfrey 1333	unknown
probable kin: Cristina 1280	
Reginald 1338-1342	
Richard 1344	

PEYSEL (PEYCIL, PENTIL)

John 1324-1354 (d)	Agnes 1324	Thomas 1327-1361 (c)	Amicia 1372
Thomas (c)	wife 1340		
probable kin: John 1356-1367 (d)			
William 1376			

PHINTE

John *le* 1281	Ivetta 1281
probable kin: Isolda Phintina 1280	

Family Name and Husband	Wife	Son(s)	Daughter(s)
PICARD			
Asbern *de* Hunts 1352	Emma 1352		
PICK (PIK)			
Umfrey 1298	Mariota 1298		
probable kin: Matilda 1280			
Emma 1282			
Simon 1282			
PIKIRING			
Robert 1282	Isolda 1282-1329		Agnes 1303
			Cristina 1303
			Phillipa 1339-1349
John 1326-1356 (d)	unknown	John 1340	
probable kin: Albrida 1284 (d)			
Roger 1335			
PISCATOR *see* **FISHER**			
PISTOR (BAKER)			
John 1282-1304	unknown		Caterina 1294
			Edith 1294
Alan 1285	wife 1285		
Richard 1280-1295	Margaret 1280-1295		
Godfrey (c)	unknown	Godfrey 1310 (c)	
probable kin: William 1283		Robert 1310	
Agnes 1301		Richard 1311	
Robert 1389			
Thomas *de* Hunts 1394			

PLOMER
John 1364-1394 (d) Agnes 1364-1369 formerly
the wife of Roger
Manipenny

probable kin: John de Westakre 1349
John 1351-1367
Simon 1391

PLOUGHWRIGHTE (PLOWRIGHT)
Robert 1330 unknown Henry 1330
Thomas de Offord Deneys Amicia 1361
1361-1367

probable kin: Thomas de Stukeley 1340-1341
Thomas, manens at ye mil cros 1356
Thomas 1356
Thomas at ye Stambourne 1360
Simon le 1350-1363
William de Hemingford 1373

PLUMBE
William 1349-1350 unknown

PLUMPTON
John 1380-1432 Agnes 1395

P'NOT
Robert 1305 Alice 1305

POPE (PAPE)
Ralph 1278-1294 unknown Eusebius 1298-1316 (c)
Eusebius (c) Agnes 1316 John 1298-1340 (c)
Agnes 1325-1329 husband called
Reginald and son John

Family Name and Husband	Wife	Son(s)	Daughter(s)
John (c)	Isolda 1340-1346	Simon 1281-1298	
Alexander	unknown		
Robert 1352-1378	Agnes 1367-1375		
probable kin: Henry 1342-1350			
William 1346			
Cristina 1347-1350 (d)			
Cristina 1354			
John 1364			
Nicholas *de* Hunts 1372			
PORTER			
Henry 1282	Alice 1282		
Lawrence *de* Walton 1335-1347	Mariota 1335-1347		
PORTHOS			
John *de* Hemingford Abbots	unknown	Walter 1340	
Nicholas 1380-1381	unknown	all his sons 1380	
probable kin: John *de* Brampton 1394			
PRECHETERE			
John 1363-1365	Sybil 1365-1380		
PRENTYS			
Richard 1391	unknown	John 1393	
probable kin: Andrew *de* Croxton 1387			
PRESBYTER (PRIEST, PRESTESSON)			
Simon 1281 (d)	unknown	William 1281	
		Reginald 1282-1299	
		John 1291	

Robert 1348   unknown   Thomas 1348
probable kin: Godfrey 1280
            Isolda 1287
            Beatrix 1296-1298
            Eustace 1306

PSALSE
Robert 1281   unknown   Luke 1281 (c)
Luke (c)   Alice 1281

PUTTOCK
unknown   Emma 1280   Robert 1280   Amicia 1280
                     Simon 1280
                     John 1316-1326 (c)

Richard *de* Yelling   unknown   John 1354-1360
John (c)   Alditha 1326   William 1354
John *de* Yelling   unknown

PYKENOT
Pykenot   unknown   Matilda dau of 1308
                                  Emma dau of 1308
                                  Alice dau of 1308

John 1324   Agnes 1324

PYSFORD
William 1377-1386   Matilda 1377

QUENYNG
Osbert 1279-1306   unknown   Richard 1295-1299 (c)   Matilda 1299
                                Henry 1299-1304
                                John 1320
                                John 1330-1339 (c)
                                Phillip 1344 (d)

Richard (c)   Matilda 1295-1298
John of London St. 1314-1329   unknown

Family Name and Husband	Wife	Son(s)	Daughter(s)
John (c)	unknown	John jun 1360-1395 (c)	
John jun (c)	Beatrix 1360-1388		
John, butcher 1325-1339	Emma 1348	John 1339-1346 (c)	Cristina 1341
		Reginald 1339-1341 (c)	Isolda 1341
		Roger 1342	
John (c)	Amabilia 1342		
Reginald (c)	wife 1346		
John of West St. 1329	unknown	John 1329-1341	
John sen of Post St. 1331-1347	unknown		Phillipa 1347
John of Mileslane 1347	unknown		Phillipa 1347
John* 1346-1350 (d)	Cristina 1346 dau of John son of Henry		
Nicholas 1350-1373	Pellagia 1362-1366	William 1361-1397 (c)	
William (c)	Agnes 1374		
John 1353-1357	Sybil 1361	Thomas 1353-1388 (c)	
Thomas	Cristina 1361-1367	John 1391	
Richard 1356	unknown	John 1367	
John	Matilda 1366 (d)		Matilda 1359
John*	unknown	Godfrey (c)	
Godfrey (c)	Amabilia 1361		
John* sen 1371-1397	unknown	John 1395	
QUENYNG DE THORLEY			
Godfrey 1288-1301 (d)	Mabel 1312	John 1294 (d) (c)	Agnes 1295, husband John Manipenny 1312
John (c)	Isolda widow 1294 re-marries Eustace de Thorley	John son of Isolda and John 1298-1313 (c)	Sybil 1302

John (c)
Eustace *de* Thorley 1294-1316

Agnes 1303
Isolda Quenyng widow of John 1294-1319

Walter son of Eustace 1302 (c)
Thomas son of Eustace 1291-1316
John son of Eustace 1299-1302

Leticia 1308
Caterina 1308
Amicia 1308
Helen 1325

Walter (c)

Ivetta 1309

Godfrey 1308-1346 (c)

Godfrey (c)

unknown

John 1324-1329
Nicholas 1324-1347

probable kin: Gilbert 1279
William 1308
Henry, tinctor living at Biggleswade 1325
Elias 1349
Thomas sen 1360-1378
Reginald 1393

Cristina 1391

DE QUY
John 1391
probable kin: John 1366

RABAT
John *de* Godmanchester 1351-1353
Joan widow 1368-1372
probable kin: William *de* Graveley 1368-1372

DE RADWELL
Simon
probable kin: William *de* Hunts 1374

unknown

Robert 1357

Family Name and Husband	Wife	Son(s)	Daughter(s)
RAG			
Edward 1297	Isolda 1297		
SON OF RALPH			
Ralph	unknown	John 1351-1377 (c)	Juliana 1361
		Henry (c)	
John (c)	unknown	Alan 1357	
Henry (c)	unknown	William 1353-1367 (c)	Matilda 1356
William (c)	unknown		
RANDOLPH			
Randolph	unknown	Henry 1342-1356	
		Hugh 1349	
DE RAVELEY			
William	unknown		Matilda 1291-1320 married to William Maddermonger 1325
			Cristina 1291-1295
John, lister de St. Neots 1342	Margaret 1342		
probable kin: John 1334			
RAVEN			
unknown	Cristina 1281-1306	John 1316	
		Stephen 1316 (c)	
Stephen (c)	Emma 1327		
RAY			
Edward 1280-1291	Isolda 1280-1291		Amicia 1291-1320
probable kin: Reginald le 1278			
Roger 1279-1280			
Godfrey 1303			

RED

Richard *le* — unknown
Nicholas 1281-1306 — unknown — Amicia 1293
    William 1313 (c)
    Robert 1325-1347
    John 1329-1360
    William 1324-1354

William (c) — unknown
probable kin: Amicia 1350 (d)
    Richard 1351
    Roger *le* 1354 (d)
    Mathew *de* Hunts 1357

REDE (RUBE, RUS, RONS)[f]

Roger 1281-1288 — wife of 1293 (d)
    Robert 1281-1294
    Simon 1281-1320 (c)
    William 1293-1315, 1317 (d)

Simon (c) — unknown
Roger (c) *de* Godmanchester — unknown
    Roger 1308-1324 (c)
    William *de* Godmanchester 1304-1316

Martin *le de* Hunts 1288-1298 — unknown — Agnes 1316-1332
    William sen 1298-1311
    William jun 1306-1311
    Ralph 1291-1346
    Martin *de* Hunts 1306-1344 (d) (c)

Martin *de* Hunts (c) — Jacoba 1325-1327 (d)
    John *de* Hunts 1343-1348
    Thomas *de* Hunts 1343-1389 (c)

[f] These variants appear only in the 1290s; by the 1300s only "Rede" appears.

Family Name and Husband	Wife	Son(s)	Daughter(s)
Thomas (c)	Matilda 1378-1382		
Richard 1292-1301	Amicia Hopay 1294-1301		
Robert *de* Hunts 1286	Alice 1286		
William sen 1333-1347	unknown	Richard 1333-1348 (c)	
Richard (c)	Sybil 1349-1353		
William jun 1329-1347	unknown	William 1329-1344	
William *de* Hunts 1345	Pellagia 1345	Roger 1345-1361 (d)	
Nicholas	unknown	John 1353	
John 1363-1397	Helen 1364-1379		
probable kin: John *le* 1281-1299			
Alice 1316			
Walter *de* Hunts 1331-1345			
Dionysia maidservant of Martin 1332			
Cristina 1340-1348			
Edward 1341			
Matilda 1349			
Robert 1352			
Reginald 1361			
Mabel *le* 1360			
William, vicar *de* Godmanchester 1387-1389			
REDELYSTER (RIDILISTER)			
William *le* 1302-1322	Cristina 1302-1303		Emma 1322
REDER			
John 1327-1347	Amicia 1327		
probable kin: John *de* St. Ives 1375, 1380			
John *de* Chesterton 1399			

REGINALD[8]			
Robert	unknown	Reginald 1278 (c)	Cristina 1322
Reginald (c)	Cristina 1278	John 1278-1316 (d) (c)	Cristina sen 1301-1316
		Godfrey 1298-1312 (d) (c)	Cristina jun 1301
John (c)	Joan 1316	Henry 1301-1346	
		Thomas 1301-1302	
		Walter 1301	
		Gilbert 1301-1346 (c)	Amicia 1301-1313
Godfrey (c)	unknown	John 1301-1347	
		Godfrey 1312 (d)	
Gilbert (c)	Elena 1329		
SON OF REGINALD			
Reginald	unknown	John son of 1316	
		John son of 1316	
		Gilbert son of 1316	
Reginald	Agnes 1329	John son of 1349 (c)	
John (c)	unknown	Reginald 1349	
Reginald	unknown	John son of 1360-1362 (c)	
John* (c)	Alice 1362		
Reginald	unknown	Roger son of 1366-1377 (c)	
Roger (c)	Agnes 1366-1377		
REINS (RENIS)			
Nicholas 1286	unknown	Robert 1286-1301	
probable kin: John 1283-1291			

[8] This is a clear indication of a patronymic change. This family began as "Robert" but soon changed to "Reginald," dropping the name "Robert." For example: Reginald son of Robert 1278; Godfrey son of Reginald son of Robert; John son of Reginald, Godfrey son of Reginald: John son of Godfrey son of Reginald. As the generations continue it was known only by the surname "Reginald." This family is not to be confused with the next one, "son of Reginald."

Family Name and Husband	Wife	Son(s)	Daughter(s)
REMER			
John 1356	Matilda 1356		
RENIS *see* REINS			
REVE			
Robert de Hunts 1311	Alice 1311		
William *le* 1334	unknown	Richard 1334	
probable kin: Thomas 1360-1395			
John 1361			
REYNOLD			
Nicholas 1317-1322	Albrida 1317-1322		
Henry 1349-1356	Cristina 1349, widow by 1361		
John 1350-1399	unknown	William 1353-1361	
		Richard 1362	
		John 1363	
SON OF RICHARD			
Richard	unknown	John son of 1278-1348	
		Thomas son of 1279	
		Eusebius son of 1278	
RICHER			
Godfrey 1302-1318	Joan 1302		
	(2nd) Matilda 1320		
RIDILISTER *see* REDELYSTER			
AD RIPAM			
Robert 1320	unknown	Richard 1326	
probable kin: Edith 1327			

DE RIPTON
unknown   William 1314-1315
             Master William 1314
             (these two are brothers)

probable kin: Godfrey 1280
               Master John 1284-1295
               John *de* Graveley, masoun 1301
               Robert *de* 1300

AD RISSIS *see* AD CIRPOS

RISSLE (RISLE)
William 1340-1348   Matilda 1340-1348
Thomas 1345-1347   unknown

Ro (Roo)
unknown   unknown   John 1351-1380 (c)
                                   William 1351 (d) (c)

John (c)   Emma 1372-1380
William (c)   Beatrix 1351
probable kin: William 1382. 1394

SON OF ROBERT
Robert   unknown   Nicholas, *de* Over 1308
Robert   unknown   John 1312-1326 (c)
                                     Godfrey 1316-1329
John (c)   unknown   Thomas 1345-1349
                                     John 1345-1376 (c)
John (c)   Margaret 1361-1375   Reginald 1360
Robert   unknown   John, *de* Paxton 1361

Isabella 1345
Pellagia 1347

Family Name and Husband	Wife	Son(s)	Daughter(s)
ROBYN			
William 1347	Emma 1347 h		
William de Hemingford Abbots	Felicia 1372		
John 1362-1382	Cristina 1378-1382	Thomas 1372-1382	
probable kin: John 1341, 1381 sen			
Thomas, butcher 1390-1394			
John 1390-1392			
RODE			
unknown	unknown	Eustace 1278 (c)	
		Robert 1278-1329 (d) (c)	
		Edward 1333-1361 (d) (c)	
Eustace (c)	unknown		
Edward (c)	Cristina 1356-1361		
Robert (c)	Isolda 1280-1287	William 1286-1295 (c)	Cristina 1297-1344 (d)
			Mariota 1297-1306
			Margaret 1316
			Isolda 1316
William (c)	Mariota 1311		
William* 1289	unknown	William 1289	
Roger 1292	unknown	Robert 1299-1302	
		William 1308	
Simon 1295	unknown	Henry 1297-1345 (d) (c)	
Henry (c)	unknown	Henry 1343-1348 (c)	

h Emma's mother's name is Elena 1347.

Henry (c)	Elizabeth 1343-1346	Richard 1316	Helen 1280
Rode 1316	Cristina wife of Rode 1316 (d)	Henry 1331-1342	
Lawrence 1326-1348	unknown	John 1335-1345	
		Thomas 1341-1378	Cristina, de Abbots Ripton 1353
			Margaret 1332-1342
			Margaret 1391

Reginald 1351 (d)	Emma 1351-1371	
Richard 1351-1375	Sybil 1351-1366	John 1351-1379 (c)
probable kin: Richard 1281		
Alexander 1295		
Reginald 1353-1389		

SON OF ROGER

Roger	unknown	Simon 1316-1340
		William 1316-1340
Roger	unknown	Simon, de Hunts 1339-1340
		William, de Hunts 1339-1340
Roger	unknown	Reginald 1361-1376
Roger	unknown	John de Hemingford Abbots 1360
Roger	unknown	

probable kin: Lord Roger, chaplain 1302

ROKYSTON

Henry 1375	Sybil 1375

ROME

Richard jun 1294-1346 (d)	Joan 1313
Richard sen 1318-1349	Pellagia, dead by 1343
John (c)	Cristina 1379-1386

RONS see REDE

ROO see RO

Family Name and Husband	Wife	Son(s)	Daughter(s)
ROTE			
William *de* Hunts 1361-1363	Agnes 1361		
probable kin: Thomas 1363			
ROWUSOR			
John *de* Bluntisham 1373	Sybil 1373		
AT YE ROYSIS			
John 1351	unknown	Henry 1351	Albrida 1354
Godfrey	unknown		
probable kin: William 1352-1357			
RUBE, RUS *see* REDE			
RUSSEL			
Henry *de* Hemingford	unknown	Godfrey 1297 (c)	
Godfrey (c)	Matilda, dau of Matilda Hus Hog 1297		
John *de* Hunts 1302-1341	Leticia 1302		
Simon 1349-1360	Sybil 1351-1360		
probable kin: Walter 1304			
William, chapman 1353			
John, chaplain of church *de* Knapwell 1387			
RYNIS			
unknown	Emma 1280		Agnes 1280
SALY			
Robert 1308-1332	Isabella 1332		
SANDONE			
Richard 1369	unknown	William 1369	

SAUNDRESSON
John 1366 (d) — Agnes 1366 — Matilda 1311-1313

SAVAGE
Simon 1291-1304 — unknown
probable kin: William 1280-1317
　　　　　　 Alexander de Stukeley 1320
　　　　　　 Andrew 1321-1324
　　　　　　 Alexander 1347 (d)

AD SCHALAM ECCLESIA
Henry 1281 (d) — unknown
William (c) — Helen 1281 — William 1281 (d) (c)
　　　　　　　　　　　　 John 1281-1282
　　　　　　　　　　　　 Amicia 1281
probable kin: William 1292

SCHOLAR
John, master de Hunts 1380 — Pellagia 1380

SCOT
Roger 1279 — unknown — Richard 1280-1299 (d) (c)
　　　　　　　　　　 Robert 1280-1301 (d) (c)
　　　　　　　　　　 John 1316-1337 (c)
　　　　　　　　　　 Robert 1312
　　　　　　　　　　 Cristina 1280

Richard (c) — Emma 1283-1333 (d) — Margaret 1302-1329, married to
　　　　　　　　　　　　　　　　　　　 John de Haveley
　　　　　　　　　　　　　　　　　 Alice 1312-1331
　　　　　　　　　　　　　　　　　 Juliana 1313-1333, married to
　　　　　　　　　　　　　　　　　　　 Gilbert Loxunt
　　　　　　　　　　　　　　　　　 Isabella 1301-1344, married to
　　　　　　　　　　　　　　　　　　　 Godfrey son of Eusebius
　　　　　　　　　　　　　　　　　 Aylred 1303

Robert (c) — Emma 1287-1295 — Cristina 1341
　　　　　　　　　　　　　　 Phillipa 1341
　　　　　　　　　　　　　　 Emma 1348

John (c) — Phillipa 1326-1340

Family Name and Husband	Wife	Son(s)	Daughter(s)
Edward *de* Papworth			
William 1281 (d)	unknown	Thomas 1280	
Alan 1301 (d)	Agnes Alrith 1281	John 1301-1316	
	unknown	Simon 1307-1335 (c)	
Simon (c)	Cristina 1312-1326	John 1312	Alice 1323
Adam *de* Hunts	unknown		Margaret 1323
Roger *de* Hunts 1342 (d)	unknown	William *de* Hunts 1340-1363	
Simon	unknown	Godfrey 1338-1346	
		William 1346-1379 (c)	
William (c)	Emma 1351-1389, dau of	Henry 1349-1377	
	William Colier		
John, bercarius 1350-1357	unknown		
probable kin: John 1279			
Hugh 1280			
Lord John, chaplain 1299			
Edward 1304			
John 1304			
William jun, *de* Hunts 1360-1368			
SEGES			
William *de* Hartford 1356	unknown	John 1353, 1362	
SELDE			
John *de* Hemingford Abbots 1372 (d)	unknown	John 1372	
		William 1372-1397	
probable kin: John *de* Holywell 1373			

SEMAN

William 1278	unknown	John 1298-1311	Helen 1314
Osbert 1279-1298	Alice 1280-1290		Matilda 1314
John 1279-1302 (d)	Felicia 1302	John 1295-1322	
		Godfrey 1298-1322	
		Reginald 1310-1337 (d) (c)	
		Stephen 1324-1331 (c)	
		Godfrey 1326-1332, 1330	
		de Arnyng St.	
Reginald (c)	Sybil 1330-1345		
Stephen (c)	Sybil 1354 (d)	William 1291-1316	
Godfrey	unknown	Eustace 1297-1329 (c)	
Simon 1297 (d)	Isolda 1297-1300	John 1297	
Eustace (c)	Isabella 1307-1345	Henry 1325	Millicent 1329
John 1321	Margaret 1321	John 1332-1342	Pellagia 1333-1349
Godfrey*	unknown	John 1329 (d)	
Thomas 1329 dead by 1346	unknown		Amicia 1345
John 1345	Emma *de* Papworth 1345	William, lockyere	
Robert, lockyere 1350-1390	unknown	1366-1390 (c)	
William (c)	Juliana 1372-1373		
probable kin: Matilda 1310 (d)			

SEREWEKS

unknown	Matilda 1347	John 1347

SEWSTERE

Thomas, masoun 1393-1395	Alice 1395
probable kin: Isabella 1373	

Family Name and Husband	Wife	Son(s)	Daughter(s)
SHEPHERD			
Nicholas *de* Papworth 1332-1347	Cassandra 1332-1347		
DE SHYRFORD (SHEREFORD)			
Simon 1302	Amicia 1302	Richard 1302	
William 1308-1309	Matilda 1308-1309		
probable kin: Walter 1291-1308			
SON OF SIMON			
Simon	unknown	Robert son of 1279	
		William son of 1279-1325 (c)	
		Godfrey son of 1280-1287	
		Reginald son of, chaplain 1283-1314	
William (c)	Amicia 1307-1312	John 1308 (c)	Amicia 1307-1312
John (c)	Ivetta 1308	William 1320 (c)	Amicia 1308
William (c)	unknown	Robert 1332	
Simon	unknown	Thomas son of 1365	
		Richard son of 1378-1389 (c)	
Richard (c)	Cristina 1382	William son of 1394-1423 (c)	
Simon	unknown	Henry 1394	
William (c)	unknown		
SKRIVEN			
SKINNER (PELLIPARIUS)			
Godfrey 1344	unknown	John 1344-1350	
Martin 1287	unknown		Isabella 1287
John 1350-1369	Pellagia 1360-1367		Cristina 1349

probable kin: John *de* Houghton 1335
John jun 1349
William 1349
William *de* St. Neots 1399

SLAIURIRE
unknown   Cristina 1280   Isabella 1280

SLY
John *de* Hemingford Abbots   Cristina 1362-1387
1362-1365
probable kin: William 1350-1373
Richard 1369-1390
Alan 1383-1391

SMITH *see* **FABER**

SOFYN
Robert 1340   unknown   John 1340

SOMAYSTER
John *de* Hunts   Margaret 1354-1371

DE SOMERSHAM
Robert *de* Hunts 1325   Margaret 1325

SOMMENOUR
Ralph *le*, *de* Offord Cluny   unknown
1297
        Lord Godfrey
        1297-1306 (d) (c)
        Andrew 1306 (c)
        Henry 1306
        Thomas 1325
        John 1306

Lord Godfrey (c)   unknown
Andrew (c)   unknown

SOMYRTON
Bartholomew 1381-1399   Cristina 1388, 1393

Family Name and Husband	Wife	Son(s)	Daughter(s)
SOUTER see SUTOR			
DE SOUTHOE			
John 1372-1379	Agnes 1379, 1390		
DE SPALDWICK			
Roger 1307	Cristina Atenok 1307		
Robert 1394	unknown	William 1394	
		Simon 1394	
		Henry 1394	
DE SPALDING			
Robert 1285	Alice 1285		
	(2nd) Mariota 1302		
probable kin: Ralph 1284			
SPARWE			
John 1350-1361	Sybil 1361		
SPICER (APOTEKARIUS)			
John 1283-1299	unknown	Reginald 1301-1311 (c)	Agnes 1292
		Edward 1302-1329 (c)	Mabel 1301-1302
		John 1334-1335	Matilda 1334
Reginald (c)	Agnes dau of Alan Lutgate	Richard 1334-1335	Cristina, married to Adam de
	1302	Robert 1338	Blaysworth 1334
Edward (c)	Cristina 1340		
probable kin: Henry 1282			
Thomas le 1300			
Alister le 1360			
Thomas de Hunts 1366			

SPRAG
John *de* Hunts 1352　　Emma 1352

SPRUNTYNG
Reginald 1295-1322　　Agnes 1295
Roger (c)　　Masceline dau of Thomas
　　　　　　　Hildemar 1311 (d)
　　　　　　　(2nd) Albrida dau of Nicholas
　　　　　　　　　　1317-1346

Roger de Arnyng St. 1311 (c)　　Isolda de Arnyng St. 1306
　　　　　　　　　　　　　　　　Isolda 1329

Henry 1301-1313 (c)
John 1300-1327 (c)
Thomas 1322-1327
Henry 1313-1325 (c)
Godfrey 1327
William 1327

Matilda 1350

Henry　　unknown

Henry (c)　　unknown

Sybil ad Crucem 1325
Isabella 1316
Rose
Agnes 1353-1366
Matilda 1367

Henry (c)　　unknown
John (c)
unknown
Henry 1350-1397
William 1367
Roger
probable kin:　Eustace 1282
　　　　　　　　William 1283
　　　　　　　　Mariota 1344
　　　　　　　　Felicia 1344
　　　　　　　　Henry jun 1358
　　　　　　　　Henry, lockyer 1372

Simon 1354-1367

Family Name and Husband	Wife	Son(s)	Daughter(s)
STALUM			
Michael *de* Waresley	unknown		
DE STAMFORD			
John 1380	unknown	William 1380	
DE STANTON			
unknown	unknown	John, chaplain 1351 / Thomas brother of John 1352	
STARTLE			
Elias	unknown	William Page 1280-1295 (c); Startle^i 1289-1298	
Willam Page	Emma Amiont 1281-1298	John Page 1303-1315 (d); also known as Startle^i	
John sen* 1298	Isolda 1311		Matilda 1302-1311 / Cristina 1302-1311
John jun 1304-1314 (d)	Cristina 1315 (d)	William 1314-1315 (d) / John 1315-1316 (c)	Helen 1314
John (c)	Amicia 1316-1317		
Thomas 1311	unknown	William 1311	
William	Amabilia 1325-1329, 1340	John 1348	Matilda 1340
John 1329-1349 (d)	Elena 1340-1388		
Godfrey 1347-1358	unknown	John 1347	
William 1394	unknown	John 1394	

^i William is known as "William son of Elias Startle" and "William Page son of Elias Startle"; as well William's son John is known both as "Page" and "Startle." This particular family is not to be confused with the "Page (Pays)" family; very likely the "Page" in this instance indicates the occupation of both William and John.

probable kin: Stephen 1291
John jun 1331-1335
Isabella 1350
John 1361, 1365
Henry 1378 (d)

STIRCUP
Nicholas 1315-1329   Agnes 1315-1329

probable kin: Adam 1345-1349

STEPHEN
Stephen   unknown   Henry 1349
Robert (c)   unknown   William 1349

DE STIRTLOE
John 1307-1345 (d)   Mariota 1307-1345   Robert 1287 (c)
John (c)   Mabel 1333-1379   Ontitius 1321
John 1378-1379   Joan 1378-1379

probable kin: Thomas 1320   John 1321-1365 (c)
Cecilia 1345
Adam 1356   Alice 1343-1348

STOKE
John 1362-1369   Agnes 1363-1372

STONDON
Paul 1335-1340 (d)   Emma 1335-1340   John 1340

DE STRATESHILL
Gilbert see GONI   Emma Goni see GONI
Adam 1310-1332   Matilda 1310-1332   Cristina see GONI

probable kin: Lord Roger, chaplain 1291-1322

Family Name and Husband	Wife	Son(s)	Daughter(s)
STRUT			
Godfrey 1326	Emma 1326		Elena 1333
			Emma 1334
			Cristina 1334
probable kin: the daughters of John 1303			
Nicholas 1329-1347			
Alice 1340			
DE STUKELEY			
William 1288-1298	unknown	William 1317-1319	
		Richard 1325	
unknown	unknown	Thomas 1332 (c)	
		Nicholas brother of Thomas 1344-1347	
Thomas (c)	Margaret Luicda 1332		
William	Matilda 1342	John 1360-1368	
Robert 1351-1385	Elena 1363, 1387		
probable kin: Alan de 1291			
Lord Walter de, chaplain 1312-1333			
STURPAYN			
Simon 1340	unknown	John 1340	
STYGENEYE			
John de Cambridge 1346	Sybil 1346		
STYKEDET			
John 1316	Amicia 1316		

SUTOR (SOUTER)

William 1280-1284	unknown	Reginald *de* Alconbury 1280-1327 (c)	Isolda 1280
			Agnes 1318
			Mariota 1318
			Sybil 1318
Reginald (c)	Cristina 1304-1307	Godfrey *de* Alconbury 1325-1327 (c)	
Godfrey *de* Alconbury (c)	Cristina 1327	John 1332-1341 (c)	
John 1280	Mariota 1280	Henry 1333-1340	
Ralph 1299-1312	Ingryd 1299		
John (c)	Agnes 1333		
William 1351-1366	Mabel 1365-1366		
probable kin: Robert 1287			
Ralph *de* Offord Cluny 1338			

SWAN *see* **SWON**

SWETMAN

Godfrey	unknown	John 1353	

DE SWINESHEAD

Henry 1278-1279	Alice 1278-1279		

SWON (SWAN)

Robert *le* 1295	unknown		Madda 1295
			Emma 1295
Simon *le*	unknown	Richard *le* 1302 (c)	
Richard (c)	Matilda 1302		
William 1332	Cristina 1332		
Reginald 1344	Sybil 1344		
John 1358	Constance 1358		
probable kin: Ralph *le* 1335			

Family Name and Husband	Wife	Son(s)	Daughter(s)
SWYNFORD			
Roger 1389	Elena 1389		
SYER			
Adam *de* Hemingford Grey 1333	Beatrix 1333		
probable kin: John *de* Hemingford Grey 1315			
SYLE			
Stephen 1353	Sybil, dau of John Colowot 1353		
TABBE			
unknown	Cristina 1325	William 1325	
		John 1325-1359 (c)	
John (c)	Alice 1339		
TABER *see* TAVERNER			
TANNER			
John 1278	Cecilia 1278		
probable kin: Thomas 1326			
TAVERNER (TABER)			
Alan *de* Hunts 1349-1366	Agnes 1366		Isabella 1349-1350
TAYLOR			
Richard 1325	Cristina dau of Roger Maddermonger 1325		
Walter *le, de* Dorchester 1344	unknown	John 1344 (c)	
John (c)	Emma 1344		

Henry 1346-1348
Bartholomew 1352-1381
Richard 1352-1353
John de Sibthorpe
Robert (c)
probable kin: Jurdan le, de Hemingford 1298-1301
William 1356-1376
Godfrey 1361
Thomas de London Street 1363, 1381
John de Hunts, fisher 1364
Robert de Ellington 1369
Walter de Papworth 1362
Robert de Pittisle (Pidley?) 1380
Roger 1380
William de Fen Drayton 1393
Thomas jun 1393
William 1399
John 1399

Sybil 1346-1348 j
Isolda 1354-1377
Margaret 1361-1367
unknown
Agnes 1372

Thomas 1359-1372
John 1366
Robert 1372 (c)

TEBAND
John de Yelling 1306
William (c)

unknown
Mabel 1306

William 1306 (c)

TESARD
John 1279-1302

Emma dau of Richard
Millicent 1279
(2nd) Isolda 1303

j Sybil's father's name is Robert and she has a sister called Elizabeth 1346.

Family Name and Husband	Wife	Son(s)	Daughter(s)
TEXTOR			
Henry 1283	unknown	Stephan 1295	
TEYE (TYE)			
Henry *de* Hunts 1366-1367	Phillipa 1361-1366		
THACHER *see* COOPERATOR ROTARUM *and* COUPER			
DE THAME			
unknown	Matilda 1380		Margaret 1380
THODENHAM *see* DE TODENHAM			
THOGOD *see* TOGOD			
SON OF THOMAS			
Thomas	unknown	John 1306	
THOME			
Richard 1342	unknown	Richard jun 1342 (d) (c)	Cristina 1342-1356 (d)
Richard jun (c)	unknown	Henry 1350-1374 (lockyer 1361-1374)	
probable kin: Walter, chaplain formerly *de* Papworth 1340			
Roger 1348			
DE THORLEY *see* QUENYNG			
THORN *see* THYKTHORN			
THRESSHERE			
Thomas 1361	Caterina 1361		
probable kin: Simon *de* Cornwall 1349			
Simon 1373			
Richard 1395			
THRUMBOLT			
John 1318	Isolda 1315	Reginald 1318	

Edward 1308-1325, 1333	Cristina 1325-1345 (d)	John 1335
Reginald*	unknown	Richard 1335-1338
		Robert 1339-1341
		Helen 1315

probable kin: Agnes 1308, 1333
Reginald 1308, 1345 [k]

THURLBY

John 1377-1388	Margaret 1377-1388	William 1393

THYKTHORN (THORN)[l]

William 1372-1396	Agnes 1374-1396

probable kin: Thomas 1376

TINCTOR

William de Hunts 1279-1280	Gunnilda 1298	
Peter de Hemingford 1281-1299	Agnes 1281-1285	Nicholas 1299-1309
Roger de Hunts 1283-1300 (d)	Mariota 1283-1299 nee Freman [m]	
Sarle 1298-1315	Beatrix 1315	John 1298
		William 1298-1299
		John 1330
Richard	unknown	

probable kin: Richard de Hunts 1279
Richard de St. Neots 1321
Lawrence, see LISTER
Herry, see LISTER

[k] This Reginald could be the son of John.
[l] This surname changes to Thorn after 1372.
[m] Mariota's brother is Reginald Freman de Weston 1299.

Family Name and Husband	Wife	Son(s)	Daughter(s)
TINKER			
Henry 1327	Emma 1327		
DE TODENHAM (THODENHAM)			
Richard 1300-1320	Beatrice 1295-1316 (d)		Joan 1316
Henry 1313-1317 (d)	unknown		Sybil 1325
Richard* 1329	Margaret 1329		
probable kin: Hugh de 1283			
Roger de 1297			
TOGOD (THOGOD)			
Godfrey 1285-1295	unknown		Emma 1301
probable kin: Bartholomew 1281			
ATTE TOWNESHEND see AD CAPUD VILLE			
TRAPPE			
Nicholas de Hemingford Abbots	unknown	Thomas sen 1374-1393	
also known as Nicholas		Thomas jun de Hemingford	
Tanower 1373		Abbots 1374	
TRIPPE			
William 1293	Agnes 1293		
TRUMPESTON			
John 1302	Emma 1302		
TURK see AUGUSTINE			
TURNOUR			
Walter 1350-1351	Agnes 1350-1351	and children 1350	
probable kin: Nicholas 1378			
TYE see TEYE			

ULF
John 1309-1313 (d)
John sen *de* Offord Cluny 1364
probable kin: John 1362
    Matilda 1388, 1393
Cristina 1309-1312
unknown
John jun 1364, 1372

UNDELE *see* OUNDLE
UNDERLESPITEL
Henry 1316-1327
Sabina 1316-1349 (d) of
Hunts 1321[n]
Emma 1332-1349
Margaret 1332

UNDERNE
Albyn 1281
John (c)
unknown
Matilda 1308
John 1281 (c)
Cristina 1314

UNDERWODE
John 1302-1321
Reginald (c)
Thomas 1329-1363
Richard
probable kin: John jun 1357
    Roger 1365
Phillipa 1302-1321
Isolda 1342
Agnes 1350-1372
Sybil 1363
Reginald 1321-1345 (c)
John 1342
John 1351-1363

DE UPTON
Roger 1286
probable kin: the servant of Roger and Mariota 1286
Mariota 1286

UTEBAND
William *de* Yelling 1307
Mabel 1307

[n] Sabina has a sister called Margaret 1316.

Family Name and Husband	Wife	Son(s)	Daughter(s)
UTTING			
unknown	unknown	John, chaplain *de* Hunts 1340	Felicia 1340-1348
VALEY			
John 1329-1362	Isolda 1329-1345	Henry 1342-1373	Elena 1345 Sybil 1345 Cristina 1345, 1373
VECHAREM			
unknown	unknown		
John (c)	Felicia 1288-1297	John 1287-1297 (c)	Joan 1287-1289
VENELLA *see* IN THE LANE			
VICAR			
unknown	unknown	Godfrey son of 1298 John son of *de* Buckden 1350	
probable kin: Lord Simon of the church of Blessed Mary 1282 William *de* St. Ives 1283 Lord Richard 1326-1345 Thomas *de* Alconbury 1335 John 1350 Walter, chaplain 1373			
AD CAPUD VILLE (ATTE TOWNESHEND)			
Ralph *de* Hemingford 1294-1324 (d)	unknown	John 1324 Simon 1324 William 1304-1340 (c)	Agnes 1324 Agnes jun 1324 Isolda 1293-1311 Margaret 1308-1317
John 1295-1316	unknown	John 1311-1317	

William (c)			
Thomas 1303	Emma 1326-1329	John 1303	
	Phillipa 1303		
probable kin: Ralph 1342			
VICELOY			
William	unknown	Godfrey 1351	
VINCENT			
Vincent 1285-1306	Isolda 1285-1306		Millicent 1304
			Leticia 1304-1321
VITING			
John *de* Brampton 1299	Agnes 1299		
WAKE			
Richard *le* 1307	Mariota 1307		
WAKEFIELD			
John 1392-1398	Idonia 1392		
SUPER LE **WAL** *see* SUPER **MURAM**			
DE WALCOT			
John *de, de* Hunts 1348	Joan 1348 (d)		
probable kin: Simon 1330			
Roger *de, de* Hunts 1348			
Richard *de* Hunts 1375			
John 1390			
WALE			
John *de* Alconbury 1341	unknown	Richard 1341	Agnes 1341
probable kin: John 1338-1353			
John *de* Swavesey 1340-1344			
WALEYS (WALEIS)			
William 1298	Isolda 1298		
Simon 1309	unknown	Simon 1313-1317	
		John 1321	

Family Name and Husband	Wife	Son(s)	Daughter(s)
William 1326-1348	Cecilia 1329-1369	William 1354-1390 John 1367 (c)	
John (c)			
Henry 1351-1357	Matilda 1374 Matilda 1382		
probable kin: Reginald 1299 Richard 1352			
WALFROM			
Robert 1360	Margaret 1360	John 1360	
WALGATE			
Richard 1391	Margaret 1391		
WALSHE			
Reginald le in Post St. 1300-1306	Mariota 1300-1306		
Simon 1332	unknown	John 1332	
Walter 1390	Emma 1390		
probable kin: Reginald 1345 David le 1347, 1398 (Walshman) Griffin Walshman 1366 Thomas 1374 John le, taylor 1374 Walshman			
SON OF WALTER			
Walter 1280	Matilda 1280	Robert 1280 (c) Godfrey 1280	
Robert (c)	unknown		Felicia 1303 Constance 1303 Matilda 1303

Walter*   unknown   Nicholas son of 1278
                                                                                             Simon son of 1296-1303

WARDE
John 1313   Albrida 1313   Cristina 1313-1327
                                                                                             Isolda 1313-1321

Reginald 1340, 1364   Emma 1364
probable kin: Reginald 1298-1301
              Margaret de Walton 1344
              Cristina 1361
              John 1392

WARENTER see MADDERMONGER

DE WARESLEY
William 1331-1337   unknown   Robert 1341   Amicia 1341

DE WARMINGTON (WERMINGTON)
William, clerk 1291-1332   unknown   Margaret 1331 (c)
unknown   Margaret (c)   Isabella 1332
Simon 1295   unknown
probable kin: Walter canon de Lincs 1316

WARYN
John 1339   unknown   John 1339 Burgess de Hunts   Robert, chaplain 1299-1326
                                                             Robert 1339
                                                             Thomas 1339 (d)

probable kin: Walter de Papworth 1295
              William de Papworth 1300
              John de Papworth Agnes 1302
              Thomas de Papworth 1341-1347
              William de West St. 1345

Family Name and Husband	Wife	Son(s)	Daughter(s)
WAT'			
Robert	unknown	John 1315	
WATERLEDERE			
Alexander 1280	unknown	Simon 1280-1291	
WEBESTER			
Robert 1315	Isolda 1315		Amicia 1329
Fulconis 1329	unknown		
Bartholomew de Vicus	Mabel 1345 °		
Canonicorum 1345			
probable kin: William 1302			
ATTE WELLE (AD FONTEM)			
Richard 1283, 1293	unknown		Isabella 1293-1348 (c)
unknown	Isabella (c)		Cristina, married to Henry son of John son of Reginald Clerk, 1315
probable kin: Isolda 1303			
John de 1309			
Walter de Great Stukeley, chaplain 1324			
William de Great Stukeley 1321			
John, smith 1373			
DE WENNINGTON			
William, clerk 1314-1316	unknown	John 1314	

° Mabel's mother's name is Cristina 1345.

WENENT' (WENNINGTON?)

Robert	unknown	John 1308

WERMINGTON see WARMINGTON

WEST

Richard de Graveley 1362-1393	Elena dau of Regnald Denne 1380-1393		Helen 1361
	Margaret 1366-1398		Caterina 1361

John 1366-1398
probable kin: William de Graveley 1361

DE WESTON

Alan de Hunts 1330	unknown	John 1330 (c)	
John (c)	unknown		
John 1351-1367	Margaret 1351-1367		Alice de Hunts 1341

probable kin: Adam, burgess de Hunts 1341-1349
            John, chaplain, prior de Hunts 1353
            John sen 1366

WETYNG (WETHYNG)

William 1369-1399	Beatrix 1380-1383

WHITMAN see WITMAN

DE WIGGENHALL

Gregory 1332	unknown	Thomas 1332

WILDE

William le 1282-1292	Cristina 1282-1292	Henry 1286-1312 (c)	Mabel 1303-1311
			Isolda 1312
Henry (c)	Juliana 1320		

WILLE

Bartholomew 1298	unknown	Walter 1290-1302	Felicia 1290
		Robert 1298	

Family Name and Husband	Wife	Son(s)	Daughter(s)
SON OF WILLIAM			
William	unknown	John 1283 (c)	
John (c)	unknown		Amicia 1282
William*	unknown	Nicholas 1283-1295 (c)	Albrida 1308
			Elena 1308
Nicholas (c)	unknown	John 1310-1316	Sybil 1308
William*	unknown	Godfrey 1298 (c)	
Godfrey (c)	Felicia 1300	Roger 1298	
William	unknown	John 1309 (c)	
John (c)	Pellagia 1309	Henry 1325-1348 (c1)	
William	unknown	William brother of Henry 1325-1332 (c)	
Henry (c1)	Sybil 1329	Henry 1349-1364 (c2)	
Henry (c2)	Emma 1364	John 1349-1397 (c3)	
		William 1352-1360	
		Thomas 1375-1390	
John (c3)	unknown	John 1331-1344 (c4)	
William (c)	Cristina 1326-1332	John 1339-1340 (c5)	
William	unknown	Godfrey 1386	
John (c4)	Matilda 1332-1338	Michael (c)	
John (c5)	unknown	Godfrey 1335	
William	unknown	Richard son of 1317	
Michael (c)	unknown	Reginald son of 1346	
William*	unknown		

probable kin: Warent 1315
Richard, pistor *de* Hunts 1328
Thomas 1333
Edward 1344
John 1377
Henry 1387-1390

LITTLE WILLIAM
William   Alice *de* Hunts widow by 1297   William 1311

DE WIMBLINGTON
Godfrey 1295-1298   Isolda 1295-1298

DE WISTOW
William 1300-1333   and wife 1300
Nicholas, butcher 1331-1333   Sybil 1333, 1382   John 1382
probable kin: Emma 1342 (d)

WITMAN (WHITMAN, WYTHMAN, WYTEMAN)
William 1283-1302   unknown   William jun 1308-1344 (c)
Thomas 1308-1350 (c)
Godfrey 1331-1367
Nicholas 1356

William jun (c)   Agnes 1327-1344
Thomas (c)   Helen Goni dau of Roger 1313

John 1350-1388 (d)   Phillipa 1379-1390 (d)
probable kin: John, chaplain *de* Hunts 1361
John jun 1362-1372
Adam *de* King's Lynn 1399

DE WOLLASTON
Thomas 1341-1399   Emma 1369-1399

Cristina 1322

Family Name and Husband	Wife	Son(s)	Daughter(s)
WOLLE			
Nicholas 1349	Sybil 1349 [P]		
DE WOODSTONE			
Godfrey 1281	unknown	John 1281-1325 (c)	
John (c)	Isolda 1316		
WRIGHT			
Eustace le 1300	unknown		
Robert 1329	unknown	John 1300	
Simon ye 1350-1371	Agnes 1350 (d)	Roger 1329	
	(2nd) Cristina 1356-1376		
John 1364-1399	Caterina 1365		
Stephen	Emma 1366		
probable kin: Godfrey le 1334			
Nicholas 1365-1372			
Roger 1372-1392			
Alan de St. Ives 1378			
WULLEMAN			
Thomas 1386-1391	Agnes 1386-1391		
WYCE			
John 1316	unknown	Richard 1316	
WYLDEBRYD			
Peter 1311-1312	Isabella dau of Benedict Buxston 1311-1312		

[P] Sybil had a brother named Peter 1349.

WYGON
John 1361-1362 — Emma 1361-1362

WYKE
Richard 1387-1395 (d) — Alice 1388

WYMER
John 1333-1348 *de* Hunts 1345 — Agnes 1333-1348 — Mabel 1304
probable kin: William jun 1346

WYN
Simon 1291-1299 — Sarra 1291-1299
John 1293-1302 — unknown
Godfrey 1295-1316 — Cristina 1295-1316
probable kin: Nicholas 1313
Robert 1321-1326
William 1321

WYNIER
John *de* Hunts 1341-1366 (d) — unknown — John 1366
William 1362[q]
Simon 1366-1382 (c)

Simon (c) — Alice 1382

WYNOT
unknown — Matilda 1346 — John 1346

WYSDOM
Robert 1339-1346 — Matilda 1339-1346[r]
probable kin: Gilbert 1342-1346
WYTEMAN, WYTHMAN *see* WITMAN

[q] William is under 15 years of age in 1362 and therefore land passes to Simon.
[r] Matilda had a sister called Agnes 1339.

Family Name and Husband	Wife	Son(s)	Daughter(s)
WYTING			
Robert *de* Woodhurst	unknown	William 1301-1315 (c)	
William (c)	Isolda 1301-1308		
probable kin: John 1312			
YACHER			
William *le de* Papworth 1302	Cristina 1302		
probable kin: Richard *de* St. Neots 1302			
DE YELLING			
Henry 1325	Helen 1325		
probable kin: Hugh 1326			
John 1341			
YONGE			
Richard	unknown	John 1324 (c)	Agnes *de* Gt Stukeley, 1313, 1324
John (c)	unknown		
YVES *see* IVES			

8

Outsiders in Godmanchester

From the band of villages around Godmanchester, from the town of Huntingdon, and from farther afield, scores of people are recorded in the Godmanchester court rolls. The record shows that the interaction between villagers and outsiders was ongoing, although for the last half of the fourteenth century the survival of the records is uneven, and the detail found in those which do survive declines. Along with the continuing process of interaction, the geographical spread among towns and villages was quite wide, as Map 2: "The Provenance of Outsiders at Godmanchester, 1278-1348" (pp. 80-81) indicates.

TABLE 27: OUTSIDERS APPEARING IN GODMANCHESTER COURT ROLLS, 1278-1399

Village of Origin[a] and Name	*1278-1300*	*1301-1325*	*1326-1348*	*1349-1399*
ABBOTS RIPTON				
Atepund, Roger	1280			
Lucas, Nicholas and				
Margeria his daughter	1299			
Ripton, Master John	1284			
Ripton, Robert	1300			
Ripton, William	1301			
Master William his brother		1314		
Emma[b] de			1341	
Heulowe, Mabel			1340	

  [a] All villages are in Huntingdonshire unless followed by an asterisk (for county unknown) or another county designation.
  [b] The "de" prefix is only indicated when the individual's surname is the actual place-name, as in Emma de Abbots Ripton. When the individual has a surname and then the designated place-name, the "de" prefix is not indicated. For certain families whose place-name surname appears through the whole period (for example, Essex, Gidding, Graveley, Barton and Mattishall), the first date only is shown. For further information on families such as these, see Table 26 "Family Data from Godmanchester Court Rolls."

Village of Origin and Name	1278-1300	1301-1325	1326-1348	1349-1399
Ladde, John				1361
Roger, Cristina				1353
ALCONBURY				
Robert de	1278			
Roger de	1278			
Wale, John			1341	
William de				1363
AMENEYE*				
John de				1374
BARNWELL (Northants.)				
Alwyne, Roger				1367
BARTON (Beds.)				
Walter de	1278			
William son of Walter de	1295			
Joan daughter of William de	1278			
BASSINGBOURNE (Cambs.)				
Dors, John			1348	
Bate, John				1382
Dogest, John				1361
Evensdon, John				1362
BATTISFORD (Suffolk)				
John de			1348	
BARKING (Suffolk)				
Berkyngg', William			1332	
BEKINGHAM*				
Staci, Hugh				1357
BEVERLEY (East Yorks.)				
Robert de	1282			
John de		1309		
BILNEY (Norf.)				
John de	1288			
Chicheni, William	1298			
John de		1321		
BLATHERWYCKE (Northants.)				
Well, John atte				1359
BLUNTISHAM				
Robert de		1318		
Cloutte, Hugh				1354
Rowuson, John and wife Sybil				1373
BRADENHAM (Bucks.)				
Alexander de	1295			
BROCKFORD (Suffolk)				
Agnes de	1281			
BROUGHTON				
Henry and sons Walter and Albric de	1297			
Somerder, John				1350
BROXTED (Norf.)				
Godfrey de	1298			

Village of Origin and Name	1278-1300	1301-1325	1326-1348	1349-1399
BRUNNE (BROOM ?) (Beds.)				
Alice de	1278			
John de				1380
Rauleyn, John				1380
BUCKDEN				
Hirne, John in ye				1365
Vicar, John son of				1350
BUCKWORTH				
Gounsaynoun, William			1340	
Ayle, Agnes and Joan				
daughters of John				1363
Hoberd, Agnes				1390
Kent, John				1381
BUMPSTEAD (Essex)				
Atemar, Peter and wife Alice	1312			
BURY				
Hugh de				1358
CAMBRIDGE (Cambs.)				
Fulco de		1327		
John and wife Matilda de		1338		
Dunnyng, Robert, burgess and				
wife Agnes		1345		
Stygeneye, John and wife Sybil		1346		
Barker, John, farmer				1378
CAXTON (Cambs.)				
York, Robert de, de				1349
CHAM*				
Robert de		1325		
CHATTERIS (Cambs.)				
Hugh, Thomas son of		1321		
Mors, John				1398
Peroun, Simon				1395
CHESTERFIELD (Derby.)				
John and wife Mariota de		1315		
CHESTR' (CHESTERTON ?) (Cambs.)				
William de				1350
CHESTERTON (Cambs.)				
Reeder, John				1399
CHYCH*				
William de		1315		
CLARE (Oxon.)				
Bory, William			1331	
CLEY (Norf.)				
John de	1294			
COCKYRMOWE*				
Peter de		1302		
COLION*				
Waret, John			1332	
COMPTON (Berks.)				
Hildegar, Robert			1337	

Village of Origin and Name	1278-1300	1301-1325	1326-1348	1349-1399
CROXTON (Cambs.)				
Prentys, Andrew				1387
DANATASTR* (DONCASTER?)				
Emma de			1332	
DICKLEBURGH (Norf.)				
Reynold, Thomas				1382
DERBY (Derby.)				
Robert de			1340	
DUNSTABLE (Beds.)				
Bury, Stephen	1278			
William and wife Joan de		1319		
EARITH				
Long, Thomas			1331	
EDENHAM (Lincs.)				
Simon son of Alan de			1330	
ELSWORTH (Cambs.)				
Adam and wife Cristina de			1334	
Walter de		1322		
Hirne, William in ye			1340	
ELTISLEY (Cambs.)				
Edward, John				1389
Fryharneys, Phillip				1356
ELY (Cambs.)				
Thomas de				1349
ESSEX (Essex)				
Nicholas de	1279			
John son of Nicholas de	1298			
Agnes wife of Nicholas de	1299			
Cristina daughter of Nicholas de	1288			
Margaret daughter of Nicholas de	1288			
John de				1353
Henry brother of John de				1359
ETON (Bucks.)				
Richard and wife Margaret de			1341	
Gold, John			1348	
Crysp, John				1363
Matilda de				1351
Solde, John				1353
Slyper, John				1363
EYNESBURY				
John son of Lawrence de				1385
FEN DRAYTON (Cambs.)				
Catelyne, John				1361
FEN STANTON				
Adam, William				1373
Felers, John				1373
Hawstyn, Henry				1392
Newman, William				1399
Ruscheton, John				1374
Thomas brother of John de				1352

Village of Origin and Name	1278-1300	1301-1325	1326-1348	1349-1399
GARFINHALE*				
Ralph de	1280			
GIDDING				
Freman, William	1297			
Henry de	1286			
William de	1282			
Hugh son of Henry and wife Elizabeth de	1297			
Phillipa daughter of Henry de	1294			
Coyper, John				1350
Adam de				1373
GILDERSOWE*				
John de		1322		
Robert de			1348	
GLATTON				
William de			1340	
John son of William de			1340	
Gate, William				1390
GRAFHAM				
John de			1332	
Hemingford, Joan				1399
GRANSDEN				
William and wife Isolda de		1301		
Reginald de			1345	
GRANTHAM (Lincs.)				
John de				1356
Robert de				1376
GRIMSBY (Lincs.)				
William de				1353
GUILSBOROUGH (Northants.)				
Roger de				1361
HADDENHAM (Cambs.)				
Eustace de		1313		
HALLYSBERY*				
Michel, William				1384
HAMERTON				
Godfrey and wife de	1278			
John de	1279			
Phillipa wife of John de	1296			
William de	1278			
Richard de				1349
HARDLEY (Norf.)				
Nicholas and wife Elene de	1288			
Richard de	1295			
Matilda, second wife of Nicholas de	1298			
HAVELEY*				
John son of William and wife Margaret Scot de	1293			
Robert son of John de		1308		

Village of Origin and Name	1278-1300	1301-1325	1326-1348	1349-1399
HEMINGTON (Northants.)				
William son of Henry de	1286			
John de		1313		
Hardy, Reginald			1338	
HIGNEY				
Agnes and Alice daughters of Alice de		1302		
HILTON				
Bate, John		1313		
Elys, William				1371
John de				1355
Maryot, John				1387
Newman, John				1389
HITCHIN (HICHIN) (Herts.)				
Robert and wife Isabella de	1299			
Robert son of Robert de	1299			
HOLLAND (WOOD)				
Peter and wife de	1281			
HOLYWELL				
John de				1391
Selde, John				1373
HOPWOOD (Lancs.)				
Clerk, Robert				1380
ISHAM (Northants.)				
John and wife Cristina de		1325		
John de				1355
Albrida wife of John de				1394
John son of John de				1394
ISLEHAM (Cambs.)				
Adam de		1322		
Simon de			1327	
KING'S LYNN (Norf.)				
Witman, Adam				1399
KEYSTON				
Richard and wife de				1356
Peryn, John		1311		
KING'S RIPTON				
Hirne, Ivo son of Hugh *le*	1299			
Hirne, Henry				1360
Hirne, John				1375
Ivo, Henry son of				1361
KINGSTON (Cambs.)				
John de				1356
Robert de				1399
LANGLEY [c]				
Richard and wife Joan de			1335	

[c] This has not been mapped as there are too many Langleys to define which county they came from.

Village of Origin and Name	1278-1300	1301-1325	1326-1348	1349-1399
LEIGHTON BROMSWOLD				
Robert and wife Cristina de		1308		
LEICESTER (Leics.)				
John and wife Emma de				1382
John de		1313		
LINCOLN (Lincs.)				
Richard de	1293			
Nicholas de	1298			
Henry de		1308		
LONDON (Middx.)				
Pulter, Alexander				1371
Reynold, John				1380
LONG STANTON (Cambs.)				
Freysol, John				1363
LUTON (Beds.)				
John de	1295			
William de				1350
MATTISHALL (Norf.)				
Roger de	1280			
Amicia de	1295			
John de	1298			
Hugh de	1295			
William de	1278			
MELBOURN (Cambs.)				
Marshall, Hugh				1360
MERTON (Cambs.)				
Simon and wife Sarra Winborn	1291			
Thomas de		1312		
Freston, William, prior of			1345	
MILDENHALL (Suffolk)				
William and wife Cristina				1350
MOLESWORTH				
John son of Robert de		1317		
MOULTON (Northants.)				
Lambert de		1310		
Elena daugher of Alan de			1346	
MUNDFORD (Norf.)				
Elena de	1297			
Eusebius de		1314		
Agnes de				1376
NORFOLK (Norf.)				
Stephen and wife Joan de		1317		
NORTHAMPTON (Northants.)				
Freman, John				1390
NORTHBOROUGH (Northants.)				
(Northborg), William				1349
OLD WESTON				
Freman, Reginald, brother of Mariota, wife of Roger Tinctor	1279			

Village of Origin and Name	1278-1300	1301-1325	1326-1348	1349-1399
Aleyn, John			1331	
John de				1350
OLNEY (Bucks.)				
Clerk, Henry				1356
OUNDLE (Northants.)				
Godfrey son of William de		1306		
Bydde, John				1377
OVER (Cambs.)				
Nicholas son of Robert de		1308		
John son of Walter and wife Agnes, daughter of William Mattishall de		1325		
OXFORD (OXENFORD) (Oxon.)				
Richard and wife Sybil de				1358
PADEMOR (Lincs.)				
William de	1279			
Alice wife of William de	1280			
Godfrey and wife Amicia de	1291			
PAGHAM (PAGENHAM) (Sussex)				
John de		1315		
PATESVILLE*				
John de			1329	
PAXTON d				
William and wife Agnes de	1279			
Walter de	1281			
Cristina de	1284			
Aparitor, Adam		1322		
Amicia wife of Paxton de		1308		
Abolot, Godfrey		1307		
		(Little)		
Herni, John				1377
				(Great)
John son of Robert and daughter Margaret de				1361
PLUMPTON (Northants.)				
John de				1380
POLEBROOK (Northants.)				
John de				1353
QUY (STOWE-CUM-QUY) (Cambs.)				
John de				1366
John and wife Cristina de				1391
RADWELL (Beds.)				
Robert son of Simon de				1351
RAMSEY				
Abbot of	1283			
Biker, Robert			1333	

d Paxton has two hamlets, Little Paxton and Great Paxton.

Village of Origin and Name	1278-1300	1301-1325	1326-1348	1349-1399
Willimot, William			1341	
Meyre, John				1399
Robert de				1349
RAVELEY e				
Matilda daughter of William de	1291			
Cristina de	1291			
Miles, John			1341 (Great)	
Braser, John				1365 (Great)
RIPPINGALE (Lincs.)				
John de				1355
RIPON (West Yorks.)				
John de				1350
RISELEY (Beds.)				
Montem, super, William			1348	
ROYSTON VILLA (Herts.)				
Sclyngeby, John				1378
RUDHAM (Norf.)				
Thomas de				1355
ST. IVES				
Ralph de	1283			
Eusebius de	1285			
John de	1288			
Maryot, Thomas		1309		
Cottingham, Peter			1331	
Earith, John			1334	
Gambourne, Nicholas			1329	
Gambourne, John			1329	
Hors, William			1340	
[P], John son of John				1349
Malot, John				1378
Paxton, John son of William		1325		
Reder, John				1375
Sacomb, William				1365
Wigar, John				1359
Wrythe, Alan				1378
ST. NEOTS				
James de	1280			
Lawrence de	1280			
Dereham, Peter son of Peter		1314		
Bele, John			1341	
Hervy, John			1329	
Abbot, Henry				1365
Coofot, John				1371

e Raveley has two hamlets, Little Raveley and Great Raveley.

Village of Origin and Name	1278-1300	1301-1325	1326-1348	1349-1399
SHERENFORD (Norf.)				
Walter de	1291			
Simon and wife Amicia de		1302		
Richard son of Simon de		1302		
William and wife Amicia de		1308		
SILVERLEY (Cambs.)				
Phillip de	1299			
Alice de			1332	
SIBTHORPE (Notts.)				
Taylor, Agnes wife of				
Robert son of John				1372
SOMERSHAM				
Robert and wife Margaret de		1325		
Toppe, John				1393
SOUTHOE				
Newman, John				1366
SPALDWICK				
Roger and wife Cristina				
Atenok de		1307		
Hill, William of the				1380
SPALDING (Lincs.)				
Roger de		1302		
STAMFORD (Lincs.)				
John and son William de				1380
STANFORD (Beds.)				
Robert de	1281			
William de		1313		
Anable, Joan			1397	
STIRTLOW				
John and wife Mariota de		1307		
John son of John de		1321		
Thomas de		1320		
STOKE[f]				
John and wife Agnes de				1351
STONDON (Beds.)				
Paul de			1331	
STOWE (LONGA)				
Millicent de			1329	
STRATTON (Beds.)				
Swethon, Hugh			1346	
STRETHAM (Cambs.)				
Robert de				1359
STUKELEY[g]				
Alan de	1291			
William de	1288			

[f] Stoke is not mapped as there are too many.
[g] Stukeley has two hamlets, Little Stukeley and Great Stukeley.

Village of Origin and Name	1278-1300	1301-1325	1326-1348	1349-1399
Houlot, Simon son of Thomas		1320		
Savage, Alexander		1320		
Richard, son of William de		1325		
Bonde, Richard			1348	
Joncer, Agnes daughter of Richard		1313 (Great)		
Yonge, John son of Richard and sister Agnes		1324		
King, John son of John				1349 (Little)
Lincoln, Margaret wife of Thomas			1327	
Thomas de			1332	
Nicholas, brother of Thomas de			1344	
Robert de				1351
John son of William de				1360
SUNDON (Beds.)				
Swafham, Thomas				1349
SWAVESEY (Cambs.)				
Wale, John			1340	
SWETHON*				
Hugh de			1346	
TEMPSFORD (Beds.)				
John de				1365
THAME (Oxon.)				
Matilda and daughter Margaret de				1380
THORLEY (Herts.)				
Eustace de	1291			
John son of Eustace de	1300			
Thomas son of Eustace de	1300			
THURNING (THERNYG')h				
Sumter, William				1351
TILNEY (Norf.)				
John de			1331	
TITCHMARSH (Northants.)				
William de	1299			
TODENHAM (Glos.)				
Beatrix wife of Richard de	1295			
Richard de	1299			
Hugh de	1283			
Roger de	1297			
Tyna, Thomas	1282			
Henry de	1313			

h This village is now in Northamptonshire, but was then in Huntingdonshire.

Village of Origin and Name	1278-1300	1301-1325	1326-1348	1349-1399
TOSELAND				
Isabella de		1307		
Turneye, John, bailiff of the hundred			1345	
William de (*manet* in Offord)				1354
TRUMPINGTON (Cambs.)				
William de	1279			
UPTON				
Roger and wife Mariota de	1286			
UPWOOD				
Heryng, William				1388
Stotherd, Robert				1381
WALCOT (Northants.)				
Simon de			1330	
John de				1390
WALTON (Northants.)				
Warde, Margaret			1344	
WARBOYS				
Garlop, Reyner son of Richard de		1315		
WARESLEY				
Stalum, John son of Michael		1311		
Newman, William			1330	
William de			1331	
Shayl, John				1361
WARMINGTON (Northants.)				
Clerk, William	1291			
Simon de	1295			
WASHINGLEY				
Fing', Robert		1309		
WENNINGTON				
William, clerk, de		1314		
John son of William de		1314		
WEYK*				
Rust, John			1340	
WIGGENHALL (Norf.)				
Gregory de			1332	
WIMBLINGTON (Cambs.)				
Godfrey and wife Isolda de	1295			
WIMPOLE (Cambs.)				
Bunch, William				1390
WISTOW				
William and wife de	1300			
Emma de			1341	
Nicholas de			1331	
WOLBOSTON*				
Richard de		1324		
WOODHURST				
Wyting, William son of Robert and wife Isolda		1301		

Village of Origin and Name	1278-1300	1301-1325	1326-1348	1349-1399
WOOD NEWTON (Northants.)				
Chapman, Reginald and				
wife Agnes			1331	
WOODSTONE				
Godfrey de	1281			
WOLLASTON (Northants.)				
John de				1350
WYTON				
Thomas de		1322		
YORK (EBORACUM) (Yorks.)				
Robert de				1349

Besides the outsiders listed in Table 27, a large number of persons closer to home — within, say, a radius of five miles — appear in the Godmanchester court rolls as acquiring land in and around the town. Table 28 is an actual list of those acquiring property and as such best indicates the consistency and variety of individuals involved in such acquisitions. It shows the number of people who appeared in the court rolls between 1278 and 1399 who ventured into the town from a radius of five miles — the agrarian zone. So that the continuing role of the greater agrarian community of Godmanchester may be seen, the families throughout the whole period have been listed in such a fashion as to illustrate the increase or decrease in numbers from the nine villages which make up the zone area (see Map 3, p. 134).

TABLE 28: THE AGRARIAN ZONE

Village and Name	1278-1300	1301-1325	1326-1348	1349-1399
BRAMPTON				
John de Brampton	1278			
Dowles, Robert	1291			
Viting, John and wife Agnes	1299			
Aula (atte Hall), Robert		1325		
Beverich, William				1378
Bonde, Peter				1361
Caune, Elias				1379
Nolly, Robert				1378
Overton, Cristina wife of				
Robert				1361
Overton, Nicholas				1397
Portos, John				1394

Village and Name	1278-1300	1301-1325	1326-1348	1349-1399
GRAVELEY				
William	1278			
Cristina daughter of William	1282			
Simon	1287			
John son of Simon	1287			
Sarra daughter of Simon		1309		
Emma daughter of John		1312		
Matilda			1342	
John and wife Isabella				1351
Isabella wife of John				1360
William son of John				1366
Alice wife of William				1371
Nicholas				1349
Bonde, William				1374
Frerbern, John				1358
Holywell, John				1394
Lucas, Mabel				1390
Newinger, Robert				1381
Robat, William				1368
West, William				1361
HARTFORD				
Crucem, Michael and wife Alice	1281			
Roger son of Edward and wife Matilda	1280			
William and wife Isolda de	1280			
Richard and wife de	1292			
Marshal, Godfrey	1282			
Oliver de		1308		
Crucem, John		1308		
Godfrey and wife Agnes de		1308		
Montem, Seginius super		1320		
Oliver, Thomas son of Matilda		1308		
Robert de			1330	
Oliver, Thomas son of John			1342	
Bole, Hugh				1380
Firmarius, Pellagia wife of John				1365
Gotte, John				1349
John de				1351
William son of Emma de				1361
Hil, Thomas of the				1365
Howlot, John				1353
Luton, the mother of Thomas				1363
Luton, Thomas				1363
Man, Richard				1351
Mason, Agnes				1354
Michel, John senior				1383
Seges, John son of William				1353

Village and Name	1278-1300	1301-1325	1326-1348	1349-1399
Seges, William				1372
Well, Godfrey atte				1372
HEMINGFORD ABBOTS (OR GREY)				
Ralph de	1295			
Newman, Robert	1295			
Russel, Godfrey son of Henry and wife Matilda	1297			
Ville Ralph ad Capud	1294			
Peter de		1309		
Ingleys, John jun		1324 (Abbots)		
Syer, John		1315 (Grey)		
Astone, William			1342	
Baggle, John le and wife Beatrix			1344 (Grey)	
Barre, Ralph and wife Cristina			1339	
Burel, Simon			1331	
Crane, John			1333 (Grey)	
Everard, Simon			1341	
Gate, Ralph atte			1339	
John de			1327	
William de			1329	
Kideman, John			1327	
Ingleys, Margaret and son Thomas			1346	
Marshall, Thomas			1341	
Marshall, John son of Thomas			1341	
Newman, Henry			1331	
Porthos, Walter son of John			1340	
Robyn, Nicholas			1341	
Robyn, John			1341	
Ryngedale, Alan			1347 (Grey)	
Syer, Adam			1333	
Wether, John			1348	
Baroun, Matilda				1366
Birche, William senior				1368
Bonde, John				1393
Cayth, John				1363
Delethorpe, John				1386
Dosyn, William				1398
Engle, William son of John				1363
Est, John				1350
Est, John				1395
Fermer, John				1373 (Grey)

Village and Name	1278-1300	1301-1325	1326-1348	1349-1399
Gate, John				1350
Hawde, Simon				1398
				(Grey)
Walter, de				1361
Ingley, Margaret				1380
Judd, Thomas				1359
Lane, Thomas in ye				1359
Marshall, Alice				1366
Marshall, John				1361
Marshall, John son of John				1394
Marshall, Margaret				1369
Marshall, Thomas son of John				1394
Marshall, Agnes dau of Thomas				1359
Martyn, William				1394
Nap, John				1360
				(Grey)
Newman, Simon				1363
Nicholas, John son of				1371
				(Grey)
Osmund, William				1385
Parker, John				1369
Roger, John				1360
Robyn, Amphlicia wife of William				1373
Selde, William son of John				1373
Selde, John son of John				1372
Selde, John				1372
Skele, John				1394
Sly, John and wife Cristina				1362
Sutton, John				1398
Tanower, Nicholas				1373
Trappe, Thomas senior son of Nicholas				1374
Trappe, Thomas junior son of Nicholas				1374
Wate, William				1394
Whate, William				1368

HOUGHTON

Village and Name	1278-1300	1301-1325	1326-1348	1349-1399
William de	1288			
Ivetta wife of William de	1298			
William son of William de	1298			
Iona daughter of William de	1291			
Edward de	1291			
Page, Lawrence son of Nicholas	1299			
Clopton, John		1321		
John son of John de		1324		
John and wife Amicia de		1321		
Richard son of William de		1311		
Ryder, Emma dau of William		1316		

Village and Name	1278-1300	1301-1325	1326-1348	1349-1399
Trappe, William		1310		
Miller, Amicia dau of Godfrey			1329	
John de				1361

HUNTINGDON

Alice, widow of William de	1297			
Rede, William son of Martin le	1298			
Rede, Robert	1286			
Rede, Martin le	1288			
Aldous, Thomas		1302		
Anfred, John and wife Matilda		1322		
Barbour, Roger and wife Joan				
dau of John de Hamerton		1314		
Begenore, William and wife Mariota		1311		
Begenore, Peter and Paul				
sons of William		1314		
Bilneye, John		1322 (d)		
Bygot, Joan		1321		
Croxton, John		1311 (d)		
Frere, John		1310		
Hamerton, John		1306		
Leter, William le		1308		
Luton, Thomas		1322		
Palmer, John and wife Matilda		1312		
Paxton, Nicholas		1308		
Peterbyn, Robert de Hunts		1324		
Prent's, John		1302		
Reve, Robert		1311		
Russel, John and wife Leticia		1302		
Scot, Alice and Margaret				
daughters of Adam		1323		
Somersham, Robert and				
wife Margaret		1325		
Abovethebroc, John			1326	
Aldous, John son of Robert			1348	
Attelaneshende, John			1332	
Alyous, Robert			1341	
Baldecote, John			1346	
Baldecote, Robert (or Roger)			1346	
Band, Nicholas			1343	
Beverle, John			1333	
Beverle, Richard			1329	
Bronne, Walter			1341	
Buldir, Henry and wife Matilda			1338	
Buldir, John			1335	
Buldir, John and wife Margaret			1346	
Buldir, Robert			1329	
Buldir, Robert son of Robert			1330	
Caxton, Walter			1345	
Cayton, William			1345	

Village and Name	1278-1300	1301-1325	1326-1348	1349-1399
Dereham, Peter			1342	
Dodington, Ralph			1342	
Dodington, William			1342	
Godoun, Thomas son of Reginald			1330	
Goldderp, Henry			1344	
Hamerton, John			1341	
Hardley, Nicholas			1327	
Haubaken, Simon			1341	
Hayilmar, John			1341	
Hemingford, William			1338	
Hemington, John			1341	
Hichin, Margaret			1341	
Hichin, Robert			1341	
Hichin, Emma			1341	
Hore, Henry *le*			1335	
Ivo, John son of			1331	
Leighton, Roger, burgess			1329	
Lister, Sybil and Margaret				
daughters of Lawrence			1340	
Lorimer, Mabel daughter of John			1333	
Luton, Emma			1341	
Luton, Henry son of Thomas			1343	
Marshall, Robert			1341	
Marshall, John			1341	
Mattishale, Agnes widow of Hugh			1329	
Mattishale, John			1347	
Mileward, Joan wife of Henry,				
son of John and dau of				
Lawrence Lister			1335	
Papworth, John de, burgess, de			1339	
Rede, Ralph			1341	
Rede, Martin			1341	
Rede, John son of Martin le			1343	
Rede, Thomas son of Martin le			1343	
Rede, Walter			1331	
Rede, William			1331	
Richardyn, John			1341	
Richardyn, William			1347	
Roger, Simon son of			1339	
Roger, William son of			1339	
Sadeler, William			1341	
Schrepprethe, William			1345	
Scot, Roger			1341	
Scot, William son of Roger			1340	
Serles, John			1332	
Shelton, Nicholas de, de			1327	
South, William			1344	
Spark, John			1342	
Thomeston, John			1341	
Underlespitel, Sabina			1341	

Village and Name	1278-1300	1301-1325	1326-1348	1349-1399
Walcot, John			1341	
Walcot, Roger de, de			1348	
Waleys, William			1341	
Waltebec, William			1341	
Wenenec, Matilda			1341	
Weston, Alan			1330	
Weston, Alice daughter of John			1341	
Weston, Adam, burgess			1341	
Wyldebef, William			1338	
Wymer, John			1341	
Wynier, John			1341	
Albon, William				1378
Albon, Joan wife of William				1394
Avered, John son of John				1349
Bate, John				1361 (d)
Bere, Godfrey				1356
Beverle, John and wife Sarra				1351
Bewschampe, Walter and wife Beatrix				1354
Bethesham, Thomas				1352
Betheleswade, William				1353
Betheleswade, Beatrix				1364
Berrer, Godfrey				1354
Blakinor, William				1372
Borel, John				1394
Bourgos, Margaret wife of Thomas				1354
Bishop, Thomas				1382
Caproun, Thomas				1362
Catoun, Thomas				1362
Cook, Margaret wife of William				1364
Couin, Gregory				1350
Cristemasse, Emma				1393
Cristemasse, Henry				1381
Dakisson, John				1375
Danyl, Thomas				1377
Davy, John				1373
Deppyng, Thomas				1367
Edmund, William				1390
Foxton, John junior				1398
Fraylynghurst, Richard				1373
Fryharneys, Phillip				1361
Godun, John son of Thomas				1360
Godman, Agnes wife of Thomas				1351
Gidding, Ralph				1359
Hadlows, Robert junior				1372
Hayrown, Nicholas				1352
Hemingford, William son of William				1354
Hemingford, William junior				1363
Hemingford, Margaret wife of William junior				1372
Hemingford, Matilda wife of William				1362
Henry, Prior of				1381

Village and Name	1278-1300	1301-1325	1326-1348	1349-1399
Herr, Godfrey				1351
Heymys, Richard				1351
Hichin, Nicholas				1354
Hobon, Robert				1356
Hor', Joan				1351
Hurleton, Robert				1380
Luton, William				1380
Lyster, Margaret wife of Alan				1351
Malisbery, John				1350
Marshall, Lucy wife of Ralph				1361
Marshall, Ralph son of Robert				1361
Marshall, Robert				1350
Marshall, Simon son of John				1349
Page, John				1350
Parvus, William				1354
Parvus, John son of William				1362
Parvus, William son of William				1362
Peddere, Walter				1363
Person, Matilda wife of John				1353
Peyntoun, William				1399
Picard, Asbern and wife Emma				1352
Pope, Nicholas				1371
Prior of				1366
Radwell, John				1374
Redde, Mathew *le*				1357
Richard, Alice wife of William				1351
Richardyn, William				1349
Rote, William and wife Agnes				1361
Rutherham?, John				1374
Sayer, John				1397
Scerlogg, John				1351
Scholar, Master John and wife Pellagia				1380
Scut, William				1357
Somayster, Margaret wife of John				1354
Sprag, John and wife Emma				1352
Styltoun, John				1350
Swynfeen, Richard				1381
Swynson, John				1395
Tye, Henry and wife Phillipa				1366
Walcote, Richard				1375
Waleys, Cecily wife of William				1362
Waleys, John son of Cecily				1367
Waleys, William				1357
Walsynggome, John				1396
Walter, William				1350
Weston, John, burgess				1349

OFFORD CLUNY (OR DARCY)

Village and Name	1278-1300	1301-1325	1326-1348	1349-1399
Edeline de	1279			
Palmer, William	1278			

Village and Name	1278-1300	1301-1325	1326-1348	1349-1399
Fryday, Alice dau of John		1301		
Howman, Robert son of Henry		1323		
John and wife Emma de		1310		
Ilgor, John		1323		
Andrew de		1317		
Mundeford, John and wife Emma		1322		
Nel, Thomas		1322		
Palmer, John		1322		
Tredgar, Robert		1301		
Bette, John			1337	
Baroun, John			1341	
Bole, Henry			1340	
Boykene, John			1330 (Darcy)	
Chapman, wife of Richard			1341	
Matilda dau of Isabella de			1330	
Alloch, John				1373
Balle, Thomas				1360
Biggleswade, John				1357
Bryte, John				1391
Chatteris, John				1373
Clerk, Emma wife of Thomas and sister of Elena West				1380
Hals, Thomas				1373
Halston, John				1381 (Darcy)
Heed, John				1393 (Darcy)
Moubray, Peter				1373
John son of John de				1351
Penyr, John				1395
Ulf, John senior				1364
Ulf, John junior				1364
PAPWORTH (AGNES) (OR EVERARD)				
Simon de	1291			
Simon son of Simon de	1291			
Roger de	1295			
Waryn, Walter	1295			
Waryn, William	1300			
Alewill, Margaret		1303		
Hockerill, John		1315		
Kem, Robert son of Walter		1321		
Reginald de		1324		
William and wife Matilda		1308		
Waryn, John		1302 (Agnes)		
William de			1341	
Aylwyne, John			1341	
Barton, Walter			1334	

Village and Name	1278-1300	1301-1325	1326-1348	1349-1399
Barton, William			1341	
Freman, William			1341	
Hockerill, John son of John			1341	
Hogon, Thomas			1341	
Ive, Margaret			1341	
Ive, Constance			1341	
Kent, William			1329	
Long, Simon			1341	
Long, Mabel dau of Simon			1342	
Long, Agnes, Margaret and Joan daughters of Simon			1342	
Squire, Reginald			1341	
Waryn, Thomas			1341	
Herne, John *le*				1380
Hunte, John				1392 (Everard)
Kyte, Agnes				1350 (Agnes)
Kyte, Emma				1350 (Agnes)
Langeley, Margaret wife of John				1363
Langeley, John				1357
Pewle, Matilda				1373
Serle, Henry				1356
YELLING				
Puttock, John son of Richard and wife Alditha	1316			
Teband, John	1306			
Teband, William son of John and wife Mabel	1306			
Uteband, William and wife Mabel	1307			
Henry and wife Helen de	1325			
Doraunt, Thomas			1341	
Horold, Cristina			1348	
Mileward, Godfrey			1341	
Bole, Nicholas				1377
Bole, Walter				1392
Bryker, John				1398
Coyder, John				1350
Church, John atte				1366
Horerd, Henry				1354
Horold, Richard				1383
Howelond, John and wife Elena				1354
Puttock, John				1354
Puttock, William son of John				1354
Wille, John				1364

Appendix 1

Godmanchester Customals, 1324 and 1465

The customals of Godmanchester may best be introduced by the remarks of Mary Bateson: "Among the fine series of court rolls at the court-hall of Godmanchester there is one which contains a Latin customal drawn up at a court for the view of frankpledge, held Jan. 2, 1324." Unfortunately, as has been noted in the Preface to this volume, this 1324 customal has now disappeared. As a result, we must be content with the material selected by Miss Bateson that has been reproduced for the first part of this appendix.

Mary Bateson continued: "There is also at Godmanchester a fifteenth-century copy of the customal, made in 1465. This professes to reissue the customal of 1324, but it contains changes and additions. The MS. is in a lamentable state, having been cruelly defaced by galls." The condition of this manuscript has certainly not improved in the interval since these words were written, so we are no more able to reproduce the 1465 customal than was Miss Bateson. However, Bateson continued: "There is also a faulty modern transcript [of the 1465 manuscript] in the Box of Charters." Mary Bateson did not elucidate the nature of these "faults," but they include the inability of the transcriber to manage parts of the text. Consequently, he left many omissions, indicated by open space in his manuscript and by brackets or ellipsis points in the following copy. Despite these faults, since this modern transcription provides us with some useful detail on town government not otherwise available, it has been thought practical to reproduce it here as well.

The 1324 Customs[1]

1. Pleading in the Court (p. 161)

   That every one pleading in pleas shall answer and be called by that name and surname by which he is most commonly called without taking exception.

---

[1] These translations are taken from the edition of Mary Bateson, *Borough Charters*, from pages as indicated in brackets after the texts.

2. Inheritance (a) male heir (p. 131)

That if any man has two sons married in his lifetime, and one of the said sons has a male and the other a female heir, and afterwards both the sons die during the father's lifetime, then, by the custom of the manor of Godmanchester, the male heir shall be the heir of the man who was the father of the said two sons.

3. Inheritance (b) age (p. 158)

When boys have come to the age of twenty, then by the custom of the manor they are of full age, and girls when they are sixteen; and then they can sell, demise, and give their lands and tenements to whom they will.

4. Inheritance (c) heirlooms (p. 141)[2]

It is decided and ordered by the full court of Godmanchester that every chief heir shall receive, as it were by inheritance, all the movables hereafter mentioned after the death of his kinsmen, if they be not specifically bequeathed, saving to the wife her dower if she survive her husband; and that nevertheless [he shall have] his portion of all the remaining utensils; to wit, the best pot of the whole house, with the best pan, a laver and basin, a mortar and pestle, a trivet, a gridiron, a spade, a shovel, a fork, a chest, a cup, a table with tressels, an axe, a bed, a table-cloth, a towel, the best cart, the plough with the irons belonging thereto, a bushel measure, a sledge, a barrow. And if the wife shall have received a part of the aforesaid things to be for her own use, she shall deposit the price out of her receipts, and shall pay to the heir, if she does any damage therein. Further, the wife shall receive her portion of all the remaining vessels and utensils except the aforesaid things belonging to the heir, doing her will therewith [with power] to assign them to whomsoever she will.

5. Inheritance (d) intestate (p. 137)[3]

If a man having the liberty [of the town] dies intestate in the said town, then his debts being deducted from the sum of his movable goods, his wife shall have a half of the residue, and the other half shall be divided among the sons, and daughters unmarried in his lifetime. And if the man dies leaving no surviving wife, then the goods which were not devised or bequeathed by him in his lifetime shall be left to the executors, one third to be disposed of as they may see fit, the other two thirds to be divided among the sons and unmarried daughters as above said, his debts and funeral expenses having been deducted from the total. And what he bequeathed in his lifetime shall be at the disposal of his executors.

[2] Mary Bateson has taken this text from the court roll of December 1312.

[3] Mary Bateson has taken this text from the 1465 customary since this matter was not treated in 1324. As a result, this text is duplicated in the early modern transcription below, but we have done this to exemplify the fact that this transcription is reasonably accurate.

6. Wife's property (a) death of wife (p. 114)

If a husband should take a wife having any lands and tenements coming to her by any kind of right, and the said husband and wife have children lawfully begotten between them, and the wife die before her husband, the said husband shall hold and enjoy all the lands and tenements for the term of his life, which tenements fall to him in his wife's right, provided that he will support the children begotten between them until such time as they can come to an agreement; and if they cannot come to an agreement, the said children may take the moiety of all the /enements, and the husband shall have for the whole term of his life all the chief messuage as it stands, and half of all the other tenements, dividing these with the children, wherever the lands may be within the liberty of Godmanchester. If no children are begotten of the marriage, the said husband will hold the moiety of all the said tenements for the term of his life.

7. Wife's property (b) will of wife (p. 110)

If no children are begotten of the marriage, the husband shall hold a moiety of all the said tenements of the wife after her death for his life. But if the wife should wish on her deathbed to bequeath in her will any part of her said tenements to any one, she may do so as touching a moiety of all the said tenements and a moiety of the said chief messuage, if the said tenements are of the wife's purchase. But if they fell to her by hereditary right, then the wife may not bequeath or alienate them, and they must descend to her nearest of blood, saving the term of her husband's life as is aforesaid.

8. Alienation (a) husband's rights (p. 104)

If a man and his wife should acquire lands or tenements, the said man can sell and alienate the said lands and tenements without his wife's leave and against her will, during his lifetime; and if after his death his wife comes to the court of Godmanchester to claim her dower of the lands and tenements which her husband sold, by the custom of the manor of Godmanchester she shall not have her dower of the said lands and tenements.

9. Alienation (b) limited to church (p. 97)

They say that no freeman may sell or alienate tenements, lands, meadows, lays of meadow or marsh-lands or curtilages, to any priests or religious men or to any foreigner under pain of loss of his freedom and of the goods thus alienated.

10. Obligations of trust (p. 163)

If any man or woman should receive lands or tenements or any other goods in perpetuity from his ancestors or from any other, and if he or she fail to maintain the said perpetuity, he or she shall not thereafter hold any right in the said property thus conditionally bequeathed, but shall have none, and then all the tenements and goods aforesaid, conditioned by the said

perpetuity, shall be handed over, according to the community's disposal, to certain persons, who are to keep up and maintain the said perpetuity.

11. Limitations of Compensation (p. 41)

That if any one incurs injury while boozing, wrestling, or quarrelling (?), he shall not be compensated by the community, and similarly each must bear his own burden as regards the loss of animals by theft.

THE 1465 CUSTOMS

Roll of Customs and Statutes
made in the 17 year of King
Edward [the son of King Edward]
Renewed in the 5th year of King Edward 4th A.D. 1465

Gumecestre

Roll of Customs or Statutes anciently made there to wit in the seventeenth year of Reign of King Edward the Son of King Edward and by the assent and consent of John Alrede and John Gylmyn Bailiffs of the said Town and of the whole Commonalty thereof renewed on Monday next after the Feast of the Conception of the Blessed Virgin Mary in the fifth year of the Reign of King Edward the Fourth:

Firstly It is statuted that two principal Bailiffs shall be elected in every year by 12 Jurors whoever they may be for that year and the said Jurors shall have [*blank*] from one View to another that is to say to elect to all offices touching the said Commonalty and to do and ordain all things touching the State of the said Town and that the two principal Bailiffs shall be elected from two Streets that is to say from Post Street and Arnyng Street one year and from West Street and East Street another year And if any one [*blank*] should hinder the aforesaid election he shall give half a mark at the next court following the said election without further delay or shall be distrained to pay the same by the Bailiffs for the time being and their officers.

Item That the Election of all officer's belonging to the said Commonalty shall be made in the full court next before the Feast of the Nativity of the Virgin Mary by twelve Jurors for the time being for the ensuing year;

Item That all Tenants of the Manor of Gumecestre shall pay their rent at the Feast of Saint Michael and at the Feast of Easter or within the Octaves of the aforesaid Feasts and if any one shall at either of the terms make default in the payment of the said farm then their land and all other their tenements lying within the said Liberty shall shall be taken into the hands of the Bailiffs for the time being until he shall satisfy the Commonalty And this shall be done by the said Consession of the Collector and so concerning [*blank*] of mills delivered by the Keeper to divers persons that the money therefore shall be paid within the Octaves of the aforesaid terms as is aforesaid.

Item That the Farm shall be set from one month before the Feast of Easter for one term and so at the Feast of Saint Michael for the other term.

Item That all the Common Rolls shall be given into the custody of the four Keepers of the Common Chest and placed in the same from one Farm to another.

Item That all common expenses shall be made by the two principal Bailiffs but of the petty expenses where they shall seem expedient for the business of the said Commonalty and if they are great they shall be allowed by the twelve Jurors.

Item That the Bailiffs shall have for the entertainment of the Bailiffs of the Hundreds according to the quantity of labour and expense done at the end of the year by the disposition of the said twelve Jurymen.

Item That all other persons labouring for the common business shall forthwith out of the Treasure of the said Town be rewarded according to the extent of their labour at the discretion of the said twelve Jurymen.

Item That all the Tenants of the Manor of Gumecestre and other persons whosoever they may be resident within the said Manor shall personally appear at the View of Frankpledge to be holden there whensoever they shall be summoned under the pains in certain leets therefore made.

Item That all persons holding common Offices shall render an account once a year to the said Bailiffs for the time being and the said twelve Jurors.

Item That no one shall retain Beasts Driven away or other profits happening to the said Commonalty except the principal Bailiffs and they shall be forthwith appraised by the said Jurors.

Item That no one shall let his Sheepfold to any Foreigner under the pain of 20s. a day for every Acre to be paid to the Commonalty to be levied by the said Bailiffs.

Item That no one shall dig or cause to be dug the Clay or Earth next the Highway under the pain of 6d. for every Cart full.

Item That it shall not be lawful for any one of the Liberty aforesaid to implead his Neighbour of the said Liberty out of the said Liberty for any trespass except concerning those things which appertain to Ecclesiastical Jurisdiction that is to say Testaments and Marriages wherefore he can have recovery in the Court aforesaid according to the nature of the Offence under the penalty of half a mark And that the said person pleadinv or pleaded shall be taxed to his loss by 12 Jurors whoever they may be for that year Provided that the said Ordinance in no wise touches the Ecclesiastical Liberty And that all these Customs or Statutes shall remain firm and inviolable for even We John Alrede and John Gylmyn Bailiffs of the Town aforesaid and the whole Commonalty of the same have to these presents put our Common Seal Dated at Gumecestre aforesaid in the Court House there as to the Sealing on the Sunday next after the Feast of Saint Thomas the Apostle in the aforesaid year of the Reign of King Edward the Fourth.

Names of the Twelve Jurors at the time of the renewing of the Customs of the time before written:

Reginald Conuff
William Alrede   Jurors Arnyng Street
T. H. Lane

William Light	
John Bowre	Jurors West Street
John Ropar	

John Baieux	
John Campion	Jurors Post Street
John Barrett	

William Fraser	
Roger Marshall	Jurors
John Alvingham	

Gumecestre

Statutes made at a View of Frankpledge in the time of John Bowre and William Frere Bailiffs there in the 18th year of the Reign of King Edward the Fourth and afterwards in the 20th year of the Reign of King Edward the Fourth confirmed by the consent of the whole Commonalty John Barnard and John Bigge being their Bailiffs:

Item That the Bailiffs for the time being shall from henceforth render their said Accounts in manner as they have formerly been accustomed and if on the day of Account of both of them either of them shall Be in arrear to the Commonalty that then the whole of the said arrears shall be fully paid to the Commonalty within a year and a day next following their next Account without fraud or deceit or further delay And if either of the said Bailiffs accounting shall make default and not pay as is before expressed then such person shall be distrained to pay the said Arrears and he shall not hereafter be put in the Election of the Bailiffs but shall be wholly deprived of that Office and shall never be restored to the said Office by prayer nor purchase nor for Gold nor Silver.

Gumecestre

Statutes made at a View of Frankpledge at the time of Reginald Conuff and John Bayns Bailiffs there in the 19th year of the Reign of King Edward the Fourth confirmed by the consent of the whole Commonalty:

Item That no one having Lands and Tenements of the said Town do from henceforth plant any Willows unless upon Lands which lye towards the Highway or the Common of the Town or upon the Ditches which are for defence of the Meadows or Fields of the Town abovesaid or upon the Common Ditches or Banks thereof under the pain of 20d. and the cutting down of the same;

Item That no Freeman shall sell nor alienate Tenements Lands Meadows Layes Grovage nor Curtilage to any Priests nor Religious Men nor to any Foreigner under the pain of the loss of this liberty and [*blank*] of the goods alienated.

Gumecestre

A Statute made at a View of Frankpledge in the time of William Frere and William Froste Bailiffs in the 22nd year of the Reign of King Edward the Fourth by the consent of the whole Commonalty:

That from the Feast of Saint Michael the Archangel until Autumn is ended no one shall put any Beasts or Cattle in the Tilth Fields under the pain of four pence for every Beasts or Cattle to be forfeited to the use of [*blank*]

Gumecestre

A Statute made at a View of Frankpledge in the time of William Aylred and John Lokyngton Bailiffs in the first year of the Reign of King Henry the Seventh by the consent of the whole Commonalty:

That if any one dwelling in the said Town having Liberty therein shall at the Suit of any one dwelling in the said Town and Liberty thereof be returned by the Officers of the Court [*blank*] then he shall immediately at the Court so returned be discharged of the Liberty which he had in the said Town And that he shall then [*blank*] before the next Court of the said return of [*blank*] so returned under the pain of imprisonment.

A Statute made at a View of Frankpledge in the time of John Bowre and William Frere Bailiffs in the 2nd year of the Reign of King Henry the 7th by the consent of the whole Commonalty:

That no one having Liberty in the said Town shall from henceforth chase or hunt after the Hare or any Beasts or Birds called Beasts or Birds of warren without the licence of the Bailiffs for the time being under the pain of losing the Liberty which he or they hath or have in the said Town except the Bailiffs for the time being or those to whom the said Bailiffs shall have given licence to keep two Greyhounds And that the said persons as charged shall not be readmitted to the said Liberty unless every one of them shall pay to the Commonalty 6/8d. without any pardon to be therefore had And that all persons having Greyhounds within the said Liberty contrary to authority of Parliament therefore made and except the Bailiffs aforesaid and those to whom the said Bailiffs shall have given licence to keep two Greyhounds shall give up those Greyhounds before the Birth of Our Lord next following after the Date of the View abovesaid under the pain of the forfeiture of 20s. for each of them to be paid to the Commonalty.

Gumecestre

Statutes made at a View of Frankpledge in the 15th year of the Reign of King Edward the Fourth also in the 16th year of his Reign by 12 jurors That if either of the Bailiffs or Officers being or dwelling within the Liberty shall be in any arrear of Account concerning his Office in any sum of money due to the Town and Commonalty he shall from henceforth be wholly deprived of the Office of Bailiff and of all Offices within the Liberty until such Officer shall be clearly discharged by the 12 Jurors for the time being and be entirely acquitted of the said Debt within a day and year after his Account under the pain of losing 20s. for every year as often as the said Accountant shall be in any parcel in arrear:

Item That the Commonalty of the said Town shall have Bulls and Boars sufficient for the Common Business And that they shall be bought sold and maintained at the Common expense by the said Bailiffs so that the Commonalty may have all the profits coming therefrom.

Item That no one dwelling within the Liberty having the Liberty of the said Town shall sell or alienate any Tenements to any Foreigner under the pain that is to say for one Acre 13/4d. for half an acre 6/8d. for one rood 3/4d.

Item That no Foreigner shall have any Beasts in Pasture within the Liberty and if any such shall be found there shall be due for every Horse pasturing 2s. for every Ox or Cow 2s. for every Sheep or Pig 6d. by the year And if any person shall be found maintaining such Beasts he shall undergo the pain aforesaid.

Item That no one shall sell or alienate Lands or Tenements for Rent of Assize nor shall the buyers of Land pay farm to any one except the Collector of the Farm.

Item That if any one shall be impleaded that is to say on a Plea of Debt he may be essoigned at the first Court And if his essoin shall be defended the said Defendant shall be amerce against the King and the same Defendant shall be distrained against the next Court following to answer And if he shall not appear in the next full Court following then he shall be distrained from day to day until he shall have justified himself and shall not be condemned in any Debt except in his presence.

Item That every Chief Heir shall take by Inheritance after the decease of his Parents the best Articles of all Utensils if it was not bequeathed by the Parents saving the Dower of a Wife if she survived her Husband And nevertheless a portion of all Vessels and when the Wife shall have received a part of the aforesaid Utensils for her own proper use or value shall be put on her receipts to be paid to the heir if any injury shall have been done thereto Moreover the Wife shall receive her portion of all Vessels and Utensils the remainder belonging to the Heir to be assigned to whomsoever he should will them for the performance of his will.

Item That if any Husband shall marry any Wife having Lands or Tenements happening to her by any right and the Husband aforesaid and the Wife aforesaid shall have between them Children lawfully begotten and the Woman shall die before her Husband the aforesaid Husband may hold and enjoy for the term of his life all lands and tenements which shall come on the part of the Wife in order that he may maintain the Children begotten between them so long as they can agree; if they cannot agree the aforesaid Children shall take a moiety of all the tenements and the Husband all the Capital Messuage as it stands for the whole term of his life and by sharing with the Children the other moiety of all other tenements wheresoever they may be within the Liberty of Gumecestre And if they should not have Children begotten between them the Husband shall hold a moiety of all the aforesaid tenements for the term of his life But if the Wife should wish by her Will to bequeath to any one at her death any part of her aforesaid tenements it shall be lawful for her as to a moiety of all the aforesaid tenements with a moiety of the messuage aforesaid; if the aforesaid tenements are of the purchase of the Wife and if they came to her by inheritance then it shall not be lawful for the aforesaid Wife to bequeath or alienate them but they shall descend to the next of kin of the aforesaid Wife saving the term of her Husband as is aforesaid all which

tenements not bequeathed by the Wife shall descend to the next of kin of the said Wife after the death of her aforesaid Husband.

Item That a View of Frankpledge shall be holden at least once a year and that the Amerciaments thereof shall be wholly paid and shall not be forgiven unless by the consent of the Commonalty And if any one for any misdemeanor or offence shall be discharged of his Liberty within the said Town by the said Bailiffs or Jurors then the Jurors and Bailiffs for the year ensuing shall not in any manner readmit him unless he is called by the Bailiffs and Jurors for the preceding year by the common consent of all of them.

Item That the Bailiffs shall weigh Breads once a Month and at the following Court they shall be taxed by a full Court and forthwith relieved.

Item That all Brewers shall sell Ale at the true value according to the Assize set under the pain next following;

Item That if any one [blank].

Item That if any Carriage shall be taken by the Bailiffs recompence shall be made to them according to their trouble when they shall return home who by their Oath shall truly acknowledge what they have received for the Carriage from the Ministers of our Lord the King or of any other Nobleman and it shall be taxed by the 12 Jurors and not of any other Captions.

Item That any one pleading or impleaded shall answer and be called by that name and Surname by which he is commonly and mostly called without any exception of challenge.

Item That if Petty Thieves shall be found within the Liberty aforesaid at any time carrying away by stealth Corn or Hay or other things it shall be lawful for them only to satisfy the Commonalty according to the discretion of the 12 Jurors And if a second time they shall forfeit for any theft then they may and shall be wholly deprived of the Liberty of the aforesaid Town and shall abjure the Town aforesaid for ever.

Item That if any person shall in any manner receive from his Ancestors or any other person Lands or Tenements or any other Goods for any perpetuity who shall make default in the said support of the aforesaid perpetuity he shall henceforth hold nothing of right but be wholly deprived of the things disposed of to him and them all the Tenements and Goods aforesaid before settled for the aforesaid perpetuity shall according to the discretion of the Commonalty be given to certain persons for performing and supporting the said perpetuity.

Item That if any Man of the said Town shall have two or three Sons by one Woman lawfully begotten the Younger of the said Sons shall be the Heir according to the usage and custom of Borough English although he may have had two or three Wives and by each of them issue the younger Son of the first Wife shall be the heir.

Item That if any man shall acquire Lands or Tenements with his Wife it shall be lawful for the said Man in his life time to give sell or bequeath the aforesaid Lands and Tenements without the licence of the said Wife And of such things Women shall not have their Dowers.

Item That Male Children shall be of full age so that they may be able to give sell and assign their Lands and Tenements when they shall arrive at the age of twenty years and Women at the age of sixteen years.

Item That if any Man shall have two Sons married in his life time and one of the said Sons shall have an Heir Male and the other an Heir Female and afterwards those two Sons die in the life time of their Father and afterwards the said Father die that the Heir Male shall be the Heir and not the Heir Female although she be of the Younger Son.

Item That from henceforth no Constable in the said Town shall discharge on Bail any Arrest for keeping the Peace at the Suit of any one unless he shall take from him arrested sufficient security by Bonds of £20 at the least and more when it shall seem fit by the discretion of the Bailiffs and Jurors for the time being And that the aforesaid Constables or either of them shall produce the aforesaid Security so taken provided that they are bound to the Bailiffs for the time being at the next Court after the Arrest made as aforesaid and the Security shall be put into the Common Chest by the Keepers.

Item That if any seizen shall be delivered into the hands of the Bailiffs for the time being for the use of any other person that the said seizen shall be engrossed on the Court Roll in the time of the said Bailiffs for that year if [blank] is delivered seisin shall be prosecuted and he shall pay the fee of his Court but it shall be wholly null and void [blank] held as nothing.

Item That no one having Liberty in the said Town shall lay snares nets or other engines within the Great Bank nor in the Riverlets which run to the said Bank within the said Liberty under the pain of six shillings and eight pence And if he be of foreign condition under the pain of one hundred shillings and those who have not wherewith they can pay the penalties aforesaid shall undergo imprisonment by the discretion of the Bailiffs and Jurors for the time being to be committed to prison by the said Bailiffs.

Item That no one shall from henceforth lodge in his house at any time of the day or night any Player of Dice for money or at other unlawful games under the pain of forfeiture of twenty shillings to the Commonalty of the said Town to be levied by the Bailiffs for the time being and imprisonment to those who have not wherewith they can pay the aforesaid pain And that the aforesaid Players shall undergo the aforesaid pain except only for the space of twelve days on the Feast of the Birth of the Lord until the eighth hour in the afternoon of each day.

Item That no one of servile condition having Liberty in the said Town shall serve out of it if any one dwelling in the said Town should wish to retain him according to the Statute of Labourers therefore made under the pain of forfeiture of his Liberty in the said Town and imprisonment according to the discretion of the said Bailiffs and Jurors.

Item That no one of the said persons elected to be the Twelve for that year shall occupy any other office.

Item That if any person shall be elected for a View to be made and he shall deny that election or shall not come being duly summoned he shall pay by distress

at the next Court after the said election or summons three shillings and four pence.

Item That if any person shall be elected and unpannelled by virtue of a Writ of Right of our Lord the King and shall be summoned and withdraw himself he shall undergo a pain of six shillings and eight pence.

Item That the Twelve Jurors and all persons holding Common Offices shall be present at the Account of the Bailiffs and others under the pain of six shillings and eight pence.

Item That the Bailiffs for the time being shall elect ordain and enpanell twelve honest men that is to say from every Street three to occupy the view and for the year ensuing.

Item That no one shall talk in the Court House nor intermeddle himself in anything to be done there except the Officers of the Said Court and those to whom the Court shall speak And if any one of the said Liberty shall do to the contrary and shall be enjoined silence by the Bailiffs Steward's Bailiffs or their sufficient deputies for the first offence shall be amerced three shillings and four pence to be levied by distress at the next Court after the said Talking for the second offence he shall be committed to prison by the said Bailiffs and Steward thereto remain until fine for the said contempt according to the discretion of the Said Bailiffs and jurors provided that the said fine exceeds the aforesaid amercement of three shillings and four pence And if the Talkers shall be unwilling to obey the aforesaid Officers he shall be discharged of his Liberty in the said Town by the said Officers and nevertheless he shall be committed by them to Prison And that such person so behaving shall in no wise be hereafter restored to the Liberty of the said Town but be wholly deprived thereof.

Item That if any man in the said Town or Liberty shall die therein Intestate that then his debts being deducted out of all his moveable goods of that which shall be remaining his Wife shall have one part and the other part shall be divided amongst his Sons and Daughters not married in his life time And if a man shall die not leaving a wife living that then the goods which had not been devised or bequeathed by him in his life time one part shall be left to his executors to dispose of according as they shall see fit the remaining two parts shall be divided amongst the sons and daughters not married as above the debts of him so dying being deducted out of the whole And what he shall have bequeathed in his life time shall be at the disposal of his executors.

Item That it shall not be lawful for any person for default of payment for any lands or tenements meadows feedings or pastures sold by him or a Testator or by his assignment to any person within the said Liberty to make entry into the said Lands unless he shall therefore petition in the Court of the said Liberty and that then they shall expel him from the entry made therein in manner as the Court shall judge and if any one shall go upon the aforesaid lands tenements meadows feedings pastures so entered And if it shall happen that Suit be made in the Said Court and he or they who shall sue shall fear that he or they against whom the aforesaid Suit is made will commit waste in the aforesaid tenements lands

meadows feedings or pastures and he shall require that he or they shall not remove any increase there until it shall be determined in full Court and it shall be granted to him by the Court and the aforesaid Defendant or Defendants being advised thereof by the Officers of the Court and shall act to the contrary without licence of the Bailiffs that thereupon they shall receive sufficient security to the full value of the aforesaid increase and more that then they shall loose the lands tenements feedings and pastures so secured for and nevertheless shall make fine for their contempt according to the discretion of the said Bailiffs and Jurors if they shall be therefore convicted Provided that the said Bailiffs do justice indifferently and speedily And that the money in arrear at the time of the Suit aforesaid so lost by him against whom Suit is made shall be paid to the Bailiffs for the time being to the use of the Said Commonalty.

Item It is Statuted and ordained that if any one of the said Liberty by any art or device shall in any manner act contrary to the customs or Ordinances abovesaid and thereupon shall be convicted by sufficient proofs he shall for the first offence be amerced at the discretion of the said Bailiffs and Jurors for the second he shall make fine of thirteen shillings and fourpence to be levied to the use of the Commonalty for the third he shall forfeit the Liberty which he hath in the said Town and nevertheless he shall make fine of twenty shillings to be levied to the use of the said Commonalty and such Offender or Offenders shall never be restored to the said Liberty neither for gold nor silver petition nor reward.

Appendix 2

Notes on Godmanchester Court Rolls

The series of court records surviving for Godmanchester until the fifteenth century were called over the greater period of the late thirteenth and fourteenth centuries the court of fines and entry fines (*fines et gersumae*). For the first years of the reign of Edward I no entry fines were assessed and the court seems to have been concerned largely with a record of property holdings for the purpose of recording obligations owed to the royal farm. Towards the end of the reign of Edward III the court record begins to appear for some sessions without entries. These courts, with the date of the court but no entries, increase in number during the reign of Richard II. During the latter reign, the court heading becomes more casual and sometimes has *Curia Gumecestre tenta* and nothing else. The language of the court evolved somewhat over our period, but not in any significant fashion. For example, *seisitus fuit* was gradually changed to *cepit seysinam*; the use of *sursum reddidit* to indicate the surrender of property into the hands of the bailiffs was current only in the late thirteenth and early fourteenth century.

As with any self-respecting town, Godmanchester exercised the right of legal jurisdiction over those non-residents engaged in economic enterprise of one sort or another with the townsmen. Unfortunately, and in contrast with the late fourteenth-century borough records of neighbouring Huntingdon,[1] Godmanchester plea records are cryptic to the extreme. Frequently the fact of the plea is recorded in the court roll without mention of the type. When debt pleas are indicated, in no instances are we told the nature of the original transaction and the amount of the debt.[2]

---

[1] The writer is now engaged in editing the Huntingdon Borough court rolls.

[2] As has been noted in the extract from the royal eyre of 1287 above (pp. 50-52), Godmanchester enjoyed the use of the little writ of right close. Use of this writ was frequent among the property holders of the town. However, there does not seem to be anything of a technical nature in the use of this writ to add to the classical study of F. W. Maitland, ed., *Select Pleas in Manorial and Other Seignorial Courts*, Selden Society, 2, 1 (London, 1888). There are many interesting incidents with respect to the use of the writ, especially a number of cases when the writ was thrown out of court for some fault in the procedure of its presentation.

Various texts given throughout this volume may be considered indicative of the substance of the entries to be found in the Godmanchester court rolls. The number and detail of entries vary widely from one court to another. No discernible seasonal pattern can be discovered in these variations. Some of the reasons for more detailed entries have been given at various places in the above chapters. These court rolls have not been catalogued in proper chronological order and as a result are difficult of ready access and for this reason, the writer has deposited a detailed index, that is to say, a list of court rolls according to date, with the archivist at Huntingdon. The court met regularly every third Thursday, and except for the year 1297, when there was a double series of records for the court,[3] the three-weekly session seems to have been the custom. Table 29 is a list of the number of courts surviving for each year. Of the 1,673 extant courts the precise date has been torn away for only 33.

TABLE 29: SURVIVING COURT RECORDS

Year	Number of Courts	Year	Number of Courts	Year	Number of Courts
1261	1	1296	15	1318	8
1271	3	1297	34	1319	10
1272	14	1298	17	1320	13
1273	9	1299	18	1321	16
1277	6	1300	9	1322	16
1278	12	1301	16	1323?	3
1279	16	1302	17	1323	5
1280	17	1303	16	1324	13
1281	18	1304	18	1325	10
1282	18	1305	7	1326	17
1283	15	1306	14	1327	20
1284	15	1307	13	1329	14
1285	11	1308	17	1330	28
1286	7	1309	12	1331	4
1287	7	1310	12	1332	18
1288	9	1311	18	1333	13
1289	13	1312	15	1334	5
1290	6	1313	15	1335	13
1291	10	1314	10	1337	5
1292	8	1315	11	1338	13
1293	9	1316	12	1339	4
1294	9	1317	10	1340	18
1295	16	1318?	4	1341	20

[3] One can make the intriguing suggestion that the locale of the court was unsettled this year!

Year	Number of Courts	Year	Number of Courts	Year	Number of Courts
1342	13	1362	15	1382	19
1343	5	1363	18	1383	11
1344	15	1364	17	1384	4
1345	17	1365	18	1385	14
1346	13	1366	18	1386	10
1347	17	1367	13	1387	11
1348	16	1368	3	1388	10
1349	11	1369	13	1389	16
1350	12	1370	4	1390	13
1351	21	1371	20	1391	16
1352	11	1372	17	1392	15
1353	12	1373	15	1393	14
1354	14	1374	15	1394	16
1355	5	1375	14	1395	7
1356	11	1376	9	1396	4
1357	9	1377	22	1397	13
1358	8	1378	17	1398	4
1359	12	1379	17	1399	13
1360	4	1380	17		
1361	19	1381	17		

33 dates unknown.
Total number of courts: 1,673.

Bibliography

Manuscript Sources

British Library, London
>   Cotton., Faust. I: Chartulary of St. Mary's Priory, Huntingdon.

Public Record Office, London
>   Gaol Delivery Rolls of Huntingdonshire, J13/various.
>   Hinchingbrook Priory, SC11/10

Huntingdon Record Office
>   Godmanchester Borough Records[1]
>   Huntingdon Borough Records

Printed Sources

Bateson, Mary. *Borough Customs*. Selden Society, 21. London, 1906.

Calendar of Patent Rolls, Henry III ff. London: Public Record Office, 1893 – .

DeWindt, Anne R. and Edwin B. DeWindt. *Royal Justice and the Medieval English Countryside*. (Forthcoming.)

Glasscock, Robin Edgar. *The Lay Subsidy of 1334*. London: Oxford University Press for the British Academy, 1975.

Jeayes, Isaac Herbert, and W. G. Benham, eds. *Court Rolls of the Borough of Colchester*. Colchester, 1921.

Maitland, Fred. Wm., ed. *Select Pleas in Manorial and Other Seignorial Courts*. Seldon Society, 2.1. London, 1888.

Oschinsky, Dorothea. *Walter of Henley and Other Treatises on Estate Management and Accounting*. Oxford: Clarendon Press, 1971.

Raftis, J. Ambrose, and Mary Patricia Hogan. *Early Huntingdonshire Lay Subsidy Rolls*. Toronto: Pontifical Institute of Mediaeval Studies, 1976.

Turner, George James, ed. *A Calendar of the Feet of Fines Relating to the County of Huntingdon ... 1194-1603*. Cambridge: Cambridge Antiquarian Society, 1913.

Secondary Sources

Ariès, Philippe. *Centuries of Childhood: A Social History of Family Life*. New York: Knopf, 1962.

---

[1] See above, Appendix 2: "Notes on Godmanchester Court Rolls."

Ault, Warren Ortman. *Open-Field Farming in Medieval England: A Study of Village By-Laws*. New York: Barnes and Noble, 1972.

Benedict, Ruth. *Patterns of Culture*. Mentor Books. Boston: Houghton, 1948.

Berkner, Lutz. "Recent Research on the History of the Family in Western Europe." *Journal of Marriage and Family*, 35 (1973), 395-405.

Bridbury, A. R. "Before the Black Death." *The Economic History Review*, second series, 30 (1977), 393-410.

Britnell, R. H. "English Markets and Royal Administration before 1200." *The Economic History Review*, second series, 31 (1978), 183-196.

Britton, Edward B. *The Community of the Vill: A Study in the History of the Family and Village Life in Fourteenth-Century England*. Toronto: Macmillan, 1977.

Dalton, George. "Peasant Markets." *Journal of Peasant Studies*, 1 (1974), 240-243.

Dawson, John Philip. *A History of Lay Judges*. Cambridge, Mass.: Harvard University Press, 1960.

Dickinson, P. G. M. "Translation of the Charter of King John to the Men of Godmanchester 20 May, 1212." *Records of Huntingdonshire*, 1967, no. 1, p. 46.

Duby, Georges. *Rural Economy and Country Life in the Medieval West*. Trans. by Cynthia Postan. Columbia, S.C.: University of South Carolina Press, 1968.

Ekwall, Eilert. *Studies on the Population of Medieval London*. Stockholm: Almqvist, 1956.

Everitt, A. "The Banburys of England." *Urban History Yearbook*, 1974.

Farmer, David. "Wages and Prices in Fourteenth-Century England." In *The Agrarian History of England and Wales*. (Forthcoming.)

Goody, Jack. "The Evolution of the Family." In *Household and Family in Past Time*, ed. Peter Laslett, pp. 10-36. Cambridge, 1972.

Goody, Jack, Joan Thirsk and E. P. Thompson, eds. *Family and Inheritance: Rural Society in Western Europe 1200-1800*. Cambridge: The University Press, 1976.

Green, H. J. M. *Godmanchester*. Cambridge, 1977.

Hanawalt, Barbara. "Community Conflict and Social Control: Crime and Justice in the Ramsey Abbey Villages." *Mediaeval Studies*, 39 (1977), 402-423.

Harvey, P. D. A. *A Medieval Oxfordshire Village: Cuxham, 1240 to 1400*. London: Oxford University Press, 1965.

———. "The English Inflation of 1180-1220." *Past and Present*, no. 61 (Nov. 1973), 1-30.

Herlihy, David. "Problems of Record Linkages in Tuscan Fiscal Records of the Fifteenth Century." In *Identifying People in the Past*, ed. Edward Anthony Wrigley, pp. 41-56. London: Arnold, 1973.

Howell, Cicely. "Peasant Inheritance Customs in the Midlands 1280-1700." In *The Family and Inheritance*, ed. Goody, et al., pp. 112-155.

Kosminsky, Eugeny A. *Studies in the Agrarian History of England in the Thirteenth Century*. New York: Kelley, 1956.

Le Roy Ladurie, Emmanuel. *Montaillou, village occitan de 1294 à 1324.* Paris: Gallimard, 1975.

Little, A. G. "Corrodies at the Carmelite Friary of Lynn." *Journal of Ecclesiastical History,* 9 (1958), 8-29.

Lloyd, Terrence A. *The English Wool Trade in the Middle Ages.* Cambridge: University Press, 1977.

Lopez, Robert S. "The Trade of Medieval Europe: The South." In *The Cambridge Economic History of Europe,* 2: 257-354. Cambridge: University Press, 1952.

Mauss, Marcel. *The Gift: Forms and Functions of Exchange in Archaic Societies.* Trans. Ian Cunnison, introduction by E. E. Evans-Pritchard. London: Cohen and West, 1966.

McKendrick, N. "Josiah Wedgwood, An Eighteenth-Century Entrepreneur in Salesmanship and Marketing Techniques." *The Economic History Review,* second series, 12 (1960), 408-433.

McKintosh, M. K. "The Privileged Villeins of English Ancient Demesne." *Viator,* 7 (1976), 295-328.

Miller, E. "The Fortunes of the English Textile Industry in the Thirteenth Century." *The Economic History Review,* second series, 18 (1965), 64-82.

Plucknett, Theodore Frank Thomas. *A Concise History of the Common Law.* 4th ed. London: Butterworth, 1948.

Polanyi, Karl, et al. *Trade and Market in the Early Empires: Economies in History and Theory.* Glencoe, Ill.: Free Press, 1957.

Postan, Michael M. *The Medieval Economy and Society: An Economic History of Britain 1100-1500.* London: Weidenfeld, 1972.

Raftis, J. Ambrose. *Estates of Ramsey Abbey.* Toronto: Pontifical Institute of Mediaeval Studies, 1957.

——. *Tenure and Mobility.* Toronto: Pontifical Institute of Mediaeval Studies, 1964.

——. *Warboys: Two Hundred Years in the Life of an English Mediaeval Village.* Toronto: Pontifical Institute of Mediaeval Studies, 1974.

——, ed. *Beyond Town and Vill.* (Forthcoming.)

Renton, David. "P. G. M. Dickinson." *Records of Huntingdonshire,* Huntingdonshire Local History Society, 1977, no. 1, part 8, pp. 2-3.

Reynolds, Susan. *An Introduction to the History of English Medieval Towns.* Oxford: Clarendon Press, 1977.

Rowe, Margery M. and Andrew M. Jackson. *Exeter Freeman 1266-1967.* Exeter: Devon and Cornwall Record Society, 1973.

Schofield, R. S. "The Representatives of Family Reconstitution." *Local Population Studies,* no. 8 (Spring, 1972), 3-17.

Sheehan, Michael M. *The Will in Medieval England.* Toronto: Pontifical Institute of Mediaeval Studies, 1963.

Thirsk, Joan. *Economic Policy and Projects: The Development of a Consumer Society in Early Modern England.* Oxford: Clarendon Press, 1978.

Titow, J. Z. *Winchester Yields: A Study in Medieval Agricultural Productivity.*
    Cambridge: University Press, 1972.
The Victoria History of the County of Huntingdon. Vol. 2. Ed. William Page,
    Granville Proby and S. Inskip Ladds. London, 1932.
Wrigley, Edward Anthony. *An Introduction to English Historical Demography.*
    London: Weidenfeld, 1966.

Index of Persons

This index is complementary to and does not include references to individuals and families in Table 22 : Godmanchester Family Units (pp. 165-179) and Table 26 : Family Data from Godmanchester Court Rolls (pp. 241-408), both of which are arranged alphabetically.

Abbots Ripton, Emma 109; Roger son of William 119
Abraham, Robert de Canonwestrete 73
Abovethebroc, John de Huntingdon 425
Acry, Agnes wife of Richard 159; Cristina wife of Henry and daughter of Reginald Denne 215; Henry 214, 215; Margaret 112; Margaret daughter of Richard 159; Margaret wife of Richard 159; Richard 111, 117, 120, 122, 125, 159; heirs of Richard 127; Thomas 110, 117; Thomas son of Richard 157, 159
Ailmer, John 99
Alan, John son of 107
Albon, Joan wife of William de Huntingdon 427; William de Huntingdon 427
Albrit, Eusebius 71, 95
Alconbury (Alk'), John 102; Reginald 109; Reginald, sutor 196
Aldous, Thomas 31; Thomas de Huntingdon 425
Alewill, Margaret de Papworth 429
Alexander, Simon son of 232
Aleyn, John 67, 75, 114; John de Papworth 429; John, fisher 193; William 73
Alk', see Alconbury
Alloch, John de Offord Cluny 429
Alred, see Aylred
Alrich, see Alryth
Alryth (Alrich), Dyonisia, mother of Isolda 21; Godfrey 98, 163; Isolda wife of Robert 21; Reginald 117; Reyner 111; Richard 163; Robert 98, 163
Althryton, William, hosier 90
Alvingham, John 436
Alyous, Robert 116; Robert de Huntingdon 425

Ameneye, John de 89
Amicia, Godfrey son of 22
Amiont, Emma wife of William Page Startle 214
Anfred (Aufred, Avered), John 77; John de Huntingdon 425; John son of John de Huntingdon 427; John son of Robert de Huntingdon 425; Matilda wife of John de Huntingdon 425
Angulo, Reginald in 97; Richard in 97
Anice (Aniz), Agnes wife of Eusebius 46; Eusebius son of Aniz 163; Godfrey son of Eusebius 46, 127, 163; John son of Eusebius 46; Nicholas 163; Nicholas son of Eusebius 163; Reginald son of Eusebius 127, 163
Aniz, see Anice
Apotekarius, see Spicer
Aston, William de Hemingford Abbots 423
Arneborn, Henry 202
Atenock, Cristina wife of Roger de Spaldwick 215; Margaret daughter of Simon 28; Mariota 163
Atequene, William 73
atte, see next word
Attelaneshende, John de Huntingdon 426
Atterissis, see Cirpos ad
Atteswodesend, Richard 200
Atthemeer, Richard 90
Aubin, Sarra 77
Aufred, see Anfred
Augustine, heirs of 129; Augustine of the Canons 214; Augustine son of 154; Godfrey son of 154; Joan Fayreheved, wife of Augustine of the Canons 214; John son of 154; Nicholas son of 154, 163; Richard son of 154; William son of 154

Aula, *see* Hall, atte

Aurifaber (Orfevere), John le 50, 78; John de Huntingdon 132, 136; Nicholas de Huntingdon 136; William de Huntingdon 136

Austy, William 105

Avred, *see* Anfred

Awnfleys (Annaipa[us]), Nicholas 73, 89

Ayleve, Elena 76

Aylred (Alred), Alan 65, 66; Alan son of "G" 103; Alice daughter of John 163; Cristina daughter of John 102; Dyonisia 127, 130, 205; Elena 205; Godfrey 33, 63, 194, 205; Godfrey son of Eusebius 214; Godfrey, taylor 192; Henry 66, 106, 111, 205; Henry son of Godfrey 163; Henry son of William 127; Isabella daughter of Robert Scot, and wife of Godfrey son of Eusebius 214; Joan 205; John 161, 205, 434, 435; Mabel 205; Mabel daughter of Simon 105; Martin 122, 126; heirs of Martin 130; Millicent daughter of Martin 126, 163; Reginald 20, 104, 163, 205; Reginald, merchant 196; Reyner 103; Richard 103; Roger 155; Roger brother of Mabel 105; Roger son of William de Arnyng Street 155; Simon 105, 205; Thomas 68, 69; William 64, 65, 75, 105, 126, 205, 213, 435, 437; William, merchant 205; William of Arnyng Street 155; William son of Reginald 41, 127, 130; William son of William 130

Aylward, Bartholomew 163; John 98; Simon 98; William son of Reginald 41

Aylwyne, *see* Aleyn

Ayshere, Roger de Hemingford Abbots 138

Baggle, Beatrix wife of John de Hemingford Grey 423; John le de Hemingford Grey 423

Baker (Pistor), Agnes 25; Joan 233; William 77

Balde, Cristina 97; John, major 97; John, minor 97

Baldecote, John de Huntingdon 425; Robert (*or* Roger) de Huntingdon 425

Balle, Alexander 98, 126, 205; Cristina 106; Cristina daughter of Thomas 126; Elena 104; Elena wife of Godfrey Bate 214; Isabella daughter of John 94; John 82, 88, 205; John of West Street 156;

John son of Alexander 197, 205; John son of Matilda 113; Matilda 106; Pellagia 48; Reginald 98; Reginald, senior 129; heirs of Reginald son of Thomas 129; Robert 73, 106; Robert son of John 194; Roger 205; Thomas 20, 31, 61, 67, 98, 205; Thomas de Offord Cluny 91, 429; William 73, 98, 204; William, chaplain 204; William son of Thomas 127

Balte, Isabella 109

Balton (Baltoun), John, carpenter 140; John de Quy 88

Baltoun, *see* Balton

Banastre, John, clerk 73

Band, Nicholas de Huntingdon 425

Barbour, Gilbert le, merchant de Sudbury 138; Joan mother of Nicholas 21; Joan wife of Roger de Huntingdon and daughter of John de Hamerton, 214, 425; John 91; Nicholas son of Roger le, de Huntingdon 21; Roger de Huntingdon, 215, 425

Baret (Barrett), John 91, 436

Barker, Elias 111, 199; John le, de Huntingdon 136, 139; John of the church of St. John de Gt. Paxton 74; Richard de Graveley 136; Robert de Gt. Paxton 136; Thomas de Huntingdon 136

Barnard, John 436

Barnwell, Henry de, mason 139; John de, le carter 191

Baron (Baroun), Amicia wife of Thomas de Merton 215; John 75, 108, 115, 196, 199, 213; John de Hemingford 92; John de Offord Cluny 429; John son of Thomas de Merton, merchant de Cambridge 138; Matilda de Hemingford Abbots 423

Baroun, *see* Baron

Barre, atte, Cristina wife of Ralph de Hemingford Abbots 423; Godfrey 129; John 156; John junior, son of John 156; John senior, son of John 156; John son of John 156; Ralph de Hemingford Abbots 423; Robert 66; Roger 75

Barrett, *see* Baret

Bartelot (Barthelot), Godfrey son of Nicholas 102; Ivetta widow of William and wife of Augustine Turk 215; John 107; Millicent sister of John 102; Nicholas 102; William 102

Barthelot, *see* Bartelot

Index of Places

An asterisk indicates that the county is not known.

[1] There are too many Langleys in England for the county to be determined.

[2] There are too many Stokes in England for the county to be determined.

Subject Index